Child Care: From Birth to Eighteen

A Comprehensive Book on the Art of Parenting

Child Care: From Birth to Eighteen

A Comprehensive Book on the Art of Parenting

By

Dr. Taher Y. Kagalwala
M.D. (Ped.), D.C.H.

ALCHEMY

Published 2005 by

ALCHEMY

An imprint of

Mehras

15, Bankim Chatterjee Street
2nd Floor, Kolkatta-700 073

4767/23, Pratap Street, Darya Ganj,
New Delhi-110 002

G-1 & 2, Ghaswala Tower,
P.G. Solanki Path, Off Lamington Road
Mumbai-400 007.

ISBN: 81-8046-023-1

Printed and bound in India by
Decora Printers, Mumbai

In memory of my mother
and my father-in-law,
both excellent parents.

This book is dedicated
to
all parents of the world:
they have only their children's good at heart.

Of Children:

Your children are not your children.
They are the sons and daughters of Life's longing for itself.
They come through you but not from you,
And though they are with you, yet they belong not to you.

You may give them your love, but not your thoughts,
For they have their own thoughts.
You may house their bodies but not their souls,
For their souls dwell in the house of to-morrow,
Which you cannot visit, not even in your dreams.
You may strive to be like them, but seek not
To make them like you.
For life goes not backward nor tarries with yesterday.

– Kahlil Gibran.

Foreword

Dr. N.B. Kumta, M.D., D.C.H.

In my professional experience of over 40 years, I have come across several books that deal with parenting and child-care. I have thoroughly whetted the book that you now hold in your hands, and I feel this is one of the most comprehensive books on the subject by any Indian Author.

I have known Dr. Kagalwala for more than two decades. As my post-graduate student, he was very diligent, hard-working and sincere. During his tenure as a student, he was always interested in the human side of Pediatrics. He would stand and patiently explain the intricacies of the illness to a sick child's parents. I frequently saw him spend time reading up on how to handle the emotional and sensitive aspects of parenting.

He started private practice in 1987. Over the years, we have interacted several times, and I have discovered that the human trait in him continues even today. He has accumulated over two decades of experience in treating sick children and in counselling parents who have approached him for advice. When he first approached me with a request to take a look at his book on parenting, I knew instantly that the book would turn out to be excellent.

I have found no reason to revise my assessment of this book. It handles all the routine subjects very well, but it also explores new areas such as advice to working mothers, adoptive parents and single parents. His ideas flow from the heart, and his use of first person in the narrative should not be construed as unscientific, for he backs up all the advice that he gives with hard facts. It is obvious that he has put in tremendous effort to impart sound knowledge to parents. His exploration of the Internet has thrown up many web-site addresses that will undoubtedly prove useful to those parents who desire to study a particular subject in greater detail.

The book will serve as a ready-reckoner for those who are looking for instant information and advice on the various issues on parenting. It will also serve as a valuable reference book for detailed knowledge on various general parenting issues. Most importantly, it will help parents who are faced with a sick child and a disease label that they do not understand: they can look up the relevant topic and get an idea of the illness that their child has or learn how to handle a "difficult" child. The book will help to dispel some of the commonly held mis-beliefs concerning child-care in Indian communities.

This book will be useful to students and teachers of Home Science, Nutrition, Pediatric Nursing, Medical Pediatrics, Child Psychology and many more faculties. It will be useful to practicing Family Physicians, Pediatricians, Gynaecologists and other medical specialities.

Above all, this book should be bought by all parents-to-be and also parents of children ranging in age from birth to 18 years. They should keep it in a prominent place in the house and refer to it whenever they are worried about their child (-ren) in any way.

I wish Dr. Kagalwala all the best in his venture.

- **Dr. N.B.Kumta**
M.D., D.C.H.

Practising Senior Pediatrician and Neonatologist,
15th October 2004.

Message

from the President of the Indian Academy of Pediatrics (I.A.P.),
Dr. Raju C. Shah

I have gone through the book "The Comprehensive Book on Parenting" by Dr. Taher Y. Kagalwala. I find the book very useful. It is a ready-to-use guide that will help all parents staying in India and its neighboring countries. Issues covering all aspects of baby, child and adolescent care have been discussed thoroughly.

The book faithfully describes all that parents need to know about normal child growth and development, the vaccines that they need to give to their kids, the nourishment they should provide to them and so on. In addition, a huge section will help them understand how to manage illnesses at home and also teach them to cope with expected as well as unexpected problems concerning their child (-ren).

I have read many chapters, especially the chapters on Infant Nutrition and Immunisation, and found all of them well-written. They are exhaustive in coverage and simple to understand.

I recommend this book whole-heartedly to all those interested in Parenting and Child-care.

I wish Dr. Kagalwala success in this endeavour.

- **Dr. Raju C. Shah,**
M.D. (Pediatrics), D.C.H.

President I.A.P., 2005
14th October 2004

Letter

from Dr. Nitin Shah

"Why one more book?" is a question asked by many when a new book like this comes out. Most of the books so far available on child health for parents have been from the western world; these suit the requirements of the parents there. There are very few such books from India and that too written by successful pediatricians. Besides, unlike in the past, the present generation of parents in India is quite aware and concerned about the health of their children. Many are confused by reading material available through internet which may not be necessarily the right type of information they should be reading. The small family norm has made every child more precious than even before. All these have led to a constant demand for this type of a book for parents, written by an expert Indian Pediatrician, in a language that Indian parents can understand, and finally addressing the problems faced by Indian parents.

This is exactly what this book is designed for; it is written by Dr. Taher Kagalwala who is an expert Pediatrician of more than 20 years standing. It is written in short chapters in a style that makes the reading reader-friendly and interesting. The size of the book is just adequate and is reasonably priced so that most of the parents can afford it. He has addressed the common questions asked by the parents in day-to-day practice and patiently tried to explain the reply by citing adequate examples and similes. I am sure every parent will enjoy reading this book and would want to keep it as a ready reckoner for day to day life while upbringing their loved little one. This book is a must on the desk-top of every house where parents care for their children!

- **Dr. Nitin K. Shah**
MD, DCH

Consultant Pediatrician, PD Hinduja National hospital, Mumbai
President Elect, 2006, Indian Academy of Pediatrics

Author's Note and Acknowledgements

Happiness is as a butterfly, which when pursued, is always beyond our grasp. But if you will sit down quietly, it may alight upon you." – Nathaniel Hawthorne

This book is a labour of love dedicated to all those men and women who decide to take the plunge into raising and/or looking after children. I am a parent myself, and despite being a Pediatrician, I have often found myself at my wits' end when faced with real-life problems involving my own children. It would perhaps be an understatement to say that I have occasionally turned to books, magazines and internet-based web-sites for advice on how exactly does one go about managing children.

It took me a while to realise that children have their own identities and neither I nor their mother could actually mould them to our own tastes and rules. Kahlil Gibran was right when he stated that children lived in the world of tomorrow ... a place we, as parents, cannot hope to visit, not even in our dreams.

I hope that this book serves the purpose for which it is designed: to provide comprehensive, yet easy to understand advice to all those who care for children. It is targeted not only at parents, but also at health workers, child care workers, crèche attendants, general practitioners of medicine and perhaps my fellow colleagues as well, who are often asked to recommend a book on parenting by their patients' parents.

The book is divided into many parts simply to compartmentalize the various topics in child care. Each chapter is complete in itself, and readers will find very few instances where they will have to turn the pages to look at another chapter. This, I hope, will benefit everyone. At the end of the book, I have supplied useful appendices as well as a glossary of commonly used medical terms so that even a person with rudimentary scientific knowledge can grasp the subject properly. Wherever possible, I have suggested links and books for the reader who thirsts for more knowledge on a particular topic.

I am grateful to all the people who made this book possible. First, my wife Nishrin and my children Inas and Hannah, who have patiently borne my nightly clicking away at the keyboard, provided me with the support and kinship I so badly needed at times and helped me to get the book published, marketed and sold too.

Second, the blessings of my own parents and family-elders, who have encouraged me to write on, read some of the chapters, and provide useful input.

Third, to the following parents who have lent me the photographs of their intimate moments with their children and allowed me to use them in this book: Mr. and Mrs. Idris Eranpurwala, Mr. and Mrs. Altaf Deshmukh, Mr. and Mrs. Ali Daruwala, Mr. and Mrs. Yusuf Kabira and Mr. and Mrs. Kailash Mohol.

Fourth, to Dr. N.B. Kumta, my Post-graduate guide and senior practising Pediatrician, Mumbai, for going over my book with a tooth-comb, pointing out ways and means to improve its authenticity, language and look and writing such a generous "Foreword".

Fifth, to Drs. Raju Shah (President, I.A.P., 2004 and practising Pediatrician, Ahmedabad), Dr. Raju Khubchandani (my friend, philosopher and guide and a practising Pediatrician too), Dr. Nitin Shah (Hon. Secretary General, I.A.P, 2004 and practising Pediatrician, Mumbai) and Dr. Yusuf Matcheswalla (Consulting Psychiatrist), who have all read portions of my book and provided me with valuable guidance and tips on improving it.

Sixth, to my brother, Mr. Murtuza Kagalwala, who scanned all the line-drawings and pictures that I sent him and e-mailed them back to me in time.

Seventh, Mrs. Sheetal Raorane, Senior Dietitian, Masina Hospital, Mumbai, for providing me with the recipes for weaning foods.

Eighth, to Master Husain Abbasi, Miss Sakina Shaikh and Miss Zahabiya Tambawala, who acted as models to demonstrate the usage of various devices that are used in treatment of childhood asthma.

Ninth, to Ms. Sharon Barsotti, LLLI Publications, for so kindly sending me photographs related to Breastfeeding.

Tenth, to Mrs. Farida Mukadam and Master Murtuza Pancha for helping me in illustrating the book.

A word to all the readers of this book. I have assigned the female sex to the babies, children and adolescents whom you will read about almost throughout the book. The reason is simple: I have two daughters and am therefore partial to girls. Also, I feel the girl-child is often at a disadvantage in our country, thanks to female feticide, female infanticide etc. and hopefully, with my emphasizing on the female sex, at least some readers will begin to look at their own daughters with a more kindly eye.

- **Dr. Taher Y. Kagalwala,**
  M.D., D.C.H.

17th October 2004, Mumbai

Table of Contents:

Part II: The First Month of Life

Part III: Infant Feeding

Part IV: See How They Grow (0-6 years)

Part V: See How They Grow (6-12 years)

Part VI: Adolescence, Teenage and Puberty

Part VII: Modern Age of Convenience – Challenges for Parents

Part VIII: Special Issues

Part IX: Medical Care

Part X: The Sick Child

Part XI: Appendices

Part I
Conception to Delivery

*If you bungle raising your children,
I don't think whatever else you do well matters very much.*

Jacqueline O. Kennedy (1929-1994), American First Lady and Wife of John F. Kennedy and later, Aristotle Onassis.

Ch. 01
Pregnancy Issues

The moment a child is born, the mother is also born.
She never existed before.
The woman existed, but the mother, never.
A mother is something absolutely new.

– Author unknown

Fertilisation/Conception:

The process of conception will occur best between the 13th to 18th day of the menstrual cycle of the mother, as this is the time when the egg is released from the ovary and travels down to the mother's womb.

The moment one of the father's sperms unites with one of the eggs of the mother, new life is said to have been conceived! This process, also called fertilisation, occurs anytime shortly after sexual intercourse has taken place between the two adults. Of the millions of sperms released by the father, just one will actually unite with the mother's egg (ovum). The rest of the sperms will perish.

The fertilised egg (*zygote*) then selects a suitable spot inside the womb and implants itself on to the inside wall of the womb for further development.

How The Baby Grows Inside Her Mother:

The one-celled zygote weighs 0.005 mg. It will grow at a phenomenal rate from the moment it is fertilised. Cells will multiply quite rapidly, till they reach a figure of over two billion at birth. Their mass will have increased 600 million times to 3000 grams or more! See the table below to get an idea.

Age of the growing fetus	Size
Conception	Microscopic
12 weeks	14 grams/7.5 cm
28 weeks	1000 grams/35 cm
Full term	3000 grams/50 cm

At 12 weeks, most of the fetus's organs are already formed and the face is almost developed. At 20 weeks, the baby begins to move, and the mother can feel the baby "kicking" inside her womb. The doctor will be able to hear her beating heart with a stethoscope or a fetoscope. However, at this stage, the baby's lungs are not well developed and the baby cannot survive outside the womb.

At 26-28 weeks, the baby is about 700 grams and if born at this stage, the baby has less than favourable chances of surviving, even with the best possible neonatal care. At 28 weeks and a weight of 1000 grams, the odds are better for the baby, and given proper neonatal care, the baby is likely to survive.

During all these days, the baby floats in a liquid known as amniotic fluid. It is free to move around inside the womb. As its size increases, however, its movements become increasingly difficult, and it settles down into one or the other position, most commonly, the head-down position, also called "vertex" (Fig.1-1). Sometimes though, the baby

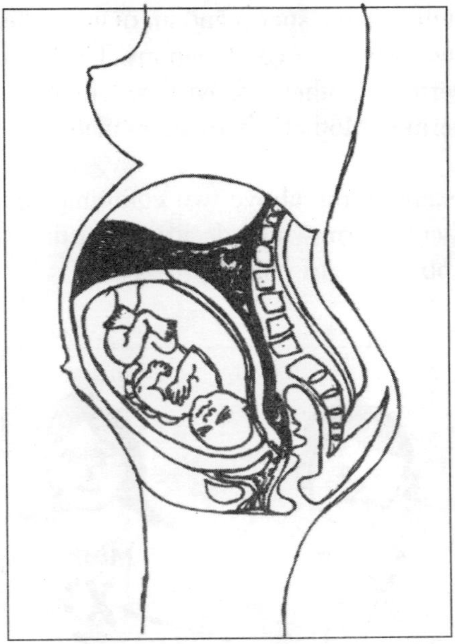

Fig 1-1

remains aligned with its head up (breech), or transversely or obliquely. In such cases, there can be complications at the time of delivery.

Sex of the Baby:

All our body cells contain the information about our inheritance in the form of chromosomes, tiny strands of protein material that contain DNA. While there are 22 pairs of general chromosomes (or autosomes), there is one pair of sex chromosomes: these are called either the X or the Y chromosomes. Males contain one of each type of sex chromosomes, while females have a pair of X chromosomes. The sperm or the ovum has only one of this pair in it, so while a sperm may have either a X or a Y chromosome, all ova have X chromosomes only.

During conception, when a sperm and an ovum unite, one can have a zygote with one of the two combinations. These are:
1. Father's X sperm + Mother's X ovum = female
2. Father's Y sperm + Mother's X ovum = male

If you closely examine the above two combinations, you will find that it is the father's sperm which decides what the baby is going to be – whether a boy or a girl (Fig.1-2).

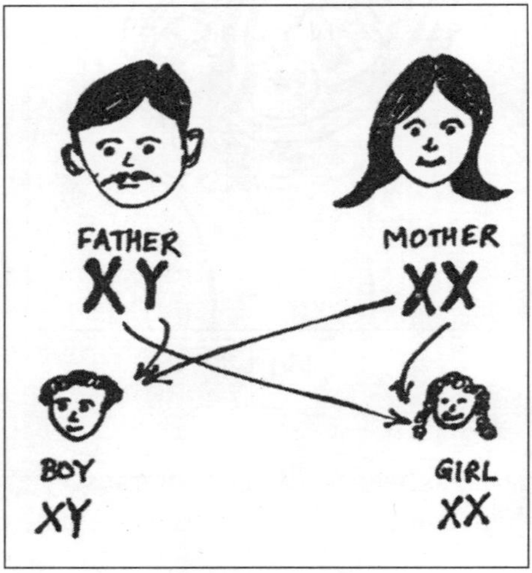

Fig 1-2

The sex of the child is not determined by the mother, but by the father.

Indian people are obsessed with the idea that a son is preferable to a daughter. This obsession has taken the lives of thousands of female fetuses (feticide), small female infants (female infanticide) and even older female children. While the male child is given the choicest food, the female child has to make do with leftovers. Even in illness, while the male child receives the best medical care at the hands of the most expensive doctor, the female child is often given "home-remedies" and substandard care. This deplorable state of affairs has resulted in **a drastic decline of the nationwide female: male ratio from an ideal of 1000:1000 to just 779:1000 as per the 2001 Census of the Government of India**.

Many people believe that while the son will be the "torch-bearer" of the family, contribute to the family's income and bring in "dowry" at the time of his marriage, a daughter cannot continue the family name, will not work on the "farm" (or other similar occupation) and will be a "financial burden" on the family at the time of marriage.

It is true that with the advancement of society, many of the older traditions are gradually dying out, but the mindset of the masses will take much longer to change. Women are educating themselves and adding their incomes to the family's kitty; many women are the family's sole bread-winners. **Dowry is illegal, and many modern grooms are refusing to be a part of this extremely retrograde practice**. Old parents are often abandoned by their much hyped sons, who think nothing of setting up new homes with their spouses and leaving their infirm parents to fend for themselves.

Blaming the mother for giving birth to girls is the name of the game, and totally incorrect, as we have just seen above. Many mothers go through childbirth again and again in the desire for a male child; marriages are broken, and males are made to marry a second time to "improve" the chance of siring a boy. This is happening not just in illiterate homes, but also in rich, elitist families labouring under a traditional mindset.

Choosing the sex of the baby:

At every conception, there is a 50:50 chance of having either a boy or a girl. There is no fool-proof method of conceiving a baby of a pre-determined sex. A Chinese calendar is supposed to correlate the date of conception to the sex of the baby. Dietary manipulations, recourse to astrological formulas, tying of the spermatic cord and many such heroic techniques have been tried, but to no avail.

The Y-sperm has a shorter life, and it is believed that a couple that indulges in sex more often (or where the father "empties" the testes by masturbating daily) has a greater chance of a male child as more sperms will be the fresher, faster Y-sperms.

There is no medicine, drug or herb which can ensure the birth of a child with a desired sex, and many such remedies may be potentially harmful to the developing fetus, as many of them are taken "after" conception has already taken place and the mother has missed her period.

There is no natural or medicinal method that can guarantee birth of a child with a desired sex.

The **only** reliable method of ensuring a male child is to go in for new technology, where a Y-sperm is identified and selected outside the body, in a test-tube, and is "made" to unite with the natural mother's ovum in it (*test-tube baby*). Once the zygote is formed, one waits for it to develop a bit more. Then it is implanted into the mother's womb, where it will develop further, like a normal pregnancy. To avoid the chance of failure of implantation, the fertility technologist will often fertilise more than one ovum with the Y-sperms, and implant more than one zygote. As a result, multiple pregnancies may also result.

The problem with this technology is that although it looks simple, it is very complex in practice and may cost lakhs of rupees. Also, the Government of India has made sex-selection of a baby a crime punishable with fine, imprisonment, or both. Thus, under normal circumstances, it would be an unethical and criminal act and a waste of resources.

The only ethical place for such technology is when there are genetic disorders in the family that affect only females. Here, sex-selection to favour a male child may be excused on medical grounds. Similarly, in diseases such as hemophilia (a type of bleeding disease), where only males are affected, the above technology may be used to select X-sperms, so that only a girl child can be conceived.

Sex Determination during Pregnancy:

Again, **it is not only unethical, but also criminal to detect the sex of the unborn child** with the help of any technique. The only ethical reason would be to give the option of terminating the pregnancy of a particular sex in case of genetic disorders that affect that sex only.

As per the above, going in for CVB (chorionic villus biopsy), amniocentesis or ultrasonography with the aim of identifying the sex of the baby is a crime that can bring punishment to both the patient and the doctor who performs it.

Antenatal care:

Routine antenatal visits to the obstetrician must begin as early after detection of pregnancy as possible. The doctor will examine the mother-to-be and call her for regular follow-up visits. She may ask for an early antenatal ultrasound examination to see if all is well with the developing embryo and to confirm if the mother's womb and placenta too are all right. She will usually ask for urine and blood tests such as blood grouping, Rh typing, complete blood counts and hemoglobin estimation, tests to rule out presence of any infections in the mother which can be transmitted to the fetus and a urine sugar test with/without a blood sugar test to rule out gestational diabetes mellitus. She will take the mother's blood pressure, weight and other measurements to establish base-line values at the first visit and repeat these at each follow-up to ensure the health of the mother. She will advise the mother about diet, use of supplements, give Tetanus Toxoid vaccine and do all that is needed to keep the mother and baby in the pink of health.

I advise you, the mother-to-be, to follow all the instructions of the obstetrician and to go for follow-ups every month till the seventh month, every fortnight from then till the ninth month and then every week till you begin to have labour pains.

Sometime during these visits, you will have to make a choice of **which maternity home or hospital to register in for the delivery**. This is a very important choice to make. Try and choose a reputed institution which has facilities for all the necessary tests and treatments that may have to be carried out on you or your baby once it is born. Along with these parameters, try and find out if the institution is a certified "Baby Friendly Hospital". BFH's are hospitals that are staffed with personnel that are trained in the Art and Science of breastfeeding. (See http://www.babyfriendly.org.uk/home.asp and http://www.storknet.com/cubbies/breast/10steps.htm for more details on the Baby Friendly Hospital Initiative.)

What to Avoid in Pregnancy:

The first two to three months of pregnancy are the ones when the baby's organs are taking shape (the period of organogenesis). As such, any adverse events during this delicate period can create problems in the baby. In the event that these actually affect the baby, the baby will likely have physical defects (congenital anomalies), mental retardation and so on.

You should strictly avoid the following during the entire pregnancy:

1. Any medication, whether to "abort" the baby, or for any illness without a doctor's opinion; a special mention must be made of certain anticonvulsants (sp. diphenylhydantoin) used by epileptics;
2. Any X-rays for non-essential reasons;

3. Any exposure to nuclear radiation (includes anti-thyroid medicines, thyroid or other scans, etc.);
4. Smoking, consumption of drugs or alcohol drinking as these can definitely affect the developing fetus;
5. Excessive consumption of tea, coffee or other stimulants;
6. Excessive use of cough and cold medicines, sleeping agents and other stuff that makes the baby drowsy;
7. Vitamin-A containing facial creams and tablets, mostly used for severe acne;
8. Getting any other family member vaccinated against Polio, Measles, Rubella or Chicken-pox vaccines. These are live vaccines and the virus may be transmitted to you, and through you, to the unborn baby;
9. Lifting unusually heavy weights or carrying out strenuous work: this can abort the baby or cause preterm onset of labour;
10. Fights and a vitiating home atmosphere: these can conceivably cause fetal distress and even preterm onset of labour; and
11. Putting on violent T.V. shows and loud music shows: these can act similarly.
12. Sauna baths: It has been shown that if the pregnant mother is exposed to ambient temperatures above 40-degrees C in the first three months, the fetus can be harmed.

Diet and Nutrition in Pregnancy:

Extra nourishment is needed in pregnancy for the healthy growth of the placenta, the uterus (womb) and the developing baby (or fetus). Blood loss during the delivery process has to be provided for. Also, the mother must create extra reserve stores of iron, calcium, fat and protein to face the delicate nursing period after the delivery of the baby.

Perversion of appetite and vomiting actually prevent the mother from eating well in the first three months of pregnancy. However, once these three months are up, the mother seems to settle down, and the appetite improves. She should then start eating extra food right till the end of pregnancy, and beyond, during lactation. The extra food includes an extra 250 calories and 30 g protein daily.

You should eat **a balanced diet** with high fibre content, high-biological-value proteins and adequate calories. In particular, eat dals, germinated pulses (sprouts), fresh green leafy vegetables, whole wheat chapatis/bread, rice, milk or milk products, (yoghurt, *paneer*, cheese, *khoya*, *kheer*, etc.) and lots of fruit (Fig 1-3). Non-vegetarians may eat eggs, mutton, chicken, fish and organ meats like liver, kidneys, etc.

Fig 1-3

Excessive intake of refined sugars and fats, such as those found in cakes, desserts, sweets, chocolates, *halwa*, *pinjiri* etc. should be avoided, as these can cause obesity and other ailments in later life.

If you eat right, you should put on around 10-12 kilograms of weight during pregnancy. You should feel active, not lethargic, and be able to carry on with normal household activities without feeling tired.

Supplements:

Folic acid supplements are very essential around the time you start planning for a baby. Use of folic acid tablets before and up to *eight weeks* after conception has been found to prevent some rather serious congenital anomalies of the baby's nervous system. You should take at least 0.5 mg/day of this vitamin throughout pregnancy.

Iron tablets sufficient to deliver at least 60 mg of iron per day are also essential during pregnancy. So also Calcium and Vitamin D supplements, which need to be eaten daily. Do take multivitamin pills containing Zinc as well.

Preparing for Breast Feeding:

Expectant mothers need **antenatal counselling** from trained persons on a) benefits of breastfeeding and b) techniques of breastfeeding. These persons can be mothers who have successfully fed their own babies with breast milk, trained health workers, nurses or even "*maalishwalis*". Such educational sessions go a long way in helping new mothers acquire the much needed skills and confidence to successfully breastfeed their newborns.

If you are a senior woman in the household and have a pregnant daughter or daughter-in-law or sister-in-law, you need to *motivate her right from the first trimester of pregnancy.* Your effort will translate into a vibrant mother-child unit which will be an asset to the entire household.

To the first-time mother, here is an important bit of advice: Size does not matter. **You can have small petulant breasts, and still be able to nurse your baby successfully**. Do get the nipples checked out by your doctor if you feel they are misshaped or "inverted". The doctor will advise you accordingly. If you feel your nipples are not protruding enough, take them between your thumb and first finger one by one, and roll them outward for a few minutes everyday.

As pregnancy advances, your breasts will start feeling fuller, bigger and heavier. Use bras with supports, choosing a bra size that fits comfortably without causing tightness. Some milky discharge may be seen in the last few months, and if it causes wetting of your dress, wear some absorbent cotton pads inside the bra while at work.

Exercise and Travel:

Keeping yourself busy with household or office work is all right, but you must **avoid over-working** yourself or undertaking strenuous tasks that may harm your pregnancy's outcome. Do take brisk walks in the mornings and evenings; cycling or swimming is also good. You may even play active games like table-tennis or badminton (at a slow pace). However, you must not play high-activity games like football, hockey etc. Participating in athletic events is also not permissible. An afternoon nap of at least 45-60 minutes is very desirable. If you have swelling of your legs, you might want to rest your feet above pillows while reclining on the bed so as to allow the extra water to get absorbed.

Travelling is also fine, but **do not carry heavy weights.** Do not travel without a companion. Avoid travelling a) over bumpy roads b) to remote villages c) in auto-rickshaws d) in crowded trains or buses and e) during the last one or two months of pregnancy.

Mental Relaxation:

The key to a healthy outcome of pregnancy is to have a continuous positive frame of mind and avoid undue anxiety, stress and negative emotion. You should occupy yourselves with any activity that keeps you happy and emotionally sound. If you are a working mother, continue to attend office as long as possible. If you are a housewife, stay away from internal family strife and keep yourself busy with jobs like knitting woollens for the arriving baby, learning new skills which help parenting, reading good self-help books, painting, cooking, or whatever else is your pleasure. Try and get at least 8-10 hours of sleep daily, including an afternoon nap. Join Yoga classes, meditation classes, Reiki classes and Lamaze classes if they are available in your vicinity. Listening to soft, soothing music will also be rewarding, and may even help the growing baby stay calm inside the womb. There is enough evidence to support the fact that whatever you can hear, the baby can, too. Hence avoid shouting, fighting and other unpleasant hearing experiences for the baby. Lastly, deep breathing must be practiced, as it will be of help in labour.

Sexual Intercourse:

There is a false belief among some people that normal conjugal relations between the husband and the expectant mother can cause the baby to abort. Normal relations can be maintained until seven months of pregnancy; thereafter, one may still continue to have relations but either with the wife on top or with both partners lying side by side with the husband penetrating from the rear or the front.

Too much nipple stimulation may cause milk to be secreted; at times, it may even cause the onset of premature labour pains. Hence, it should be avoided, especially after seven months of pregnancy. The couple may elect to abstain from sex in the last 2-3 months and instead concentrate on the emotional aspects of a lasting, loving relationship.

Symptoms to worry about:

The following danger symptoms should cause you to immediately contact your physician or obstetrician:

- Sudden bleeding per vaginum
- Severe nausea or vomiting, esp. in the first three months
- Burning sensation while passing urine
- Blurring of vision or seeing white or black spots before the eyes
- Severe or persistent headache

- Unusual abdominal pain that comes and goes, but without anybowel movement
- High fever (more than 100° F) without any obvious common cause
- Reduction or absence of baby's movements
- Fainting or dizziness
- Accidents, falls or injuries to the abdomen from any cause
- Marked swelling of the feet and/or other parts of the body

The above symptoms may indicate either that your pregnancy is experiencing some difficulties or that you have some other undesired complication or infection. Pregnancy related complications include retention of fluids and rising blood-pressure, excessive weight gain, urinary infection, premature onset of labour, abortion, placental bleeding, distress to the fetus, pregnancy-related diabetes in the mother, fetal demise in the womb and many others. For complete details, please consult your obstetrician or look in an appropriate pregnancy book. Some useful web-sites are given below:

✔ www.pregnancy.org
✔ www.childbirth.org
✔ www.pregnancy.about.com
✔ www.pregnancyguideonline.com
✔ www.pregnancy-info.net

There are many good books available also. A few are listed here:

✔ The Mother of All Pregnancy Books: The Ultimate Guide to Conception, Birth, and Everything In Between (U.S. Edition) by Ann Douglas.

✔ The Pregnancy Journal – A Day to Day Guide to a Healthy and Happy Pregnancy by A. Christine Harris, Ph. D.

Ch. 02
Preparing the Home and the Heart for the New Arrival

Making the decision to have a child is momentous.
It is to decide forever to have your heart go walking around outside your body.

–Author unknown

Every marriage begins on the premise that it will lead to the expansion of the family and the "patter" of tiny feet in the household. Anxious about this, "*kundlis*" are matched between prospective pairs as much for their ability to have healthy children as for their internal compatibility. The commonest blessing bestowed on a newly married couple is for them to have a string of bonny and healthy children.

Mothering is an instinct that is as old as the history of mankind, only older. Even lower animals love their children unabashedly. The cat which eats part of its litter loves her offspring as much if not more than a mother who showers affection upon her newly born baby. In human beings, the arrival of a baby and the start of an extended family are looked upon as the ultimate gift from the Almighty. Families become rapturous on hearing that their daughter/daughter-in-law is "in the family way". *Pedhas* and other sweets are distributed, long-distance calls are made, "leave" is taken by all the working members, and the *kulvadhu* is sternly exhorted to stop going to work/college as the case may be, to stop doing all household chores and to avoid climbing up/down stairs. The charged atmosphere continues as the news of pregnancy is sought to be confirmed by an early visit to the doctor, the carrying out of the pregnancy test and the frantic visit to the child-care paraphernalia shop (as if the baby will arrive the same day!).

Such then is the magic of the anticipated arrival of a new baby in Indian culture. I am reasonably sure it is the same all over the world. This chapter will look into the nitty-gritties of preparing for the arrival of the baby once pregnancy has been confirmed.

Motherhood:

God could not be everywhere, so he created mothers.

– Jewish Proverb

Every woman feels "incomplete" if Nature or Fate denies her the chance of becoming a mother. The instinct of Motherhood is so strong that a woman will do all she can to find herself a suitable life-partner who can help beget her (a) child/children. Motherhood involves tremendous effort and sacrifices on the part of the mother. It is no cakewalk at all. She is prepared to undergo the physical strain of "carrying" her tiny baby inside of her for all of 280 days … even if it means restriction on her daily pleasures and abstention from many of her normal activities. Enduring days and nights of remaining alert for any signs of the baby being in any trouble, enduring the changes in her body, the unseemly weight-gain, the mis-shapening of her arms, face, breasts, hips and what have you – are all things that she will embrace with a smile. On top of this are the **other responsibilities** that she must continue to balance: looking after her other child (-ren), doing all the physical and social chores that she has been doing and in some of them, continuing their jobs. Other family members, friends and relatives can help by sharing some of her concerns and tasks with her so that she remains cheerful and positive throughout her pregnancy (see below). Mother-support is required before, during and after delivery (Dr. N.B. Kumta, personal discussion).

Mothering is instinctive but mother craft has to be learnt. It is imperative to know so many different things about the upbringing of children. Although we have a tradition of learning from our elders, this method has its limitations. The real-life experience of bringing forth a new life into the world and then looking after her every need and desire is so mind-boggling, no words or tomes can fully make an expert out of us. Yet, all these resources do point us in the right direction. A mother who suddenly has to balance her baby, her in-laws, her husband, her work and her own needs is sure to get bewildered and confused by it all. Hence, I feel books on parenting, internet web-sites etc. all have a very important role to play in today's times.

The need is all the greater because of the breaking up of joint families, the difficulties of commuting in large cities and the pressures of living.

Let us collect everything that is needed to welcome the new mother and baby home. Some of these items will be needed immediately, but others will be needed as the baby grows up.

The Home:

The home in which the baby will be welcomed should also be readied for her arrival. Babies sleep for long hours, so loudly chiming doorbells, raucously ringing telephones and noisily opening doors of almirahs and cupboards should be replaced or repaired so that they become quieter.

An area should be cleared for the mother and her nursing baby in a small house. (In a larger house, the parents' bedroom can be used for the same purpose.) The area should be well ventilated, clean and large enough to accommodate the mother, her baby, a baby cot, the baby's daily supplies and all the other paraphernalia needed for both the individuals. Preferably, this area should be as far away from the kitchen as possible. It should have proper lighting, preferably with dimmers so that the intensity of the lights can be adjusted according to the waking and sleeping cycles of the baby (and the mother).

The paint on the walls should not be fresh, as its toxic fumes are harmful for the baby. Emphasis should shift from *dusting* the house to *wet-mopping* when the baby arrives, as dust can enter the baby's respiratory passages and cause her to have cough and sneezing. Alternatively, one can use a vacuum cleaner to have a dust-free environment in the house. Purchase one that is sturdy and reasonable in cost. Check to see that it is not very noisy when it is switched on.

Fans and air-conditioners should be serviced to see that they operate without noise and are free from dust and dirt on all surfaces.

Clothes:

In a nutshell, **baby's clothes should be comfortable and easy to put on and remove**. They should be light, white or light-coloured, made from cotton, soft to the touch and have no sharp or protruding buttons, appliqués or unnecessary piping, embroidery or embellishments. Velcro® can be used instead of hooks and buttons. Many mothers stitch baby clothes on their own, using fresh or old saree material. Sometimes, new babies wear clothes of their elder siblings or cousins, and rarely, even of their own parents! In summer, the above clothes should suffice. In winter, woollens are needed as well. The necessary items include socks, mittens, cap and a sweater/pullover. Bonnets and caps are not very essential unless it is planned to take the baby outdoors often, but they do look so pretty on the baby, don't they?

Clothes should be such that they are a little large for the baby, since *the baby grows very fast.* If you buy too many newborn sized clothes, you will be in trouble in just a few months, as they will all become tight for the baby. The types of clothes babies need include shirts, night-gowns, long gowns and shoulder-less strap sacks. Stretch-suits that snap from the neck down to one leg and button up the groin area are also popular. They can be used as day-wear as well as night wear.

Napkins (diapers) should be comfortable, made from soft, absorbent cotton material and have strings or Velcro® to fasten them. They should be large enough to prevent leakage of urine or stool. Diaper pins should have a safety-lock in its head. One should prepare or buy at least two dozen or more napkins as most babies urinate up to 8-10 times a day and pass 5-6 stools daily. **Plastic napkins worn over the cotton ones should be removed as soon as possible**, but are essential when going out. Plastic underwear is also readily available.

Nowadays, *disposable* napkins are available. They are costly but quite easy to put on and remove. They are highly absorbent. However, the incidence of rashes has not declined with their use because mothers become complacent after putting them on their babies.

Babies' bibs, booties and frocks are other optional items that you might want to purchase. Choose those that are light, made from cotton and not padded with too much cotton or covered with lace or plastic.

Toiletries:

One dozen small towels and two fluffy bath towels should be procured for the baby. Cotton should be bought and small cotton balls prepared for wiping the baby's eyes and private parts during her bath. The soap should be mild and non-irritating as well. There are special shampoos for washing the baby's hair. Baby lotions and creams may be used only if the baby's skin is dry. **Cheap and untested baby oils should generally be avoided**. Olive oil, coconut oil and other herbal oils are available for a daily baby massage. Mustard oil is very irritating and should not be used. **Massage with *besan* flour (usually given to remove the downy hair that are normally present on the forehead, shoulders and face in most babies – hair that are normally shed off naturally by three to six months)**

is NOT needed by normal babies. It can cause the skin to react with boils and rashes. Thus, this *pratha* (tradition) is to be abhorred. Infant scissors with blunt tips or nail clippers should also be obtained. Talcum powder should be used sparingly on the genitals and in the joints of the limbs. Baby powders are better, but any good talc is all right.

Bed, Cot and Bed sheets:

Most middle-class families cannot afford to buy a separate baby cot; they do not have the space needed in the house either. In a sense, this is a blessing because "bedding-in" of the baby on the mother's bed brings the mother and the baby closer and leads to more successful breastfeeding as well.

However, many families have ancestral baby cots. These are all right, but ***palanas* which can be rocked should preferably be avoided as rocking the baby creates a habit that is difficult for the baby to give up**. If you are planning to buy a cot or get it fabricated, see that it is long enough and big enough to last the first three to five years of the baby's life. The height of the cot should be as much as the mother's bed, so that the mother can lift up the baby easily to feed her at night. The side railings should be lowerable for the same reason. It should have a horizontal protruding arm just above where the baby's eyes will be, so as to mount toys like the "merry-go-round" on it. There should be a facility to cover the entire cot with a mosquito net in areas where mosquitoes or other insects are commonly present.

The bedding (mattress) should be soft but firm. It should be covered with a plastic cover. If the baby rolls over on to her tummy in sleep, the firmness will prevent the nose and face from getting smothered. You will need three to four bed sheets and two or three small blankets. A pillow is not recommended for babies. A shawl that doubles up as a cover to wrap around the baby is a good purchase, as is a sleeping bag made from cotswool material. In lieu of a shawl, one can make do with an old *sari* or *dhoti* that is long enough to be folded into a large triangle into which the baby can be swaddled.

Other Items:

A bassinet made from plastic is needed for a baby to be given a bath in. This should be large enough to last at least a year or two. A baby bag big enough to hold extra dresses, napkins, drinking water, milk feed (in a Tupperware® or similar glass), hand towel (s), tissues, medicines and the doctor's file is a very useful buy. An infant carry-cot (Fig. 2-1) with a sturdy handle can be carried much like a suit-case from your hands and is very convenient for daily use outdoors. A sling or back-carrier is good for carrying a baby at least 4-5 months old and up to about 10-12 months of age. It frees both hands and is good when the mother needs to go out to purchase things.

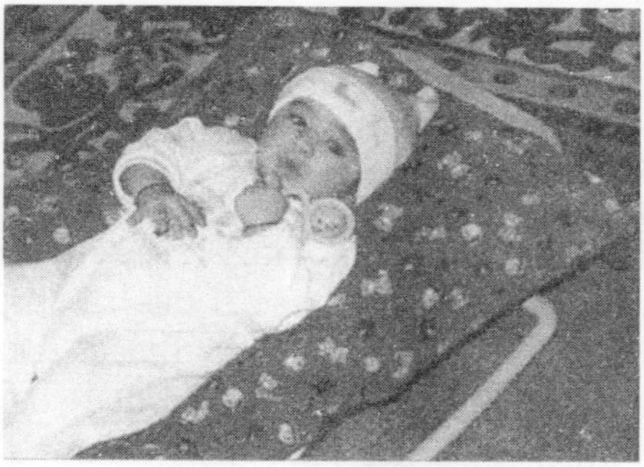

Fig 2-1

A baby-pram (Fig 2-2) is a luxury that not everyone can afford, but it is certainly handy if you are likely to go out to a park or on a walk everyday. It should be a folding pram if you are going to a distant place in a four-wheeler. A stroller is a pram in which an older baby can be made to sit up. It has straps which are used to harness the child in.

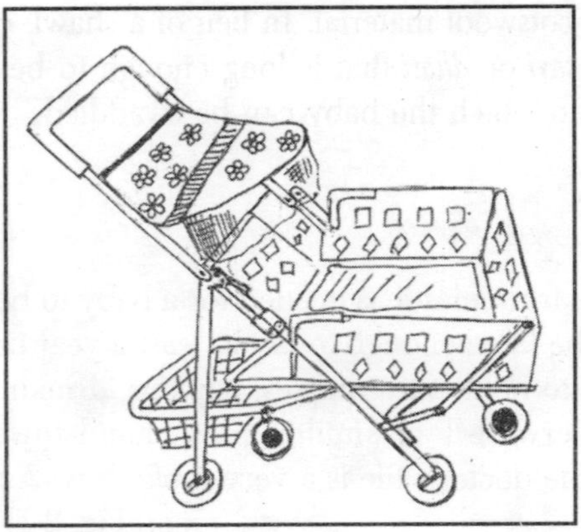

Fig 2-2

A nose syringe with bulb suction is useful to clear out a blocked nose of a baby with the cold. Safety pins with a locking device are also necessary to secure napkins. Automobile seats may be purchased by those who have their personal cars. These seats with harnesses are to encourage greater safety for the travelling infant. If the baby is kept in a separate room from where the mother usually spends the day, you might wish to have a two-way speakerphone so that you can hear her crying and go to her assistance immediately. Baby's room should have a smoke-alarm if possible. An air-conditioner is all right if you are used to it for most months in a year. Go in for a model that comes with a good filter and operates at minimal noise. For areas where humidity is very high, one may go in for a dehumidifier as well. However the last two items are costly and meant only for those who can afford them. If you still haven't got one, apply for a telephone or a mobile phone immediately. Also get yourself a telephone diary where you must prominently mention all the important numbers, including those of your obstetrician, pediatrician, general practitioner, the nearest hospital with child care facilities, your maternity home numbers, Ambulance service, your own parents' and in-laws' phone numbers and the like. A mixer-grinder, if you haven't already got one, is also an essential buy after 4-6 months of the baby's life.

An infant-walker is NOT recommended. Infants learn to balance themselves naturally as they walk, and use of walkers can, in fact, delay the acquisition of these natural skills.

A thermometer is also a good buy. There are many types available (see Chapter 31 *B* for details). You should go in for a branded *digital* thermometer that is very easy to use. Nowadays, *forehead strip* thermometers and *ear* thermometers are also available. They give you readings in less than 5 seconds. Fancy thermometers that resemble a *pacifier* and digitally record the mouth temperature are also available. They are imported from China or Taiwan and are reasonably priced but not very accurate. Old *mercury thermometers* should not be used as they have to be kept for too long a time inside the armpit and they are difficult to read as well. *Rectal* thermometers may be a good option in preterm babies where the risk of a low body temperature is really high, especially in winter. Consult your Pediatrician to decide which thermometer will be best for your baby.

Visitors' Timings:

The arrival of a baby is, as discussed above, a cause for celebration and an army of known as well as unknown friends, associates, neighbours and relatives will descend on your home-mat the day you bring the baby home from the Maternity Home. Handling and kissing by so many individuals is definitely not desirable, and it is therefore reasonable to announce this well before delivery in as polite a manner as possible. You may use your Pediatrician's name to restrict the hordes of people who arrive to "bless" the baby. Children should also be similarly restricted. Special timings may be declared-say four to five p.m. on all week days for visitors.

Helpers, Maids and Sitters:

In joint families, there is no need to worry about hiring professional helpers, but in nuclear families, it is always better if you can begin to look for a good helper who can either come in for some hours daily, or stay with you all day or reside in your home all 24 hours *exclusively* to look after you and/or your baby.

You should make enquiries about their level of education, their familiarity with the languages spoken in your home, their familiarity with the telephone, their ability to give and receive messages on the telephone, their past experience in looking after a baby (maids who have been mothers already have an upper hand), etc. *Sitters* are paid workers who will look after the baby when you are away for some time. All those whom you appoint should necessarily have good personal hygiene, stay nearby, be accessible by phone (or a similar method) and be conscientious and punctual.

Grandparents make the best care-takers for the baby since their care is peppered by their natural affection for the baby. However, if they are themselves infirm, you should provide a back-up in the form of a professional maid/house keeper.

It is wrong to rely on the *maalishwali* to give advice on child care and to help you, the mother, to manage the baby's illnesses. For this, you must consult the baby's pediatrician.

Older Siblings:

Right from the days of pregnancy, you should begin preparing your older child (-ren) for the arrival of a "new" brother or sister. If the older child is too young and still breast feeding, you should begin to wean him/her. Making him/her feel your tummy where the baby has begun to 'kick' may engender feelings of love and affection in his/her tender mind and thwart the natural feelings of jealousy and ill – will which are detrimental to the sibling relationship.

Take him/her with you when you go to purchase clothes and other items for the baby. Involve him/her in choosing these items, and you are more likely to have a more supportive older child. Buy a large baby-doll for the older sib and let him/her "look after" the doll as if it were a cuddly baby. This will help him/her participate in taking care of his/her brother/sister with less jealousy and more affection. Whenever you can, balance his/her desires against the more pressing needs of the newly arriving baby. Take him/her to the movies, purchase some new clothes or toys for him/her and occasionally, treat him/her to a bar of chocolate or candy.

Once the baby is born, click a photograph of the elder sib cheek by jowl with the newborn, or in a similar intimate pose, and put it on a prominent shelf in the baby's room or in the family's living room.

I must warn you, however, that no matter what you do, some degree of sibling rivalry is unavoidable. At least, however, with all the above measures, you can blunt its sharpness.

Ch. 03
Delivery

There is only one pretty child in the world,
and every mother has it.

– Chinese Proverb

The following items should be packed in a small overnight bag or suitcase and kept ready for transportation to the Maternity Home as soon as the mother is in labour. I am listing mainly the items needed for the newly arriving baby. In addition, the mother's medical papers, night-gowns, pads etc. also need to be carried.

a) Frocks, Vests, caps, woollen items
b) Baby napkins and safety pins
c) Baby soap, cream, lotion and talcum powder
d) Bath towel, face towel, cotton balls
e) Plastic sheet, bed sheet and blanket

Onset of Labour:

Most babies are born after a gestation period of 39-41 weeks in the womb. This means, roughly, nine months and 7 days after the first date of the last menstrual period. The end of pregnancy is heralded by the onset of labour pains. These are modest and infrequent to start with, but as labour advances, the pains become more and more frequent and also severe in intensity. The first sign that labour has begun is the appearance of a bloody mucus substance at the vaginal opening. This is called the "show" and it may precede or just follow the first painful contraction of the womb. Soon thereafter, the pains recur again and again. At some point, the bag of water that surrounds the baby "breaks" and fluid starts trickling down the birth canal. At this point, contact your obstetrician, and call for transport to the Maternity Home.

Labour is a **physiological process** and if it progresses normally, it generally does not cause undue stress to the baby or her mother. To make it less painful, some of the natural methods tried include delivering the baby from a sitting position, delivering the baby with the mother lying on one side, delivering the baby underwater and delivering the baby at the parental home. Nowadays, new methods are used, such as use of strong pain killers, spinal anaesthesia and delivery by operation (the so-called Cesarean Section or C-section). Before using any of the above listed alternative methods, do read up on them from a book or on the net.

Here are a few net resources:

- ✔ http://www.pennhealth.com/health_info/pregnancy/labordelivery/articles/deliverypos.html
- ✔ http://www.waterbirth.com/whywater.html
- ✔ http://health_info.nmh.org/HealthNews/reuters/NewsStory0127200310.html

It should always be remembered that **using strong pain killers or anaesthesia can affect the health of the unborn baby**. An operative delivery has its own complications. Remember also that most women the world over give birth naturally and are none the worse for it. Proper breathing and relaxing between the painful contractions can enable the anxious mother to brave the pain and difficulty of normal labour.

Normal Delivery:

The baby usually emerges head first. As labour progresses, the baby is pushed out more and more with each contraction of the womb. The nose, face, mouth and chin are followed by a slight pause, after which the shoulders, trunk and legs are delivered, sometimes with a little assistance by the maternity nurse and/or doctor. The mother experiences a rush of relief once the head is out; the rest of the process is comparatively easier. The baby cries as soon as its head is delivered. After the body is out, the umbilical cord is clamped by the person conducting the delivery. A short while later, the afterbirths (placenta, amniotic membranes etc.) are delivered.

There are many studies that show that early skin-to-skin contact between the mother and its just-born baby has many long-lasting benefits for both the mother and the baby. Even more, it creates the right *milieu* for successful initiation and maintenance of breastfeeding. In most nursing homes and maternity set-ups, the baby is swaddled in warm linen sheets and dried and covered with a fresh sheet. She may need some suction of her mouth and nostrils to remove the fluid that she may have incidentally swallowed during her passage down the birth canal. The eyes are wiped with a sterile cotton swab dipped in salt water. After this, the cord is tied and the extra length removed with sterile scissors. The baby is wrapped in a clean sheet and *then* offered to the mother for breast feeding as soon as possible.

Assisted Delivery:

The first time a mother delivers a baby, the process of labour may take from 6 to up to 16 hours. With subsequent deliveries, the process is much faster. A 4th time mother (a rarity these days) may deliver the baby so soon that she may not even reach the hospital in time.

The first time mother may need a cut to be placed on the edge of her birth canal to facilitate the delivery of the baby's head. This is called an *episiotomy*. This is preferable to getting a vaginal tear by accident. After the baby is delivered, the cut is stitched under local anaesthesia.

At times, there is an undue delay in delivery of the head of the baby. Delay in progress can threaten the well-being of the child as well as the mother. In such cases, the doctor may use either a vacuum pump or a pair of forceps to pull out the baby's head. This is usually safe, but at times, the undue pulling effect may cause internal brain swelling or even bleeding in the baby. Because of this risk, more and more doctors as well as patients are preferring delivery by a Cesarean section (operation).

In a study of birthing practices all over the world, it has been conclusively shown that interventions like episiotomy, forceps and Cesareans have a negative impact on secretion of *oxytocin*, a milk-ejection hormone secreted by the mother; this can lead to breastfeeding problems.

When the baby has turned around inside the womb, she may be born bottom first or feet first. This kind of delivery is called a breech delivery. The head is born last, and may need either physical assistance or the application of forceps or vacuum. In some cases of this type, the labour process may get arrested because the baby's cord drops through the birth canal to the exterior (a cord prolapse), or the foot of one of the legs emerges by the side of the bottom (a footling presentation). These two complications may warrant an emergency cesarean operation.

Cesarean Section:

Truly speaking, a C-section is only indicated to save the life of either the mother or the baby. However, nowadays, increasing numbers of operative deliveries are taking place on the request of mothers who do not wish to undergo a painful labour process or on the suggestion of an unethical obstetrician (a very rare breed) who desires an additional income or has no time to wait for a natural progress of a delivery.

Arrested labour, complicated presentation, multiple babies and threat of distress to the unborn baby are the commonest indications for a C-section. A placenta that lies low in the birth canal and obstructs the passage of the baby (placenta praevia) is another common indication. A mother who is suffering from toxaemia of pregnancy (wherein she has a very high or unstable blood pressure, besides having severe swelling of the body, and a threat of having fits) may also need a C-section.

Some mothers are taken up for a C-section as a planned mode of delivery. This includes placenta praevia, mothers with a very narrow outlet, a first-time mother with a breech presentation, and a mother with two or more previous babies delivered by C-section. This type of planned surgery is called an *Elective* Cesarean Section.

The decision to do a C-section should be left in the hands of the doctor. Consent must be given for it if it is clearly evident that either the mother or the baby is at risk. The baby is expertly removed in a C-section and apart from the fact that she may need her stomach to be cleaned out, she receives no other special care.

Following a C-section the first time, it is not mandatory to do a C-section for the next delivery, unless there is a narrow outlet or some other recurrent cause. However, most obstetricians would advise a C-section for the third baby if the first two were delivered by surgery. On such occasions, the parents may also be offered the option of getting the mother sterilised by cutting off her fallopian tubes. If your family is complete, you might wish to exercise this option so as to be permanently free from the tensions of child-bearing and contraception.

Care after delivery:

Attention to vaginal hygiene, general hygiene, rest, and intake of a well-balanced diet are the most important issues that face the new mother. She should drink plenty of water, avoid too many fried or heavy foods and use laxatives if she has constipation (a common complaint). Care of the breasts is explained in the chapter on Breast Feeding. Toning exercises and aerobic training like cycling, badminton and tennis may be undertaken after six weeks of delivery to regain the pre-pregnancy weight and figure. Exercises for the muscles of the vagina and the perineum are also important to tone them for a possible future pregnancy. Feeding the baby on the breast is in itself a good stimulus for the mother to lose weight. It is a faulty notion that breastfeeding spoils a mother's "figure". If at all, it enhances it, as a nursing mother will lose upto 600-800 calories worth of breast milk each day.

Sexual activity may be resumed anytime after four to six weeks following delivery as long as there is no soreness or pain in the vagina. You should consult the doctor about using a contraceptive device even though you may be breast feeding and there are no periods. Generally, you should avoid taking pills as you are feeding the baby. Using a medicated internal device such as a loop is acceptable, as is a condom used by the husband.

Part II
The First Month of Life

A baby is God's opinion that the world should go on.

- Author Unknown

Ch. 04
Care of a Normal Baby

Every child comes with the message
that God is not yet discouraged of man.
– Rabindranath Tagore

When an expectant mother who is in labour pains is finally wheeled into the labour room, the other relatives, including her husband, other children, parents, siblings and in-laws of all hues and colours go into a tizzy; while some immediately begin praying to the Almighty for a smooth passage for both the baby and the mother, others are busy making arrangements to receive the newborn into a happy, safe and well-planned home! There are all manners of expectations: birth of a son, birth of a "healthy" baby, birth of a "fair" baby and birth of a baby that "resembles", say, the recently deceased grandmother, are but a few of them.

You should remember that most of these desires are deep-rooted in superstitions and wrong notions of the usefulness or otherwise of a "particularly" aligned baby, whether it is a matter of its sex, its size or skin colour or it being vested with the "spirit" of a dead relative. Whatever happens happens with the will of God, and you should be ready to accept His bounty, whether it is in line with your wishes or not. In fact, you may as well remember that the sex of the baby has already been decided by the father at the time of conception – and the mother has no say in the matter, at least biologically!

When the baby is born, a cry is heard – a cry that is welcomed with laughter, joy and merry-making by all those awaiting the "good news". Telephone calls are made, *pedhas* are distributed and so on. Thus a normal birth is a momentous event in the life of a family, to be rivaled perhaps only by that child's marriage after a couple of decades!

The doctor or nurse who appears out of the labour room is immediately surrounded by the eager relatives of the just born baby, and bombarded with questions like:

Is it a boy or a girl?
What is the weight of the baby?
Did it cry immediately, or was there any delay?
Is the baby healthy?

The baby at birth (Fig 4-1 and 4-2):

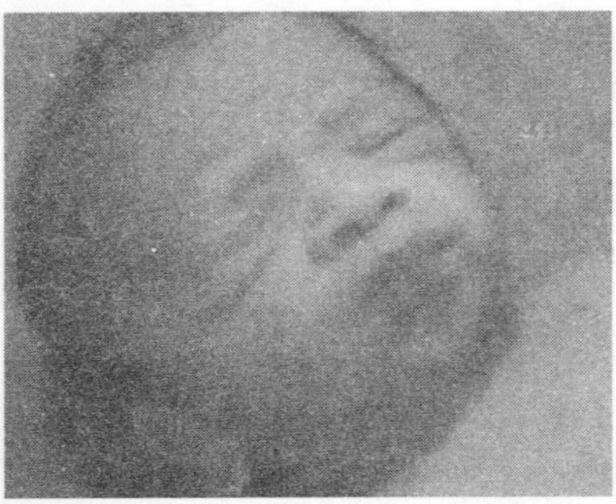

Fig 4-1

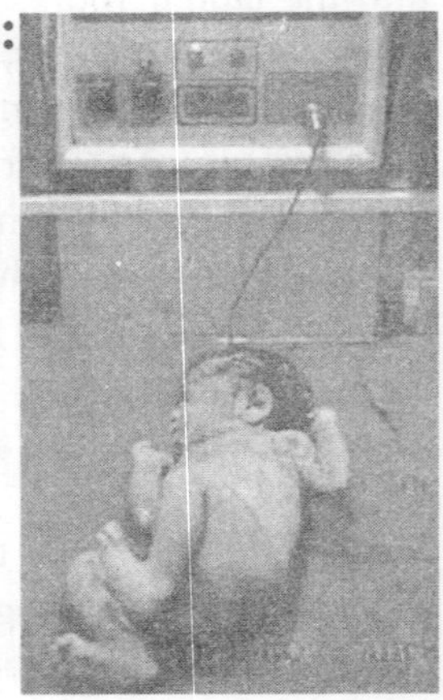

Fig 4-2

The average baby who is born at full-term weighs about 3 kg (6 ½ pounds), measures 50 cm. (20 inches) from head to heel and has a head size of about 35 cm. (14 inches). A very large baby is often born to a diabetic mother, while a small baby probably did not receive adequate nourishment from her mother during pregnancy.

At the time of birth, the baby's head often has some soft bumps, owing to the difficult passage through the birth canal of her mother. These bumps are harmless and tend to disappear within some days or months. The eyes are closed at birth, and the lids are swollen. The hands are outstretched and the fists are often closed, but they may be open.

If no problem has occurred during the delivery process, the baby is dried with a warm towel by the delivery nurse or doctor. Her mouth is inspected for any secretions, and a suction machine is used to remove them if present. After this, the child is dressed up with a full-sleeved top, diaper, cap and, if need be, socks. *If the baby appears clean at birth, a baby bath is not needed.*

In normal deliveries, the baby is handed over to the mother soon thereafter, and nursed next to her (*bedding-in,* see Chapter 2). This is because early skin-to-skin contact, face-to-face contact or whole body-to trunk contact between the baby and the mother encourages "bonding" of emotional ties between them and lays down the foundation of a mutually loving and caring relationship. If the father also joins the duo, then it is like the proverbial icing on the cake: the family bond is strengthened further.

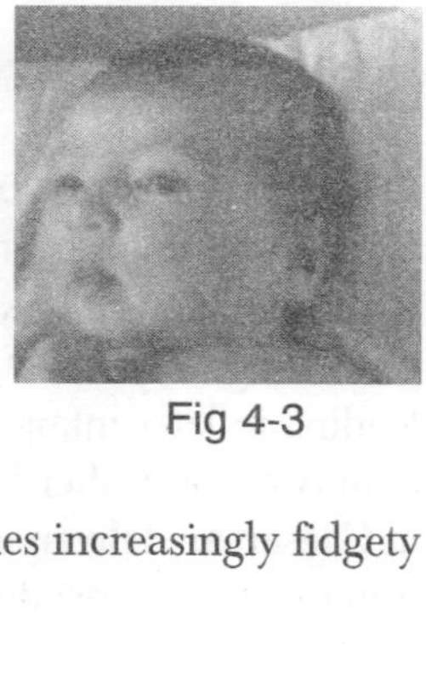

Fig 4-3

After an alert phase of about 45 to 90 minutes (Fig 4-3), the newborn baby will lapse into a state of sleep; this may continue for hours thereafter. In fact, the normal baby mostly sleeps, even in excess of 14-15 hours per day. She will wake up only when she wants a feed, when she wants to evacuate or when she is feeling uncomfortably warm or cold. Before the baby becomes hungry, she looks alert and quiet. As her hunger increases, she becomes increasingly fidgety and restless. If not fed soon, she will begin to bawl and cry. After taking her feed, she needs to be "burped" (see below); after that, she may again go to sleep! The baby sleeps like this through most of the day, but gets up to feed almost five to six times during the night. This is because Nature has provided the highest milk flow only at night.

If you look at the baby in good daylight, you may notice some of the following on the baby's tender skin:

- Red spots on her eyelids, forehead and/or on the nape of her neck
- Pin-point yellow dots on her nose, chin and at times on her forehead and cheeks too.
- Raised red blotches with a boil-like centre on the second day of life.
- Soft downy hair on her forehead, arms, shoulder, back etc.
- Bluish-black areas over her buttocks, legs and lower back.
- Peeling skin over the tips of her fingers, palms, toes and heel.

All the above "curiosities" need no treatment, as they are not harmful in any way. Each of them will disappear without any treatment after a variable period. These minor variations are discussed further in Chapter 5.

Breastfeeding (see Chapter 7):

Once the baby has been handed over to the mother, she should, without wasting any time, immediately put the baby to the breast. Early initiation of breast feeding (within ½ to 1 hour after birth) will go a long way in engendering successful maintenance of breast feeding in later infancy. The baby should be put to the breast in less than two hours after birth in normal deliveries, and within 1-4 hours in Caesarean deliveries. No pre-lacteal feeds, like honey, water, sugar-water or tea are needed. The milk secreted by the mother in the first

2-3 days is yellow, thick and appears "dirty". This milk, also called **"colostrum" is rich in protein and immunoglobulins (protective factors); it should NEVER be denied to the baby. It is the baby's first immunisation.**

Once the milk "comes in", the mother should feed the baby "on demand"; usually, the baby will take feeds almost every 2-3 hours, although some may demand feeds either more or less frequently. In the first 1 ½ to 2 months, babies should be fed both in the day as well as night, but more so at night, since there is a natural surge in the secretion of milk during nights. As the baby grows a bit older, one can train her to feed during the day, and to sleep during the night.

Exclusive breast feeding is recommended for the first six months of life. Not even water needs to be given, as breast milk is 89% water, and adequately meets the need for water in most babies.

Routine Handling and Care:

It is best to allow the baby to sleep with the mother in the latter's bed, as this permits the mother to feed the baby whenever she wants in whatever position of comfort she desires. It also allows the mother to detect when the baby is wet or has passed stool; when the baby is uncomfortable because she is feeling either warm or cold; or when the baby just needs to be held or cuddled.

In normal deliveries, the baby is generally given to the mother within an hour. It must be breast-fed at once. Afterwards, the baby is nursed WITH the mother in the latter's bed. This is called **rooming-in** or **bedding-in**. For a low-birth-weight baby, we advise mothers to cuddle the baby *at all times* upon their own chests/abdomen. This is called **kangaroo-care**. It is excellent for the small baby as it allows her to get her mother's body warmth and can hear her mother's heart-beats. Thus, it aids in feeding, in development and in thermal control of the baby.

Many parents are scared to pick up the baby for fear that they may hurt her. Believe me, the baby is much hardier than you think: it can withstand some rough handling! Thus, don't be scared if her head goes back on her neck when you pick her up from the armpits, or if her back gets arched – she will usually be all right. The **best way to pick her up** is by first putting your hand under her back, then gently "loading" her on to the same forearm; then transfer her, head first, on to the other hand, and you are done. If you wish to carry her against your shoulder, support her wobbly head from behind. You may want to use a carry-cot or a back harness while taking her out: this is perfectly all right.

Babies tend to become cold in winter as their body's temperature regulation system is not yet well developed. In cold climes, protect the baby from drafts of cold air, and if necessary, use a room heater to keep the baby warm and comfortable. Woollens should be used, and a cap on the rather large head is a must, since babies can lose considerable body heat by radiation. The tips of her fingers and toes may turn bluish if a sufficiently warm environment is not created for her.

Conversely, in summer, there is a possibility of the baby becoming hot and feverish if she is not kept open and cool. Coolers, open windows, fans and even air-conditioners are welcome if the heat is unbearable. Loose cotton dresses are recommended in this case. Sometimes, the baby may even be left naked for a short while.

Body Massage:

Touch therapy is being re-discovered as one of the most pleasant methods of treatment for all kinds of ailments in all age-groups. An oil massage is touch-therapy, but it is much more: it improves blood circulation, tightens the lax muscles, relieves tiredness, reduces skin dryness and in small, premature babies, it may even allow absorption of calories through the delicate, thin skin. Touch, in fact, sends pleasant signals to the developing brain, and this may aid in development of the baby's nervous system.

Fig 4-4

A baby-massage need not become a point of conflict between the family and the Pediatrician - if it is an act of love that is passed on from the mother to the baby, and if the baby enjoys it too. This implies that the baby's mother should be the one who gives a massage and not a professional masseur or *bai* (Fig 4-4).

Generally, the baby should be at least 3.0 kg in weight before massage is begun. Any non-irritant oil, such as baby oil, coconut oil, olive oil or almond oil can be used. Mustard oil is irritating to the eye and has an unpleasant smell as well, but we have known many communities where it is used. Massage should be given before the baby is bathed; the oil should be warmed if it is cold; it may be rubbed between the palms to warm it before it is applied on the baby's skin. The baby is laid on her back, and the massage is begun by symmetrically moving both your hands over the trunk of the baby (Fig 4-5). The hands should move away from the midline, and the movement must encompass one horizontal region of the trunk after another in a rhythmic way, using gentle pressure. As the hands move towards the upper trunk, they should move outwards over both the arms of the baby, which are massaged similarly, from shoulder down to the hands. The fingers are also given a gentle tug one by one, as is the thumb. The wrist, elbow and shoulder joints are moved in all possible directions, thereby giving a "passive" exercise to the baby. This is then repeated with the legs as well.

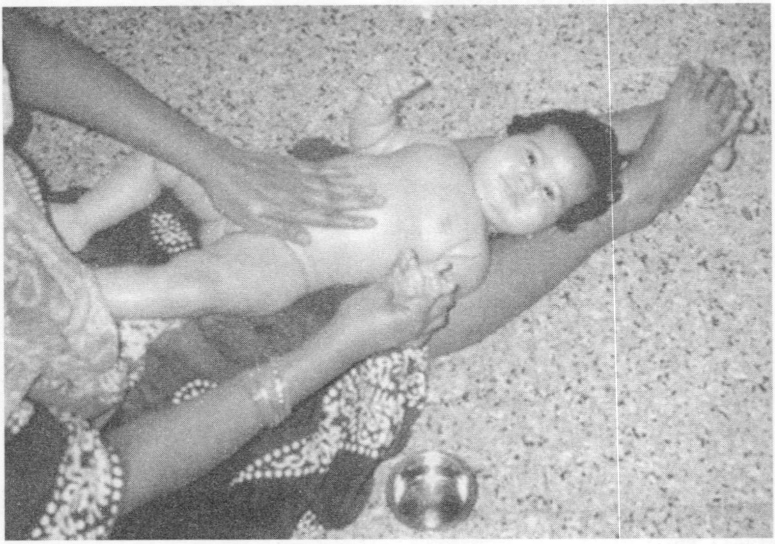

Fig 4-5

Most babies enjoy the massage and make pleasurable, cooing sounds during the massage, especially when she is talked to. After the massage is over, the baby may be left for a short while in sunlight. Care should be taken to see that the rays of the sun do not directly fall on the baby's eyes as this may hurt her. Sunning the baby allows the skin of the baby to manufacture Vitamin D, which is necessary for the health of bones and teeth.

Bath:

At birth, a newborn baby is covered with a light, creamy cheesy material called *vernix*. This vernix is not dirt, but a barrier that protects the delicate skin against the assault of germs. Hence, a baby bath at birth is NOT recommended *unless* the baby is covered with mother's blood or her own feces (stools). The skin, even in such a case, may be gently wiped off with a soft towel. The bath can, in fact, be put off till the second, or even the third day. Even later on, a bath is not really necessary on a daily basis; in cool climes, it may be given but two or three times a week, although most households have a daily massage and bath routine in place by the time the baby is brought from the maternity home.

In the initial few days, when the umbilical stump is still attached to the baby, a **sponge bath** is recommended. The baby is swaddled in a warm, soft towel, and the part(s) to be sponged are successively exposed and cleaned with a soft sponge damped with a mild soap. The face may be sponged without soap. Creases, armpits, groins and the head behind the ears are given special attention. In the end, the private parts are cleaned, first with soap and then with clean warm water.

Once the cord has fallen off and the navel has dried, one can start giving **dip baths**. Select a warm area in the house which is free from cold drafts of air. Keep all the needed items by the side and then pick up the baby to start the bath.

You will need a soap, one large towel, two napkins or washcloths, cotton balls, baby lotion/powder, dress, pins and diaper/napkin.

Fans and air-conditioners should be put off. Lay the baby on your straight legs; first check if she has soiled herself. If so, remove the nappy and first clean the nappy area before beginning the bath. The basin should be 2/3rds filled with warm water.

Now, supporting the baby with one hand, lay her in the tub with her head and face out, and begin by washing the head with a mild soap. As you do so, keep an eye for soapy rivulets running down her forehead. The eyes should be protected at all times! Wash off the soap with a mug of water. All the time, keep one hand on the baby's forehead so that the soap does not enter the eyes. Next, proceed to clean the face, the area behind her ears, the trunk, the extremities and finally, the bottom and her genitals. The routine must involve alternate scrubbing with soap and rinsing with warm water until the entire baby has been bathed.

If you do not have a tub to give a bath, you can proceed by sitting on a plastic sheet. Keep your legs straight in front of you and lay the baby on your legs with her face down. Apply soap and water and wash her back first. Then turn her around, and do the face and head, taking care again to see that the soapy water does not run into her eyes or ears. Next, finish the bath with a wash to the trunk, followed by the upper limbs and the fronts of the legs of the baby. Genital cleaning is a part of the bath and is discussed separately in this chapter.

The fun and enjoyment for the baby may be enhanced by talking to her all the time, tickling her in the ribs, making pleasant sounds, splashing a little warm water on her chest and showing her toys like ducks, dolls etc.

Afterwards, cover the baby with a warm fluffy towel and begin drying her by dabbing her rather than wiping abrasively. Once dry, you may apply a bit of talcum powder by taking it on your palm, *away from the baby*, and gently rubbing it on her neck, armpits, groins and genital areas. It is time now to brush her hair, dress her up, perhaps offer her a feed (if she is so inclined) and then let her go to sleep.

<u>Use of hair-oil is NOT recommended.</u>

A word about hiring professional services for the massage and bath. Most "*bais*" are partly or fully illiterate; they know their jobs well, but their advice should not be sought for ailments that the parents do not understand. It is not correct for these women to offer "household remedies" and "medical advice"; for this, the child's doctor should be contacted. In the final analysis, it is much better if the baby's mother herself gives the massage and bath as these two activities bring the mother and baby emotionally nearer to each other.

Care of eyes, mouth, ears and nose:

Many caretakers fuss over these openings for no reason at all. Natural mechanisms already exist for keeping the baby's various special organs clean and functioning well. For example, wax protects the eardrum against any object or insect that accidentally enters the ear canal. Thus, putting buds in the baby's ear canals is not only unnecessary, but also dangerous. In the same way, the external nostrils of the baby are her only route for inhaling air with each breath. Yet, many a times, I have witnessed massage-*bais* putting oil drops in the baby's nostrils. This will choke up the only inlet for baby's breath, as babies cannot breathe with their mouths open. Secondly, as the baby inhales the oil drops, these descend into her lungs, where they may then cause a chronic cough, or even "oil pneumonia", which is very difficult to treat!

The eyes have tears – a natural cleansing liquid, which forms a protective film over the baby's delicate eye surface. No attempt should be made to put *kajal*, *surma*, etc. in the baby's eyes. These substances can introduce infection in the eye, and there is no truth to the old women's tales that they "enhance" vision in any way.

In the same way, you do not have to clean the nostrils or the mouth unless you find definite problems. If the nose is choked with sticky secretions, instill salt-water drops in them, and gently insert a wisp of linen or cotton-bud to remove the softened secretions. If the tongue looks whitish, and the patch (-es) do not go away even after the baby has taken a feed, remove them with a linen or cotton dipped in a little glycerine.

Care of the genital area:

It is very essential that the area of skin demarcated by the genital structures is kept immaculately clean and dry at all times. As soon as the baby has passed urine or stools, the bottom should be cleaned and dried immediately. If this is not done, nappy rashes may develop;

if infection occurs in these rashes, girls can even develop a urinary tract infection. In boys, rough handling of the foreskin over the tip of the penis may cause scarring and ballooning of the tip of the penis area – a condition that can cause you to run to the doctor for urgent relief.

To clean the genital area in a small baby, use cotton wool or soft cloth dipped in water. In girls, the wiping is done <u>from the front to the back</u> to prevent soiling and infection of the tender urine area. Direct washing of the bottom in running water is also not a bad idea in a slightly older baby. Only, take care that the water is not too cold, and does not gush out too fast from the tap. After cleaning, pat-dry the area with a soft towel. If necessary, put a little powder into the cleft below the bottom, and within the groins.

If a rash is already present, consult the doctor for advice on creams that can be used for relief. Remember, if you keep the nappy area open and dry, the rash will heal faster!

Care of the skin and nails:

Since the newborn's skin is very delicate, you should be very sparing in the use of cosmetics, powders, lotions etc. Clothes should be thoroughly rinsed to remove even small traces of detergent from them; preferably, the baby's clothes should be washed separately.

Nails should be trimmed either with blunt-nosed baby scissors or with nail-cutters very carefully; this should be done at least once a week, although trimming may be needed more often in the first few months of life since nails grow more quickly initially.

Care of the navel:

The umbilical stump may fall off anytime between the 3rd to the 14th day after birth; do not bandage it or dress it in any way. Clean it with surgical spirit daily to help keep it dry. After the cord falls off, the navel may remain moist for a few days; continue to clean it with spirit till it dries up. If the wetness persists for more than a few days, consult your pediatrician for further advice. If there is a small bud of wet tissue (called an *umbilical granuloma*), it can be treated with application of a small pinch of table salt two to three times a day for some days.

Sometimes, the umbilical area swells up like a balloon whenever the baby strains at stool, or cries a lot. This is nothing but an *umbilical hernia;* it occurs because of an intrinsic weakness of the baby's stomach area muscles. No coins or bandages should be used to press the balloon down – it is not only useless but also dangerous to do so, as sometimes, the baby's bowel can get trapped in the herniated balloon, and the baby will become very sick indeed, or may even die. Generally, as the baby starts sitting or walking, such hernias subside *on their own* -- usually by one year of age.

Bowel movements:

A normal newborn passes dark green sticky stools known as meconium on the first two to three days after birth. After this, usually on the fourth day or so, the baby is prone to pass large, watery, liquid stools which are greenish yellow in colour; as suddenly as they started, these watery stools return to normal within 24 hours. They are called "transition" stools and are a normal development. As such, they do not warrant *any* treatment.

Soon thereafter, a normal baby's stools become what are known as "breast-milk" stools. These are golden yellow in colour; they are passed almost each time that the baby feeds. The usual timing with respect to the feed is when the baby is actually suckling, and their passage is heralded by the rather loud sound of evacuation of gas. The stool is semi-solid, appears to be composed of large-sized yellow granules accompanied by a small quantity of water. It is passed effortlessly, and is approximately as large as to cause the nappy to have a stain 2 ½ to 5 inches in diameter. It is sticky, but only just, and it smells like curd, not foul. The baby may pass 8-10 such stools in a 24-hour period, since it feeds that many times. Since passing of the stool creates wetness and soiling of the nappy, the baby immediately becomes "uncomfortable" and begins to cry to remind the parent to "clean" her up!

There are babies who pass some stool with every gas movement, and this becomes a nuisance for the already tired mother, who has to change the nappy almost 20-40 times in a 24-hour day. Often, in such cases, parents worry if their baby has diarrhea, and consult the doctor, who may, if he is not aware of the "normalcy" of such a bowel movement, prescribe antidiarrhoeals or even, God forbid, antibiotics.

One thing more: The bottom must be always cleaned as soon as you become aware that the baby has passed a stool. See "Care of the Genital Area" above.

Frequently, babies also pass urine *along* with stools. This may cause them to cry before passing the stool as well.

Lastly, remember that some babies may not follow the above norm and pass stools just once a day, or once every 3-4 days. As long as the stools are of normal colour and appearance and the baby is thriving, it needs no treatment. The same is true for some babies passing normal, but slightly greenish stools.

Urination:

You may already be aware of this: most of the fluid in the mother's womb in which the baby floats during pregnancy is the baby's own urine. Not only does the baby pass urine regularly while inside, she also keeps "drinking" the urine continuously. After she is born, she will usually pass urine almost immediately. Thereafter, she may not pass urine for the next 24 hours or even 36 hours. This is because she does not get much liquid (mother's milk) inside her during this time. Once the mother's breast milk is established, the baby will pass urine more frequently, say almost once every 1-3 hourly, but even up to 5-6 times in 24 hours is all right. Some babies may pass urine even 15-20 times in 24 hours.

While passing urine, or sometimes, even before doing so, the baby may cry because of a full bladder or because of the nappy becoming wet. She will stop crying as soon as she has been attended to.

Immunisations:

Usually, large hospitals and government or municipal maternity homes arrange to give the baby her first vaccines before she and her mother have been discharged from there. These vaccines include the B.C.G. vaccine, the zero polio-dose and the first injection of Hepatitis B. Later vaccines are given in the clinic. For further details, see Chapter 30 and Appendix b.

Care of a Low birth weight Baby:

A baby which is born with a birth weight of less than 2500 grams is considered to be a low- birth-weight (LBW) baby. LBW babies are either under-nourished or born prematurely. The first category of babies is called "small for dates"; this may be due to maternal malnutrition or some disease like tuberculosis, high blood-pressure or something else.

Preterm babies, or "preemies" as they are called, are usually sent home after some period of stay in the NICU (Neonatal Intensive Care Unit). At the time of their being sent home, they have usually become normal with respect to their ability to take breast feeds, remain warm under blankets, be free from the perils of prematurity like shaky hands and feet, fits, jaundice etc. and sleep and wake at normal times to satisfy their hunger and other needs.

During the early days following the arrival of a small baby at home, the main things to take care are:

- The baby should be kept adequately clothed and covered to avoid "hypothermia", a condition where the baby becomes cold due to a cold environment and rapidly takes a turn for the worse. Cold drafts of air from a fan or air-conditioner should be strictly avoided.
- The baby should be given frequent, regular feeds on her mother's breast – at least once every two hours – both during the day *and during the night.*
- *Rooming-in*, where the baby sleeps with the mother in her cot, is recommended because the mother will be better able to monitor the baby in this case, and attend to her various needs more quickly. *Kangaroo-care* is even better (see above).
- If the baby is unable to feed directly at the breast, the mother should remove some milk from her breast by manual expression and feed it to the baby with a small spoon, dropper or *palada.*
- Everyone, including the mother, MUST wash their hands with soap and water before handling or lifting the baby, as the baby is most likely to catch germs from the care-taker's hands, rings etc. As the baby's body defenses (or *immunity*) are weak, such germs may cause them to become sick rather soon … although the same germs are harmless inhabitants on the skin of the adults!
- The cot, mattresses, pillow and her clothes should all be clean and maintained hygienically, with the covers changed regularly to avoid contamination of the baby with germs.
- On the day of discharge from the NICU, the preemie should get all his vaccines which the full term baby would have received within the first few days of life.

Conclusions and Final Words of Advice:

It is a full-time occupation for a mother to look after her baby, and in recent times, it is heartening to see fathers too contributing in the care of the newly arrived baby. In some ways, this was unavoidable, since more and more families are becoming nuclear and "shunning" the presence of grandparents in their homes. Old people may be slow, choosy about what they eat, need tender loving care and "be in the way' of youthful enjoyment to a young, merry-making couple, but once the baby arrives, they learn very quickly that the patience, wisdom and fortitude of old age are indispensable. It is all too easy to brush away one's aging parents quite literally "under the carpet" on days when guests come to party, but it is at the time of the arrival of the baby that their worth is realised and their attention and "services" are sought by the young parents.

Fathers of babies can certainly help in so many ways: they can help dress/ undress the baby, they can help soak the soiled nappies, they can create a home environment that is conducive to a peaceful mother-child relationship, they can fix up doctor's appointments and participate in their baby's pediatric care, they can even make simple weaning foods for the baby with basic kitchen skills! On top of everything, fathers can iron out the differences that may arise between their wives and their mothers: this allows for a happy household unit!

A final word. The parents of the baby should realise that the moment the baby was conceived in the mother's womb, **their lives have been altered forever**. They have to forget everything else, and learn to live for their baby. No amount of time-management, maid's help, foster-care, *ayahs* etc. can actually release time for the parents to pursue their pre-parenthood hobbies and dreams. If they try to balance their babies against their personal aspirations, the baby WILL suffer in some way or the other. The first three years are crucial for the cerebral development of the baby, and parents must do all they can to provide a stimulating and loving environment for their baby so that she can reach her full potential. The sooner the parents realise this, the better it is for themselves *and* the baby.

Ch. 05
Developmental Variations and Minor Problems in the Newborn Baby

Children are the living messages we send to a time we will not see –
Author unknown

From the time the baby is born, it is a natural tendency for the parents, the grandparents, the siblings and all other relatives to gather around her to look at her closely. The analytical person will examine her to see who she resembles most. The loving person will ooh and aah over each and every aspect of the baby's appearance. The cynical fellow will immediately try and identify flaws in this latest "creation" of God. The mother will tenderly touch the baby to pass on her unlimited love and compassion.

Such inspections and examinations may cause one to observe some unexpected lumps, boils, coloured marks, hairy areas and other curiosities on the baby. Either you have already seen them before, and are blasé about it, or you have never seen such astonishing and worrying things and are immediately anxious about what they could be.

We shall go over some of the more commonly observed variations and skin changes on the newborn baby. Rest assured, most of these will have no lasting effects on the baby!

The aftermath of the baby's passage through the birth-canal:

It is indeed surprising that such a large baby can emerge almost unscathed through what seems at first glance to be such an inadequate passage! However, Nature has designed the pelvic bones, the muscles and the womb in such a way that while it looks "compact", it can expand as per the need of the descending baby. In spite of this, sometimes, one can see that the baby has had a tough time of it all. She may show one of the following:

1. A mis-shapen head with the skull bones all clumped over each other (moulding);
2. A boggy feel to the entire scalp, or a part of it (caput);
3. Small superficial cuts and bruises as well as marks of instruments like forceps or vacuum;
4. A large, soft swelling overlying a limited portion of the head (cephalhematoma);
5. A darkened, swollen face, rump, or genital area in some babies

Most of these "anomalies" are the effects of pressure on the baby's delicate tissues. While superficial cuts and small bruises don't mean a thing, the large scalp swellings are certainly frightening.

Moulding and caput formation are temporary and are due to pressure of the birth canal on the babies's head. *Moulding* refers to the bunching together of the bones on the top of the skull, while a *caput* is a collection of clear liquid just under the scalp. They are seen just after birth and disappear in one to two days without any treatment.

At times, there is some blood collection under the outer covering of the skull bones. This kind of swelling is well demarcated and may be as large as 3-5 cm in diameter. It is called a *cephalhematoma*, and it slowly reduces in size without any treatment over 2-4 weeks. It should not be "excised" or "incised" under any circumstances.

Depending upon which part of the baby emerges first from the birth canal, there may be swelling and dark discolouration of it. Therefore, the face will be affected if it was a "face-down" delivery, and the genital area will be affected if the baby was a breech.

Some babies develop *small bleeding spots* under the *conjunctival membrane* of the eye(s). This appears as a red spot when the eye of the baby is opened. It is seen over the white part of the eye. This is absolutely harmless and needs no treatment.

When a vacuum is used to extract the baby's head, a rather large well-defined swelling may appear where the suction cup was applied. This is called a *chignon*, and needs no treatment. Similarly, in a baby whose heads is delivered with a forceps, small, red lines may be seen where the forceps was applied. These too will disappear and need no further treatment.

Downy Hair:

Most babies have a soft covering of downy hair on their bodies. These hair are usually most prominently seen on the forehead, shoulders, arms and upper backs. Some may have them on the lower back, in the groove below the buttocks, and over the pubic area as well. Downy hairs tend to fall off as the baby grows, and in most cases, they have disappeared by the age of 6-8 months. Therefore, I do not recommend application of gram flour (*besan*) on the baby's skin to remove these hair. In fact, besan may provoke a very frightening allergic rash, which will need separate treatment.

Skin Pigmentations:

Many babies have bluish black areas on their arms, buttocks, backs of the legs, lower backs, and elsewhere too. These are called "*Mongolian spots*" and they represent a developmental stage in the maturation of skin pigment. They disappear over 6-24 months of life and need no treatment at all. Children with darker skins have greater numbers and areas of these "spots".

Some babies have smaller areas of dark discolouration, while others have pale, red, port-wine or black spots over their skins. These are called birth marks or *nevi.* Most nevi are harmless, but some may be pointers to an internal disease.

Other Skin Curiosities:

Milia are tiny yellowish white pimples that are seen on the baby's nose, chin, and sometimes, forehead. They disappear on their own after a few days.

Some babies develop *acne-like pimples* on the face; this is due to the effect of mother's hormones in the baby's blood; they will disappear on their own in a few weeks.

On the second day, some babies have a red eruption on their bodies. The rash resembles boils, but is in fact sterile and needs no treatment. It will vanish in the next 24-48 hours. It is called *erythema toxicum.*

Jaundice:

Over 60-70 % of all normal newborns develop a yellowish discolouration of the skin and the whites of the eyes on or around the third day of life. This is called physiological jaundice, and it occurs because of a rapid removal of red blood cells (containing "fetal" hemoglobin) from the baby's blood. The hemoglobin is broken down into many components, one of which is called *bilirubin.* It is yellow in colour and causes this jaundice.

The jaundice increases over the next few days, and then begins to subside on its own. By the end of the second week of life, the child's skin colour has returned to normal. The resolution can be hastened by exposing the child to early morning or late evening sunlight. This exposure not only reduces the blood bilirubin level, but also allows the skin to manufacture Vitamin D, which is needed for the healthy growth of bones and teeth.

In some breast fed babies, the jaundice may climb a little too high to call it physiological. If the doctor cannot find any other cause for it, he may conclude that this is due to breast feeding and he may advise you to take the baby off the breast for a few days and then resume it. This may bring about the required reduction of jaundice.

In some babies, the jaundice may continue to increase beyond the physiological levels described above. Although there are many causes of this "pathological jaundice", the most common reasons are a baby who is not getting enough breast milk inside her (either because of maternal reasons, or some problem with her), a mother-baby blood group incompatibility (mother is O and baby is A or B group; or mother is Rh-negative and the baby is Rh-positive), a G-6-P D deficiency in the baby and an ill baby, most often with some type of general infection or liver disease.

The occurrence of jaundice under the age of 24 hours, a rapid rise in the yellow discolouration of the body and deep yellow eyes seen in a newborn less than 3 days old -- all indicate pathological jaundice. It is a potentially dangerous condition as the high bilirubin level in the blood can cause permanent brain damage, fits, deafness or cerebral palsy. Treatment of severe jaundice needs the urgent attention of a Neonatologist. He may either put the baby in special lights (*phototherapy*) or arrange for the baby to undergo a special form of blood transfusion known as an *exchange transfusion.*

A baby who has undergone either of the above two treatments is likely to recover fully. However, she will need a close neurological follow up to rule out any subtle effects of the high bilirubin that she had in her neonatal period. Particular attention is paid to looking for high-tone deafness, presence of a developmental delay and any learning difficulties she may have once she attends school.

Note: Some exclusively breast fed babies develop a high bilirubin due to the presence of a hormone in the breast milk of their mothers. Such babies are advised to continue breast feeding unless the levels become too high. This condition is called *breast milk jaundice* and is exceedingly rare and familial in nature. The hormone, and therefore the jaundice, tends to disappear over three to four months.

Lastly, congenital or neonatal *hypothyroidism* (a low thyroid level) (Chapter 45) and *Mongolism* (Down syndrome) (Chapter 25) can also cause a prolonged and heavy jaundice.

Sleep and Wake Cycles: (See Chapters 4, 11 and 14)

It is not unusual for a newborn baby to sleep 12-16 hours out of 24. She may get up to take a feed, and after she has been burped, she may promptly fall back to sleep. Usually, a newborn baby tends to alternate between states of waking and sleeping throughout the day and night. She is unaware of what day or night mean to us adults. She will therefore be expected to wake up periodically to get the next feed regardless of the time. Often, this irritates not only the parents but also the grandparents, the baby's older siblings and in some cases, neighbours. The hungry baby awakens them all when she begins crying.

We should remind ourselves that the mother secretes different quantities of milk at different times of the day. Her milk is usually at its highest at or around midnight and gradually declines till it reaches a minimum level in the late afternoon of the following day. The response of the baby is to therefore stay awake through the night to derive the maximum benefit from her mother. In fact, she will sleep for up to 5-6 hours in the day time after her massage and bath. This is normal for the first 2-3 months, by which time most babies "learn" to sleep uninterrupted at night for six to eight hours.

The best time to prepare to feed the baby is when she is not yet fully hungry, that is, when she is awake and about 15-20 minutes "away" from crying. In this alert, active state, she will also be most receptive to close eye to eye contact and a loving interaction, as she "lures" you, the mother, to pick her up and feed her!

A baby who sleeps more than usual, and appears lethargic and dopey most of the time may either have a low thyroid function (cretinism), or be mentally retarded. On the other hand, a previously active baby becoming dull and inactive has a more than likely chance of having a serious acute illness. She should be taken to the doctor immediately.

Excessive Crying: (See Chapter 6)

A normal neonate tends to sleep during daytime and remain awake at night as we have seen above. Part of this is because of hunger, but it is also a fact that during the entire time the baby was in the womb, she would sleep in the day and move and be active in the night. This habit "spills" over into the first few months of life. After two to three months, babies adjust to night time sleep.

Most babies cry when they are hungry, but a baby may well cry excessively for other reasons. See Chapter 6 for details.

Regurgitation of Feeds: (See Chapter 39)

Many mothers complain that their babies vomit milk all the time. In spite of this, they find that they (the babies, I mean) remain "healthy" and cheerful. Not only that, they gain proper weight as well. This is because some amount of regurgitation of milk (throwing up) is normal for a baby. She will take her feed, you will carry her on your shoulder to burp her and next thing you know, she has brought out some of that milk along with a curd-like substance back through her mouth (and sometimes, even through her nose.

Do not be alarmed. Just wipe the stuff away and carry the baby till she settles down. After she has burped, lay her in her bed on her right flank and leave her like this as she goes to sleep.

<u>If the baby vomits forcefully or continuously, or if the vomit is green (like bile), or has blood in it, or if she rapidly gets constipated and develops swelling of the abdomen, it is time to urgently see the doctor.</u>

Oral Curiosities: (See Chapter 36)

The roof of the mouth sometimes has **pearly white spots** arranged in a vertical row near the midline. They disappear in a few days. Some babies have **blisters** inside the mouth from sucking movements inside the uterus of the mother. Occasionally, babies are born with soft, **neonatal teeth** (or more often, a single tooth). If they are soft, and covered with the skin that covers the inside of the mouth, they are unlikely to hurt the mother while feeding. They may then be left alone. If, however, they are firm, they may need to be removed (otherwise, they can get detached and go down the wind pipe and choke the baby).

Bottle-fed babies, and less commonly, breast fed ones sometimes develop a whitish, patchy discoloration of the tongue that is hard to wipe off, even with a flannel cloth. If you try wiping it forcibly, the areas may show pinpoint bleeding too. This is due to a commonly existing mouth fungus called *candida* or **thrush**. It can interfere with feeding as it is painful. The baby may get the infection from her mother; conversely, the baby may infect the mother's nipples and cause her to avoid feeding her. The condition can be easily treated with anti-fungal creams and lotions.

A tiny lick of mucosa is often seen to be "binding" the tip of the tongue to the floor of the mouth. This is called a **"tongue-tie"** and many people believe it may interfere with the baby's future speech development. This is not true, however, and it should not be operated upon.

Eye Problems: (See Chapter 37)

To read about **sub-conjunctival bleeding**, see above under "The Aftermath ..." paragraph. Some other eye conditions are discussed here. Babies' eyes often get infected either from germs acquired in the maternity home, or after discharge. Such infection is called **conjunctivitis**. It can be prevented if all care-takers wash their hands thoroughly before handling the baby. The eyes should be swabbed clean at the time of bathing. If, however, infection does take place, a few drops of mother's colostrum (the milk that comes from the mother in the first few days) instilled into the baby's eye is said to be specially useful If it does not work, one will have to ask the doctor to prescribe antibiotic drops.

Occasionally, some babies have **constant watering** from one or both eyes. This may be due to a blocked tears channel that is located in the inside corner of the eye. A blocked naso-lacrimal duct is the diagnosis. The easy way to remedy this problem is to gently massage the inner corner of the affected eye with gentle but firm pressure using your thumb. The massaging movement is from above downwards and reverse. It should be done many times during the day. If this does not solve the problem by one year of age, you should visit an ophthalmologist, who may then choose to "open" the blocked hole with a probe and a syringe filled with normal saline. He will, quite literally, flush out the debris from the blocked canal and restore patency.

Tremors of Hands:

Some healthy babies show a very fine tremor of their hands and feet, as also quivering of the chin when they are stimulated or handled roughly or when they are startled awake from sleep. This tremulousness or jitteriness may be due to low blood calcium or a low blood glucose level, especially if there has been a delay in onset of feeds or when the baby is small. Usually, jitteriness disappears within 2-3 days.

Hiccups:

The diaphragm divides the internal body cavity into the chest and the abdomen. It is a large, sensitive muscle that helps the normal person to breathe in and out regularly throughout life. It can easily get irritated by the distending stomach, as after a milk feed or a weaning food. When irritated, the diaphragm contracts suddenly in an "attempt to remove the irritant stimulus". This sudden contraction causes the baby to take a breath in, create a sharp noise and draw in her tummy. This is called a hiccup. Hiccupping can occur several times in a day; it is perfectly harmless. Proper burping of gas will reduce its frequency.

Sneezing:

Most babies sneeze and even cough in the first few days of life. They are "trying" to remove mucus, water and amniotic fluid that they may have inhaled in their lungs. Such sneezing is NOT due to cold and does not need any treatment. Even afterwards, sneezing may continue off and on, and may cause you to seek medical help. When sneezing is accompanied by cough that is moist and keeps coming both during the night and the day, the child may be having a viral sore throat or cough.

Yawning:

Yawning will occur before going to sleep or after waking up. It is a normal physiological behaviour and needs no further care.

Boils: (See Chapter 38)

Pus-filled small boils are sometimes seen on the skin of the babies, particularly on the face, groins, armpits, neck etc. They are caused by bacteria, most commonly the staphylococcus. The baby often gets infected by coming in contact with care-takers who do not wash their hands before touching her, as also by contact with infected napkins, towels, soaps, etc. Small, isolated boils can be ruptured by the doctor to drain away the pus followed by advice to apply an antibacterial ointment over the area. If there are too many boils, consult your doctor as the child will need antibiotics by mouth.

Cradle Cap: (See Chapter 38)

This is a form of dandruff that occurs over the scalp of babies who have an oily skin. The baby develops yellowish crusts and scales on the scalp. This is unsightly and itches as well. Try and soften the scales by applying coconut oil over it for a few days and then remove them with a soft comb. Shampooing may be done after oil application. Hair oil should NOT be applied. The treatment should be continued for a few days or till the problem is ameliorated.

Fever: (See Chapter 31)

Sometimes, full term healthy newborns start running a moderate temperature of up to 100 to 101° F without any apparent cause on the 2nd or 3rd day of life. This is most likely to occur in the hot months when the outside temperature is over 40° C. If you find that the baby is otherwise all right and is accepting feeds properly, do not panic. Just keep the baby under a fan or in the AC and let her cool down. Paracetamol rectal suppositories can be used too. Most of the times, once the baby feeds well on her mother's breast, the fever decreases very well. If fever persists beyond one or two days, or if the baby stops feeding properly or shows symptoms of illness, show the doctor urgently.

Vaginal discharge and/or Bleeding:

The girl child carries her mother's hormones in her blood for a few weeks; as a result, her body organs may show some changes which normally occur in adult females. Vaginal discharge of a whitish nature and menstruation-like bleeding are symptoms of the same condition. These do not need any treatment.

Breast enlargement can also occur due to the same reason. No attempt should be made to "remove" the milk from the breasts as the swelling will disappear after a few days. Squeezing the breasts can, in fact, lead to a breast abscess in the baby.

The tight Fore-skin: (See Chapter 42)

In boys, the prepuce or the foreskin appears "stuck" to the penis and cannot be retracted. This is actually normal. No attempt is to be made to "pull" back the skin as this can cause tremendous pain and lead to complications later on.

Final Words:

By now, you must be totally confused about what is and what isn't normal in a newborn. Remember that a sick-looking child is most likely definitely sick, while a well looking child is most likely, well, well. The danger signals which indicate that you go to the doctor are already enumerated and should be memorized so that you can take a decision about seeking medical attention.

Ch. 06
The Crying Baby

Parenthood is a lot easier to get into than out of.
– Bruce Lansky

Most babies will cry almost daily throughout their infancy, and it would be wrong to assume that there is something wrong with them each time they cry! **Crying is the only way of communication babies know** – not counting their absolutely adorable body-language when they coo and smile at you! In fact, most of the times, you will be totally clueless as to why your precious one is on a "crying spree".

The worst that can happen is that the crying baby "reveals" her illness to you over the next 8-12 hours and you can then consult the doctor about it. No baby ever "died" because she cried, although if the reason for her crying was a serious illness, you may have trouble. My sincere advice to you is to call her Pediatrician if she hasn't stopped crying in 45 minutes to one hour or so. The other indication to call up her doctor would be when it was obvious that she was ill, for example when her limbs turn cold and blue, or her lips turn blue when she cries, or when her crying intensity goes down to a whimper as her illness (whatever it may be) takes a firm grip on her well-being.

The distress that parents, the extended family and neighbours experience when their baby wails is too much to put adequately into words. As it is, many parents do not HAVE an extended family's support, many work long hours to make both ends meet, and on top on that, they have to deal with an irritable, fractious infant ... it would make any person insane in no time!

It is now believed that babies may be "letting off steam" or venting their frustrations when they go on one of their crying spells.

Reasons for Crying:

Hunger and thirst are the foremost reasons for the baby to cry. Wet or soiled nappies are next, followed by pain in some or the other part of the body, discomfort due to under- or over- clothing and even such things as plain, simple boredom. Many babies cry just before passing urine; some do so before evacuating their bowel. Over - stimulation and fatigue may cause some to cry. Sometimes, babies cry due to the movement of crawling ants, bites of bed-bugs, or the buzz of an insect that is trapped inside the external ear canal.

The abnormal causes include simple ones like teething; viral infections like a cold, skin infections (such as boils), and earache due to middle ear fluid collection can all cause excessive crying. Babies cry after receiving their DPT (or almost any other vaccine, but less so), after having some cough and cold medicines and when they have fever or dehydration. If the child cries while feeding, or when offered a feed, she may be having ulcers in the mouth or oral thrush. If the child cries when she is being picked up, she may have a muscle, joint or bone problem such as inflammation of these structures or a fracture of the bones of the shoulder girdle or limbs (e.g. fracture of the collar-bone during a "vigorous" oil massage by an untrained or over-enthusiastic masseur)

At night, the baby becomes more "aware" of the things around her. She may react to these by crying. Examples include pin-worms emerging out of the anus and causing irritation of the vulva in a girl, the effect of a nose-block which interferes with easy breathing, the presence of insects inside the baby's clothing, and so on. Night time is also the time for extra hunger in small babies, so they may stay up through most of the night, demanding feeds. This can prove to be a very frightening and tiring experience for the parents. A poking object that hurts the baby may be all the reason for her crying!

However, by far the most important and least understood reason for crying in small babies is what is called "evening colic". We shall come to it later.

What to do?

Firstly, do not panic. Pick up the baby and cuddle and caress her with gentle rocking movements. Try to soothe her by holding her close to your chest and grasping her jittery limbs. Some babies do well if they are stroked on the forehead, the top of the head or on the temples. Try and see if she is hungry. Offer her a feed on the breast or with a cup and spoon to check if she is hungry. Next, open her clothing to see if she was too tightly or loosely packed. See if she has wet herself or passed a stool, and if so, change her. Look for wandering ants or other insects, an open diaper pin that may be hurting her or for an anal rash.

Evening Colic:

This condition is so common that even first-time mothers with a nuclear-family background are aware of it. Whether it is actually a colicky abdominal/intestinal pain or not, the baby is seen to suddenly bend her thighs over her abdomen and make her tummy tight; she then lets off a scream that continues in fits and bursts over the next three or four minutes. Episodes of this occur intermittently for the next 3-4 hours, daily, for the first three to three and a half months of life.

The crying leads to swallowing of air (*aerophagia*) which then worsens the crying in a queer vicious cycle sort of way. The spell winds down after three hours or so as the baby gets tired from crying and whimpers off to sleep. One must remember that "colic" may actually be due to milk allergy, an over-sensitive baby, over-stimulation of the baby by parents/grandparents, anxiety and stress among the parents etc. More crying simply increases the anxiety.

What to do?

Once you have ascertained that there is no other problem with the baby (see above), you may do the following in a rough sequential order. First, try and soothe her by talking to her. Then, lay her on her tummy (prone) on your crossed legs. Gently stroke her back till she stops crying. If this does not work, you might want to apply asafoetida (*hing*) mixed in water on the baby's stomach in slow circular movements. If possible, give her carminative medicinal drops at this stage. These drops do NOT have spasm-relieving agents which are found in anti- spasmodic drops. The latter are not recommended as excessive use of anti-spasmodic drops can reduce the normal movements of the gut and precipitate a crisis. **Gripe-waters (which contain alcohol or bicarbonate of soda and lull the baby to sleep) and *janam-ghuttis* (which contain the addictive substance opium) are also NOT recommended.**

We also do NOT recommend the use of pacifiers. These come in plain and honey-containing varieties. They are prone to catching bugs from the floor of the house, carpets, table-tops, etc. This may produce infections of the middle ear (otitis media) or episodes of diarrhoea. Also, if the baby is hungry and quietens down with a pacifier, you will end up NOT feeding her – and that is inexcusable. Even in babies, pacifiers can reduce the desire to demand a breastfeed.

Part III
Infant Feeding

A baby is a blank cheque
made payable to the human race.

– Barbara Christine Seifert

Ch. 07
Breastfeeding

God could not be everywhere, so he created mothers.

– Jewish Proverb

Why Breastfeeding is best for the baby:

Breast is best. How many times have you heard that? Perhaps it irritates you when your pediatrician extols the virtues of mother's milk and practically passes judgement on your capabilities as a successful mother based only on one criterion: Did you breast-feed your baby/Are you planning to breast-feed your baby? How long?

Look at all mammals: Be they big or small, herbivores or carnivores – cats, lionesses, mice, kangaroos, bears – you name it: they all breastfeed. Then **why is it that a highly evolved human mother, especially from a higher socio-economic family cannot breastfeed successfully?** Come to look at it from the baby's point of view and you will see the wisdom of our elders, who almost always managed to successfully breast-feed their progeny for one, or even, two whole years. How did they do this? What was their secret formula?

The truth is: they had no secret formula. They did not follow any special regimens of diet, sleep, exercise or rest. They lived their normal lives, as to them, Breastfeeding was but a normal routine activity that they did-as naturally, as perhaps changing the baby's nappy, or cooking family food. With the advent of modern times, mothers are increasingly failing at this most incredible, natural and time-honoured activity simply because they consider it a "chore" and not a pleasurable activity. They call it their "duty" to feed the baby; to them, giving the baby breast- milk is a "sacrifice"!

And yet, it is a miracle that almost 95-98 % of all mothers DO breast-feed their babies successfully. This is so because they stop worrying about whether their babies will get enough milk or not, whether they are putting on weight adequately or not and whether they are "healthy" or not.

Successful infant feeding requires cooperation between the mother and the baby, beginning with the first feed, and continuing throughout the child's period of dependency. Promptly establishing comfortable, satisfying routines contributes greatly to your baby's emotional well-being. Feeding times should be pleasurable to both mother and baby.

When to start:

As soon as possible after birth, the baby should be put to the breast for feeding. This will enable her to acquire the needed energy to successfully transit to extra-uterine life, promote mother-infant bonding and decrease the risk of the infant getting a low-blood sugar, jaundice, low blood calcium levels and many other metabolic problems. It may be possible to make mistakes, and give the baby too much or too little milk. She may then vomit (too much) or become feverish (dehydration fever) (too little). **Babies usually begin to breastfeed within half to one hour after birth**, although some may start after 4-6 hours. After this, the baby may feed "on demand", that is, whenever she is hungry. The interval between feeds may vary from one child to another and even in the same infant from time to time, and will depend on the time it takes for her stomach to empty after a feed. However, by the end of the first fortnight, your baby will have established a reasonable schedule of feeding. Feeds can be considered adequate if your baby stops losing weight by a week and regains her birth-weight by 10-12 days.

It should be remembered that babies cry for reasons other than hunger too (Chapter 6), and on no account should the baby be fed every time she cries. Nor should you immediately suspect either that the baby is ill, or that you are not having enough breast milk.

Advantages of Breastfeeding:

Everyone knows that breast milk is the best milk for the baby! But few mothers realise that it is also best for *them*!
I shall enumerate its advantages here so that you may realise just how good it is for your baby and for you as well.

Advantages for the baby:

1. It is the natural food for her. It is always available at the right temperature and needs no preparation. It is always available – at any time and at any place. It is fresh, free and has no contaminating germs which could produce attacks of diarrhea.

2. Cow's milk often causes allergies, characterised by intestinal bleeding, anemia, diarrhea, spitting up, colic, or even wheezing or eczema. Infants fed breast milk have no such problems. They also suffer less from middle ear infections, pneumonia, meningitis and some other illnesses.

3. Human milk is full of antibodies against disease-causing germs. These antibodies protect your baby within the gut as well as in the body from an attack by many different kinds of bacteria and viruses. Besides antibodies, human milk has

many other immunity-boosting chemicals and hormones that protect the baby from an onslaught of diseases. Breast-fed babies have a 14-fold reduction in the incidence of deaths by diarrhea, 4-fold reduction in deaths by acute respiratory tract infections and 3-fold reduction in deaths by other infections.

4. Milk from an adequately nourished mother will supply most essential vitamins and minerals (especially iron, calcium and zinc, which are so essential to the infant's all-round health and immunity), except, perhaps fluoride (in the West), and Vitamin D (after several months).

5. Certain ingredients in breast milk actually help the baby gain more intelligence than top-fed babies. Visual development is also better in a breastfed baby.

6. Breastfed babies have a lower chance of developing heart, blood-pressure, obesity and diabetes-related ailments in later life. The chance of having some forms of malignancies is also reduced in a breastfed baby.

7. Breastfeeding has tremendous psychological benefits for both, the baby, and the mother. The mother feels a sense of accomplishment at having nourished and nurtured her baby; the baby is provided with a close and comfortable relationship with her mother.

Advantages to the mother:

1. Breastfeeding hastens the healing of the womb; it is said to impart a sensually happy feeling to the mother; it also promotes a better shape to the bust of the mother in later life; it may actually **protect against breast and ovarian cancer in the mother**; and finally, it provides some protection against an unwanted pregnancy for a variable

length of time, as long as the mother is nursing. **The efficacy of contraception due to lactational amenorrhoea is a staggering 98% in the first six months.** After six months, though, conception may occur despite this, so some other form of contraception is then recommended. This is because when a baby is conceived, the expectant mother misses her *next* period and not the previous one.

2. Breastfeeding provides **emotional bonding** between the mother and baby, which will stand both of them in good stead when they face emotional crises in the family. The mother is less likely to beat or abuse her daughter/son if she has fed him/her her milk.

3. Mothers who have breastfed their babies have a **lower incidence of fractures due to osteoporosis** in the fourth and subsequent decades of life.

4. There is a definite **economic saving to the family**, as the cost of buying feeding bottles, teats and milk powder are added to the cost of sterilisation and cleaning of the bottles, the cost of treating the infective illnesses and the time-cost of preparing the feeds.

Establishing and Maintaining Milk Supply:

The most satisfactory way of maintaining adequate lactation is to feed the baby regularly to empty the breasts. During the initial days, although the mother may feel that she has less milk, she should continue to put the baby to her breast every time she cries, or at least every 2-3 hours, so that the baby stimulates the production of more milk. Some babies may sleep longer, but there is no need to worry, as such babies will take MORE milk when they wake up.

Remember: *More suckling means more milk. Sometimes, the baby may suckle just for comfort and not for milk. Happily, this will increase milk production too.*

Once the mother's lactation is established, she will easily produce more milk than what the baby requires. Breast-feeding should begin as early as possible after birth, and preferably within the first few hours. The baby may be given to the mother whenever she cries, or at least every 2-3 hours. About 75% of the milk that has been taken by the baby in the previous feed gets replenished in the next two hours.

The first two weeks are crucial for the successful establishment of breast-feeding, and unnecessary supplementation by bottle-feeds, raising doubts about the adequacy of milk flow, giving "other" foods like honey etc. and cracks in the nipple or other breast-related problems can compromise the success of breast-feeding. Hence, please JUST PUT THE BABY TO THE BREAST. Do not do anything that can take her away from the mother's breast.

Worry and unhappiness in the mother are the most potent dampeners of breast-milk flow. Fatigue, tenderness (pain) in the nipples, full, engorged breasts, tensions about the home, other children/husband etc. can all create nursing problems. Hence support from the husband, other family members and relatives can go a long way towards making breastfeeding more successful as well as enjoyable.

<u>Care of the breasts:</u>

The breasts should be washed once a day and the nipple area must be kept dry at all times. A comfortable brassiere, with support at the bottom, and absorbent pads under the cup to absorb leaking milk will allow the mother to stay comfortable.

What should a nursing mother eat?

The nursing mother should eat a well-balanced, varied diet that imparts health to herself and to her baby. Her diet should be supplemented (if needed) with extra calcium, iron etc. in consultation with her obstetrician. She may find that the baby has gas or loose motions when she (that is the mother) eats legumes, tomatoes, onions, certain berries, spicy food or chocolates in excess.

She must completely stay away from alcohol, smoking, recreational or addictive drugs and sleeping pills.

What to do if the mother is ill?

By and large, the mother can continue to breastfeed her baby provided she has the strength to do so. She may even take most medicines without any fear that they may affect the baby. Before taking any drugs or going for any special X-rays, the mother should consult the doctor about whether breastfeeds need to be temporarily withheld.

The conditions where the mother needs to stop breast-feeding are when she is critically sick, she has cancer and is receiving anti-cancer medicines, or she has AIDS. Some drugs taken for heart problems and thyroid diseases are also contraindications for breast-feeding.

Technique of Breastfeeding:

Fig 7-1

At the time of feeding, the baby should be hungry, dry, neither warm nor cold, and be held in a comfortable semi-sitting position with the back erect and supported by pillows or the back of the bed (Fig 7-1). The mother should also be comfortable. The baby is held in the crook of the elbow of one hand, while the same-side breast is supported by the other hand in a C-grip (that is with the thumb above and the other four fingers below the breast). The nipple is brought near the baby's searching mouth (The *Cradle* hold). The baby's neck should be slightly extended and she should be "brought" to the mother's breast to feed. Her lips should be everted and her mouth should cover more of the areola below the nipple than the one above it (Figs 7-2a, 7-2b and 7-3). **Correct attachment is the key to successful breastfeeding.**

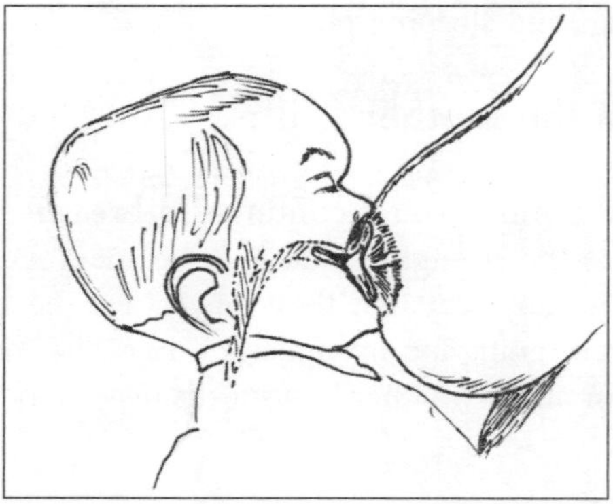

Fig 7-2a

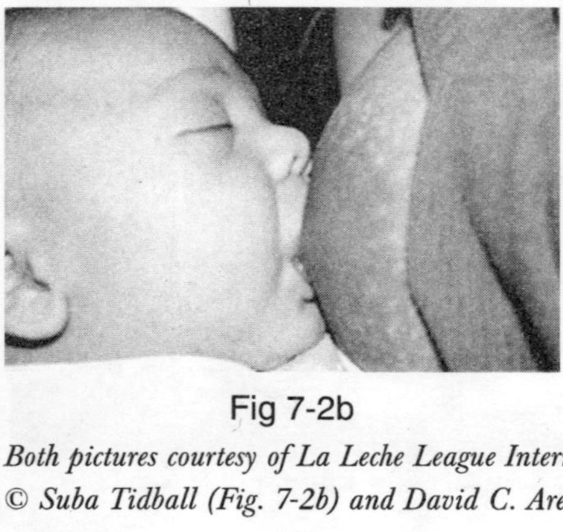

Fig 7-2b

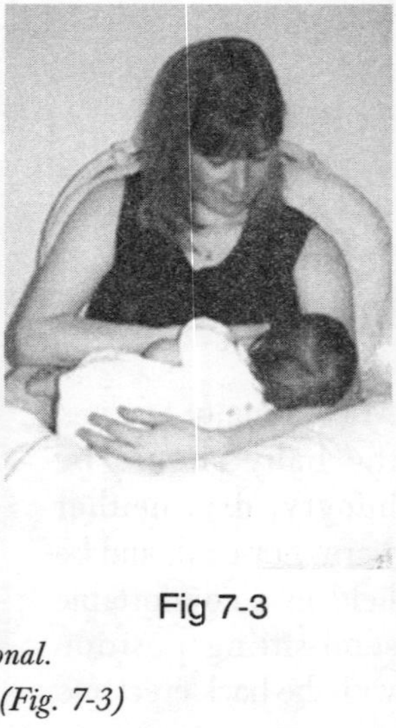

Fig 7-3

Both pictures courtesy of La Leche League International.
© Suba Tidball (Fig. 7-2b) and David C. Arendt (Fig. 7-3)

You should realise that if the baby is hungry, she will energetically "root" for the nipple, and her sucks will be deep and accompanied by a thrusting action to enable the easy expulsion of milk. In fact, the baby presses the mother's areola between her tongue and hard palate and literally "squeezes" the milk out into her mouth! On the other hand, a baby who does not "root" for the breast, or does not suck vigorously, is either not hungry or is sick. Usually, the baby gets the major part of her milk in the first few minutes after she begins to feed; almost 80-90% has been already ingested within the first 4 minutes. However, the baby should be permitted to suckle till she is satisfied. She should never be "pulled" away from the breast, for this may cause nipple cracks or tenderness. If it is necessary to interrupt a feed, just insert your finger inside the baby's mouth gently; she will loosen the grip on your breast and you will be able to take her off the breast. Waking a sleepy infant "to feed" is also usually inappropriate and unsuccessful.

At the end of the nursing, the baby should be held erect, either on the shoulder or mother's lap for assistance in expelling swallowed air (burping). Her back may be gently rubbed or patted to aid the process. When the burping is completed, the baby must be laid in her cot on her back, or on her right side to aid the digestion process. If a baby never s2wallowed any air during her feed she will not burp at all!

I suggest that every mother should learn about the skill of breastfeeding from the free videos that can be viewed on/downloaded from http://www.breastfeeding.com.

Are there any other positions the mother may feed her baby in?

Yes, the mother may elect to take the baby in three other positions:

a) Cross-cradle position (Fig 7-4): Here, the mother holds the baby with the hand opposite to the side of the breast which she offers the baby to suckle.

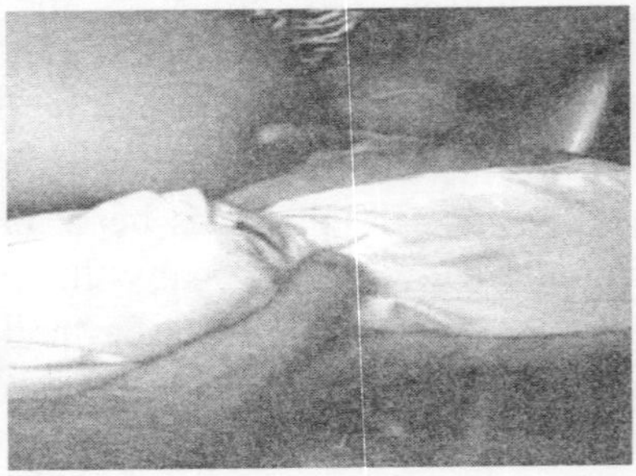

Fig 7-4

b) Football position (Fig 7-5): Here, the mother holds the baby in such a way that the baby's legs are out instead of in – that is to say, she holds the baby in a direction reverse to the general one. In this way, she can feed twins simultaneously (Fig 7-12)!

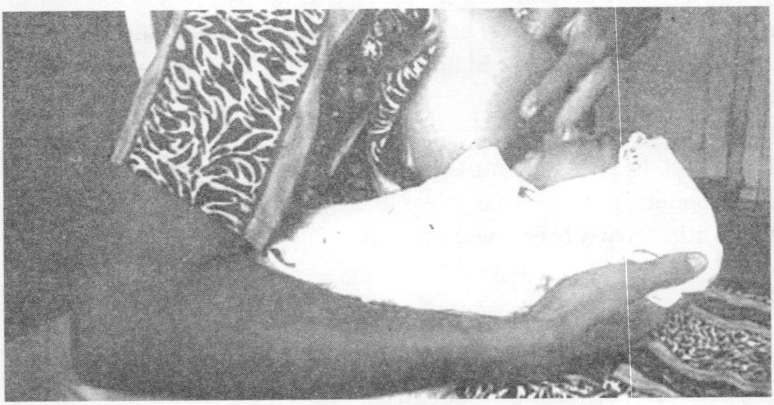

Fig 7-5

c) Side-lying position: This is very useful in the first few days when the mother may be too weak to sit up and feed the baby. She can feed her lying on one side.

What is burping and how is it done?

Burping is the process of aiding the baby to expel the gas which she might have swallowed into the stomach while feeding or crying.

Most babies tend to swallow some air when they are very thirsty or hungry and are sucking vigorously. The likelihood of gas being ingested is increased if the mother's milk flow is too fast, too slow or too chaotic; when the latching-on position is not correct; and when the baby is irritable and feeds in fits and starts or cries a lot while feeding.

If this ingested gas is not removed, the baby will, upon being laid in her bed, become restless and vomit a large amount of milk and curd. Therefore, you should, after the baby has been fed, lift her up in front of you, and make her sit either on your abdomen or in your lap, and gently stroke her back till she expels gas. Another alternative is to carry her on your shoulder and stroke her back till she burps.

What to do if the baby is sick?

Breastfeeding, if it can be done by the sick baby, should be continued as before, since breast milk is also ideal for a sick baby. If she does not suckle because she is weak, the mother can remove her milk manually and feed it to the baby using a cup and a spoon.

How to remove milk from the breast?

Removing milk from the breast is an art that a mother should learn as soon as possible. There are two ways to do so.

The manual method is the more popular of the two basic methods. In this method, we take advantage of the fact that the milk collects in small sacs just under the areola before it is ejected or sucked out by an energetic normal baby.

The actual removal, or "expression" as we call it, involves two movements. In the first movement, you should massage the entire breast in a centripetal direction (from outside towards the centre), and try and loosen the lumps of milk and move the milk to an area just under the nipple. Do not forget to bring milk from the breast tissue that extends into the armpit and that which lies in the lower fold of the breast.

Just under the areola, the milk ducts are enlarged into so-called "sinuses" or sacs, where the milk collects prior to it being ejected into the baby's mouth when the baby suckles the breast (Fig 7-6). If you continue to massage this area forwards, towards the nipple, the sinuses get compressed, and the milk will not flow *outward* but stay *within.*

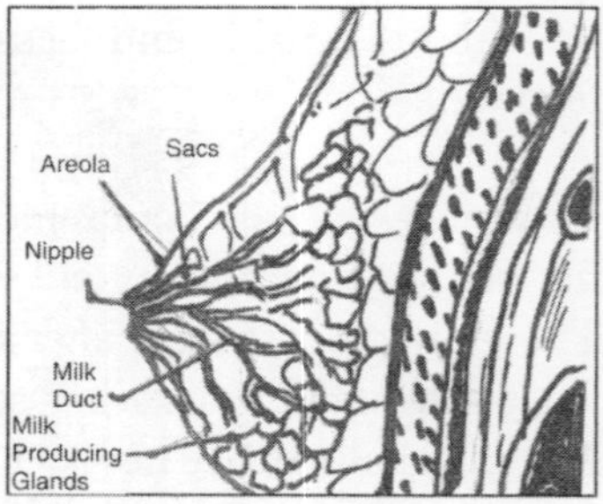

Fig 7-6

Thus the second movement: in this, you grasp the areola just behind the nipple with a thumb and an index finger, and move these backward and towards each other on to your rib-cage. This backward movement will help to empty the sinuses very effectively. Initially, this process may be painful, but as you practice it, you will be able to express your milk easily. Sometimes, the milk flows in a trickle, and sometimes it flows so liberally that lots of it can be collected without any difficulty.

The second method is through use of a pump, which can be either mechanical or electrical. The *mechanical* pump (Fig 7-7) consists of a large glass syringe which has a narrow, tubular mouth at one end (to which a rubber ball is attached), and a large hole at the other end. You apply the large hole over the breast with the rubber ball pressed hard; the areola and the nipple are both within the glass. Now you slowly release the rubber ball; the milk will flow into the syringe because of negative pressure. The syringe often has a small receptacle inbuilt into the glass on one side, and this allows the milk to collect in it while continuing the suction process.

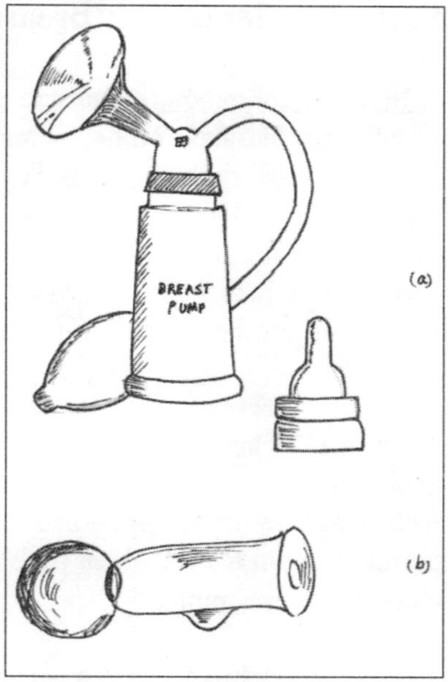

Fig 7-7

Electrical pumps (Fig 7-8) are available in India, and if you can procure them, they are hard task masters and achieve complete removal within minutes.

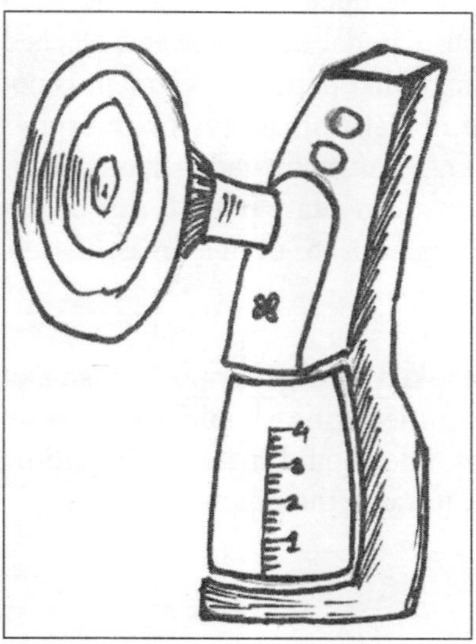

Fig 7-8

Early Problems with breast-feeding:

1. Breast-engorgement: This can happen after the milk "comes in". The breasts feel full and heavy and hard lumps can be felt in them. The lumps are nothing but milk, and all that is needed is to allow unrestricted suckling to the baby. If the engorgement is too painful to bear, the mother will not be able to feed the baby comfortably, and the tight breast tissue makes it difficult for the latter to "pull" the areola out into her mouth to feed properly. This can create a major problem.

What to do? The right thing to do is to remove some milk from the breasts, either by manual expression, or with the help of a hot bottle with a narrow neck applied to the areola (as it cools, it creates a partial vacuum inside, which pulls the milk out), or with a manual or electrical breast pump.

2. Milk fever: Engorgement can produce fever in the mother, and this usually subsides within 48 hours. If the fever persists despite removal of milk, consult the doctor.

3. Blocked duct: Sometimes, one of the ducts that bring milk from the secretory glands to the milk sinuses under the areola gets blocked by thick milk. This generally occurs if that particular segment is not being emptied properly because of tight brassieres or improper position of the mother while feeding. Left untreated, a lump forms inside the breast. The undrained area can cause pain. It can be the beginning of a breast inflammation (mastitis) or even a breast abscess (pus formation).

What to do? The mother should be asked to vary her position so that all the areas of the breast get emptied. She should wear loose, comfortable brassieres and clothes. She should massage the lumpy area and try and "move" the milk towards the nipple.

4. Mastitis and abscess: A hot, inflamed breast can be a harbinger of an abscess. To prevent mastitis from progressing to an abscess (pus formation), the mother should be shown to a doctor, who should begin a course of effective antibiotics and anti-inflammatory medications. Feeding at the breast need not be stopped. If, in spite of all this, an abscess does form, it will need surgery: the pus will HAVE to be drained.

5. Sore nipples: Soreness of nipples is due to improper attachment of the baby at the breast. Using soap to clean the nipples or too frequent washing of the nipples can also do the same. The pain hinders feeding, and this can cause milk production to decline too.

What to do? You should seek help to see that the position of the baby's mouth on to the breast is proper and that the baby latches on comfortably. Once this is done, you will be pleasantly surprised to see that the pain will disappear, the baby will feed better and the problem will vanish. If the pain persists for more than 5-7 days, examine the baby's mouth and your nipple for small, white spots; these can be due to a fungal infection called *candidiasis* or thrush. See the doctor for advice on treating it.

6. Cracked nipples: A persistently poor suckling position leads to development of cracks on the nipple. These can be around the base, across the tip, or both. The cracks are extremely painful.

What to do? Seek help to improve the baby's latching position and continue feeding her. If one breast is less painful than the other, nurse the baby on the less painful side. Usually, this is sufficient to heal the crack(s). Leave the nipples open to allow them to dry. Do not wash them too often. It will help if you leave a drop of your hind-milk on the crack. It has healing properties. If the crack still does not heal, you may have to stop feeding the baby temporarily, and remove the milk from the affected breast using any of the methods discussed on p. xx till the crack heals.

7. Blood in the milk: Although this is frightening, it is harmless, and is due to a slight leakage of blood from one of the ducts inside the breast. Continue suckling the baby and the problem will disappear on its own.

8. Flat nipples: Since the baby suckles the breast and not just the nipple, the length of the latter is not really important (Fig 7-9). The reason is that when the baby suckles in the correct latch-on position, she takes in not just the nipple but also a considerable portion of the areola: this part of the areola gets stretched into what is called a "physiological nipple". If your nipple looks too small, do not worry. Grasp it with your first finger and thumb and pull it. If it comes out, then there is no problem at all and the baby will be able to pull it into her mouth and feed easily. If it does not come out, try pulling it frequently when you are free. This "exercise" will allow it to come out properly in a few days. Your husband can do the job of sucking the nipple out if this is acceptable to the two of you.

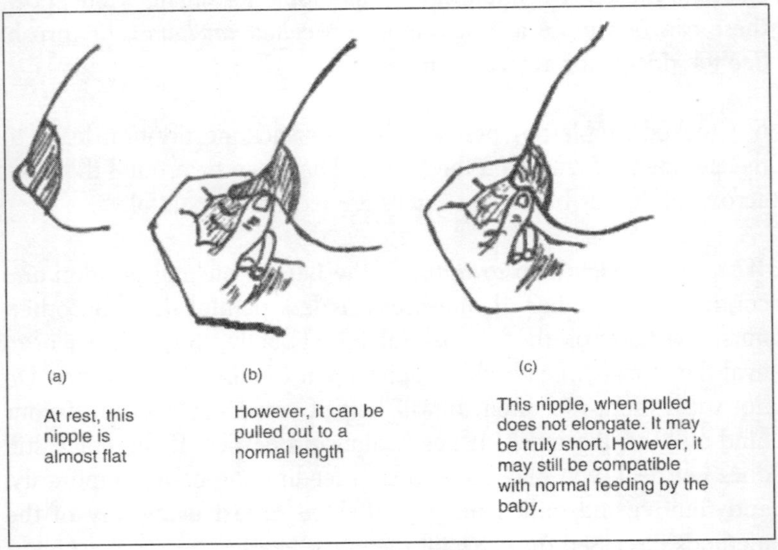

Fig 7-9

9. <u>Inverted nipples:</u> In some mothers, the nipples turn inwards when an attempt is made to pull them out. Such true inverted nipples are rare (Fig 7-10). To help such mothers, doctors have an unusual remedy.

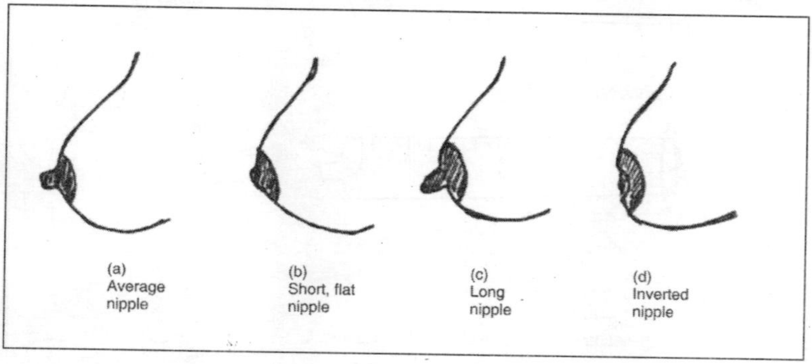

Fig 7-10

What to do? (See Fig 7-11)

- You take a 5- or 10-milliliter plastic syringe (the device doctors use to give injections).
- The outer tube is cut near the tip after removing the inner piston. The end with the tip where the needle has to be attached is thrown away.
- The piston is re-inserted from the broken end and the smooth end of the outer tube (with a flange) is then put over the affected nipple so that the flange rests around the nipple on the areola.
- You then try and pull the piston out so that a negative pressure is created within the syringe. The inverted nipple also gets pulled out with the piston. Try and keep the suction for a few seconds till you can no longer bear the pain.
- Then slowly release the piston. Some milk may have also come into the syringe. Pull the syringe away and remove the milk; then repeat the process again.

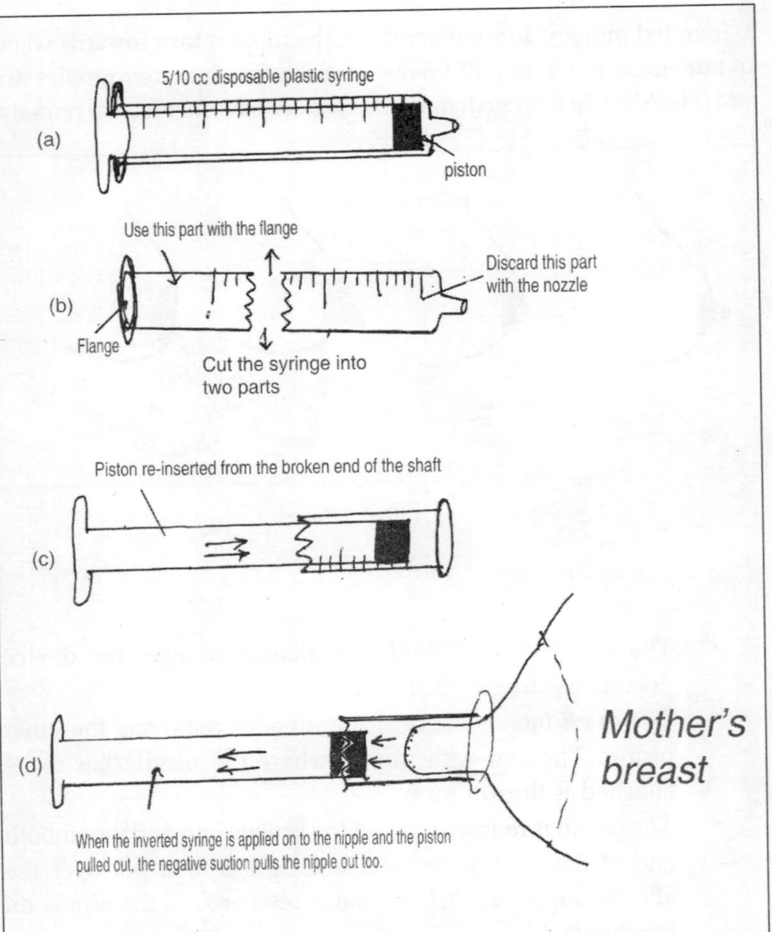

Fig 7-11

Over one or two days, with patience and perseverance, the inverted nipple will become everted.

A Baby who refuses to suck:

There are many reasons why a baby may not suck.

These include:

a) The baby may be ill. This can be serious. If she has any other symptoms of illness, consult the doctor immediately.
b) The baby may be too small or weak. If she weighs less than 1500 grams, she may not suck well. You may have to remove your milk manually and then feed it to her with a dropper or a cup and spoon. All the same, the baby should still be offered the breast for what is called "*non-nutritive sucking*". This will help milk production as well as milk ejection.
c) The baby may have a *blocked nose due to a cold.* Babies cannot breathe through their mouths, and get into trouble if their nose is blocked. Help them to remove the blockage by instilling salt-water nose drops inside both the nostrils. To prepare salt-water drops, dissolve a pinch of salt in a glassful of water, boil the water and allow it to cool. Fill it into a bottle with a dropper. Your old vitamin drops bottle will do. Nowadays, ready-made saline nose drops are available with a squeeze bottle.
d) The baby may have a fungal mouth infection (*oral thrush*). This can be treated with anti-fungal mouth solutions applied with a gauze-piece over the affected areas of the mouth.
e) The process of breast-feeding has gone wrong somewhere along the line, and the baby is frustrated.

    i) The milk may be coming too fast – in this case, the mother should pinch the nipple with her first and second fingers and control the flow of milk.
    ii) The milk is coming too slow and the baby is getting tired – here, more and more suckling is the answer, but the mother can help the baby by dripping some of her milk (or any milk) over her

breast and nipple so that it flows into the baby's mouth; this helps to increase the milk production as it allows the baby to feed without any idea that the milk is coming from an external source.

iii) There was a delay in starting the first feed, or the baby was separated from her mother for some days – just be patient, and the baby will take the feeds properly.

iv) There has been some emotional or physical upheaval in the mother's life – and she has had no time to feed her baby, or is emotionally too upset to feed her.

v) The baby is also being given bottle feeds or a pacifier – if that is so, it must be stopped forthwith. **Even one bottle-feed at night can come in the way of successful breastfeeding.**

vi) The mother has restricted the feeds to the baby or she is sticking to a rigorous "*schedule*" – this causes the baby to get confused and frustrated, so don't do it.

Later Problems and Other Issues:

1. <u>Insufficient Milk</u>: There are many instances where the mother, or more often, the other family members – most likely the baby's grandmother – look at the baby crying, or feeding frequently, or for a longer duration – and announce that the *mother has insufficient milk.*

Sometimes, someone sees a baby sucking her fingers or thumb and say the same thing. Sometimes, someone actually prepares a bottle of top-milk, and because the baby takes that milk and instantly becomes quiet, they say it's because *the mother has insufficient milk.* After the engorged breasts of the first few weeks, the breasts become relatively softer: mothers may interpret this as a sign that the milk flow has reduced. This is totally incorrect. The same interpretation may be given to the fact that after the first few weeks, the "leakage of milk" from the other breast too comes down.

So how to decide if you have been giving enough milk? If, while feeding on one breast, the milk leaks from the other one, then the milk production and ejection is probably adequate. The next easiest way is to check the baby's pattern of urination. If she is passing normal amounts of urine at least 6-8 times in a 24-hour time-frame on exclusive Breastfeeding, then she is getting enough breast milk.

A baby who is putting on sufficient weight, say 200-250 grams in a 10-day time-frame is getting enough breast milk.

What if she isn't getting enough? If the above tests tell you that the baby isn't getting enough milk, it is time to study the problem further.

a) She may be weak or ill or have congenital heart disease.
b) The mother does not feed frequently enough.
c) The baby does not want to feed longer because of discomfort or improper attachment.
d) The mother has already started early supplements.
e) The mother cannot breast-feed properly because she is in a public-place and feels shy to feed in view of others.
f) The mother lacks confidence in herself.
g) The mother has cracks or fissures in the nipple and due to the pain that she gets, she does not feed the baby completely.
h) The mother is uninterested in giving breastfeeds but won't say so because of social constraints or because the baby is "unwanted" due to any reason.
i) The mother herself is undernourished.
j) The baby does not suck properly because she is mentally subnormal or has congenital anomalies like a cleft palate.

In all the above cases, proper counselling and advice will go a long way in turning the case around. One can approach the right authorities to get other forms of help such as **engaging a wet nurse** (a lactating mother who agrees to feed someone else's child) or getting milk from a **human milk bank** (there is one at the LTMGH, Sion, Mumbai).

2. <u>Crying Baby:</u> The only language that the baby can communicate in is the cry. She cries only when something is wrong. In relation to breast-feeding, there are several reasons why the baby may cry. However, one must remember that hunger is not the only cause of crying.

Before you begin to doubt that your milk is not enough or it is not "suitable" for the baby, check out the following:

a) See if you are allowing the baby unrestricted, unlimited feeding times and schedules.
b) Is the baby latching-on properly?
c) Is your mind at ease or filled with tensions?
d) Has the baby wet herself or soiled her nappy?
e) Is she crying because she has fever, blocked nose, or any other illness?

At times, due to rapid growth, the baby may temporarily face a lactation crisis around 2-3 months of age. Let the baby continue to suckle, and the crisis will pass off as milk production will once again "catch up" with the baby's needs.

Babies who do not get enough "hind milk" (the last portion of a feed, which is thick and filled with calories) will be calorie-deprived and will cry more often for feeds. This happens when you try and shift to the second breast before the first breast has been properly emptied. The initial milk flowing from the breast ("fore milk") is thin and watery and is meant to quench the baby's thirst, while the hind-milk is thick and satisfies the hunger and calorie needs of the baby. So, if you are switching sides before the first breast has been fully emptied, the baby will cry for milk sooner, pass more urine, and often be constipated, as she isn't getting enough milk solids.

At times, the baby may cry because some substances ingested by the mother, and passed to the baby through breast milk do not agree with the baby. Cow's milk, *dals* and legumes, or any other food may produce such a problem. Try eliminating some of these foods from your diet to see what substance was the cause of the baby's crying.

Some babies are literally "crying babies". They cry for no apparent reason, fidget a lot while at the breast, "fight" at the breast, and generally create a "tense" environment. For such babies, my advice is simple. Wait till she is three or four months old, and the problem will disappear on its own. You might want to carry her a lot, or rock her, or sing to her – anything may just work, or nothing may.

Occasionally, babies get "frightened" by the jet of milk that literally threatens to "overwhelm" the baby and suffocate her. This is specially so in mothers who have a very strong ejection reflex. It may help to squeeze the areola with a scissors-like grip to regulate the flow of milk in such cases.

Last but not the least, some babies cry only because they feel "lonely" and desire only your company and closeness. They quieten as soon as you pick them up, and stay quiet as long as you carry them; conversely, they begin to scream the moment you put them down.

3. <u>Working Mother (Chapter 26 *B*):</u> If you are a working mother, then you need guidance on how to maintain breast-feeding even when you resume work. Most mothers get a three-month maternity leave. During these three months, give exclusive breast-feeds. Have some good person to take care of the baby in your absence. Teach her how to give EBM (expressed breast milk) or any other top milk with a cup and spoon.

To collect EBM, you should first give your baby one or two morning feeds directly at the breast; after this, sit comfortably and remove your milk from each of the breasts successively to the maximum limit. This milk can be kept in any clean container, covered with a muslin cloth or saucer and left in a cool corner, or in the refrigerator (if available). It should be given to the baby without heating, as heat destroys the anti-bacterial chemicals in the milk.

Some mothers are able to express as much as 400-500 ml. of milk and leave it behind for their babies. If this stored milk is not enough, cow's milk or powder milk can also be used.

Mothers should, if their breasts fill up, remove the milk formed in them in their office or work place, and either throw or collect it in a clean thermos flask, and take it back home to feed it to the baby in the evening.

4. Twins: Mothers have been known to successfully breastfeed both the babies on their breasts without using top milk, even up to six months (Fig 7-12)! If this is not possible, you may continue to breastfeed both of them and supplement the deficiency with top milk given with a wait and a spoon or with a bondla or sipper.

Fig 7-12

How long to breastfeed:

There is no hard and fast rule on the duration of breast-feeding. Most traditional views recommend exclusive Breastfeeding for the first six months, after which supplements can be begun, of either top-milk or other weaning foods. After six months, breast-feeding is continued for as long as the baby takes it … even up to two years or more.

However, there are some babies who themselves leave the breast by one year of age, without any trouble to their mothers or anyone else.

Any other crucial advice?

Just one. Do not start a feeding bottle "just like that" for the baby who is successfully breast-feeding. It can mean the end of breast-feeding. This is because the baby quickly "learns" to prefer the easy, passive means of feeding over the more "difficult" active method involved in feeding at the breast. The baby will rapidly "unlearn" what it took her days to master; soon, she will suckle less and less at the breast, and as a result, the mother's milk production will decline.

Unnecessary use of the bottle even once a day can ring the death knell for breastfeeding.

There are many excellent books and web-sites dedicated to helping mothers successfully breast-feed their young ones. A list is appended below. If you do not have the time to look up all these sources, you may elect to just look at all the other animals on this planet: how they deliver their babies naturally, and begin to instinctively breast-feed their little ones within moments of birthing, and how they continue to successfully nurse their babies for months together without any professional advice!

The miracle that is breast – feeding is all around you! Learn from it!

Suggested Reading:

- ✔ http://www.breastfeeding.com
- ✔ http://www.aap.org/policy/re9729.html
- ✔ http://www.lalecheleague.org/
- ✔ http://www.vh.org/pediatric/patient/pediatrics/cqqa/breastfeeding.html
- ✔ http://www.bpni.org
- ✔ "The Womanly Art of Breastfeeding" by Gwen Gotsch, et al (September 1997)
- ✔ "The Breastfeeding Book: Everything You Need to Know About Nursing Your Child from Birth Through Weaning" by Martha Sears R.N., William Sears M.D.
- ✔ "Eat Well, Lose Weight While Breastfeeding: Complete Nutrition Book for Nursing Mothers, Including a Healthy Guide to Weight Loss Your Doctor Promise by Eileen Behan (October 1992)
- ✔ Jellife, D. B., and E. F. P. Jellife. 1978. *Human milk in the modern world.* Oxford: Oxford University Press
- ✔ "Helping Mothers to Breastfeed" by Felicity Savage King (1992).

Ch. 08
Artificial Feeding

You invite illnesses when you start bottle-feeding for the baby

– Dr. Kagalwala

In the seventies and eighties, bottle-feeding finally became a fashion, and even healthy mothers with adequate breast milk began to "take" to it in an attempt to look "modern". Mothers from U.S.A., Britain, Australia, and many other developed countries "switched" from breast to bottle. Female emancipation ruled the day, and the babies were damned to artificial nourishment, often at the hands of a maid or some other care - taker. The winds of change arrived at the shores of developing nations such as ours, and urban mothers began to emulate their counterparts in affluent countries. Soon, disaster struck, as child after child fell ill with pneumonia, otitis media, diarrhoea, dental caries, malnutrition, and so on. Bottle feeding, a method designed to free women from the yoke of breast feeding, was now a curse, as it took the lives of innocent children.

Times have changed. The wheel has turned a full circle. Doctors are extolling the virtues of the breast as never before. As more and more research findings are uncovered, it is becoming clear that breast milk is a miracle feed, and nothing else can come even close to it.

Knowing well that mother's milk is species-specific, tailor-made for each baby, loaded with protective factors, able to satisfy both the thirst and hunger of the baby and full of nourishing nutrients, many mothers still begin bottle feeds on their babies for no more a reason than that "I am not getting enough milk and my baby should not go hungry". This is an appalling state of affairs. No reasons, save the direst ones, can actually justify the penchant of some mothers to introduce a feeding bottle in their babies.

The Need for Artificial Feeding:

As we have seen in Chapter 7, almost all mothers can raise their babies exclusively on breast milk for the first six months. There are, however, cases where the mother or care – taker has to start the baby on top feeds, that is, milk other than breast milk. This may mean introducing dairy milks available in plastic pouches or Tetra packs, loose milk sold by milk sellers or powdered formula made for babies.

These are the various reasons where such feeds need to be given:

1. The mother is seriously ill
2. The mother really has insufficient milk
3. The mother is on anti – cancer medicines or she has AIDS
4. There are social constraints to successful breast feeding
5. The mother has borne twins, triplets or more babies
6. Breast feeding has been stopped because of breast abscesses on both sides
7. The mother has to go to work and crèche facilities are available
8. The mother dies/leaves the household.

Which milk to give?

As explained above, any milk that is readily available and economically affordable may be used. Most mothers have a false notion that "outside" milk needs to be diluted before giving to the baby, as otherwise, the baby is liable to be constipated or have colic. Nothing can be more wrong.

The milk of cows, buffaloes, goats or (as in desert areas) even camels can be used. The milk so procured must be boiled first. At least two teaspoons of sugar should be added per 250 ml of the milk. The milk must then be allowed to cool to room temperature. Then, if possible, it should be transferred to the refrigerator and allowed to stay inside for at least 4 hours. The cream is now skimmed off the top. The milk is now suitable for giving to the baby without further dilution. This process is also called ***humanising animal milk***, because with these steps, the composition of the milk loosely resembles that of human breast milk.

If formula milk is used, the instructions on the container should be followed to get liquid milk of the right composition. Generally, one flat measuring spoon obtained from the container is added to about 30 ml of pre-boiled warm water.

The milk obtained from cows and buffaloes is a little different from human breast milk. The former contains more cream, less sugars and a different, more difficult to digest protein (*casein*) as compared to human milk which is a bit thinner, has less cream, is sweeter and has an easy to digest protein (*lactalbumin*). Hence, some authorities recommend adding water to animal milk in the first few months; however, I feel this is unnecessary once you have humanised the milk. Bovine milk also contains *lactoglobulin*, another protein; this one can cause allergic manifestations in some babies.

How much milk to give?

In contrast to a baby who breast feeds naturally, the top fed baby's needs need to be worked out so that the baby does not end up being under- or over-fed. Generally, in the first month, the baby will consume 30-45 ml of milk at each feed; thereafter, the quantity can be increased by 30 ml per feed each month. In this manner, the baby should be drinking 150-180 ml per feed by six months. Around this time, one can begin to introduce complementary feeds (see Chapter 9). The frequency of top feeding will then begin to decline. By nine to twelve months of age, the baby should be taking 3-4 feeds of 210-240 ml or so. In addition, she would be eating most home foods.

Some babies drink more and some drink less milk. If the baby's weight gain is all right, one shouldn't worry about absolute quantities of milk intake. If you have offered, say, 150 ml of milk at one time, and the baby stops drinking milk and leaves a small quantity behind, do not worry. Either discard that milk, or have another family member drink it up. The fact that the baby stopped on her own is sufficient evidence that she got enough in that feed.

What method to use?

The traditional way to give top milk is by using **a cup and a spoon**. This method is less cumbersome and more hygienic as compared to bottle feeding, but it is more time-consuming initially as it is more proactive and a little difficult for the baby to learn. The *plus* points of this method also include a fairly easy process of just washing the steel or glass utensils in detergent and water. There is no need to sterilise by boiling or pressure cooking them. The *minus* point of this method is that a very hungry baby sometimes gets so frustrated awaiting the next spoon that she begins to cry, or to fret so much that the milk gets spilt from the spoon. This is a real drawback, no doubt, but it can be easily eliminated if you begin the feed **before** the baby begins to wail for the milk. Catch her when she is just waking up for the feed, and you will find that she will take spoon feeds without much ado. It also helps if you immobilise the baby by holding her arms with your free hand and "gripping" her legs between your crossed legs. The other minus point is that one cannot spoon-feed the baby while travelling in a bus, or while being outdoors, say, on a picnic. It is true that this does become an inconvenience, but if you plan your outings properly, you should be able to get around the problem. If the baby is suckling at your breast, you can discreetly feed her on the breast when outside; if not, you can offer her a glucose biscuit dipped in warm water to tide the crisis. If absolutely necessary, you might want to keep a feeding bottle with you for emergency use.

Another way to deal with the first minus point above is to use a ***bondla*** **(Fig 8-1) or a *palada*.** This is a *diyaa* shaped stainless steel spoon with a long snout. It can hold 10 or 15 ml of milk depending upon its size. If your baby gets too fretful with a normal spoon, then this is the right method for her. You can trickle the milk down her throat by gently pouring it down the snout between the gums and the cheeks. She will sense "satisfaction" as there is a lot more milk for her to swallow as compared to the 3-5 ml available in the spoon. You can get this very useful "device" from any utensil vendor!

Fig 8-1

The third, and by far the most "popular" method of feeding among parents is **bottle feeding**. I say popular because in spite of the repeated admonitions by health care workers, nurses, doctors, pediatricians etc to NOT use it, it continues to be used by parents from all socio-economic strata. We do not advocate bottle feeding at all because it brings with it a whole lot of problems. Some of these problems are listed in the next section. In spite of this, if one wants to use a feeding bottle, I can only pray that the baby is not a victim of her mother's folly (or the father's or the grandmother's ... it does not matter).

Technique: The bottle should first be filled with pre-boiled warm water up to the needed mark on it. Next, milk powder should be added to it. The bottle top should be closed by using the flat lid provided with the bottle, and the contents shaken till the powder dissolves in the liquid. Check the flow of the milk through the teat. There should be an initial stream of milk, after which, milk should flow in drops and NOT as a stream. Allow some drops to fall on the back of your hand so that you can check the temperature of the milk. If it's too hot, or cool to the touch, modify this by waiting/heating for some time. Next, you can feed the baby. Tilt the bottle sufficiently so that the teat remains full of milk at all times, and there is no danger of swallowing air. You should pay full attention, *always keep the baby's head high*, and check the milk flow intermittently till the milk is over or till the baby leaves the teat.

Remember to never "prop up" the bottle on pillows and leave the baby to suck on her own from it. The risks include the risk of the baby swallowing a lot of air and the possibility of the milk being aspirated into the baby's lungs (choking).

Disadvantages of bottle feeding:

1. If proper hygienic precautions are not taken, bottle feeding can lead to all sorts of infections. Diarrhoea, vomiting and dysentery are the consequences of G.I. infection. They occur because of inadequate sterilisation of the bottles and teats. Many a times, such infection can lead to hospitalization or even death.

2. The Eustachian tube connects the back portion of the mouth to the middle ear, and its function is to help hearing. It also equalises the pressure of air on both sides of the delicate ear drum. A small lump of tonsil surrounds its internal opening. See Chapter 36 for a picture of this tube. When you bottle feed the baby, the thin jet of

milk hits this tonsillar tissue and effectively causes germs to grow on it. Over time, the tonsillar tissue grows in size and blocks the opening of the Eustachian tube. The result is accumulation of fluid and pus in the middle ear, and eventual perforation of the ear drum. (Perforation = hole). This can lead to permanent hearing loss in the affected ear.

3. Sometimes, the angle of the bottle is not sufficient to guide the remaining milk into the baby's mouth. Air is then swallowed by the baby. This causes stomach discomfort, leading to crying, leading to further aerophagia (swallowing of air). Bottle-fed babies are therefore more fretful and irritable in the first three months of life, as they have more gas problems.

4. One of the most important drawbacks of bottle feeding is the development of baby bottle tooth decay (BBTD, see Chapter 45), along with dental malalignment and malocclusion. In severe cases, such children have difficulty in chewing, articulation and appearance.

5. Bottle-feeding is very easy as compared to breast feeding. While the latter is an active process in which the baby has to "draw" the milk out of her mother's breast(s), the former is an entirely passive process, in which the baby doesn't have to "do" anything; she merely has to keep her jaws open, and the milk will flow inwards automatically. As a result of this basic ease of feeding at the bottle, the baby slowly starts preferring the bottle to her mother's breast. She feeds less frequently there, and when she does, she stays on the breast for a shorter time. When a top feed is given, she takes it more energetically each time; as a consequence of this, the breast milk goes on decreasing, and eventually, the breasts dry up because the sucking stimulus drives the production of breast milk.

Once the bottle is introduced, sooner or later, the breasts will dry up. This is the most unfortunate outcome of bottle feeding. The baby stops getting all the known and unknown benefits of breast feeding, and is liable to fall ill more often because of this.

6. Bottle-feeding becomes a hard to leave habit over a period of one year. Infants who are still feeding at the bottle at two years of age (or even three) are not so rare to see. They will demand their bottle at any odd hour of the day or night. They are stubborn, irritable and more often than not, fat for their age. They will take the bottle with them all over the neighbourhood. They will drop the bottle on the ground, then pick it up from the filth, and promptly put it back in their mouths.

7. As bottle feeding is a passive act (see above), there is a very good chance that the baby will completely empty the bottle at each feed even though she is not that hungry. This risk of overfeeding is real, and may lead to obesity in the child.

8. Babies love to feed at the bottle. As a result, many babies will ignore weaning foods presented to them. The mother gets confused as to why the baby will not eat such an attractively given plate of rice, or cream biscuit or the like. Some mothers get so frustrated about this, that they start force-feeding the baby. The result: irritability in the baby, torture to the mother, and often vomiting by the baby.

9. Sterilisation of feeding bottles and teats is a cumbersome process. The water must first reach boiling point, then the cleaned and scrubbed bottles are put inside it; the water is allowed to boil further; then the cleaned nipples are added to the boiling water. The gas is switched off after two minutes.

10. Due to economic reasons, many hard-pressed mothers end up over-diluting top milk. This can lead to malnutrition in the infant.

As can be seen from the foregoing list, the problems of bottle-feeding do not begin and end at infection alone.

Further tips on cleaning and hygiene of bottles:

It is better to purchase 3-4 sets of bottles and teats. Sterilise them together by putting them all in a big container filled with water and boil the lot for at least ten minutes. As an option, the bottles may be put in first, and the teats may be added after 5-8 minutes.

In a method known as terminal sterilisation, the bottles are all filled with the requisite amount of milk, and then capped with inverted nipples mounted under the flat covers. These are then kept upright in a large pressure cooker, and pressure cooked for 8-10 minutes. After some time, the cooker lid is opened and the pre-sterilised feeds are stored in the refrigerator. They can be removed about half an hour before the anticipated time for the baby's next feed. When the baby demands the feed, the cap is opened, the nipple is "righted" and the baby is given a completely hygienic feed.

Remember that hand washing has no substitute. It should be done rigorously before preparing any artificial feed for the baby. The inner areas of the wrists, the back of the hands, the hollow of the palm and the grooves between the fingers should receive a little extra scrubbing.

On no account should the "balance" milk in the feeding bottle be kept for the baby's next feed; it should always be either discarded or taken by an adult member.

Those who have scarcity of gas for boiling and cooking can keep the cleaned bottles and teats in Milton's sodium hypochlorite solution for at least three to four hours. This is adequate to sterilise the equipment, but after this the bottles and teats must be washed with hot water before milk is filled inside them.

The important task of sterilising the bottles etc. must never be left for the maid to perform. You should do it on your own.

Ch. 09
Complementary Feeds in Infancy

Parents are often so busy with the physical rearing of children that they miss the glory of parenthood, just as the grandeur of the trees is lost when raking leaves.

- Marcelene Cox, American Writer

Of all the worries that assail the minds of young parents, the baby's eating habits are the most important, at least to the parents themselves. This is because they associate eating with growth. Quite often, the Pediatrician's focusing on the eating habits of the child plays on the minds of the parents to such an extent that the latter keep worrying about whether they are doing right by their babies.

Most of the times, parents think that they need perfect, dish by dish instructions, exact time-schedules and so on so as to bring up their babies correctly. This is a wrong notion. By and large, the things printed in Pediatrician's files and in childcare books (such as this one) are merely guidelines and not the Gospel Truth. You would be perfectly right in deciding to follow just the broad guidelines and make your own dishes, timings and schedules. Most likely, nothing wrong would happen to your baby!

Three things determine the health of a child: her genetic endowment (what she got as inheritance from both her parents); the adequacy of nutrition; and freedom from illness. Thus, if the baby's parents are both short in height, it is unlikely for the baby to grow tall even if she gets the best nourishment and remains free from any disease. Similarly, even a slightly less-eating Punjabi boy will continue to grow to a formidable height (and weight), since he is born of Punjabi parents.

Since children grow all the time, they need much higher quantities of nutrients compared to adults; a three kg. newborn baby will triple her birth weight in just one year, quadruple it by three years and will reach a weight of over 30 kilograms by ten years and over 50 kg by adolescence. (See Chapters 13 and 16).

Breast milk is the best food from birth up to six months, and until this age, an exclusively breast-fed baby needs little else (see Chapter 7). After six months, however, the baby's increasing nutritional needs cannot be met with breast-feeds alone, and hence, weaning foods are started to provide taste, nourishment and variety to the child's diet. If weaning foods are not begun, the child's growth may suffer, in addition to the fact that she may develop deficiency of selected nutrients, most specifically, an iron-deficiency anemia (Chapter 44).

The Art of Weaning:

Weaning foods are complementary in nature - that is, they complement mother's milk. The basic purpose of introducing these foods is: a) to provide taste and variety to the baby's diet; b) to provide the "missing" nutrients; c) to teach the baby swallowing, chewing and eating skills; and d) to habituate the baby to the exact taste and flavour of home meals.

The ultimate purpose of weaning is to provide a smooth, systematic and gradual transition from breast-milk to a full diet in a loving, disciplined manner.

You may begin with liquids initially, then go on to semi-solids and finally to normal home foods to enable the child to enjoy a full diet. By the age of ten months, the baby should be eating an almost full vegetarian diet, while babies who are brought up in non-vegetarian families will be eating flesh foods only after crossing their first birth anniversaries.

Baby foods should preferably be only mildly flavoured and taste as neutral as possible. Unduly sweet, sour salty or pungent foods are not recommended, as they alter the eating preferences of the baby subtly but irreversibly. Wafers and chocolates are examples of foods which must NOT be used while weaning. Home-based baby foods are always preferred over readily-available cereal mixes and fruit/vegetable pulps sold in cans or bottles. The latter are imported from the Middle East and Europe. The reason for this is that cereal mixes are so tasty to the baby that a breast-feeding baby *stops nursing in preference to these foods*. At the same time, the canned or bottled foods may be packed with preservatives or other artificial agents to prolong their shelf lives. There have been reports of contamination of baby milk powders and weaning foods with potentially lethal bacteria and even deaths of babies on whom such products were used inadvertently.

Utmost care to maintain good hygiene is a must while preparing, storing and serving home foods to the baby. Hand-washing, for example, is a must, as is proper washing of raw vegetables, especially in monsoon, and serving the food in clean, easy to use stainless-steel or food-grade plastic trays. It is always better to serve freshly prepared food; previously prepared food may be kept in the refrigerator; it may be thawed when needed over a slow flame or in the micro-wave oven; never put thawed, left-over food back in the refrigerator. I do not have to remind you to keep food always well-covered and protected from house-flies and other pests, and to teach the baby to wash her hands before and after eating, after using the toilet, and even otherwise, at frequent intervals, to reduce the risk of contamination and infection.

Water should be offered with weaning foods. The water should be clean and hygienic. *Boiling* for ten minutes kills all common disease causing germs, but has a drawback, in that, it irreversibly de-sweetens water and makes it bland. *Water-purifiers* are great, but most of them cost a lot of money. *Tap-fitted iodine-resin purifiers* are satisfactory, but their use is associated at times with an iodine-like smell in the water. They are economical, and purify up to 8000 litres of water, thereby lasting for nearly two years.

Plain *candle filters* rarely eliminate bacteria and viruses, but may be all right if no other options are available. *Cloth filtration* at the tap is too inadequate, and must be deplored. *Mineral water* and *bottled water* are quite often given to babies, but the purity of these has recently come into question, as many of these are not mountain waters, but underground, bore-well supplies, and some even contain very high, unacceptable levels of pesticides.

Once clean water is retrieved, it may be stored in the refrigerator in bottles, or in vacuum flasks for almost 6-10 hours. It may be given with a cup and spoon to the baby at the conclusion of a session of feeding her with a weaning food. Alternatively, the baby may be given a cup with a snout and a lid (called a feeder or sipper in domestic circles (Fig 9-1). This feeder should NOT be used for milk feeds as the milk often sticks to the inside of the snout, and acts as a focus for bacterial contamination.

Fig 9-1

While feeding, it is essential that you and the baby are both comfortable and relaxed. If there is undue anxiety in the mother, or if she has set a tight schedule for herself, for example, she has put milk to boil, or the pressure cooker to cook some food while attempting to feed the baby, she is more than likely to become impatient with the baby, or make some blunder or force an accident.

Spilling is unavoidable, and you should be prepared for it. It would be better if you put a bib around the baby's frock or dress, and sit with her on the FLOOR on a clean plastic sheet. She may either be in your lap (if less than eight months old), or sitting opposite you, with pillows to support her back and sides (if above the age of nine months). Offer the food slowly, in small morsels, either with your fingers (if solid) or with a spoon (if semi-liquid or liquid). Talk to the baby, smile with her and make pleasant expressions so that the baby will sit quietly. Try not to push the food in; rather, wait for her to open her mouth and accept the offered food. Switch off the T.V. or radio, so that the baby's attention does not get diverted.

Do not expect the baby to swallow much food. She is still learning to chew/swallow the food, and there will be times when she seems to be "refusing" the food, or even "throwing" it back out, when actually, she is just unable to co-ordinate her mouth and tongue movements sufficiently enough to put the food inside. Mashing of foods is essential, and a blender or mixer comes in handy too. As the child grows older and teeth erupt (say 8-9 months), somewhat less mashed foods should also be given, so that the child learns to appreciate the differences in the texture, hardness and shapes of different foods. At the same time, avoid mixing too many foods together, although standard mixes like dal + rice or curd + rice are all right.

You should begin the weaning process with just one food, say a steamed tomato, or a boiled potato; give this food daily for the next three to four days. See if she is able to eat it, digest it and remain free from any allergic symptoms like coughing, loose motions or rashes. After the four days or so are up, you can start with another new item. In this way, build up her range of foods week by week, month by month. A food item that does not agree with her can be RE-TRIED after some weeks. In case of families with a history of food allergies, atopic eczema, drug intolerance etc, new foods should be tried with caution.

First Weaning foods: 6 - 8 months:

Soups and Juices:

There are two schools of thought with respect to the starter foods. Some nutritionists allow mothers to give non calorie-rich soups and juices (within preset limits), while others prefer to start straightaway with cereals. You, as a mother, are the best judge. I feel that there is nothing wrong in giving the child limited quantities of home-made soups and juices, besides giving her cooked-rice water, coconut water and buttermilk in the first weaning months.

The basic tomato soup needs only the following ingredients. One medium-sized tomato, a few black peppercorns, some sugar crystals, salt, a few mint leaves and some butter. Add all but the butter to a cup and a half of water and pressure-cook for 3-5 minutes on a high flame. Turn off the gas, and once the cooker lid opens up, strain the soup through a sieve, squeezing the tomato so that its juice gets into the soup as well. The butter is added at the end for taste.

In the subsequent weeks, one may add one vegetable after another to improve the taste, consistency and texture of the offering. Non-vegetarians may add bones of chicken, mashed, pre-cooked chicken liver, lamb bones or other types of meats to the soup.

Instead of using plain water, one may use rice-*kanjee*, chicken stock or *palak* stock to prepare the soups. Moong-dal soup is another excellent alternative.

Juices of sweet-lime, oranges, water-melon, pineapple, etc. are all very nice to give to your baby in the weaning period, and even later on. These should be preferably made in the house using strict hygienic methods.

I am personally against steaming apples, pears, etc. and then giving their pulp because steaming will destroy most of the water-soluble vitamins. However, many childcare books do allow mothers to use the steaming process so as to get the child to have other nutrients from the fruits. I think the baby can be straightaway given fruits like bananas and *chikoos* even if they do not have any teeth. Even an apple may be given by grating it or by scraping some of it off the main fruit with a spoon. The baby will easily eat it.

Excessive use of fruit juices in infancy and early childhood is NOT recommended because it has been shown to cause a predisposition to childhood obesity. That is not acceptable, because many children who are obese in childhood grow up to be obese adults.

<u>Semi-solids:</u>

Porridges and milk-based *kheer* made from rice flour, *rawa* flour, *nachni* flour or wheat *daliya* are all very good semi-solid foods to be start with. On the salted side, one can give mashed, boiled egg yolks, boiled mashed potatoes, mashed soft-cooked rice with or without yoghurt or dal, mashed *idlis*, *upma* and milk-dipped, soft slices of bread. Other foods that can be given include mashed vegetables, custard, and so on. *Khichri* is a very "Indian" versatile food that can be modified in so many different ways. You can use it with curd, *kadhi*, gravy of chicken, *kheema*, and so on. Children enjoy mango juice, biscuits, puffed rice (*kurmura*) (babies love to chase flying *kurmuras* all around the room on all fours!), cream from the cake toppings and even ice-cream, should they get to eat it.

Bhujias (*gathiyas, sev,* etc.) are also well-liked, but these are not to be encouraged, as they are fried foods. Egg protein or albumen should be given only after 8 months as the younger babies may find it difficult to digest; there is also the risk of developing allergy to these foods. Dosas, dhoklas, besan ka halwa etc can all be given as weaning foods. *Choori* is a North Indian weaning food made from chapattis, sugar or jaggery and pure ghee. It is a very good weaning food, but it is rich in calories and should be given in limited quantities.

Remember to use the cooked food as quickly after cooking as possible and to protect it from flies and cockroaches when it is kept aside.

Pre-cooked Artificial Cereals:

Occasional and judicious use of marketed, pre-cooked commercial cereals is fine, as long as you don't make a habit of it and feed your baby with such tasty cereals everyday. In fact, you are doing great disservice to the baby, because she will not learn to eat home-based foods properly; besides, the baby may prefer these artificial meals so much that *she may refuse breast milk*. This is definitely NOT desirable.

At the same time, she may become so fond of the cereal that she may eat more than what she needs and become overweight. That is why, as a general rule, I do not recommend artificial weaning foods.

Age 8-10 months: Increasing Experience:

By this age, the baby will accept a larger variety of foods, and be able to use her lips to clear the spoon, her teeth to chew the food and her tongue to effectively move the food inwards to swallow it. She should be able to eat *paneer*, *chappatis*, breads and even soft *parathas*. As the baby has learnt to chew her food, it will no longer be necessary to blend the foods or to mash them before putting them in her mouth. One may give her all types of vegetables (except those with fibre or soft pips like *bhindi*, sweet potato or brinjals) and fruits (except pomegranates, berries and figs). One can give whatever fruit is fresh, freely available and cheap. Guava juice, strained to remove the hard pips, is an excellent source of vitamin C.

It is very important to allow the child some liberty in choosing the food, in the speed at which she eats her meal and in a few other things besides. At the same time, some limits must be set and adhered to. For example, it would be foolish to allow the child to spill all the milk on the carpet and then laugh with her, calling it a "prank". Thus, setting disciplinary limits allows the child some freedom, and at the same time, allows the parent to operate with a cool, rational mind.

I may as well add here that one should never force the child, or even urge her, or even coax her to eat a particular food or a particular quantity of food. At the risk of repeating myself, let me state once again:

Never, ever force-feed the child. Period.

It is also unwise to distract the baby's attention and then put a morsel of food inside her mouth on the sly (Fig 9-3). Such tactics do nothing to train the baby to eat on her own, and in fact, spoil her for ever. Meal-times should be a pleasant time for both, the baby and her care-provider; they should not become an opportunity to fight a *Mahabharata!*

Age 10-12 months: Geared to eat everything:

By the time the baby is ten months old, her dependence on breast feeds has already diminished to just 3-4 feeds in a 24-hour period. As she has begun to eat most foods, it makes sense to make her sit at the family table and grant her her own high-chair with a harness to prevent her from falling. She should be encouraged to self-feed from the offered plate. Bibs and such other spill-over garments should be draped over the baby so that she can eat with less sloppiness. Appreciate her attempts to eat by praising her, talking to her and loving her all the time.

At one year, the baby is eating all the foods from the family pot; therefore, it will not be necessary to make separate foods for her. The child who is given non-vegetarian food may be already having kheema, mutton, chicken and fish. She will eat whatever is cooked for the rest of you all. Babies should not be given tea, coffee, soft-drinks, chocolates, boiled sweets, too many costly nuts, etc. (Small food items can get inhaled into the lungs and choke her).

Ch. 10
A Balanced Diet

Children have never been very good at listening to their elders, but they have never failed to imitate them.
– James Baldwin, 1924-1987, American author

The Foods We Eat:

Some wise man once said, "We are What We Eat". So true is this aphorism that most people know what foods are "good" for them and what foods are "bad". Yet, so often do we see people eat the "wrong" things – and that includes you the reader, and unfortunately, sometimes, me the writer too!

Devising a balanced diet, that is, a diet that gives all the necessary nutrients to an individual is at once a simple and complicated task. This is because the knowledge of **what** contributes to a balanced diet is very simple; but **how** to offer it to a given individual requires tact and wisdom along with knowledge!

The list in the accompanying Table contains all essential nutrients needed by human-beings.

Water	Minerals	Vitamins
	Sodium	Vitamin A
Carbohydrates	Potassium	Vitamin B Complex
	Chloride	*Thiamine (B1)*
Fats	Calcium	*Riboflavin (B2)*
Linoleic and Linolenic Acid	Phosphorus	*Niacin (B3)*
	Iron	*Pyridoxine (B6)*
Proteins	Magnesium	*Cobalamine (B12)*
Essential Amino – acids:	Manganese	*Pantothenic Acid*
Histidine	Iodine	*Biotin*
Leucine	Fluoride	*Folic Acid*
Lysine	Cobalt	Vitamin C
Phenylalanine	Molybdenum	Vitamin D
Methionine	Selenium	Vitamin E
Threonine	Sulfur	
Taurine	Zinc	
Valine		
Tryptophan		
Isoleucine		

Calories: The energy found in food is used for growth, activity and development of all human beings. The unit of energy in human life-sciences is the Kilocalorie. It is also called a kcal or a Calorie (with a capital C). A newborn baby needs 120 kcals of energy for every 1 kg of his birth-weight everyday. This is expressed as 120 kcal/kg/day. At birth, her demand will be for about 350-400 kcal/day. By adulthood, the energy demands have increased overall, but the actual per kg demands have fallen to just around 40 kcal/kg/day. At one year, the baby will be having a 1000 Calories/day, and thence, this total will go up by 100 kcal/day per year to 5 years, then 50 kcal/day per year to 10 years, and then 20 kcal/day per year to adulthood.

Fat has the most Calories (about 9/g), while carbohydrates have less Calories (about 4/g), but the energy from carbohydrates or carbs is available instantaneously while that from fats takes some time to be released. Proteins, if "burnt" for energy, have as many calories as carbs do, but our body prefers to use the protein in another way – for growth rather than energy.

From the above discussion, it must have become apparent to you that the human body needs all the three main forms of food, viz. carbohydrates, fats and proteins, for optimum growth.

Carbohydrates:

Carbohydrates, or sugars, are found in cereals such as rice, *jowar*, *bajra*, etc., tuberous vegetables like potatoes, *arbi*, beet root and sweet potatoes, fruits of all kinds which are sweet and of course, refined sugar. In fact, fruits are a source of ready energy, and juices can work wonders to a tired body.

Cereals, preferably whole and unpolished, also provide fibre in our diet, while potatoes are mainly composed of complex starches, and are good for children and adults. Even among the foods that contain carbs, there are some whose carbs are considered "good" while others whose carbs are considered "bad". This difference is based on the ability or otherwise of a certain food to release large quantities of glucose (after that food is ingested) into the blood-stream. This is called that food's "glycemic index". To give you an example, the carbs in whole wheat bread are good and suitable even for a diabetic patient as they do not release a lot of glucose into the blood-stream after being ingested. On the other hand, the carbs in sweet-lime juice are, to that extent, called "bad" as they lead to a glucose "surge" in the blood-stream within minutes of being ingested.

Fats:

Fats, available in ghee, butter, oil etc. are the richest source of energy. Children need fats in order to grow. Fats containing long-chain fatty acids are essential for the development of the brain. At the same time, childhood obesity is mostly due to the excessive and indiscriminate intake of chips, wafers, cakes and chocolates, besides cheese, butter and fried stuff like *samosas, wadas, hamburgers, pizzas, hot-dogs, puddings* etc. It should be remembered that obese children have an earlier onset of blood-pressure, diabetes mellitus and heart problems (than fit children) in adulthood, and they tend to remain obese in later life. Hence, you as parents MUST remain on guard to see that your children do not just munch these junk foods and take larger quantities of protective foods like fruits and vegetables.

Flesh from beef (and other red meats) is also a rich source of fat, and its intake should be avoided as far as possible. Non-vegetarians should bring up their children more on fish, less on white meats (chicken, lamb) and least on red meat (beef).

Proteins:

Amino-acids are the building blocks of the growing child, and their supply must continue unbroken throughout their growing years. At the same time, as pointed out earlier, if fats and carbs are not available, the body uses either external or internal proteins to digest the food and provide energy. This leads to "wasting" or loss of flesh and muscle mass from the body.

Animal meats, eggs, milk, and milk products (esp. cottage cheese or paneer) provide the best proteins. These contain almost all the "essential" amino-acids (see table above). Vegetable-sourced proteins are of a poorer quality, but one can mix and combine the vegetable sources to get all the needed amino – acids. This is called "complementing" foods. The vegetable sources include dals (lentils) and legumes, wheat, and to a lesser extent, rice. Legumes (whole dals) contain up to 25% of their weight as protein, while oil-seeds like groundnut and soyabeans have even more protein (up to 26% for groundnuts and 40% for soyabeans).

Vegetarian Is Better:

If one looks at the way our bodies are designed, one will realise that it is designed for a vegetarian diet. We have hardly any canines, most of our teeth being the cutting (incisor) or grinding (molar) type.

At the same time, many human-beings subsist on non-vegetarian foods on a daily basis. The world is going vegetarian, and loving it!

There is increasing medical evidence to show that eating non-vegetarian food causes a higher incidence of high blood pressure, strokes, heart attacks, gout and perhaps cancer too. It is believed that non-vegetarian food causes minds to be more passionate, aggressive and cruel, while vegetarianism is free from this type of effect.

A well-balanced vegetarian diet is adequately geared to provide all the essential nutrients. For example, fruits are rich in vitamins, minerals, anti-oxidants, fibre etc. The single exception to the above statement is the low content of Vitamin B12 in vegetables and fruits. However, those who drink milk and/or eat eggs will get this vitamin too in adequate quantities.

Minerals and Trace Elements:

Of all the minerals listed above, iron, calcium, iodine and zinc are the most important, while sodium, potassium, and chlorine are freely available in most foodstuffs.

Iron: Iron is needed for the formation of hemoglobin, an important component of red blood cells. Hemoglobin helps to transport oxygen from the lungs to all the cells of the body. Deficiency of iron affects the health of the red blood cells and causes anemia. This can affect growth, general development and intelligence in small babies (see Chapter 44). Iron is found in *bajra*, *nachni*, wheat, eggs, meats, organ-meats (esp. liver), green vegetables, lentils and germinated pulses.

Calcium: This mineral is needed not just for the growth of bones and teeth, as most of you know, but also for the proper functioning of many critical systems of the body, such as the coagulation system, the beating of the heart etc. Milk and milk products like butter, cheese, etc. are the best sources, but one can also get calcium from nachni, bajra, green leafy vegetables and other vegetables.

Iodine: Iodine in small traces is a must for the healthy growth of a child, as it is needed for manufacturing thyroid hormones in the body. Deficiency of dietary iodine in many parts of India is responsible for mental deficiency, large thyroid swellings of the neck (goiter), and growth stunting (see Chapter 45). This is mostly due to low iodine in the natural water springs and rivers in hilly regions of the country. Good sources of iron include fish, meats, green vegetables (esp. spinach), cereals and milk and milk products. The government of India has made it mandatory for manufacturers of table-salt to add iodine to it (iodine-fortified table salt).

Zinc: Poor wound healing, skin infections, reduced body immunity, growth failure and poor sexual development can all be the result of zinc deficiency. Fortunately, zinc is available in a wide variety of foods and its deficiency is not so common. The foods include wheat, milk, nuts, eggs, cheese, grains and meat products.

Salt: Perhaps the most important communication I can share with you is to reduce the intake of salt (sodium chloride) in the diet right from infancy. A higher than normal salt intake is one of the most important risk factors for development of high blood pressure or hypertension. For adults the goal is less than 6 g of salt per day. Most of the salt we eat is naturally occurring in foods. Eating processed foods like *papads*, pickles, chips, wafers, sauces, biscuits, soups, pizzas, etc. can increase the salt intake tremendously. 80-90% of the salt we get into ourselves is derived from cooking, while up to 20% comes from salt added at the table. This last component should be avoided as far as possible.

An interesting side-light is that potassium containing foods act in the opposite way and may help to reduce the blood-pressure in hypertensive individuals. Thus, one can encourage the intake of potassium-rich foods like potatoes, pulses, dried fruits, tomatoes, orange juice, oatmeal and fresh vegetables.

Vitamins:

Vitamins are naturally occurring substances in foods that are essential for the proper functioning of the many complex chemical processes inside our bodies. Literally, vita = life, and amines = type of chemicals. Deficiency of any vitamin can produce symptoms and diseases, some of which are potentially fatal in nature. On the other side of the spectrum, excessive intake of certain vitamins may also produce disease. Thus, nutritionists have advocated optimum intakes of most vitamins. The requirements change with age. See Appendix d for recommended requirements of the vitamins by age.

All vitamins are divided into fat-soluble and water-soluble vitamins. It is important to know this, because heating and washing or soaking of vegetables in water can destroy the water-soluble vitamins. This is why it is recommended to wash the vegetables before dicing them and to steam them rather than cooking them in open vessels. Polished rice is also devoid of the B-complex vitamins as these vitamins reside in the outer husk, which gets removed while polishing (see later).

Vitamins A, D, E and K are fat-soluble, while Vitamins B-complex and C are water-soluble in nature. While the fat-soluble vitamins are found in fatty foods, some of them are found in leafy vegetables and dairy products too.

<u>Vitamin A:</u> This vitamin is needed for healthy eyes, and it has anti-infective and anti-oxidant properties. It is found as natural vitamin, and as a pre-vitamin Carotene in many foods. These include ghee, butter, oils, esp. fish-liver oils (along with Vitamin D), green leafy vegetables, yellow fruits and vegetables (these contain carotene), such as carrots, papayas, mango, apricots, yellow bell-pepper, egg yolk and milk and milk products.

Deficiency of Vitamin A leads to night-blindness initially; if this is not recognized, the disease can progress to complete blindness of one or both eyes. The child also develops skin problems, keeps getting respiratory infections, and fails to grow normally.

Vitamin D: Because Vitamin D regulates the metabolism of calcium in the body, its main role is to promote the health of the bones and teeth. A chemical in our skin can get readily converted to Vitamin D by the action of direct rays of the sun upon the exposed skin. In addition, Vitamin D is also found in fish-liver oils (cod, halibut etc.), milk and milk products, ghee, butter, egg-yolk and liver.

Deficiency of Vitamin D produces rickets, a condition characterised by reduced strength and easy breakability of bones, deformation at the joint areas and failure to put on height. In advanced cases, there can be deformities of the skull, rib-cage and other parts of the body.

Children must get an opportunity to play in the sun, as this will allow the body to make natural Vitamin D automatically. In children with rickets, the vitamin must be supplemented medically too.

Vitamin E: This is quite freely available in natural foods, and its deficiency is virtually unknown. It is an anti-ageing, anti-oxidant vitamin found in wheat-germ and other vegetable oils, eggs, liver, peanuts and dairy products. The role of this vitamin is not clear.

Vitamin K: This vitamin is needed for the proper clotting of blood. It is made by the intestinal germs in our body, but its final work can occur only when the liver makes it usable in the body. Dietary sources include dairy products, cabbage, spinach, cauliflower, beans, peas, potatoes and liver. Since newborn babies do not have a fully functional liver and breast milk is relatively deficient in this vitamin, all newborn babies are given an injection of this vitamin soon after birth.

Vitamin B-complex: The Vitamin B-complex consists of many different vitamins, labeled numerically and otherwise. B1 is Thiamine. B2 is riboflavin. B3 is niacin. B6 is pyridoxine. B12 is Cobalamine. Apart from these, we have folic acid, pantothenic acid and biotin. All these are water-soluble vitamins and are found in vegetables and fruits, milk and milk products, wheat, meats, fish and nuts. If allowed to sprout, legumes become very rich in these vitamins. Polishing the rice removes the endosperm, which is rich in the B complex vitamins. Green leafy vegetables are rich in folic acid (Folia = leaf) too. Cooking vegetables in open containers, dicing the vegetables before washing them, throwing out the rice water while cooking and so on are cooking and handling practices that may destroy or leach the B-complex vitamins from a healthy diet.

Deficiency of the different B vitamins affects the health of the mucus membranes, skin, nervous system, heart and almost all other systems of the body. Beriberi, pellagra and pernicious anemia are diseases caused by deficiencies of Vitamins B1, B3 and B12 respectively.

Vitamin C: This is also called *Ascorbic acid*. It is necessary for the healthy growth and functioning of teeth, gums, blood vessels and for healing of wounds. As it cannot be stored in the body, it must be had in the daily diet in sufficient quantities. It is found in *amla*, guava, citrus fruits like sweet-lime, oranges, lemon, grape-fruit etc., tomatoes, potatoes etc.

Deficiency of ascorbic acid causes "scurvy", or bleeding gum disease. In this, one may find, as the name suggests, easily friable bleeding gums, swollen hands and legs, anemia and bone pains. Breast-fed babies get sufficient Vitamin C.

Eating and Drinking the Healthy Way:

There are so many things to learn about eating and drinking the healthy way. I am going to try and enumerate only the most important of these here:

Timings: Train the children to eat at proper times. The newborn baby drinks milk from her mother almost 10-12 times in 24 hours. By six months, this has already reduced to 6-8 feeds, and by one year, to 2-3 feeds per day. Eliminating night-time feeds is an important training step, and most babies self-learn this by four to six months, but some don't. They need to be taught that night time is for sleeping and NOT for drinking milk or eating food. Babies do eat solids by seven to eight months, but not many are trained to eat at fixed timings, a thing that most parents must strive to achieve. The usual system is to offer a breakfast, a mid-morning snack, a lunch, a mid-evening snack and a dinner. This is adequate for the majority of children above two years of age.

Quantity: The amount that a child eats will depend not upon what you give her, but what she wants. This is dictated by her body's needs (hunger). If you train your child to eat at fixed times and give a good variety, most children will eat what they want when given a meal or snack. You should avoid "rewarding" a child who does not eat well by "offering" tasty snacks/toffees and so on. It makes sense to put a small quantity on the plate and let the child eat that first; and to offer a further helping afterwards. **Never force the child to eat against her will.**

Variety: Most children are put off meals if some variety is not seen on the plate. I am not for serving 36 varieties, but at the same time, some variety is essential for the child to "choose" what she wants to eat and hat she does not. The foods that we keep on the plate should be fresh, wholesome and rich in all nutrients, rather than just good to look at, or full of empty calories.

Speed: Encourage the child to eat neither too fast, nor too slow. She must chew each morsel properly, whether she has some urgent activity or not. A usual meal should last 15-25 minutes.

Presentation: An attractive presentation of food goes a long way towards a satisfactory meal intake by the child. The art of food dressing cannot be overemphasized! Dressing up a pair of half-fried eggs to look like the face of a man is one example; tomato ketchup is used to highlight a smiling face and pupils of the eyes. Similarly, radishes, carrots, peas and grapes can be utilised to create human faces, animal shapes etc. Tomatoes and spring onions can be cut to look like roses or other floral shapes; coriander and mint leaves over the lamb curry give it a very appetizing look, while a cherry atop a milk drink can work wonders!

Behaviour: It is very important to start early training for good behaviour. Children create a mess, talk constantly, watch TV, spill milk, and do all sorts of unacceptable things at the family table. They should be disciplined rigorously, and thereafter, you should give them a "gentle" reminder as soon as they join you at the table to "not to repeat their bad behaviour" again. You as parents should also follow proper table etiquette so that your children learn to do the right things. It is always easy to criticize others but very difficult to spot our own mistakes! Lastly, discourage conversation while eating food that needs meticulous chewing and cleaning, say fish or porridge. If the child talks while chewing, she may choke on the food. In general, tell your child not to talk with her mouth full.

Ambience: At eating times, the family MUST sit together and eat. The television set should be switched off, the lights in the other areas of the house should be dimmed, the telephone should be taken off the hook (if possible) and the curtains of the room drawn to allow everyone to "put their heart where their mouth is"!

Water: It is perfectly acceptable to offer small amounts of water during the meal if the child asks for it; it is, however, wrong for the child to always sit with a big bottle of water next to her and to continually drink water from it. The child should be asked to wait till she has completed her food, and to have water only after brushing her teeth. Avoid drinking carbonated beverages while eating; if need be, encourage the intake of *chaas, lassi,* fruit-punch or other similar drinks. Always sip these slowly and carefully to avoid the danger of inhaling them into the lungs. This should be your message to the child.

<u>Hygiene:</u> Train the baby from a very tender age to clean her hands with soap and water every time she returns from the toilet, and before sitting down for a meal. She should also brush her teeth for at least two minutes with a brush after each meal. You should teach her not to eat the food that has dropped accidentally on the floor or the table. Hand-washing after a meal is, of course, common sense, but you will be surprised how often children do NOT wash their hands after having snacks: they merely wipe their hands on their dresses! This should be censored immediately.

<u>Illnesses:</u> Continue to feed the child even when she has fever, loose stools or any other common illness. This rule is applicable even to the adults in the household. Many wrong beliefs inhibit mothers from giving the best seasonal fruits; for example, bananas and oranges are available in the winter in our country: they are not offered since they are perceived as "cold" foods. Similarly, mango is believed to be a hot food, and although available in summer, many mothers will not give it since it may cause boils. This archaic thinking should be discarded. Curds are very good for building up the baby's intestinal immunity. It is said that a cupful of curd taken daily will prevent gastrointestinal illnesses very effectively.

Ch. 11
Schedules and Supplements

Before I got married I had six theories about bringing up children; now I have six children, and no theories
– John Wilmot, 1647-1680, British Courtier and Poet.

Many mothers are able to understand their babies' whims and preferences early on in life. However, there are some mothers who are at sea on the subject of sleeping and waking patterns of their babies and get confused by the changing patterns of a growing infant. This chapter is dedicated to these mothers. I hope they will benefit from it. We will describe a normal day in the life of a baby, recommending schedules for feeding, resting, playing and sleeping along the way.

Newborn Baby (0-28 days):

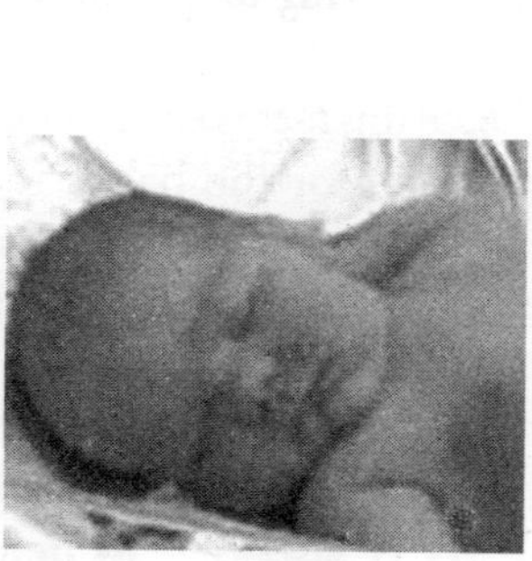

Fig 11-1

As noted in Chapter 4, the newborn baby is born alert and crying vigorously. She remains active and quiet for almost 45 minutes to two hours after birth. After this, she may cry for milk, or unusually, she may go to sleep. Thereafter, for nearly a fortnight, the baby will wake up only for her feeds, and lapse back to sleep as soon as she has had enough (Fig 11-1). However, because the feeding pattern of newborn babies more closely resembles that of predatory mammals, they take most of their feeds at night times. As a result, babies sleep almost throughout the day, but remain awake at night to feed.

Many families are "annoyed" with this nightly "performance" by the baby, as the other adults have their day-time schedules cut out for themselves. They have to get up early, grab their breakfasts, get ready and run to catch their trains or whatever – to reach their place of work in time. In their place, I would also be similarly bewildered and perhaps a tad annoyed that the new arrival just did not let me sleep! I would cast aspersions on the mother's abilities, on the quantity of milk she was getting, on the fact of the baby perhaps being mentally subnormal or even perhaps that it was a punishment for past sins committed by me!

I can assure you that none of these is true. It is the inherent nature of a newborn to awaken at night because she "knows" that her mother's milk will flow well after 6 p.m., and the amount of flow will keep increasing to reach its maximum by midnight. She knows this because this is programmed into her memory even before she was born. Because she knows this and because she knows that her mother will be by her side at night (and not working in the house), the baby keeps crying to get more and more milk at night.

Once this fact is clear to you, the mother, you will be able to "prepare" yourself for the baby. Try and sleep at least 2-3 hours during the afternoon everyday. Learn to remember when and how frequently the baby wakes up at night to take feeds, and wake up ahead of her and be ready to feed her as soon as she begins crying. In this way, you can be more composed, less confused and always ready to welcome the baby at your breast. The family also wins because the baby is attended to before she has time to wake up the entire household, the neighbours and sometimes, the occupants of the whole building!

Thus, the baby's "day" begins when she wakes up from a long spell of sleep in the evening. She passes urine, maybe stool, and then cries for some time before taking a feed. You are prepared for her and find it a pleasurable thing to do. You feed her; she plays for sometime, not willing to be "put" to sleep by rocking, stroking and what not! After an hour or so, she will cry for yet another feed; she then goes to sleep for a half hour or so. She is up at half past eight, feeds as per the mother's schedule and goes back to sleep. These sleep-wake cycles go on throughout the night. She hardly sleeps 2-4 hours during the night. She is wide awake in the morning. You should then sit and feed her from time to time. By 10 a.m., take her into the bathroom for her massage and bath routine. Upon emerging from the bath, your baby will look vigorous; she soon becomes drowsy and can be put to sleep in her cot. Most babies sleep for 4-6 hours after this – to awaken later at about 5-6 p.m.

The Young Infant (1-3 months):

As the baby grows, she begins to absorb information like a sponge; her mind is developing very fast. She learns to appreciate differences in her environment between "night" and "day", and slowly but surely learns to stay awake in the day and sleep at night. By three to four months, her total sleep time has already declined from a huge 16 hours to about 13-14 hours per day, and she is taking 2/3rds of this sleep at night. Thus, you will find that she may sleep uninterrupted at night, maybe from a late-night feed to an early-morning one.

The usual day begins with a morning feed; the baby has 4-5 briefer-than-before sleep periods all through the day, with the longest one (after her bath) being about 3-4 hours in duration. There are small periods of arousal in each spell of sleep. These arousals are periods of REM sleep*, and are interspersed with restful sleep.

After her first feed of the day, the baby remains playful and alert till she gets either hungry or sleepy. Then, she will either cry till she is fed, or be irritable till she is put to sleep. It is important that you let her do what she "wants" and not force her to feed or sleep, because this will enable her to learn faster on her own. She will not need "props" like stroking, carrying, back-rubbing or rocking to fall asleep.

After her bath and massage, she will still fall asleep for 4-5 hours as before, but she may not sleep as fitfully as she did earlier. She may wake up in the early part of the evening, and demand a feed or want to play with you. Eye contact and social smile are now her "tools of play" and she will use these optimally to engage you and other "admirers" in "conversation" for hours on end! She will look at objects shown to her very intently, and if she likes what she sees, she may make cooing sounds of pleasure and even squeal with delight.

By 8:00 p.m. or so, she will take her night feed and retire for at least 2-3 hours. Thereafter, a last feed at 11:00 p.m. will see her through the night.

The Not-so-young Infant (4-9 months):

As the baby grows, she starts interacting more and more with you and begins to remain awake for longer spells; she shows a greater interest in her surroundings, begins reaching out for dangling shiny

---

**The normal sleep cycle of a human being consists of sleep with Rapid Eye Movements (REM) and sleep without REM. REM sleep is essential for the "rejuvenation" of tired brain cells, and marked by agitation, eye movements, eyelid movements, fast breathing and occurrence of dreams, while non-REM sleep is deep, less easy to arouse from, and characterised by loosening of the muscles of the body and slow, deep breathing. For more details, read "Solve Your Child's Sleep Problems" by R. Ferber, M.D., Simon and Schuster, 1985 (ISBN 0-671-46027-7).*

objects that are brought near her and turns her head to see the source of any new sound(s). It may not be a surprise to find her bending her head nearly backwards to watch the television program you are watching, for example.

She sleeps comfortably through the night, though some babies have still not mastered this, and will continue to wake up to take night-time feeds. It all depends on your approach to the problem. Whether you are willing to be woken up or not will decide how fast the baby will train herself to sleep at night. A mother who learns early to "ignore" the baby's cry for a while will, in effect, train her baby to sleep for longer durations at night. This does not mean that such a mother is "heartless" and needs a rebuke from her in-laws. At the same time, she should try and explain why she ignores the baby so that a lot of misunderstanding can be avoided. The husband's support will go a long way in such cases.

After waking up in the morning, the baby will take her feed and remain awake for almost three to four hours thereafter; You may bathe her then; usually, a baby of this age really looks forward to the bath and enjoys it immensely (Fig 11-2 and 11-3); after this, the baby

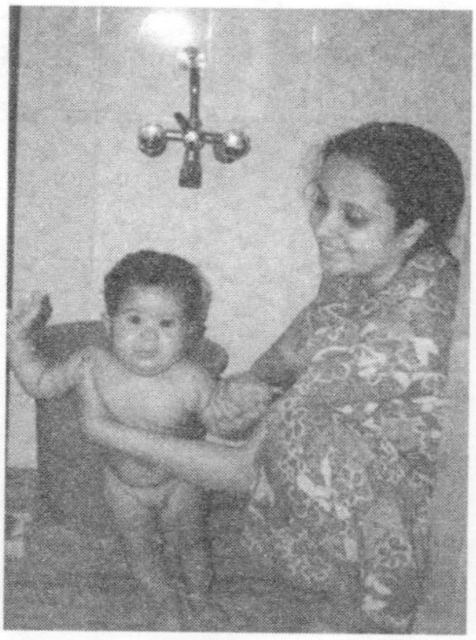

Fig 11-2

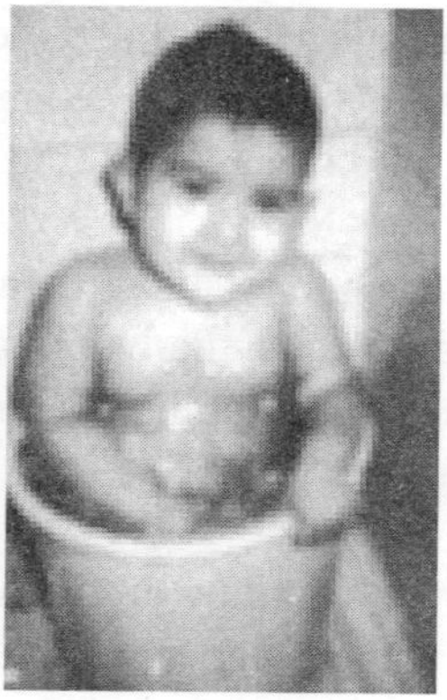

Fig 11-3

will go to sleep for about 2-3 hours and wake up again at about 1-2 p.m. in the afternoon. Sleep-wake cycles will continue through most of the afternoon and evening. She will retire to bed for the night by 8 p.m. if she has quiet in the house. In most urban households, she may stay awake till 10-11 p.m. as the T.V./ radio is on and everyone is active till that time.

By six months, it is time to introduce semi-solids and liquids other than milk in your baby's diet. I have found that most mothers finish their basic kitchen and cleaning work by 10:30 to 11:00 a.m., so this is an appropriate time to prepare something fresh for the baby and give it to her. Be sure that you have time on your hands. Don't try to "do" other house work or anything else when you sit with the baby to feed her. I have seen mothers put on the T.V. set, start cleaning rice or wheat, heat milk, supervise the older child's studies, and what not, while at the same time feeding the baby. This is NOT advisable.

The baby should be talked to and played with while feeding her the "new" food so that she accepts it in a playful milieu. Touching her, tickling her on her face, singing songs to her and generally entertaining her will enable you to feed her much more easily than if you feed her in a restrictive, unplayful environment.

I generally recommend the massage and bath after this weaning food. Cleaning the baby becomes easier that way. I also suggest giving any medicines or vitamin drops etc just before the bath.

The second weaning meal should be given in the early part of the evening, after the baby has woken up from her afternoon nap. The principles for doing this remain the same as for the morning weaning meal.

Always continue any new weaning food for 4-6 days before trying out yet another new food. (See Chapter 9)

The Older Infant (10-12 months):

By nine to ten months, infants are already trying to stand up on their own, speaking meaningless bisyllables and understanding simple parental commands. It is hard to put them down as long as they are awake. Over 90 % of them are sleeping full nights by now and waking up by 7:00 a.m., or even later. They take just 3-4 daytime feeds of milk, though some babies may take a few more than that. At each robust feed, they suckle for about 4-5 minutes or so. Their attention is often diverted by the sights and sounds around them, and at times, they will refuse a feed simply to see, hear or take active part in something that is happening around them. You may find it very frustrating if, after making something special to eat, your child just does not want to sit and eat it; she wants to play peek-a-boo with her grandma instead! You should remember that the child has acquired new physical, mental and emotional skills, and her world is fast expanding beyond the focal length of her eyes and the reach of her ears. She no longer gets limited by the stimuli reaching her: she wants, in fact, to reach out *to* the stimulus!

While she has begun to take interest in the things around her, she is also learning new skills like speaking, conversing and handling small objects in her fingers. The newly acquired skill of holding very small things with her thumb and first finger (the prehensile grasp of advanced mammals or apes) enables her to explore so many new things around her like her frock buttons, pens, pencils, marbles, chick-peas (*chana*), ground-nuts (*seeng*), scraps of paper and so on. She may want to put her fingers inside electrical sockets, into various holes in the walls and inside her own ears and nostrils.

At this time too, she is learning to control her urine and stool; you may find that while she might have waited till she went to the toilet to evacuate her bladder, she actually won't do so because of her spirited nature to get distracted while she is sitting on her potty (see Chapter 14). She will get up from it and run to check out the latest "happening" thing in her immediate surrounding!

As such, therefore, it is very difficult, but not impossible, to plan schedules for an older infant. What are needed are innovative child-rearing practices, a willingness to alter the schedules if the child is not "co-operating" with you, and a slightly stern approach to discipline. It is my belief that children are perceptive enough to recognise what problems you as a parent are facing. They won't even mind a little disciplining if it is done with empathy and explanation of what is being demanded of them. This would be the right approach for them.

You should continue to give them breast feeds, offer at least two top liquid feeds and three to four solid feeds and do all this only in the waking hours. Night-time feeds should NOT be given as a rule.

The Second Year of Life:

What is true of the 11-month old is truer still for the 13-24 month old child. It is no mean task to make the child sit for meals at precisely planned times. However – and this is the crunch – this is *exactly* what you should try and do. Fix meal times for them and expect them to abide by the rules.

Once your child is given simple instructions, you will find that she will actually be more responsive and less rebellious. Expecting her to learn the rules after stating them just once is, however, too much. You may have to reiterate the rules again and again till it becomes second nature for her to follow them.

This is the age when the child is absorbing information from all the nooks and crannies of her world that is your home. At the same time, she has a chance to further her "education" by listening to the radio/cassette player/disc player and watching television programmes. Try as much as you want, but today's child cannot be kept aloof from these entertainment devices. Hence, it becomes your responsibility to choose the programs that they can listen to/see. Then again, I have seen toddlers spending time on playing with other electronic devices like mobile phones, pagers and the like. Discourage them from touching these gadgets.

Encourage the child to play with child-safe toys. For more details, see Chapter 13. Join her in this activity. Read books to her. Select books with pictures and sounds. Show her how to do simple tasks around the home. All these activities should be done around 11:00 a.m. to 1:00 p.m., when the child is alert and demands time from you. You are also free from the morning duties of cooking etc. Hence, good interaction is possible between you and the child.

In the evenings, try and take her outside the house on a walk to a garden or any open space. If you reside in a colony, even the ground inside (the compound) is adequate, as the child wants to run around to vent her excess energy and to exercise her body.

Eating times should generally be restricted to breakfast, lunch, mid-evening snack and dinner. Milk should be given twice a day, once at breakfast and once at bed-time. Toffees, boiled-sweets, chips and wafers are considered non-nutritive and classified as "junk" foods. Their consumption should be carefully monitored and restricted. If at all, they should be given just after a meal, and the child should be trained to clean and brush her teeth immediately after eating them.

Vitamin and Iron Supplements:

Breast milk is perfect almost to a fault. Even nutrients which are less in it are almost 100% bio-available to the baby. Not only that, nature has designed the baby's digestive system in such a way that the said "deficient" nutrients can be easily assimilated by the body. The baby's digestive enzymes are somewhat different from those in an adult. This enables the baby to extract maximum quantities of needed nutrients and thrive despite there being a relative lack of these substances in the mother's milk.

For example, the physical amount of iron is less in breast milk, but it is highly bio-available to the body. Hence, no iron deficient state develops in the body. Breast-fed babies therefore do not need any vitamin drops or tonics during their first six months. Most animal milks also contain adequate amounts of most nutrients; however, boiling may reduce the quantity of water-soluble and heat-labile vitamins like the B vitamins and Vitamin C. Thus, babies fed exclusively with cow/buffalo milks should be given vitamin supplements. Powdered infant milk formulas are already enriched with vitamins, so no additional supplements are needed. Calcium supplements are normally **NOT** needed by normal babies.

Once the weaning process has begun, babies fed with any of the above methods will need iron supplementation. Iron drops are readily available in the market. Most drops contain 1-1.25 mg of iron per drop of medicine. The growing baby usually needs up to 2-3 mg/kg/day of iron. The dose can therefore be easily calculated.

Babies who are ill, or are on antibiotics repeatedly, will need vitamin supplements. These are available as drops with a dropper. The dropper has markings for 0.3 and 0.6 ml. Most babies need 0.3 ml once a day. Give the medicinal supplements just before taking the baby for her bath. The actual administration should be unhurried. You should try and put the dropper in the groove between the gums and the inside of her cheeks. Prop her head up during the process so that the drops go in properly.

At times, vitamin drops – and specially iron drops – may produce intestinal hurry or lead to slight constipation. If reducing the drops does not help, you may have to change the brand, or even stop the drops altogether.

Ch. 12
Eating Problems in Children

There is no finer investment for any community than putting milk into babies.
- Winston Churchill, 1874 - 1965, British Statesman and Prime Minister.

By their very nature, children are honest when it comes to eating. They will accept even the simplest foods when they are hungry, and reject the choicest delicacies when not. This makes the topic of discussing their eating problems very easy. Yet we find that most of the concerns of parents are about their children's eating "troubles". This is quite surprising, considering that most children will grow up into perfectly normal adults whether they ate well or did not during their childhoods!

I cannot overemphasize the next point: most eating problems are NOT genuine problems, but a burning question inside the minds of the parents. They continue to "feel" that their child is not feeding/ eating well, and that she is not "putting on sufficient weight". To a mother, her own child is always weak or not eating enough and in need of "tonics", "appetite stimulants" and "tests" to rule out internal diseases.

Why parents are concerned about their children's eating:

If parents had their own way, their children would never be allowed to get up from the dining table! This implies that if children did not have an automatic control over their appetites, most children would end up being obese and out of shape. However, and this is equally true, even all children who eat a lot do not always become fat. Some children become fat even when they eat less, while others maintain their lean build even though they are gluttons!

The reason for the variable response to increased food intake is the genetic build of an individual; children have varying rates of metabolism and therefore grow at different rates despite eating the same type and same quantity of food. Since parents are not aware of this basic fact -- or are aware but will not acknowledge the fact -- they run from pillar to post to find the elixir that will make their child a *pehelwan.*

The fussy eater comes from a well-to-do family:

It is sad but true that problem eaters come from well-to-do families with caring, educated parents. As I have mentioned in Chapter 10, each meal time is a time for waging a war between the spoilt, overbearing child on the one hand and the coaxing, cajoling, threatening and screaming parents on the other. There are trade-offs, understandings, deals and compromises galore before the meal is done.

Why does this happen? The *chief reason* is that parents want their children to be "healthy" and they equate obesity with healthiness. This is a wrong premise since, as we saw above, all children do not grow at the same rate. The *second error* that parents make is to assume that if the child eats more, she will put on more weight. This too is a fallacy, as we have just read.

The *third reason* is that most well-to-do families have the time, money and patience to "be after" the child and satisfy her every whim and fancy. Thus, we see that the parents bribe the child to eat, they promise toys and outings in return for the child favouring them with eating food properly, they seldom beat the child (a good thing, no doubt) and they often feed the child with their own hands – a clear act of pampering. All these actions say to the child in very "loud and clear language" that what they are doing is correct; that if they demand something, it is correct; that if they fret and fume, their wishes will be granted; and that if they so choose, they can make their parents dance on their little fingers!

The *fourth reason* is that most homes where fussy eaters are "born" are homes where mid-meal snacking is a rule rather than an exception. Parents and grandparents will collect their children and grand-children around the dining table and have a feast of specially cooked or prepared *chaats*, samosas, *kababs*, etc. at 11:30 a.m. and at 5:30 p.m. Children love the unusually prepared foods so much that they have a hearty meal of these items. Naturally then, they do not eat the regular meal that is offered at 1:00 p.m. and 8:00 p.m. This leads to a curious state of affairs: as the child does not eat well at lunch, the mother plies her with biscuits, chocolates, *chaats*, and so on in the evening. Then, the child eats well, and decides to again eat less at the dinner table! *This drama is played out almost everyday in many homes*. Parents then bring their wards with the complaint that "my child does not eat well"! Can you see the obvious paradox here?

How parents can make their children eat more:

You have to "unlearn" the wrong habits that you have been practising: that is, of making your child eat more by forcing, diverting her attention, coaxing, cajoling, threatening and screaming. You may have even struck your child when she did not eat. I am surprised at the number of parents who admit to having beaten their children if they did not wipe "their plates clean".

What you should not do:

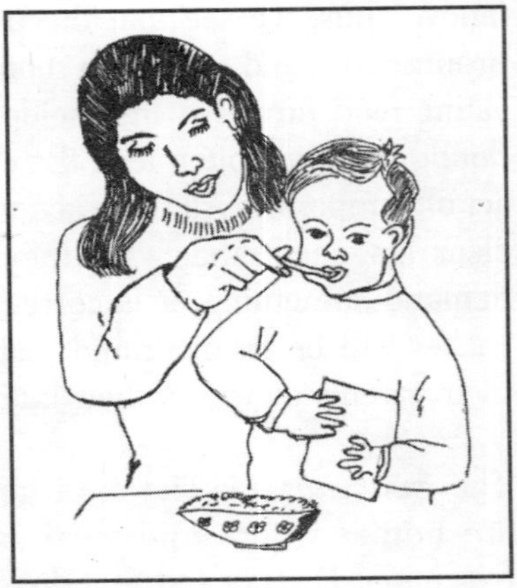

Fig 12-1

Clearly, these are wrong techniques and you should make an effort to change yourself before you try to improve your child's intake of food. Do not feed your child with your hands (Fig 12-1). Make her independent. Do not ever force the child to eat food. Don't do this when she is eight months old, don't do it when she is three years old, and don't do it when she is seven years old. In short **never force her to eat when she does not want to.** Bribing her, coaxing her, cajoling her, sitting before her with folded hands, falling at her feet and diverting her attention to a "bird outside the window" or to " a comical scene on the T.V." and then pushing the morsel down her throat are all inadmissible as strategies. Going after the child with plate in one hand and a dripping morsel of food in the other is also NOT allowed. Threatening her with dire consequences, shouting at her, "making angry eyes" and screaming your lungs out at her are also to be deplored.

What you SHOULD do:

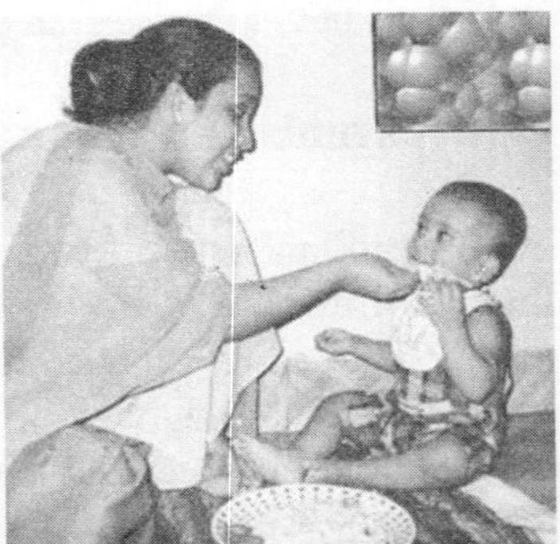

Fig 12-2

To feed an <u>infant</u>, the mother or the care-taker must allocate sufficient time to complete the task. She must spread a plastic sheet on the ground, sit the child on it, and arrange the food attractively in a large plate and bring it to the baby. If the baby is less than a year old, the mother may feed her with her hands (Fig 12-2), but an infant who is more than a year old should be allowed to feed on her own. She will only then learn the skills of eating.

To make an <u>older child</u> eat well, one should stop all the wrong things and institute a proper eating time-table; one should "reward" the child for eating well. Let me explain each of these in more detail.

- About fifteen to twenty minutes before the appointed meal time, remind the child that she has to join you at the dinner table in a short while.
- She must be told to wash her hands and sit at the table/ floor-mat where she dines everyday.
- Before food is served, explain to her that she will have to eat from the items that are to be served regardless of her likings or dislikings.
- Present her with a choice of at least two or three different items, at least one of which she loves to eat.
- She must be told that she will get about twenty to twenty-five minutes to eat whatever she wants. She must be told that she will be politely asked to get up from the table at the end of that much time and told to "go and wash her hands and brush her teeth".
- She must be told that if she misbehaves or throws a tantrum, she will be asked to leave the table for a set time (say, two minutes) and return to the table thereafter; that the two minutes will stand deducted from her rationed time of 25 minutes. Not only that, she will stand to lose two minutes each time she misbehaves, and no concessions will be allowed therefrom.
- Once she begins to eat, switch off the T.V. and other such devices. Join her with the rest of the family to eat at the same time whenever you can. Take the telephone off the hook (if possible) and switch off the door-bell (if feasible). Turn to the task of eating the meal.

- Serve small portions of food on her plate. Once she empties her plate, ask her if she wants more. Do not insist on her "wiping her plate clean". Consider her effort to be a success even if she finishes about 60 – 75 % of the food on her plate.
- If she has done so, **"reward"** her immediately with praise, kind words, a declaration of the tremendous love you have for her, a serving of her favourite dessert, or a helping of chocolate or some such "snack" item.

If you talk too much, you encourage the child to talk while eating and also to get distracted. Hence, keep the flow of conversation to a minimum. **Do not bring topics like family feuds, office matters, politics and stories of horror and crime to the dining table**. Converse instead about pleasant matters that do not create too much excitement. Involve her in the conversation, while reminding her that she should chew the food slowly, and NOT TALK WITH HER MOUTH FULL. Remain with her till she finishes eating, even if you have already done so.

Continue to praise her for hours afterward; do so even when she is with her friends. This will increase her self-esteem much more than any other single thing that you might have already done. At snack-time, offer her that day's snack with a reminder that she is getting to eat her favourite snack because she ate her meal properly. I can assure you that such *positive reinforcement* will work wonders for your child!

Some more guidelines and recommendations:

Remember the following:

1. You may want to take the child with you to the market to make purchases, so that she feels important
2. Stick to previously declared meal-times.

3. Do tell her the rules for eating just before she begins eating. Do so gently, with a smile, but convey with your body language that you are serious about each of those rules.
4. Train the child to eat with her own hands.
5. Involve the child in all meal – time discussions
6. Present an acceptable choice of foods from which the child can "independently" make a selection.
7. Restrict the meal-time to 25 minutes at the most.
8. No mid-time snacks in the space after a meal in which the child did not eat well.
9. Positive reinforcement is the name of the game.

The Overeating child:

There are some children who tend to eat more than what is necessary for their own health. In the beginning, parents are only too happy to see the child eat as if there is no tomorrow. However, they soon realise that the child's eating pattern is abnormal. They find that the child often does not "hear" them when she is eating. They find the child not participating in play in the house, building compound or outdoors.

They find the child often discussing food and food preparations most of the time. The child's favourite topic on the T.V. is the Afternoon cookery show. I could go on, but I am sure you get the drift. My concern is fully justified as overweight infants become overweight toddlers, overweight toddlers, overweight children, overweight children, overweight teenagers and overweight teenagers, overweight adults. This last category is at increased risk of early onset of obesity-triggered diseases like high blood pressure, heart attacks, diabetes, breathlessness and so on.

Children of genetically overweight or obese families are generally more prone to obesity themselves, but poor controls by parents may also cause overeating. Parents should exercise reasonable controls on their children and provide them with a balanced diet. Offering butter, cheese, sweet-meats and ghee or oil-based items in excess is not advisable. Frequent intake of chocolates and potato and other chips are also responsible for children putting on excess flab on their bodies. The television culture has increased the threat of obesity across all age groups, and children are even more vulnerable because parents feel that "if my child is eating, there is no problem as he is growing, and he will not put on weight". Nothing could be more wrong. Children *will* put on weight if they eat haphazardly and excessively.

Thus, **encourage your child to have more fruits, vegetables and nuts, while at the same time curtailing the intake of chips and chocolates to a bare minimum, and that of butter etc. to a reasonable level**. Also, make your child participate in more active play, outdoor sports etc. so that she can use up the unwanted calories.

The selective eater:

Some children are extremely selective in their eating habits. Part of this problem may be genetic, and it is not unusual to find one of the parents also very choosy about the type of food they eat. However, some children become choosy because the wrong types of foods are introduced in their diets in infancy. The usual way in which this occurs is that parents give selectively tasting food like sweets or salted foods etc. What happens is that the infant develops a liking for that particular taste and this gets ingrained as a preference throughout life.

Once such a preference has taken root, it becomes very difficult to undo it. In fact, even as adults, such children continue to eat only those foods that they like, and in their turn, foist the same habits on *their* children!

The only way to remedy this problem is for the parents to start eating all foods in turn, and make their children eat them too, by leading with example. There are no medicines which can really help in this matter.

Role of tonics, appetite stimulants and protein supplements:

The Indian pharma industry manufactures hundreds of tonics and appetite stimulants each year, and almost 30 – 40% of the shelves in a pharmacy are filled with such preparations. These belong to all streams of medicine, viz. allopathy, ayurveda, homeopathy, *unani* and what not. There are exotic medicines like *Chyawanprashes* containing gold, silver, saffron, etc. and they all promise wonders. The actual fact is that tonics and appetite stimulants are NOT really effective, and even if they are, they produce unacceptable side-effects. For example, Cyproheptadine, a commonly prescribed appetite stimulant can produce neurotoxicity. It has a very poor margin of safety, and even twice the recommended dose may produce toxicity. The same is true to some extent with Buclizine. Some tonics contain **alcohol** as one of the ingredients. This is definitely not acceptable.

A lot of direct marketing companies (like Amway and Modicare) have come out with protein powders which are no better and no worse than freely marketed products like Bournvita®, Complan® and Horlicks®. Use these if you wish, but I generally recommend using prescription protein supplement powders only as these are nutritionally more powerful.

Ayurvedic prescriptions and such other preparations may not work at all. Some health workers prescribe vitamin supplements and other nutritional products, but most will have not the slightest effect on a child's appetite. If a child has iron-deficiency anemia, *iron supplementation* may improve her appetite.

The bottom line: **Barring iron preparations, all other preparations are NOT recommended**.

Part IV

See How They Grow (0 – 6 years)

The greatest poem ever known
Is one all poets have outgrown:
The poetry, innate, untold,
Of being only four years old.

– Christopher Morley, *To a Child*

Ch. 13
Normal Growth and Development (Age 0 - 6 years)

You don't really understand human nature unless you know
why a child on a merry-go-round will wave at his parents
every time around - and why his parents will always wave back.
– Author unknown.

A "Biopsychosocial" model of development and growth has replaced the earlier models where the argument was between "nature" and "nurture" alone. As per this model, biological factors (or genetic endowment) continuously interact with psychological and social factors to bring about net growth and development. For example, a baby endowed with genes for an eventual height of say, five feet ten inches, may not achieve this final height because of lack of love (psychological factor) or because of poverty and lack of food (social factor). Conversely, with proper nurturance and care, even an orphan child may reach 90 to 95% of her genetic potential.

Hence, while it may not be possible to artificially increase a baby's height or intelligence with tonics or love, it will always be feasible to help the baby attain her full genetic potential by properly looking after her needs and continuously showering her with love and nurturance.

The Newborn:

Immediately after birth, the newborn baby has a quiet state of alertness. She looks around, and responds to her mother's touch by making pleasurable sounds and slow back arching movements. If offered the breast, she will root for the nipple and begin to suck her mother's milk. This quiet alert state lasts nearly 40 to 45 minutes, and as a mother, you are advised to feed the baby if possible during this phase. After this, the baby goes to sleep. Later on, she will be found in different states of alertness and wakefulness all through the first month.

The baby has amazing capabilities at, or soon after birth. She can see, hear and feel things around her. Her vision is 6/60, which is very poor by adult standards (a mere 10%), but with this vision, she can see her mother's face very clearly as she suckles on the latter's breast (a focal distance of 9-10 inches). She has a preference for seeing a human face (a roundish moving structure with two eyes and a talking mouth) and for hearing and recognising her mother's voice too.

During the first week, the baby may lose up to 10% of her birth weight owing to various reasons; this weight is then regained over the next seven days. After this, the baby is expected to put on 28-30 grams daily for the next 45 days or so. During these early months, she may add up to 3.5 cm/month to her body length.

Sleep patterns may be such that during the first month or two, babies may sleep almost twelve to sixteen hours daily. This may consist of a long sleep of nearly eight hours, plus 3-4 naps of 40-50 minutes each in between. As the baby grows, the night time sleep remains constant at about 7-8 hours, but she will take fewer and shorter day-time naps. Even during the night time, she may wake up for feeds, and this is perfectly normal.

During the first few months, the child is easily startled by loud sounds, bright light or rough handling. She may even cry when exposed to such stimuli suddenly. Often, one finds that she will not only cry, but also open out her hands and extend her arms outward, bend her legs and arch her back. This response is called a *Moro response* and is actually one of the signs that the baby's reflexes are sharp and she is unlikely to have any serious problem. On the other hand, a crying baby is *quickly calmed and consoled* when picked up and gently stroked or soothed with cooing sounds in her ears.

Baby crying without any apparent reason (see Chapter 6) is why most mothers get poor sleep and rest during the baby's first three or four months. While many such crying episodes are due to what has been called "infant colic", some babies will cry in spite of being properly fed and burped. Crying activity peaks -- at almost 3 hours of crying per day -- by about 6 weeks of age, and then gradually declines to 1 hour or so by three months of age. On the other hand, involuntary smiling is also seen in one-month old infants.

Sensory achievements include recognition of mother's voice and smell of mother's milk, gazing pleasurably at mother's face while suckling and conveying the felt feeling of "trust" in the mother's ability to look after her urgent (hunger, wet nappy)as well as non-urgent (desire to be cuddled or burped or just carried in the arms) needs. The moment the baby sees her mother approaching her, her crying ceases and she will expectantly await her needs to be satisfied.

Age 2-6 months:

The emergence of a voluntary smile and increased eye contact with you will mark a watershed change in your feelings for your baby. You will feel as if she is returning your love back to you. During the next 3 to 4 months, the baby will achieve many movement (motor), mental (cognitive) and social milestones.

Between 3 to 4 months, the growth rate will slow down to about 20 grams per day. Her length will also grow less rapidly, say about 2.0

cms/ month. By the age of 5-6 months, most babies will double their birth-weight.

The baby will begin to see objects hanging before her and will try and reach out for them, albeit imprecisely. She will enjoy looking at her mother (Fig 13-1) or anyone within her field of vision and will wait expectantly for something favourable to happen (such as being picked up to be fed milk). Rolling over from the tummy down (prone) to the back down (supine) position becomes possible at around 4 months, while the reverse roll is achieved a little later at 4 ½ to 5 months of age. Head control improves so that by 3 -3 ½ months, the head does not need to be supported by your hand. Now the baby can be made to sit up in your lap to allow you to either feed her from a cup, or for her to look around. At the same time, her vision has improved too, and she can see a larger field as well as more depth.

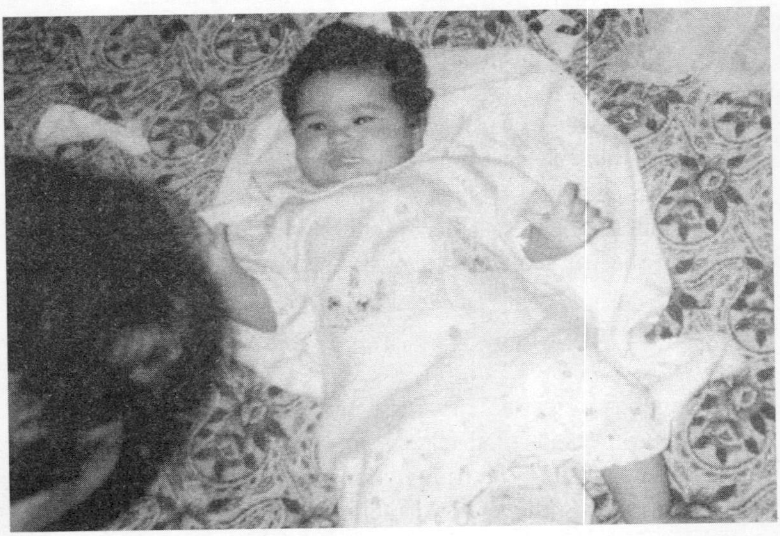

Fig 13-1

Movements of a small infant are more complex as compared to those of a newborn. She can raise her head and neck when laid prone (Fig 13-2) and look at objects dangled before her eyes at an angle of about 25-30 degrees above the cot. When she is happy, or tickled, she will laugh aloud, thrash her arms and legs or make gurgling sounds. She enjoys gentle bathing (see Fig 11-2) and being fed. Mouthing behaviour is seen by 5 months or so. The baby will be found to put almost anything in her mouth to experiment.

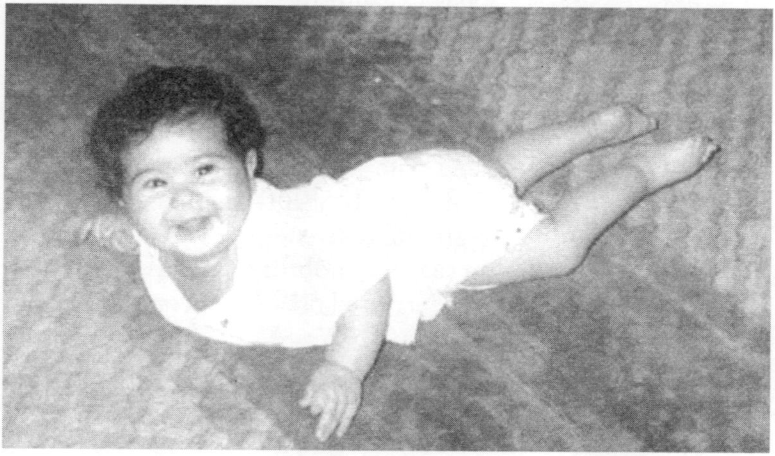

Fig 13-2

She can be made to stand (with your support) on her feet with her legs straight. She may begin to throw one toy from her hands when offered another one to hold. Sleep patterns are almost the same as before, though the day-time naps may be reduced in frequency and/ or length.

Socially, the baby is beginning to appreciate things outside the field of her mother, and gets distracted easily while feeding. She tries to "engage" an adult in a "conversation" and will try to lure the adult back to her if the former looks away. She will smile at her own reflection in the mirror.

Self-exploration is also seen from this age onwards. The baby will often "play" with her face, hands, feet or genitals. Finally, the baby will begin to exhibit emotions like anger, sadness, joy, etc., but these will get further refined after about 7 to 8 months of age.

Age 6-12 months:

Fig 13-3

The child's growth slows down further, to about 15 grams/day of weight and 1.5 cms / month of length during this period. By the end of her first year, she will have trebled her birth weight. She will begin to sit up without your help by 7-8 months (Fig 13-3), stand with support by 8-9 months, stand unsupported by 10-14 months, and finally begin to take steps by 12-15 months. Increased mobility means increased opportunities for exploration, increased risk of injuries and disinterest in feeding or other activities.

Around 6-7 months, the first tooth (usually the lower central incisor) erupts, and then the other milk teeth erupt over the next two years or so (see later in the chapter, p. xx). Tooth development goes hand-in-hand with skeletal growth.

Your baby has now begun to clearly pick up any object within the range of her hands, and will put that object immediately into her mouth. Before doing so, she may inspect the object, pass it from one hand to the other, bang it, drop it, etc. What appears to be purposeless activity is actually a learning process for her, and will advance her understanding of the offered object(s). She will be able to hold her cup of water or milk, or a piece of *chappati* or bread and "play" with it or put it in her mouth. She will even hold a spoon but won't be able to coordinate the movements of putting it in her mouth without spilling anything contained within.

By the age of nine months, the infant knows that an object that is not "visible" may actually be "hidden" and she will "uncover" the object from under a towel, cup or whatever else may have concealed the object (such as a coin or a marble). At the same time, she will begin to differentiate between familiar and unfamiliar people, and "stranger anxiety" may cause her to cry inexplicably when, for example, your US returned brother wishes to hold her in his arms. She will scream for no reason, and will not quieten till you take her back from his hands.

Finally, your baby will begin to assert her independence by asking to be allowed to hold her own glass or spoon while feeding. Tantrums may also be seen as she tries to become autonomous. Socially, she has begun to understand simple words spoken by you. She will respond when her name is called. She will play games like "peek-a-boo", hide and seek and can clap her hands (without much sound). She can wave her hands when asked to say "bye-bye" to someone. When asked to return something that she is holding in her hands, she may willingly do so.

Speech is in the form of babbling syllables like ma, *ba*, *da* etc. without actually knowing their meaning. Some inflections may reflect your native tongue, like *aai* for mother. One or two meaningful words may also appear and you will find them used with a specific person or object.

At this age, picture books provide an ideal context for verbal language acquisition.

Age 12-18 months:

The growth rate declines further to 8 grams/day of weight and 1.0 cm / month of length. Her appetite declines. She burns up her baby fat, while her mobility increases. By 12 months, she would be walking independently in most cases, although a few will achieve this milestone by only 15 months of life. At first, she will walk with a wide-based gait, almost "toddle" (hence toddler!). Frequently, she will stumble, or lose balance and fall. **This, along with her "lean" appearance and "poor" appetite, is a frequent cause of worry for the parents; however, this is a normal phase in her development.**

Her stomach will be out in front, the knees, slightly bent and feet will strike the ground flat. As she develops the walking skills further, her gait becomes more stable and the protruding stomach gets tucked in. The child will then walk straight, with arms swinging by the side of the trunk, and she will be able to stop, turn or stoop without falling. By the age of 18 months, she can run around and go up and down stairs without help from you. Initially, her stair climbing activities may be on "all-fours", but as she develops further, she will hold on to the banisters and go up or down.

Toddlers advance their thinking processes further. As a result of her exploratory quests, she may come to you with odd objects and things that she has "curiously discovered" from virtually inaccessible nooks and corners of the house. She will play with blocks, making towers of up to 3-4 cubes. She enjoys playing with pulling and pushing toys. She may want to "join" you in dusting, sweeping and mopping activities. Your baby will often be discovered playing "appropriately" with things: she will use a comb for the hair, the keys for the cupboard, and so on. She will enjoy arranging and re-arranging stacks of things such as blocks, books, video-cassettes, spoons, etc.

With this ability to "control" objects comes the need to exercise the "power" to explore the home, and to "go away" from parents. She may inscribe circular arcs of exploration around you or even "orbit" out of your field of vision.

As far as language goes, the child's understanding precedes her expressive abilities. She will respond appropriately to no, yes and bye-bye before she is one, and point out body parts, pictures of animals etc, by 18 months of age. She will use 15-20 words with meaning and use proper nouns too.

She has awareness of her bladder and bowel movements and may indicate her toilet needs by pointing to the potty, walking to the toilet and pulling down her panties (or making an attempt to do so) or with other similar gestures. Some children will achieve complete bowel control before 18 months of age, while most will do so within the next few months. Day-time control is achieved earlier than night-time control.

Age 18-24 months:

The growth rates that applied for the first half of the second year of life apply here as well. By the end of this period, the child would have quadrupled her birth weight. What increases most in these months is the ambit of motor development. The child has learnt to run and to climb stairs; she may even begin to jump.

An important cognitive change is the understanding that she may get separated from her parents. This causes her to increasingly cling to them. The child will not permit her parents to go anywhere outside without taking her in tow. When her mother goes to play with another child, she will experience jealousy and will immediately indicate her displeasure by screaming, fidgeting or "having it out" with her mother for "ignoring" her. In parents' absence, she may cling to a transitional object that represents the parents such as a blanket or a toy. This attachment to objects will remain for at least this period, and will go as she grows older and her feeling of parental permanence is fully internalised. It is recommended that you change her blankets, dolls and other objects frequently during this period to avoid object attachment.

Self awareness and concept of self/image difference will appear in this period. If your baby sees a blemish on her face in the mirror, she will reach out for her face rather than for the image in her reflection, and try to remove the blemish.

Perhaps the most dramatic change will be her rapid strides in language development. From a vocabulary of about 15 + words at 18 months, she will be able to vocalize and understand almost a hundred words by the age of 2. She will begin to join words and form sentences. She will understand a two step command, such as "Remove your shoes and come to me". She will use her index finger to point at objects and indicate with her gestures that she doesn't want the object, but merely wants to know what it is. She may even ask, "What is that?" Picture books continue to provide new input to her knowledge.

With a pencil, she may make crude vertical and horizontal lines. She may learn to recognise some or all the letters of the alphabet and may even attempt to "write" them, albeit with little success. With blocks, she will be able to make a tower of 6-7 cubes. She may put cups inside larger cups with some success. By two years of age, some children have become adept at "dissembling" and "re-assembling" toys; it is another matter that their re-assembled toy may not resemble the original version at all!

She will easily remove her shoes and socks by herself and pull down her shorts too. She will refer to herself by her own name and will love songs and nursery rhymes.

Age 24 – 36 months:

By the age of two years, the child is almost completely independent while mobile. She continues to put on weight and height, albeit at a much slower rate than before. During the third year of life, she will have added about 2-3 kg weight and about 5-7 cm height.

She continues to explore her surroundings, only now, her surroundings will include neighbours' homes, the back yard and the front porch! She can climb up and down stairs more rapidly, using an upright posture to do so. She climbs up one step after another by placing her feet alternately on the stairs; on the other hand, she will climb down the stairs by placing both feet on each step. She jumps with both feet, she can ride a tricycle, and she can dress and undress herself (except buttons).

Most of the times, the child will have lost interest or will soon lose interest in blocks and other games of infancy, and will, if offered, choose games that invite him/her to compete against other children in the house and neighbourhood. Games of running, games with the bat and ball and in case of boys, toy cars, and in case of girls, dolls become their favourite toys as well as companions of solitude. The child will often be seen talking to herself in the company of her favourite dolls. A boy will occupy his free time when alone with all his toy cars laid around him. With these, he will play in different ways. He may make the cars race against each other, or he may "grant them life" and make them characters in his tales of fantasy. He may also bang cars against each other, or he may "enact" stories where cars, animals or simple glass marbles become his main story characters.

She is usually fully toilet trained by this time. Socially, most children, by the age of 2 ½ or so, have outgrown their anxiety for strangers, and will participate actively in any event with lots of new people to interact with. They love to join in and listen to the elders talk, gesticulate and argue.

Their curiosity is at a high, and they will frequently approach you to ask you a string of questions. Try and be patient as they ask first simple, and then, increasingly complex questions. If you are unable to give them a satisfactory answer, you should say so, but you should almost never lie to them.

Your child will talk a lot and may even be able to count up to ten on her fingers or with blocks or objects. She will sing advertisement jingles, nursery rhymes and movie songs. She will become aware that she is female.

Age 3-6 years:

Over the next three years, the child learns many new skills, eats on her own, plays with her own friends, and as she begins to attend nursery classes, she rapidly starts gathering knowledge. At three, the child is at home, except for a few hours when she may attend a play school. At six, she attends school for almost three to five hours, so her day is distributed between home and school almost equally. At three, the child watches TV, but with little comprehension; at six, she understands issues much better and may ask her parents to put on her favourite programmes.

Physically, the child grows as before, with a speed that is slower than in the first three years; in fact, she may grow very little in these three years. She gains just about 2 kg/year and 6-8 cm/ year of weight and height respectively. By six years, a boy will have dimensions of 21 kg and 115 cm, and a girl, 20 kg and 114 cm.

There are no obvious new motor or fine motor skills that the child will learn between three and six years, barring some unusual things such as the ability to hop on one foot, jump from a height of about two to three feet and jump over heights of 70-90 cms high obstacles. She may also learn to ride a small hand-held scooter and a small bicycle with side wheels. By six, a child may even learn how to ride a bicycle without side wheels.

By four years, a child will learn to tell small stories and play with simple musical instruments like drums, small pianos, flutes and the harmonica. The actual skill will depend upon whether the child has exposure to such instruments and how much training or instruction is given to her. Your encouragement and support will go a long way in fostering hidden talent in the young child.

PRIMARY TEETH: DEVELOPMENT AND CARE

Development of Teeth:

Humans have two generations of teeth. The first set, called "deciduous teeth", "milk teeth" or "primary teeth" erupt between 6-30 months of age; they are 20 in number. By six years or so, these teeth have "outlived" their usefulness. Hence, they are shed off (in more or less the same sequence in which they erupted) from the age of 6-6 ½ years, and up to about 10-12 years of age. In their place grow "alveolar teeth" or "permanent teeth" or "secondary teeth", which will stay with the person from the age of eruption to the end of life or till they are knocked out by an act of violence or disease. No natural replacement of the permanent teeth can ever occur.

<u>Primary Teeth:</u>

Although the usual age of eruption of the first tooth is six months, this age depends upon the child's own genetic makeup (and therefore, the family's genetic background). In a child with delayed dentition, inquiry will often reveal a similar delay in one or both parents. Although this can limit the kind of foods that you may be able to give the baby, medically, the delay is not significant as the tooth buds are already present within the jaw (as an oral X-ray will show); the timing is, as said above, a genetically determined limitation, about which nothing can be done.

Generally, one of the lower central incisors (the teeth are named from centre outwards as is shown in the table) is the first to erupt; the other one comes in next, followed by the upper jaw incisors; the lateral incisors are next, at about 7-10 months; the first molars make their appearance next – by 10- 12 months, followed by the canines at 15-20 months and the last molars at around 2-2 ½ years.

Table: Sequence of eruption of teeth

Primary Teeth	Age of eruption
Lower cent. incisors	5-7 months
Upper cent. incisors	6-8 months
Lower lat. incisors	7-9 months
Upper lat. incisors	10-12 months
First molars	10-15 months
Canines	15-20 months
Second molars	20-30 months

In general, the teeth of the lower jaw erupt before those of the upper jaw. By 1 year, the child has 6-8 teeth, and by 2 years, about 16. The last molars erupt by 2 ½ years. Milk teeth are smooth, softer than the permanent teeth and white in colour.

Secondary Teeth:

The secondary, or permanent teeth as they are called, start coming in at about 6 years of age. Further discussion of the sequence is taken up in Chapter 16.

Teething:

Teething is a physiological phenomenon; it has been much maligned for its propensity to occur with diverse illnesses like cough, cold, fever, diarrhoea, vomiting, weakness etc. which also tend to occur during this phase of the child's life. Parents tend to believe this so much that they seek homoeopathic, ayurvedic, unani or even magic remedies for the prevention of all these problems (see below).

Neonatal teeth: On rare occasions, teeth covered with oral mucosa have been noted even in the newborn. Such neonatal teeth are soft and do not cause any problems; the mother can even suckle the baby without any fear of injury to her nipples. Occasionally, neonatal teeth may have to be removed as loose teeth can come off any time and enter into the baby's wind-pipe and lungs (aspirated) with disastrous consequences.

<u>Eruption of the first tooth:</u> The usual age of eruption of the first tooth, which is one of the lower central incisors, is 6-8 months. This time is, however, variable, and I personally know many children whose first tooth erupted after their first birthday! (A delay beyond 15-18 months should prompt referral to the Pediatric dentist.) The commonest way in which a parent or a care-taker discovers that a tooth has erupted is when the child exhibits one of the symptoms listed below; however, it is not uncommon to have NO SYMPTOMS AT ALL; in such cases, you may suddenly hear a "ting" sound when you are feeding your baby food with a spoon; or you may actually feel the tooth with your fingers if you use them for feeding your baby. To see the full sequence of eruption of these "primary" or "milk" teeth, see Appendix f on Page xxx.

<u>Common symptoms of teething:</u> The eruption of teeth may be associated with the following common problems:

1. *Irritability and crankiness*: This occurs due to the erupting tooth "cutting" the overlying mucosa and coming out. Local irritation produces drooling of saliva. It also provokes the child to rub her gums with her own fingers, or try and chew on hard items like bread-sticks, teething rings, plastic keys and so on. General crankiness causes the child to have disturbed sleep, feeding difficulties and reduced playfulness.
2. *Mouthing behaviour*: As discussed in the foregoing paragraph, during the process of teething, the baby may want to put anything inside her mouth – including potentially harmful or sharp objects like pencils, pointed sticks etc. Some of these objects may well be dirty or covered with germs. This can lead to secondary infection – and consequently, sore throat, loose motions or vomiting.
3. Barring the above reasons for the myriad difficulties experienced by the small child, teething does NOT cause loose motions or a severe respiratory illness. On the day of

eruption of the tooth in question, there may be *one or two slightly large or liquid stools*, with a greenish tinge. Frequent, prolonged diarrhoea is NOT due to the eruption of teeth. *Slight fever* may also occur in some, but not all babies.

What to do?

Teething powders, syrups and tablets have NO role to play in reducing "teething troubles", as they are called. Do not keep sharp items or small, movable items within reach of the baby. This will help avoid many accidents. Instead, offer soft plastic teething toys like rings, keys etc; or, alternatively, give her carrots, toast, *rusk* or other hard biscuits to bite on. Glycerine, available with most chemists, can be applied to the painful gums for temporary soothing effect. Do not use aspirin containing gels (such as Zytee® or Gelora®) as aspirin is not good for children. In case the child is too cranky, give her a dose of paracetamol or a safe sedative on advice of the doctor. If the child has a few loose stools, do not fret; nor if she has a mild fever. If, however, she has high fever or many stools, contact her Pediatrician for further advice.

Taking care of teeth:

As soon as the baby starts cutting milk teeth, you should buy a soft baby tooth brush and begin to clean her teeth with the same *without* a tooth paste.

Brush her teeth gently, from side to side, twice a day, on waking up in the morning and just before bedtime in the evening. Circular movements are also recommended (see below), so that the child learns these movements early in life. By three years, you may allow the child to use a tooth paste. Any toothpaste that has an acceptable flavour is all right; unflourinated tooth pastes are fine for children in our country as most of the water supply in our country contains sufficient fluoride to prevent any deficiency. In fact, the fluoride content in some places is too high and an illness called "fluorosis" is possible in children who use fluorinated pastes. Encourage her to brush her teeth *after every meal* in addition to the morning-time brush, but if not every meal, then at least twice a day as discussed above. **Also, ask her to *massage her gums* with the fingers and then actively *rinse her mouth after every meal and snack* that she takes**; this should be done always if brushing is not done. If your child has eaten flesh foods, allow her/ advise her to use a soft *tooth-pick* after the meal. Show her how to use the tooth-pick to dislodge any fibres that may have got stuck in between the teeth. The commonest site where dental caries occurs is the surface of the tooth that faces the adjacent tooth; hence, the use of a tooth-pick in the manner described is very useful. Even more useful is to use a *dental floss* – a thread made from synthetic material that is used regularly to clean the spaces between the teeth. This should be taught in older children above the age of six. Eating fibrous fruits like apples, bananas, pear, guava, fig etc are all useful to clean the debris between the teeth and nutritionally super too.

<u>How to brush the teeth:</u>

1. Gently start the brushing process by placing the paste laden brush parallel to the lower teeth.
2. Start brushing side to side for a few strokes and then move on to up and down and to and fro tiny circular movements in all parts of the mouth.
3. Clean the inside surfaces first, then the biting surfaces and finally the outer surfaces of the teeth.
4. Brush the tongue gently with a soft tongue cleaning device.
5. Check the child's breath to ensure that there is no foul smell.
6. Make sure that the child brushes her teeth for at least 2 minutes.

To read about problems related to the teeth, see Chapter 45.

Ch. 14
Problems and Challenges
A. Growth and Development

No matter how calmly you try to referee, parenting will eventually produce bizarre behavior, and I'm not talking about the kids
– Bill Cosby, Fatherhood, 1986

Normal growth and ideal development are mirages, as each and every baby will face some or the other hurdles in her advancement to adulthood. The intelligent parent is not one who raises her child (-ren) as per the wisdom of books or past knowledge, but one who will raise her child (-ren) as her own, despite the knowledge obtained from books or documents. In short, modifying events and facts to match one's own peculiar state of circumstances and acting according to the instinct are the name of the game in these matters.

For example, a couple whose only target is to see their son (or daughter) put on 20 kilos in the first five years of life will often try all possible things to make their child put on weight. Gymnasia, cooking of daily delicacies and giving appetisers will all mean the world to such parents. On the other hand, a couple who wants their son (or daughter) to be a happy, active and educated darling will spend that much more on getting their child books, games, fun stuff and so on, because to them, a happy child is a healthy child, irrespective of the weight she has put on.

If all this sounds correct to you, I am glad, because I wish to make this very clear to everyone that quality of life means much much more than mere quantity. And this applies not just to wealth and material possessions but also to physical dimensions of a child! Several studies on obese children have shown that they go on to become obese adolescents, and also, obese adults. As you well know, obesity in adulthood is responsible for so many ills, namely, diabetes, hypertension, ischaemic heart disease and stroke. On the other hand, if a child has a familial thin stature and is eating well, no amount of force-feeding, coaxing or urging her to eat more will make her put on weight. On the contrary, the child is likely to refuse food and vomit out what has been forcibly fed down her throat. For more details, see Chapter 12.

Who is healthy?

Let me therefore define the term "healthy". A child who is happy and full of energy is healthy. Her weight is not an issue as she keeps gaining weight and her health record reflects this. Her growth curve shows a normal pattern (see Appendix a, p.xxx). She eats when she is hungry, rarely falls sick and takes her vaccines as per the schedule. She shows a fairly normal advancement of milestones of development. She is naughty, active and playful. Her emotional and cognitive development is in tune with her age as well as her socio-cultural background.

Growth-related Issues:

Weight and Length Gain

The growth rate of a baby is never the same. It is maximal in the first few months, and as she grows, the rate of increase (or velocity) starts falling. From a rate of gain of 1 kg/month in the first three months, the weight gain velocity, for example, declines to just 250 gm/month by the age of 6-9 months. In the same way, the increase in length/ height also declines from a high of 25 cm/yr in the first year of life to just 5-7 cm/yr at six years (Table 1).

Table 1 Growth rate (velocity) in children

<table>
<tr><th colspan="3">Velocity of Height and Weight gain in the first six years of life</th></tr>
<tr><td>At birth</td><td>2.75 kg-3.5 kg</td><td>47.5-52 cm</td></tr>
<tr><td>0-3 months</td><td>800 g-1 kg / month</td><td rowspan="3">25 cm / yr</td></tr>
<tr><td>4-6 months</td><td>400 g-500 g / month</td></tr>
<tr><td>7-12 months</td><td rowspan="4">200 g-300 g / month reducing to 100 g-150 g / month later on.</td></tr>
<tr><td>13 months-2 years</td><td>12.5 cm /yr</td></tr>
<tr><td>25 months-3 years</td><td>8-10 cm /yr</td></tr>
<tr><td>37 months-6 years</td><td>5-7 cm / yr</td></tr>
</table>

The absolute gain in weight and length also depend on racial and genetic factors. For example, a Punjabi infant grows more rapidly as compared to one from, say Karnataka. This is pure racial difference and cannot be wished away any way.

Let us now examine growth-related issues.

1. My child is not putting on weight: This is perhaps the commonest complaint of parents. As I have discussed above, there are many determinants of weight or height gain which are *outside* our control, such as genetic factors, inheritance from parents and racial differences, plus factors that we *can* control, such as availability of nutritious food, knowledge of care-takers regarding preparation, preservation and presentation of food, parental expectations, and so on. Just as all five fingers are never the same, children are all different from one another. One of the most important points to remember is that even if children eat the best, most nutritious food, they need not put on weight to the same extent.

Hence, one should not pay heed to absolute values or compare one's own child with other children. See above to understand what constitutes a healthy child.

2. What will my child's adult height be? There are several formulae to predict the adult height of a child. The easiest one is as follows: Adult height = twice the height of the child at **two** completed years = 1.35 times the height at **three** completed years.

Height of the child can also be computed from the height of parents. First we find the average height of both parents (say H*p*). Now the predicted height of the child will be as follows:

For boys: Adult height = $0.545H_c + 0.544H_p + 14$
For girls: Adult height = $0.545H_c + 0.544H_p + 10$
(Where H*c* is the height of the child at 3 years). Here all the values are in inches.

Remember though that the actual adult height may fall short of the above target if the child has illnesses, poor nutrition or other forms of physical or psychological handicaps in life.

3. I want to increase my child's height! It is, in short, impossible to increase a child's height beyond his/her potential. The potential is determined by all the factors we have just seen, e.g. genetic, racial, nutritional, emotional, health etc. No tonics or medicines can make children tall, not even if they advertise these products using U.S. Basketball players, giraffes or the like.

Here I would just like to make a point: it may sometimes be wise to check out the hormonal status of a short child who looks otherwise normal. This is because a **growth hormone deficiency** may have no other signs or symptoms other than a short stature. However, this is a decision that must betaken by a Pediatrician, and not parents.

4. Will my prematurely born baby grow like a normal child? Initially, a prematurely born baby would grow a bit slowly, as she is a few weeks to a few months behind in development as compared to a full term baby. After some months, however, a prematurely born baby's growth velocity becomes faster than a full term baby's, and so, within a year, or two at the most, she will "catch-up" with a full term baby.

5. My child is growing too fast/she is obese: This is fast becoming an area of major concern, especially in recent times, with the arrival of Western culture in our countries, the availability of fattening foods, the opening of hamburger, pizza and "subs" joints and the fast pace of life in metropolitan and large cities. The problem has affected even children from middle-class families, as junk food has become freely available and is affordable too. The potato couch mentality of sitting before a TV set and watching movies has not helped any in encouraging activity and outdoor play.

It is necessary to take steps to prevent obesity in childhood itself, especially when one or both parents are obese. Do not introduce weaning foods early; do not offer excessive quantities of high calorie foods like jams, cakes, butter, ghee, sweets, etc; avoid giving snacks and junk food; encourage the child to play outdoors and avoid home-based sit-down activities like card games, etc; keep the TV off except for an hour or two daily; have the child eat more salads, greens, vegetables, fruit (not fleshy fruit like banana or mango though), lean meats (fish or chicken), pulses and dals and eggs. Cook with the minimum amount of oil and if you plan to make her diet, be slow and do not ask her to go on a fasting binge, as this will be useless in the long run, and the child will put on the lost weight once again.

Development-related issues:

Development of a child from a frail, completely dependent baby to an independent, exploring, naughty and rambunctious toddler is one of the most wondrous acts of nature. As she grows in height and weight, so does she develop, gaining milestones almost every week!

The rate of development varies from child to child. It is partly determined by heredity, and the child's own genetic endowment, and partly by the environment around her and the way she is challenged and stimulated. Undoubtedly, the food she eats and the love and nurturance she gets all shape her advancement process.

Her special senses help her to absorb, assimilate and react to her external environment. A child who sees, hears, smells, touches and tastes her world is more likely to form impressions and respond to these stimuli than a child whose world consists of indifferent, unloving people whose interaction with the child is minimal, and at times, even traumatic! An extreme example of such a mean environment would be a poor, unmotivated orphanage. Here, the lovelorn baby is deprived of almost all stimuli; she grows, but only just. Her eyes look vacant, her smile is scarce and she sits in one place, all lost and unconcerned. She reacts slowly, she is unable to save herself from danger, and she is unable to laugh at a funny incident. Hence, it is no surprise that she develops at a slower pace than a more privileged child.

Let us now move on to the various issues.

1. Is my child developing properly? One of the most serious concerns of a parent is to be assured that her child is developing just fine. While the sequence of development is more or less the same in all children globally, the rate of such development varies (see above). Hence, the anxious mother will often perceive that her child is not developing as well as, say, the baby next door, or say, her other cousin who stays somewhere else. Also remember that the preterm child will lag behind in all milestones by approximately the period of months she was born prematurely.

2. When do I label my child as developmentally delayed? Isolated delays in one or another particular sphere of development can be normal. For example, many children sit and walk at a normal age but speak very late; some children speak early, but have some delay in cognitive milestones. This is NOT referred to as developmental

delay. A child who shows an inordinate delay in *all* spheres of development may be developmentally delayed, and needs further investigations.

3. How does one check if the baby sees and hears well? Absence of blinking when a bright torch is shone on the baby's face should alert one to the possibility of reduced vision in the baby. Other indicators include purposeless roving eye movements, presence of a squint beyond the age of six to eight months and delay in the development of social milestones such as smiling. If you find your baby showing any of these symptoms, see a Pediatrician or an Ophthalmologist immediately.

When you play with the child and make sounds, the child responds to these overtures by looking towards you and smiling, or by turning her head to look at the source of the sound. Calling her by name, making sounds like "sss… sss…" and "haa! … haa!" are the standard noises to be made by you if you wish to check if the baby is hearing well. Make these sounds from behind the child, standing about 4 feet away, and make them with a medium intensity normal inflection voice. If the child fails to show any change in behaviour or fails to turn her eyes or head towards you, take her to a Pediatrician or an E.N.T. specialist to get her hearing tested.

4. What are Developmental Quotient (DQ) and Intelligence Quotient (IQ)? During a developmental assessment the psychologist will ask the parents the age at which different developmental milestones were achieved, and also try and see to which chronological age the child's developmental level actually corresponds. This age, divided by the actual age and expressed as a percentage, is called the Developmental Quotient (DQ). The normal child has a DQ of 85-115. Anything below 85 suggests a developmental delay; anything above 120 suggests precocity of development.

To further assess the mental status of a patient referred to them, the psychologist carries out certain standardised tests of intelligence; from the performance results, she calculates a "mental age" for the child.

Then the IQ is expressed as: Mental age/ Chronological age expressed as a percentage. The average IQ is 85-115. IQ's below 70 suggest a mentally challenged child, while IQ above 120 is above average; above 150 suggests a genius; and IQ's above 175 suggests a super-genius or an exceptionally gifted child.

It is important to remember that:

a) If the child performs the intelligence tests in a relaxed and quiet atmosphere, she will perform better. b) If the child does not understand some of the instructions for doing the tests, she may show a falsely low IQ. c) A child from a rural or backward region may not show a correct response because of lack of understanding of some of the tests. d) Prior experience with Intelligence tests improves the child's performance in subsequent tests.

5. How can I make my child more intelligent? Most of the development and growth of the human brain occurs during fetal life, and by the age of one, almost 90 % of the growth is already completed. It is true that genetic endowment confers the potentialities and the limitations of the growing mind, but proper nutrition and correct stimulation can improve the performance of the child's mind tremendously. Although the height of the intelligence cannot be increased, the child's full potential can at least be realised.

Nutrition: Right from pregnancy it is essential for the mother to eat a well-balanced diet rich in proteins, iron, vegetables, fruit and so on. She must avoid smoking and drinking. She should take vitamin and iron supplements. After birth, the baby should also be offered a proper nutrition. She must receive breast milk for as long as possible. Vitamin supplements are not needed, but iron supplements should be considered after the age of 4 months.

Stimulation: Our brain has a left side and a right side. Our left brain is where we have the seat of intelligence. Speech, reasoning, logic, mathematics, language and erudition are essentially the left-sided brain's functions, while the right-sided brain deals with art, fine art, creativity, spirituality and extrasensory perception. To enable the child to realise her full potential, we as parents *must* allow equal stimulation of both sides of the child's brain. Thus, early exposure to alphabet and language are good, but we should not ignore music, dance, painting and story-telling.

In fact, the stimulation process can begin even before the baby is born. By sitting in a rocking chair and gently rocking, the expectant mother is actually stimulating the yet to be born child. The same effect is seen with playing music, reading nice books and singing soothing songs during pregnancy.

During infancy, the baby may be stimulated by touching, cuddling, massaging, bathing, playing good music etc and also by giving her toys, blocks, objects that have attractive colours like wool, plastic animals etc. Many parents purchase cribs and prams. I recommend that they line the inside of these with soft toys, and also hang some shiny, colorful toys (like the winding type of merry-go-round) from a stick tied to the top of the crib/pram. The baby will get plenty of stimulation from these and will learn fast! Playing peek-a-boo with the baby, showing her pictures from a book, exposing her to programs on the radio set or TV and letting her eat on her own and taste food with different textures are other examples of stimulation that are recommended.

6. What toys are suitable for the child? The world of small babies is changing fast. Toys that parents played with are not even seen in urban markets. Many a parent have experienced that when they bring traditional, ethnic toys from their native place, *their child will not even look at them.* Why has this happened? This is so because toy business is big business and the child is literally bombarded with unlimited choices of electronic toys and gizmos that cost a lot and teach nothing (Fig 14-1).

I advise parents to purchase *simple, educational toys* for their children. Do not just buy a toy that says "Educational Toy" on its box! See whether it really does have educational qualities. The toys should be safe, have no sharp corners or edges, no small removable parts and be colorful and attractive. They should be commensurate with the age and developmental progress of the child. Toys with visual and auditory appeal, for example, will be more suited to the infant, while toys which encourage the child to "interact" and "solve" will thrill the pre-school toddlers and older children. Guns, pistols and darts may cause hurt or injury to children, and I urge parents to be very careful before deciding to purchase them. Toys should be painted

Fig 14-1

with "safe" colors, so that an occasional child who "eats" the paint off his/her toy(s) will not end up with lead poisoning. **Avoid** toys with button cells, toys that run on electrical mains, toys that move very fast, heavy toys, toys that need long threads to pull, toys that have too many removable parts, toys covered with stuck-on paper (which the child might remove and swallow), small toys like marbles, beads etc, toys that teach children to hate people with different religions, attires, cultures or habits, toys made from hunted, endangered animals or their body parts and toys that are so complicated that the child soon gets bored of them. (See also Chapters 21 and 22)

Table 2 is a partial list of acceptable toys for children of different age groups.

Table 2: Suitable Toys by Age

Age	Suitable toys
0-3 months	Soft rattles, merry-go-round, squeaky toys
4-8 months	Soft toys, rattles with visible colorful pieces, Washable picture books Grasping toys and teething toys
9-15 months	Cubes, pails, sand-play tools, soft dolls, soft animals, ring towers, picture books, unbreakable mirrors and light, plastic balls
16-24 months	Soft dolls or animals, picture books, alphabet cubes, bath toys (like floating duck, plastic ball), beach activity toys, vehicles (mostly for boys), push and pull toys, balls, connecting chains and blocks, sand box, portable swimming pool, mini-trampoline and simple musical toys like piano, clarinet and violin (all made of plastic, of course)
25-60 months	Art and craft sets, mini-doctor/police/carpenter/painter sets, tricycles and toy scooters, story books with pictures, play house, dolls and dresses (for girls), cricket sets with plastic ball and bat (for boys), clay modeling, jigsaw puzzles and memory cards, musical instruments like flute, piano, keyboards, etc.
Any age after 2 years	Educational and entertainment CD's to play on the home computer.

Developmental Challenges (for parents and care-takers):

A. Toilet Training:

I have come across two types of parents. The first types are the single child - upper middle-class parents, living in a nuclear household: the parents are aggressive and overbearing in training the child to urinate and defecate in their "self-contained" flat's toilet. The other are the lower middle class happy-go-lucky couple with three older children, who won't even tie towels on their child; they will just make the child wear a flimsy panty and allow her to pass urine all over my examining bed! Needless to say, both the approaches are incorrect. I have enumerated them here just to bring home the lesson that ignoring the problem or being fanatic about it is equally harmful to the ultimate learning process for the baby.

During the first six months, no attempt should be made to train the baby. Some mothers do carry the baby to the toilet and hanging them by holding them behind their knees, they make funny noises or pour water on the baby's genital areas to make her pass urine. This is all right up to a point. It is a useless exercise from the long term point of view.

Kids will be kids, and it is pointless to think that they will train easily. I have personally experienced this. At a family get-together where my cousin brought his 14-month old to demonstrate her trained status, she embarrassed him by passing stools **on** the dining table (where he had put her to show the relations how nicely she ate)! Always persevere, but do not get frustrated. Learn to smile at yourself and take things in your stride. Punitive training is OUT. Don't even think of it. Do it with love, understanding and a firm but polite attitude.

When to start? How to go about it? The right time is when the child has begun to sit on her own, say 8-9 months of age; put the child on a plastic potty with smooth edges and an attractively coloured design.

Do this daily in the morning, afternoon, evening and night. The baby may be shown picture books or talked to so that she remains in the potty for at least 10-12 minutes. Pick her up after this, regardless of whether she "used" the potty or not.

In addition to these fixed times, look at the baby for signs that she has a "full" stomach and needs to evacuate her bowels. She will go quiet, leave her toys, make a flustered, red-looking face and signal you with her eyes or hands or by holding her panty or the lower part of her trunk. This may be accompanied by the sound of gas being expelled. Lose no time and put the baby in the potty! At the same time, try and divert her mind by talking to her or by showing her a picture book. Show her how to "strain" by mimicking the act; let her stay in the potty for about 15-20 minutes, or till she herself gets up and shows that she has "done" what she was meant to do, or that she is plain "tired" of sitting there and "doing nothing" because she may not *want* to pass bowels as of then!

Don't let the training become rough; that is, do not force her or be angry; do not lose your temper if she remains dry when on the potty but gets up and goes to the room's only expensive rug and passes her motion there! This is all part of the training and learning process. If she does evacuate in the potty, appreciate her so that her good action gets encouragement and gets reinforced.

Aggressive training can, on the other hand, create a psychological hurdle to proper stooling habits. The child may "learn" to avoid passing stools; she will retain fecal matter within her large bowel. This may lead to constipation or passage of hard stools with formation of cracks and fissures in the outlet area and pain on defecation, with further constipation. Sometimes, the bowels become so full that the child may involuntarily pass liquid stool in small quantities frequently. This is called *encopresis.* Both the above situations require the intervention of a psychologist and/or child psychiatrist.

Most children are bowel-trained by 2 years and become dry by day (urine) by the same time too; some may take longer. Night-time dryness takes another 1-2 year in some children, and it is not unusual for some children to occasionally void at night even up to 5-6 years of age.

B. Sleep-Related Problems:

We have already read in Chapter 11 about the normal sleep pattern of infants and young children. Every child's sleep pattern is unique, but it follows certain universal trends. Sleep durations are longest soon after birth, and gradually reduce as the baby grows older. The type of sleep (deep sleep versus dream or REM sleep) also changes as the baby grows. By 10-14 weeks of life, a large majority of infants are already attuned to a long sleep period at night, but they continue to sleep for about 4-5 hours in the day, with the longest nap being the one after their massage and bath. Parents can help their children to form consistent and friendly sleeping habits by being themselves consistent about feeding their children at the right time, by making the nightfall times conducive to sleep and by reducing social and cultural activities in the house after 8 p.m.

A child who keeps waking up for night time feeds every hour or two even after six months of age can be easily trained to not do so. All that you need to do is to allow her to cry for, say 10-15 minutes once she wakes up for the feed, and then feed her. Delaying the feed by such an interval on a daily basis will allow you to initially reduce her awakenings, and later, to stop such awakenings altogether. Providing a regular "24-hour rhythm" to your baby is very crucial; if you do not remain consistent, the baby will begin to function with a 25-hour, or even a 26-hour rhythm, and start waking up late, getting to sleep later and so on. Fine tuning her bath, feeding and playing routines will allow you to "reset" her biological clock back to the normal routine.

Falling asleep: Children take some time to wind down at the end of an active day. Hence we need to make allowances for the same by giving them a pressure-free, relaxing and comfortable sleep environment. Providing them with their favourite toy to hold or a nice picture or story book to read is welcome. So is reading them a story or singing them a lullaby. Adults often continue their own evening activities like watching T.V. and talking and laughing in the same room as the child who is trying to fall asleep. Such activities should be curtailed, or if feasible, taken to another room. Rather, the child should be made to sleep in another room if possible. Distractions like flickering neon lights, noises and smells from the road outside, sounds of neighbours and others may all add to the agony of falling asleep. On the other hand, some children start "demanding" certain rituals everyday! These demands may be easy to satisfy initially, such as "give me some milk" or "read me a story" or "tell me a story", but as time goes on, they may become a nuisance for the parents who themselves need time to unwind at the end of a hectic day. Thus some children find it increasingly difficult to fall asleep.

What to do? It is very tempting to smack the baby and let her cry to sleep, or to give her a "sleeping medicine". However, this is incorrect. Try and find out why your child is finding it difficult to fall asleep. Remember that a hungry stomach, a bored mind and uncomfortable surroundings are the three main causes of this problem. Try not to "excite" the child by telling horror stories or reading from very scary or adventure-filled picture books. Do not offer bribes or rewards for falling asleep. Nor should you castigate her or beat her for not doing so. Understand that the child needs the love of both her parents and if the father customarily arrives late, the child will keep making excuses to stay awake till he does, so that she can get to be close to him. If possible, do something about it; if not, take it in your stride and learn to cope with it. It is likely that sooner or later, the child will also learn to cope with it and stop making such a big issue out of it. She may either learn to sleep without seeing her father, or sleep late everyday, regardless of what you do to make her sleep early.

Nightmares and Night Terrors:

There are two different night-time events that children experience. *Nightmares* are very scary dreams that wake up the child and leave her feeling frightened and anxious. Even a year old child can have them. They occur during REM or dream sleep and are therefore maximally seen toward the early hours of morning. The child wakes up fully, and the older child may actually tell you what she dreamt about. The content depends on the child's mental stage of development, emotional conflicts that she is facing at that time in her life and specific day-time events that seemed particularly frightening to her at the time she experienced them.

All children have nightmares at one time or another. Most nightmares concern the fear of loss of loved ones, appearance of monsters, falling dreadfully sick , scenes of dying or death, insect attacks, etc. The occurrence of nightmares is high between 3-5 years of age and at or around the ages of 11-15, i.e. during adolescence (see chapter 19).

What to do? The younger child, who cannot describe or put into words what she just dreamt of will wake up thoroughly scared and will be either screaming or crying. All you need to do is to hold her, reassure her that everything will be all right and ask her to "go back to sleep". A toddler may be asked to describe her dream, and telling it to you will act like therapy for her, and ease her anxiety. If you reassure her and allow her to leave a night light on, for example, her worries will fade away. In almost all cases, you might have to stay with her for a while as her fears are calmed and she goes back to sleep. During day time, study what drives her to nightmares in the night. If her toilet training is too aggressive, then you should relax it. Likewise, moderate her viewing of sexually or physically aggressive programmes on television. This would include cartoon films, which are, in fact, filled with the maximum possible violence!

Persistence of frequent nightmares beyond the age of six may indicate the presence of phobias or irrational fears and may require counselling.

Night terrors or *sleep terrors* occur during the deepest part of non-dream sleep. They occur early in the night, and are different from nightmares in that they are unstructured, have no recall, are marked by the child crying out and sitting up but still in a sleep state from which *she is not yet fully awake.* Even if you hold her and comfort her, she will not recognise you, or be comforted. She may even become more agitated and push you away. Once the state of terror passes, she will go back to sleep immediately, with no need for further comforting. In the morning, the child will have no memory of the dream or the event, but she may remember being comforted by you or waking up partially for no apparent reason.

What to do? Essentially, nothing needs to be done for night terrors. The child will go back to sleep on her own.

Sudden Partial Wakings:

This is a term applied to a spectrum of behavioural problems that occur toward the end of deep sleep and includes sleep terrors (see above) and sleep walking. Some authorities include non-specific thrashing, enuresis (bed-wetting, see below), and talking in sleep. While some children merely mumble something, turn over and go back to sleep, others become agitated, sit up in bed, get up and start walking calmly or even worse, run amok around the house wildly and frantically.

The best way to describe these occurrences is to imagine that the child is awake and asleep *at the same time!* Thus, although she is asleep, she talks, walks, goes around the house and so on. An older child may even open the front door and walk out (*somnambulism or sleep walking*).

It is believed that these wakings are simply developmental aberrations and a sign of a maturing sleep/wake pattern. They have no lasting physical or emotional impact, at least in children less than six.

What to do? For thrashing and moaning, just let the event run its course. See that the child does not injure herself. Tuck her in between the covers once she calms down and let her go back to sleep. Don't discuss this with her the next day. For calm sleepwalking, just try and guide the child back to the bed and tell her to "go to sleep". If she wants to urinate on the way back, help her to do so by leading her to the bathroom etc. If she is agitated, stay at a safe distance and monitor her to prevent injuries or walking out of the house. In both cases of sleep walking, refrain from ridiculing her in the morning or making her feel strange or bizarre. For all categories except talking in sleep, consider counselling. For severe cases, temporary medication should be considered.

C. Bedwetting (Nocturnal Enuresis)

Voiding of urine during sleep is called bedwetting or nocturnal enuresis. Control over urine at night is a developmental process. Some children acquire early night time control, while some continue to void urine in bed even at three to five years. At times, due to some emotional disturbances, a child who had achieved night-time dryness regresses to start voiding in bed again (secondary enuresis), while in most cases, there is a time delay in learning night-time voiding control (primary enuresis). We label the child as having bed wetting only if she continues to wet herself beyond the age of five years. This condition is seen in almost 5 % of all children.

What causes enuresis? Delayed maturation of the child's nervous system, coupled with a small bladder capacity, emotional upheavals in the child's family in the first two or three years of life and to some extent, heredity, are all considered responsible for primary enuresis. Medical illnesses, change of house, divorce or separation among parents, death of a parent and such other events may precipitate secondary enuresis, particularly on a temporary basis. Sometimes, bedwetting is a symptom of a medical disorder or a congenital malformation of the urinary tract. Rarely, infection of the urinary tract may cause temporary enuresis in a previously dry child.

Consequences of Enuresis: Bedwetting can be emotionally very depressing on the child. It can undermine her self-confidence and make her worried about going to her friends' places for an overnight stay or go to an overnight school outing. It can make the poor child emotionally insecure and unable to make friends, join groups and enjoy outings. Ultimately, it may turn her into a social recluse. The problem occurs even if you as a parent are able to understand her problem and are empathetic and supportive and do not mind changing her sheets etc. It still makes her feel "not in control" of herself; it makes her embarrassed and ashamed.

Some parents do not understand the problem, and in fact become punitive and hostile to their own child. They may even punish her or ridicule her in front of their other children or her school or neighbourhood friends.

What to do? The treatment of nocturnal enuresis is a combination of counselling, behavoiur modification and use of alarms and medication, used judiciously and under professional guidance. Even with all these modalities, however, not all enuretics will achieve 100 % cures, and some may continue to occasionally wet their beds even as adults.

Solving the problem requires everyone's cooperation and assistance. The first step is acknowledging this fact so that the guilt trips and punishments are stopped forthwith. Behavioural treatment envisages giving more household responsibilities to the child (like clearing the dishes etc), giving her more responsibilities concerning the bedwetting itself (like changing her pajamas, changing the sheets and doing her own laundry), treating her on par with other family members, using plastic sheets over her mattresses, restricting her fluid and water intake by 20 % or so after 6 p.m., and setting up a system of rewards for dry nights; the rewards should be written down on paper and put up where she can read them. For every consecutive dry night, the reward should be (though not necessarily) proportionately bigger. Silver or golden stars on the calendar are very useful motivational tools for the child to aim higher.

Bladder exercises: These include training the child to increase her bladder capacity by "holding back" her urine for successively longer durations, making her practice urine stream "starting" and "stopping" exercises, and challenging her holding capacity by making her drink bigger quantities of water during the day time.

Enuresis Alarms: These are conditioning devices which are used with good success rates. They essentially have pads that "sense" wetness and trigger off an alarm that immediately wakes up the child. These are usually more helpful after 7 years of age when the child herself has begun to cooperate and work with you to solve the problem. She must herself wear and turn the alarm on at the time of going to bed. Once she wakes up, she can go to the bathroom herself. The system must be used every night for it to be successful. In general, 25 % become dry in just 2-6 weeks, and by 4-6 months, over 85 % will have become dry.

Medications: A relatively cheap, older remedy is to try oral medications. Nowadays, inhalations of a hormonal preparation are available for the treatment of enuresis. These inhalers are used through the child's nose, and are extremely effective; however, they are expensive when compared to oral therapy.

Other methods: Do not forget to ask the child to "pray" to God for help, as this might just prove to be the missing trick in treatment. A few other suggestions include a) lifting the child to take her to the bathroom and b) asking her to go to the bathroom about 1-1 ½ hours after she falls asleep.

D. Speech Problems:

There are three types of problems concerning the development of coherent and lucent speech. The first problem is the problem of *delayed speech development.* As we have seen earlier, most often, this can be normal, or familial. The only important thing to remember is that at times, **delay in speech development may lead to a hearing problem**. Hence, hearing must be checked in every child who has speech delay. I have seen many normal children who have a normal intellect and a normal cognition, and yet they start speaking relatively late, say after 2 ½ -3 years. However, one must remember that **childhood autism** may present with an apparent *hearing* problem as the child simply does not register what is being said to her. In this condition, the child will have poor eye-to-eye contact and other symptoms too.

The next two problems are related to defective speech.

Baby talk refers to the inability of an older child to correctly articulate certain consonants and to make them sound like a baby's language. I have personal acquaintance with many adults whose speech remains unclear throughout their lives. Some examples of defective consonants include r, k, l, kh, j and ch. The speech sounds different and babyish. When a child talks in this manner, the best thing to do is to ignore her fault and to not ridicule her. You should speak to her normally, and never try and imitate her way of talking. Most children outgrow this way of talking as they grow up.

Stammering is most often seen in children aged 2-4 years, and is characterised by the increasing difficulty of the child to start a sentence or to participate in a friendly conversation. The disorder may be familial, and affects boys more than girls. Most children outgrow their problem within 3-6 months of its starting, but in some, it may persist for a much longer time. The stammering may start because of some emotional upheaval in the child's life, and it may occur in a child who spoke normally in the past. It becomes worse when the child is ill, anxious or excited. On the other hand, when the child is alone and plays unobserved, she may speak absolutely normally.

Stammering is usually temporary, and care takers must not draw the child's attention to it, ridicule her or try and launch any punitive programmes. The child must be encouraged to speak slowly, and you, as a parent, must listen to her patiently and attentively. Ask her to practice speaking in front of a mirror, so that she will closely observe herself and learn proper articulation.
If the problem persists beyond 6 months of its onset, or beyond 4 years of age, the child should be taken to a speech therapist for further intervention

Ch. 15
Problems and Challenges
B. Habit and Behaviour Disorders

A torn jacket is soon mended; but hard words bruise the heart of a child.
- Henry Wadsworth Longfellow (US poet (1807 - 1882)

In this chapter, we will study some habit and behaviour disorders in children aged 0-6years.

Habit Disorders:

A. Thumb or/and Finger(s) Sucking:

At first, finger or thumb sucking may be a sign of hunger. Haven't we all seen our babies taking their thumb, finger, or fist in their mouths as soon as their feeding time is due? As the child grows and starts taking objects in her mouth, she puts her finger(s), thumb, toes and even whole of the fist in her mouth. The reasons could be hunger, painful gums (because of teething), boredom, fatigue or sleepiness. The habit seems to increase over the next one year or so; after the age of 1 ¾ to 2 ½ years, the habit declines. Most children have given up this habit by 3 years. Persistent and compulsive sucking of finger or thumb beyond the age of 3 years is abnormal and needs evaluation.

The most likely reason for an abnormal finger or thumb sucking problem is a feeling of insecurity, but boredom and sleepiness may also be responsible. Infants may also take to compulsive thumb sucking if they are deprived of a sucking stimulus such as the breast, a pacifier or a bottle. In some cases, thumb sucking may be familial.

Impact of finger/thumb sucking: Besides looking unsightly and causing embarrassment to the affected child, thumb or finger sucking can cause calluses to develop on these digits; it can lead to skin maceration and development of infection; finally, it may produce malalignment and malocclusion of the front teeth, which will need dental care.

What to do? Since most children leave the habit by 3-5 years of age, nothing needs to be done. The only thing to remember is that use of bandages, bitter liquids and so on is not likely to be of any help. For children beyond 3 years of age, counselling may be needed to discover the underlying cause of the problem. In the meantime, the child should be provided with avenues to remain "occupied" in doing what she likes to do. Do not nag her to remove her thumb; do not ridicule her in front of others; and do not ignore her. Older children can be reasoned with to "drop the habit" as it is very childish and annoying to parents.

B. <u>Nail-biting:</u>

Nail biting may start at any age, even in a 3-4 year old child, but usually it appears after the age of six. Girls pick up this habit more than boys. Some may even chew toe-nails. This habit is also secondary to boredom, stress, anxiety or a sense of insecurity. The habit is socially unacceptable. The approach to the treatment is similar to that with thumb sucking (see above). Avoid ridiculing or shouting at the child. Appeal to her better sense and wisdom. And insist on keeping nails well-trimmed on a regular basis.

C. Pica:

Eating non-edible stuff like mud, chalk, peeling plaster or paint, hair etc. is called Pica. Pica is an extremely common habit disorder in infants and small children. Children can develop worm infestation and gastroenteritis by eating mud. People have a misunderstanding that pica is due to calcium deficiency; some children, in fact, have an iron deficiency in their bodies! This is also a pointer to the treatment (see below).

Impact: Apart from the risk of infection and infestation, pica may reduce the intake of nutrients and food. Some children also end up getting gastric upsets, recurrent stomach pain etc.

What to do? Once again, it is better to provide a safe environment for the child to play in. Paints and plasters should receive attention when they start peeling off walls and furniture. If you have a garden or plants in your house, see that the child does not gravitate to these spots and "enjoy" eating mud. Try and provide better distractions or be with her to spend her (and your) free time. Iron supplementation may also be tried.

D. Masturbation:

Playing with one's own genitalia is a completely normal developmental milestone, and is temporary in most children. Aggressive techniques like beating the child or "burning" her "there" should never be used. In older children, one should check to see if there are rashes, boils or other local problems in the genital areas. If found, these should be treated by a doctor. If nothing is found, it is assumed that the activity is likely to be due to boredom or due to the child not finding anything more interesting to do. In such a case, the child should be given more opportunities for play and participation in other interesting activities.

E. Tics:

Tics, or habit spasms, are awkward, repetitive, semi-purposeful or non-purposeful movements of the body. They are usually seen in older children, but may occur in 3-6 year olds as well. Their onset may be after some physical illness, but they may start without any apparent cause. The movements may be mimicry of similar movements in some other family member, or they may be totally "new". The commonest examples are shrugging of shoulders, frowning, blinking of eyes and twisting of the neck. The incidence of tics is greatest in children whose parents are strict disciplinarians. Tics are absent in sleep, and increase when the child has an audience. As a rule, tics subside on their own after some weeks to months, but some may remain for life if managed poorly. At times, one type of tic disappears, to be replaced by another type of tic.

What to do? It may be helpful to find what causes stress or anxiety and remove that cause; also, as with other habit disorders, do not ridicule the child, shout at her, admonish her etc. If tics persist beyond a short duration, the child should be taken for a physical and a psychological evaluation.

F. Biting:

A tense, frustrated or unhappy child may indulge in biting other children of her own age, or even smaller or bigger children of the household. If this problem persists beyond 2-3 months, or if some selective children are her target, an attempt must be made to understand why she is doing what she is and try and take corrective steps. At the same time, prevent such encounters by separating your child from her potential targets. The child should be provided distractions in the form of play, and her good behaviour rewarded with appreciation.

G. Rocking and Head Banging:

Some infants start body rocking and head banging movements once they begin to sit and crawl. While physical causes should first be ruled out, they may be totally absent and the problem may be a habit-related problem. Many parents get worried as to whether head banging will injure the child's developing brain and/or lead to mental disorders or handicap. Rocking of the whole body in the sitting position may be related to a need for self-stimulation. It may also reflect boredom or stress.

What to do? Normally, you should take care that the child does not injure herself when she indulges in head banging or rocking. If the problem persists, consult a Pediatrician or a child psychiatrist.

H. Teeth Grinding (Bruxism):

Some children are known to grind their teeth in sleep. The cause of this is not known, but it may be an expression of tension or anger. Some mothers believe that grinding of teeth is due to intestinal worms. However, this is not true. Teeth grinding has no consequences for the child.

What to do? No treatment is needed. Allow the child to freely show her anger or displeasure in social interactions. Make her sleeping time rituals relaxing and comforting. If possible, talk with her to unravel her unpleasant daytime experiences.

Behavioural Problems and Disturbances:

Discipline is a symbol of caring to a child. He needs guidance. If there is love, there is no such thing as being too tough with a child. A parent must also not be afraid to hang himself. If you have never been hated by your child, you have never been a parent. - Bette Davis, 1908-1989, American actress, producer.

Let us now move on to the second half of this chapter. In this part, we will discuss "normal" aberrations in behaviour as well as certain "abnormal" deviations.

A. Temper tantrums and Breath-holding Spells:

Temper tantrums: Which parent has not seen his/her child throwing a temper around when she is denied a treat that she feels is "rightfully" hers? In fact, even those of you who are unmarried may have seen it or perhaps thrown one as well! Development of the child's "ego" is responsible for these tantrums. Basically, if the child has to endure some "hardships", or forgo something she so keenly wants, she is likely to start grumbling. She may start yelling, cry or scream and often bang her head on the wall or slap her hands on her forehead repeatedly. Children who are bottle-fed, stubborn by nature or emotionally disadvantaged or deprived in some way are more likely to have temper tantrums.

What to do? The child with a tantrum is protesting against the overriding of her desires by her powerful parents. She is calling attention to herself. She is trying to make her opinion "count". Hence the best thing to do is to make light of it if possible or to ignore her tantrum with an intellectual withdrawal from the scene of the tantrum. Keep an eye out so that she does not break any household things or accidentally injure herself (although that is *most* unlikely). Do not go and satisfy her every demand; let her "cool off" on her own. Encourage her to talk about her frustrations and show her alternative approaches to her problems. Be polite and firm about the fact that no amount of posturing by her will make you change your decision.

Avoid using a feeding bottle right from infancy as that engenders stubbornness in later infancy. See that the child takes adequate food and gets proper sleep, including the afternoon nap. This will allow her to be more restful and less demanding, and will reduce tantrums.

Breath-holding: Occasionally, a temper tantrum causes the child to cry uninterruptedly for a longish time, and then to stop breathing and become pale or blue. To the alarmed parents, this looks like a catastrophe that needs emergency care. They will start screaming themselves, summon help, call for a doctor, etc. The stoppage of breathing will sometimes be so severe that the child may throw a fit (convulsion). After a variable interval of 2-6 minutes or so, the "spell" is broken and the child resumes crying or whimpering on a softer note. The parents usually "give in" to the child's every demand in the next hour or so for fear that otherwise the "breath holding attack" may be repeated.

What to do? Do not give in to the child's wishes, or else her blackmailing cycle will continue to dominate all future interactions between you and her. Try pinching her leg or smacking her on her rear to draw attention away from her demand and on to the pain that she is getting. Or simply, put her down on a firm mattress on the floor and walk out of her room (or the room where she has had the spell). Remember that the child will come to no harm if the spell is not broken by you, because she will break it herself as her blood carbon-dioxide levels go up due to lack of breathing. There will not be any neuronal loss, so intellect or memory will also remain normal in future. Iron supplementation has been found to be of some help in some cases.

B. Dishonesty in thoughts, words and deeds:

Parents are the role models of their child (-ren). Because parents frequently lie and behave dishonestly, children too learn to be dishonest. The problem gets compounded when the child, not realising the impact of the wrong deed or word by her, continues to do it again and again.

Parents often ask their children to participate in lying and cheating; for example, sometimes I ask my child to ignore the ring of the telephone when I know whose phone it is but I do not want to answer it. Or, when we promise to take our child somewhere on "some other day" because we want her to stop nagging us to take her there today.

Parents must inculcate values of truth and honesty by being good role models. They should stand upright if they are to mould their child's moral values, as the child does not know the difference between truth and lie, or honesty and dishonesty. By telling them stories of heroes of the past or even fictional characters who were truthful, honest, courageous and righteous, one can build a wall of virtues around one's child! Condemn lying and cheating people at every turn of life, so that they realise that these are undesirable qualities in people.

If a child is caught after the act of stealing or lying, you should try and first understand why she did what she did and then unravel the knot so that she does not do the same thing again. For example, she may deny that she broke the expensive table vase simply because she is scared that you may beat her. Once she realises her mistake, and you realise why she wouldn't tell you the truth, the conflict has already got resolved and you can look forward to a more honest revelation the next time she makes a similar error.

Stealing more attractive pencils and erasers from the partner's box is another frequent occurrence in many children and stems from the innate human desire to have something that "looks" better than one's own stuff. Once discovered, the child may try to come out of the situation by lying or by claiming that she did not know how "that thing" came to be in her compass box! You need to be firm but not violent; tell her that you don't care how that thing got to be in her compass box, but that you fully expect her to return it to whoever's it is, or to give it to the teacher for final disposal. Corporeal punishment is useless as it will just make her more hardened in future.

Some children continue this habit of "lifting" things that do not belong to them. They indulge in it in shops, department stores, at their friends' places or elsewhere. This soon becomes a compulsive behaviour and they often try to outdo their own previous "performance" in an attempt to earn self respect for their own "capacity" inside their own heads. This kind of compulsive stealing is called *kleptomania* and needs professional counselling. Such children often get caught, what with modern surveillance in big shops. This may spoil their entire future.

C. Rivalry and Envy:

While a healthy rivalry is good for the human spirit and encourages people (and children) to excel and outperform their rivals, unhealthy envy or rivalry can actually destroy an individual. Children instinctively dislike anyone who is a bully, or who stops *their* creative activities or physical endeavours. Thus, elder or physically more robust friends, cousins or siblings are the main objects of their dislike. The child makes attempts to overtake these "rivals" in every field; if the result is positive, the child's ego is boosted and vice versa. *Sibling rivalry* is in a class by itself, and begins even before the younger sibling arrives in the house. As the younger sib gets first attention of the mother almost all the time, the older sib feels neglected and left out. A rivalry then ensues, which may lead to the older sib actually physically assaulting the younger sib, or bite or harass him/her when the parents are not observing.

When parents compare siblings in front of each other, a feeling of envy and resentment is caused to the slighted sibling, and a feeling of superiority is seen in the favoured sibling. The resentment may be expressed in the way described above, or it may be repressed at that time – only to surface later on in life. Such life-long rivalry among sibs has led to broken homes, fights and even murder.

What to do? Preparation for the baby-to-arrive must include generating positive vibes in the heart of the elder sibling. You should tell the elder sib that she is going to be blessed with a younger brother or sister only if she agrees to let the new baby stay with them, and does not harass her. No bribes should be offered to the elder sib to "accept" the new arrival.

For feelings of rivalry in older children, it is imperative for parents to not ridicule the children, but to empathise with them and to encourage them to use the example of their better achieving rival(s) to excel in their endeavour! If you "ask" the child not to be jealous of her rival, you will only end up making her more tense and frazzled. Instead, explain to her that she must use these feelings to generate positive energy to overtake her rival and become an achiever. At the same time, do not exert undue pressure on her to make her achieve her goals.

D. Aggressive vs. Shy Behaviour:

Children learn what they live with, but at the same time, genetic, racial and community influences all mould her to be what she becomes in life. To give you an example, a child whose parents are over-protective and indulgent tends to be a shy person, while a child whose parents never bother about her, often beat her for slight mistakes or even fight among themselves is likely to turn a shade aggressive.

Arrogance is also a likely outcome if a child from a rich family sees her parents degrade their home staff and make them do demeaning tasks. Such a child will frequently throw things she doesn't like, speak to elders with disrespect and generally behave like a boor.

While a shy child remains timid because she gets no opportunities to learn new skills by herself, the aggressive one fends for herself most of the time. Both situations lead to danger for the child. For example, the timid child will not be able to get out of danger's way on a traffic-heavy road; the aggressive child will try to negotiate the heavy traffic. Both are likely to get involved in an accident.

The aggression of some children is limited to their homes where they are king; outside their homes, these children become scared to face challenges. In other cases, a child who is timid at home may behave quite differently at home! So, all shades of behaviour are possible.

What to do? Proper upbringing requires a balanced approach. The child should neither be over protected nor left to herself completely. The child must be taught to face adversities with courage and encouraged to devise ways and means of extricating herself from dangerous situations on her own. She should be inspired to participate in concerts, music programmes, contests and other competitions. She should be told that while a win in sports is a desirable outcome, it is better to have played than to have not.

E. Destructive behaviour:

In small children, destructive behaviour is often a developmental aberration which soon passes as the child learns that breaking things and spoiling the house etc. will be frowned upon by parents and will often cause injuries of all kinds to themselves and others. However, many children who are careless or clumsy end up destroying household property too frequently to be "condoned" and become the target of parental anger. They often receive beatings at the hands of the parents. You should remember that children are naughty and clumsy as such, and therefore, you should take ample precautions to see that breakable and expensive items do not fall in their hands. Other kids will actually open gadgets and boxes to see "what's inside"; they will dismantle or break battery-operated toys and small electronic items to see "just how the box made music" or how "the doll walked with lights on in her dress"! Elders might be prompted to say that "he is going to be an engineer when he grows up"! The curious streak in children makes them do all this, so you should get him/her toys that can be assembled/dissembled; at the same time, you can expose him/her to the world of engineering by showing him/her books, CD's and movies that allow him/her to understand the inanimate world around him/her. A suggested web-site is www.howstuffworks.com. You may also buy books like the "How Things Work" series.

Lastly, allow access to articles and material that can be torn, mutilated, destroyed and defaced with immunity, such as old clothes, old magazines, cardboard boxes and cartons, thermocole packing from boxes that you got from purchase of electronic goods and so on. She can do what she likes with these things and yet NOT rile you. In fact, set her a perfectly enjoyable goal: create something with the items at her disposal and bring it to you – a sort of "best" from "waste"!

As the child grows older, she should be made to understand the impact of breaking things on the beauty of the house, the cost escalation, and such other issues.

Children with crossed mental wires who go about destroying things deliberately may need professional counselling.

F. Phobias:

Phobias or fears are real problems in children. While some children are not scared of "anything", there are others who quiver even when the wind blows through the window. To such children, any sort of noise or disturbance is enough to send them running to hide. Most children are innately scared of the dark, of the night and of strange animals and weird insects, for example. Children whose parents are also scared of things will intrinsically be scared of similar or other things. Phobias do run in families.

By definition, a phobia is an *irrational* fear of something. Many a times, parents or other family members are responsible for engendering fear in the heart of their own child. For example, a child who is always told that she will be taken away by "the boogeyman" if she does not behave well will naturally be scared of a knock on the door at night, of opening cupboards at night, of entering dark rooms and of old people with beards, knapsacks and what not. Similarly, if you always tell your child that if she harasses you, you will take her to "doctor uncle" to get an "injection", she will dread her visits to the pediatrician!

Fear of death is another big fear that most often occurs when a near and dear one, frequently a grand parent of the child passes away in front of her eyes. You should take out the time to console her and explain about the inevitability of death and about how one should accept it as a will of God. This will soothe her mind.

What to do? It is very difficult to change a child's basic nature, and we know pretty well that as the child grows older, she will "outgrow" most fears, either through development of courage or wisdom; or she may "feign" a studied indifference to an object she was "once" afraid of, and yet be secretly scared of it!

What you should do is to be there for her. Provide her the assurance and the confidence that she lacks to face her fears. Do not laugh away her fear or ridicule her, for her fear is very real. Teach her to remain calm, count to ten and face the fear *while you hold her hand reassuringly.* Try and identify the "trigger" that caused her to be afraid of something, and then try and eliminate it or explain it to her.

For example, she may have once seen a movie in which bats were shown to be large, fearsome, blood-sucking, human-eating monsters. She will then always be scared of the dark, and of anything that flies in the dark, on say, an evening walk to the garden. Encourage her to tell her story. Once you find out about that movie, you can demystify her by showing her a stuffed bat in the museum, or showing her pictures of bats, or, if possible, real bats in the wild. The fear will most likely vanish once she learns that bats are mostly vegetarians and so small that they cannot eat even a cat, let alone a human.

Read these web-pages for more information on fears and phobias:

- ✔ http://www.americanbaby.com/ab/story.jhtml?storyid=/templatedata/hk/story/data/2053.xml
- ✔ http://www.phobialist.com/
- ✔ http://www.pe2000.com/fears-phobias.htm
- ✔ http://www.psych.org/public_info/phobias.cfm

Part V

See How They Grow (6 – 11 years)

Raising kids is part joy and part guerilla warfare.

– Ed Asner

Kindly read the above line (6 - 11 years) as (6 - 12 years)

Ch 16
Normal Growth and Development
(6 – 12 years)

You know children are growing up
when they start asking questions that have answers.
– Author Unknown.

Once the child is about six years old, she is studying in Std. I. The days of happy infancy, kindergarten and romance with the new sights and sounds of the mundane world are over, and the child is at peace with the physical world around her. She is no longer wowed by what her parents are doing. Parents have become "normal" human beings, and their worship is just about over. There is no God-like aspect about them, and rebellion is just brewing around the corner. The child of six is intelligent, warm and caring, but also naughty, rambunctious, rowdy and intolerable.

You have seen how children are very receptive before six. They learn rules of behaviour and discipline from you. They repeat whatever you ask them to – may it be nursery rhymes or simple stories. They are happy with inexpensive gifts or toys, and they marvel at even the simplest of things with a complete childlike demeanour. However, after six, they have begun to use their heads to get more of everything. They are competitive in all respects. They want toys that are bigger than their neighbours' toys; they look at simple things and almost scoff at you for thinking so little of their status, intelligence or abilities. Ask them a question like "Can you climb that wall?" and you are sure to receive a mocking derision and perhaps a sentence that stings or a tone of voice that cuts ice. "Of course, Daddy!" she will shout, making you feel thoroughly miserable. This then is the age when the child begins to grow up and acquire a personality of her own.

GROWTH:

After the age of six, children continue to grow in weight and height, but marked differences are now apparent in the growth rate of boys and girls. On an average, the pubertal spurt in girls begins some years before it does in boys, so that the spurt in physical growth is earlier in girls than boys (see Chapter 19).

At the end of 12 years, the average boy will be 138-144 cm tall and weigh about 38-45 kg; the average girl will be 142-146 cm tall and weigh about 43-50 kg.

Towards the age of 10 years, **girls** begin to show physical signs of puberty, but their body physiognomy starts changing even before that when they are about 8-9 years of age. There is a re-distribution of body fat from general areas to the thighs, upper arms and shoulders; the carrying angle of the elbow gets more accentuated, and breast buds start forming. In **boys**, the physical changes of puberty have more to do with the sprouting of sex hair, the darkening of the private parts and the cracking of the voice. By twelve, the average boy would already be half-way "there". However, mentally, not many Indian boys are aware of the opposite sex or are aware of their own sexuality. These physical, mental and socio-psychological changes will be discussed in more detail in Chapter 19.

DEVELOPMENT:

Parental Independence: It is not that the child does not love her parents, but the running theme now is to seek independence from their "surveillance and discipline". As the child can now think for herself, she tries to assert her mind on the things that her life rotates around. Not only does she "do" things on her own, she extends her influence on her younger siblings, on her pet(s) (if any) and on the servants and maids in the household. She no longer mimics her parents and no longer openly adores them; her love remains deep, but the outward manifestations are absent. She resents the parent of her sex (the mother) because the latter vies with her for her father's affection. (The reverse is true of the boy, who resents his father in a similar fashion.)

They trust not the wisdom of the parents but that of other adults who they are in constant touch with, such as their class-teacher, their paternal uncle or their youthful neighbour. As they are now comfortable about their sexuality (i.e., they know they are male or female), they do not feel comfortable with children of the opposite sex, or love-scenes in movies or such other issues. Thus, they are more than eager to pursue indifferent matters like language, arithmetic, science and so on. This is one of the reasons why children are so interested in studies at this age.

Ill-manneredness and Verbal abuse: Children test the authority and upbringing of their parents by misbehaving in all possible ways. They will "accidentally" drop things, spill milk, bring dirt on their shoes inside the house and so on. Do not be surprised or annoyed if they appear at the dinner table with dirty hands, or present themselves to your important guests in an unseemly manner in dirty dresses or nightwear. This rebellious attitude stems from their desire to be independent of your "overbearing" influence and not because they mean you any disrespect. It is a very natural reaction for you to be angry at such open defiance, but believe me when I say that deep down, they do not mean to annoy you or to show disrespect. It is just natural for them to rebel against authority in any form.

Children often hear abusive language when they go out in public places and the careless abandon with which these words are hurled by the abuser and the meek acceptance of them by the victims is something that the children feel is very "groovy" and the "done thing". Initially, they mouth the words in their minds, then openly when alone, and finally, with their friends in school or at play. The words fall off their tongues so effortlessly that they are emboldened to say them to more and more of their acquaintances. One of them squeals to you and you suddenly realise that your child has got "spoiled" or is in bad company! Nothing could be further from the truth. Neither is his "company" bad, nor has he gotten spoiled. He realises perfectly well that whatever he is doing is morally wrong and he may get a punishment if he were to get caught; at the same time, he gets an inner feeling of "controlled power" when he uses those words. For now, he will willingly take a punishment for being complained against. If the punishment is insincere or punitive, or physical, he won't learn anything from it and go and abuse again. However, if his punishment is handled sensitively – as if you are simply reminding him of his error – and not *talking down to him* – he is more likely to behave better the next time.

Forming gangs: A gang is a group that comes together with a common purpose, usually identified by society as something that is negative: for example, a gang may decide to trip all the electric meters, or close the door-latches on all the neighbourhood homes; a gang may decide to make fun of all the sissy kids or tease all the girls staying in that street. We are talking about children forming gangs. Yes, they too may do negative things, but if their hand is held and they are guided correctly, such gangs may become totally different. With a clear purpose in hand, the kids' gang may sweep the street, help old people, or take up the challenge of educating the illiterates in their neighbourhood.

Thus, it is clear that forming groups is a normal thing that young boys and girls do. Often, such groups become "enduring" – i.e. they continue even beyond childhood and adolescence right into adulthood. Even if they don't endure, however, their primary purpose is to "conduct" activities *without* the interference of adults. It is this need to self-regulate that is the essence of such group formations and thus, it is your duty to help the children form useful groups. After all, children are tomorrow's citizens, and the work they do will help them immensely in their organisational skills in adulthood.

Permanence: This word summarises what parents need to provide to their growing child in life. Permanence of relationships, permanence of residence, permanence of friendships and acquaintances, permanence of values and permanence of their own marriage! Most children between 6 and 12 feel utterly comfortable if there is no change or minimum change all around them.

It is imperative not to change the house that you all stay in too frequently, their school, your house caretakers etc. Anything that is changed too fast allows no leeway for the child to establish relationships, form groups, gather confidence and make friends. At the same time, you should provide high ideals and high moral standards for the child, so that this shows up in her character in later life despite the rough childhood activities and the temporary phase of bad behaviour that she is passing through at the present time.

Encouragement and Impetus: To encourage your child further, you, as a parent, can be pro-active too. Help your children make friends in the society you are living in by celebrating her birthday with the other children; call the other children over to your house for snacks; co-organise a fete or a fun-fair with the children with the help of other co-operative adults in the society; take one or two of the children whom your child wants to be friends with with you to the movies or for an outing. In such ways, your child will gain immeasurably in social prestige and peer acceptance. At the same time, some imposition of limits is also required.

At school, to make your child sit with "desirable" children, you might have to break ice with his/her teacher and negotiate with her about shifting your child to the desired seat. If this is not possible, you can still do a world of good to your child by speaking to his/her teacher about changing your child's partner(s) as soon as possible.

Orderliness and rules: Most children want their play activities, eating, dressing, their rooms, their study area etc. to be well ordered and properly planned. Hence, parents should, while not directly interfering, help their children achieve their goals in a reasonable way.

The obsession with orderliness and rules allows children to compete with their friends and colleagues in competitive games and sports. They dread, but at the same time, in a queer sort of way, relish the rules and restrictions that make games so enjoyable to people of all ages. The challenge they want to master in any game is this: I must not make an error; otherwise I will have to start over again! Bringing orderliness also allows them to start collections of various items like stamps, books, pictures, etc. You as parents must assist him/her in acquiring these items, at a cost if necessary.

It is the same fetish with orderliness that makes an eight year old suddenly rearrange everything in her cupboard, or tidy up her room, or straighten up her hair or arrange her books in a neat stack; it is the same fetish that enables mothers to teach their nine or ten year olds how to manage pocket money, how to draw graphs and charts and how to organise the kitchen. The orderliness and the curiosity to learn new skills, coupled with the child's innate interest in handling food, makes a child learn new skills like cooking, fruit and vegetable decoration, table-setting and so on.

On the other hand, orderliness and a fetish for rules may also cause obsessiveness and compulsion in the child. For example, a child will walk on cobblestones with an obsession that she should never step on the joint lines between the stones; or she will climb only even-numbered stairs (she would have mentally numbered them on an earlier occasion); or she will touch every fourth picket on a fence; these obsessions usually reduce, and even disappear over time, but in some cases, they won't, and the child continues to be compulsive in later life. Such children will need the help of a psychiatrist, as will children whose entire day is spent on a compulsion and how to satisfy it: for example, a child who keeps washing his hands, or one who mutters numbers all day long.

Schooling and Education: As discussed earlier, the age group specific to this chapter is conducive to learning. We shall explore this aspect in detail in Chapter 17.

TEETH: ERUPTION OF PERMANENT TEETH

As we have seen in Chapter 13, the permanent teeth make their first appearance around 6 years of age, and they gradually replace the existing milk teeth, which are sequentially shed by the body. The problems associated with teething of primary dentition are, surprisingly, absent. The child may have a slight pain and tenderness of the gums for a day or two, but there aren't any constitutional symptoms like high fever or loose stools.

Sequence of eruption: This is shown in the table below and in Appendix f

Table: Permanent Teeth Eruption

Permanent teeth	Age of eruption
Central incisors	6-8 years
Lateral incisors	7-9 years
Canines	10-12 years
First premolars	10-12 years
Second premolars	10 ½-13 years
First molars	6-7 years
Second molars	12-13 years
Third molars	17-23 years

Around the age of 7-9 years, it is not unusual to see new front teeth erupting and forming a crooked row in front of the old milk teeth which have not yet fallen off. The child may look quite "unsightly" when she smiles. This is a normal event, and parents must not worry unduly because of the same. As the milk teeth fall off, the countenance and smile of the child will improve. By 12-13 years, 28 teeth have already erupted, and it will be many more years before the final 4 wisdom teeth or third molars will cut through (if at all). Eruption of wisdom teeth may be a problem event if they do not "find" place on the jaws to come out. Sometimes, they cause so much pain and agony that the dentist may have to "help" their eruption by cutting "away" the mucosa, or, in severe cases, even remove the tooth/teeth altogether.

Care of the teeth and gums:

See Chapter 13 for details. Children of school-going age must be taught how to use dental floss. They should also be explained why they should not eat boiled sweets and other "sticky" stuff like gum endlessly, as this can cause serious dental disease. Chewing gums containing baking soda are useless for whitening the teeth. Their use should be discouraged.

Dentists nowadays apply dental sealants on the chewing surfaces of the back teeth to prevent the occurrence of cavities in the teeth; in fact, if decay has already begun, sealants will help prevent further damage. Dental sealant is a plastic coating that seals the tooth from accumulation of food debris and bacteria and prevents development of tartar and plaque. Both these are precursors to formation of dental cavities.

A 6-monthly visit to a dentist is recommended for everyone whether or not there are any acute problems.

Ch 17
School and Education

If there were no schools to take the children away from home part of the time, the insane asylums would be filled with mothers

. – Edgar W. Howe

We are apt to forget that children learn more from example than from preaching

–.Roy L Smith

It is not for nothing that we become so emotional when we remember our school days. We grow nostalgic and a lump rises in our throat; I feel my gut is being tightened by a wrench. Truly, school is our second home between the ages of five and fifteen, but it is more than that. We are impressionable and teachable, naughty and incorrigible, studious and playful, friends and competitors; we are so many things all at once! We live, breathe and feel the school in our blood!

What the school does for the child:

It is a temple of learning, said one great thinker. However, if by that one meant only mastering the three R's, viz. Reading, 'Riting and 'Rithmetic, we would be wrong. The school moulds our persona, our character and our very soul in the ten odd years that we spend in it. A child learns how to face the real world in school by dealing with inter-personal challenges at every turn in her life. By studying with children from different religions, different cultures and different socio-economic backgrounds, the child prepares to meet the world on her own terms. She learns to not merely co-exist, but to flourish, with such a wide variety of her friends in a peaceful manner.

By providing stimuli to the fast-expanding mind of the school-going child, the school, is, in fact, creating better citizens of tomorrow.

Admission to a School:

With each passing year, India's tiny tots and their parents have to literally dance to the tune of the schools at the time of admissions. Hefty donations are demanded in the name of some "charity" or the other in many schools; in yet others, the parents are put under the microscope to see if their child is "fit" to enter the hallow precincts of such an "accomplished school"! In other schools, a not inconsiderable amount is demanded just to issue a form, with no guarantees about whether the child will get admitted. Further, this amount is non-refundable, so that a large corpus of money is collected every year. Admittedly, not every school gives quality education, and not every school demands such donations; but the trend is there for all to see, including the mandarins of the Education Ministry. The government has tried in vain to regulate minority educational establishments and private unaided schools, but the problems seem to increase with each passing year. In such an environment, we hear of schools that demand "registration" of a baby when she is born, or within 24 hours of birth!

Is it therefore any surprise that admission to schools ranks as the most troublesome issue among new parents? I sincerely and honestly feel that school admission formalities must be made simpler, more transparent and more liberal, so that tomorrow's citizens are not deprived of the best possible opportunities to learn.

What is the procedure for admissions?

Usually, each school first puts up a notice for admissions to the Nursery and K.G. standards about 4-5 months before the start of a new academic year. Parents are required to collect forms, and return them as per the schedule. They should then await the putting up of a new notice, with the names of those children who will be called for an "interview". At the interview, the child and the parents are asked questions; after some days, the "successful" candidates' names are put up on the same notice board, with the exhortation to "pay the whole academic year's fees" if the parents wish to accept the said admission.

Preparing for the interview:

It is imperative that parents do not unduly pressurise their children while preparing them for the upcoming interview. While it is perfectly correct to revise the alphabet, numbers, nursery rhymes and picture recognition, it is unfair to expect the child to remember the names of say, the Indian Prime Minister or the "full name of the play-school from which she came". Of course, it is even more unfair of the school teachers to ask the child the aforementioned questions, but we have all become victims of an extremely insensitive system, and we have to live with it. Groom the child and yourself on the day of the interview, and reach well in time, so that you are able to grab seats on the few available chairs/benches and can help the child to "relax" sufficiently before she is called "in".

Take some light snacks and drinking water with you, as well as a change of dress in case the child needs to change her dress before the interview.

If the child is called in alone, you should gently propel her away from you and into the arms of the person who has come to fetch her; at that time, make eye contact and smile encouragingly, and reassure her that all will be fine.

When she returns, take her in your arms and shower your love for her. Do not even "try" to "find out" what she was asked inside, for she needs your love more than anything else after those trying moments in front of strangers.

If you are a teacher, and are reading this book, try and be as gentle and sensitive with the child as possible during the actual interview.

This quote by Aristotle (384 B.C.-322 B.C.) is a tribute to the teachers who are reading this book:

He said "*Those who educate children well are more to be honored than parents, for these only gave life, those the art of living well.*"

Play-school and Kindergarten:

With each passing academic year, this author has witnessed further and further lowering of the entry age for play-schools, especially in big cities in our country. Some ten years ago, children were admitted to Kindergarten after they completed three years of life. This age has been halved in recent times, and it is not unusual to see 1 ½ year olds travelling to "school", either in their mother's arms or in a special bus, tempo or taxi. It is a disturbing trend among metropolitan parents, who, in their quest for super-kids, have abandoned common sense and are sending children who are barely out of the potty into a structured, strange environment of a play-school. Be that as it may, the trend has met with the tacit approval of the powers-that-be in the corridors of the Ministry of Education. The age at entry into the K.G. has been now lowered to 2 ½ years, so that a 1 ½ year old has an advantage if he/she has completed one year of play-school already. Not just that, there is such a long waiting list for admission to reputed schools that the school authorities take an "oral test" of the aspiring children and use the performance therefrom to decide about which children will get admitted to their school. Moreover, many of these play-schools are unregulated and charge exorbitantly, knowing fully well that the parents (who are often working and "want" some free time for themselves) will shell out the dough without grumbling.

These social issues aside, this author is firmly convinced of the need for parents to realise that the toddler's place is in the home, by the side of her mother; the kind of "education" the mother can give far surpasses the rote learning that is the name of the game in nurseries all over the country. Yes, undoubtedly, informal and non-structured learning is VITAL for the all-round development of the child's rapidly growing mind.

Try and choose a play-school that has a relaxed atmosphere and that emphasizes in such informal learning methods, and you might just escape the pressure-strung environment of an average play-school where the child is taught how to dot the i's and cross the t's. The child's motor skills, cognitive powers, creativity and artistic abilities must be allowed to bloom in play-school and nursery. Children, in short, should enjoy play-school and learn while they play, colour, paint and sing.

A play-school as well as a nursery should have ample space, a play-ground, a garden or some greenery, attention to hygiene, proper sanitation and a good collection of audio-visual material, soft toys, and so on. Teachers should be well-versed in handling children; they should be kind-hearted, tolerant and loving. They should have a good grasp of child psychology. They should know, besides Maths and English, art, drawing, craft, music, dance and other similar activities.

<ins>Games:</ins>

The children should be allowed to play different types of outdoor games. Games should be such that they encourage the children to play fairly, enthusiastically and with just a hint of competitiveness. At the same time, teachers should supervise the children to see that they play with a proper spirit, that they participate actively in the game (and not sit by the side), and that they do not get injured. If they *do* get injured, the teacher should either administer or arrange for someone to administer first aid immediately. After doing so, the teacher may call up the child's parents to inform them about what happened and what action was taken.

Snacks:

Either the school or the parents must provide nutritious snacks to the child for her to eat at break-time. This is important, because children tend to eat better in the company of their fellow-mates than when they are asked to eat alone. The table below tells you what snacks to give and what to avoid. As can be seen from the lists, all types of fruit and vegetable items constitute healthy snacks, while fried foods, chips of all kinds and foods with cream and sugar etc. are the unhealthy foods.

Table: Snacks for children

Healthy Snacks	Unhealthy Snacks
1. *Poha* 2. *Upma* 3. Chutney-Sandwich 4. Cucumber/Tomato Sandwich 5. Apples 6. Grapes 7. Diced fruit 8. *Idli/Wada* 9. Sprouted legumes (*moong*, etc.)	1. Cream biscuits 2. Potato *Wada* 3. Jam sandwich 4. Potato chips 5. Junk food 6. Chocolates and toffees 7. Cakes and sweet meats 8. Fried stufflike samosas etc.

In view of the fact that the child will eat in the play-school, many parents have started sending unrealistic portions of the food in their child's snack boxes. Please do not fall into this trap, and always put a realistic amount of healthy stuff in her snack box.

The satchel:

Do try and buy a satchel that is easy to carry over the child's back; it should be made of light material, be attractive to look at, and be able to hold at least a couple of books, a panty/shorts and T-shirt (which many play-school owners expect the child to carry everyday), a pencil box and a snack box (in case you are sending home-made snacks with the child). Write the child's name prominently on the satchel with a permanent marker. The satchel should preferably have a slot to take the child's water bottle as well, so that the child need not carry two items, but just one.

Fears and Crying:

Most first-timers cry heavily when they begin to attend school. Children who are more attached to their mother and first-borns are affected much more as they receive much more attention and closeness at home. There is a two-fold fear: that of "leaving the mother" and that of "meeting strangers". For such children, the preparation begins with a couple of trips to the school in the weeks before the school actually starts. The child sees the colourful environment, the open spaces and the various games available (such as the slide, the swing and so on). Afterwards, the parent(s) should accompany the child to school for the first few days. Another useful trick is to prepare the child for school right from the previous night. You should prepare the child "mentally" for the delightful time she is going to have "at school". You should have the child externalize her fears and choose the dress and snack she is going to use the next morning. The same method should be utilised the next morning too. Such encouragement and prior preparation goes a long way in making the nervous child come to terms with the reality of school.

Leaving and Picking Up:

Most parents try and choose a play-school that is located near their residence, and they then go personally to leave and to pick up the baby. Some, however, are not so lucky, and choose a more distant school, with "bus" facilities. While this is not a bad thing in itself, you should make sure that the child does not lose much time in commuting. This is because, at this age, the child cannot be subjected to so much loss of time. She needs time to relax, time to eat lunch, time to play and time to sleep, all before it is evening time. Then, she needs play, merriment and snack times once again! Finally, she will have some more games and fun, take her dinner (by eight or so) and go to bed before nine p.m.

Regular School:

Where a child has already secured admission at the Nursery level in a High School (that is, one that goes up to the tenth standard (Board Exams)), the child automatically gets promoted to Std. I after completing higher K.G. The problem occurs when the child has been admitted to a Nursery/Kindergarten school. As soon as Nursery/ K.G. is over, the parents have to once again start hunting for schools to admit their child to one. High schools that are run privately are costly, and not many parents can afford them. They charge anything from Rs. 500/= to Rs. 3000/= per month! In addition, there are "activity fees", "term fees", "stationery fees", "excursion fees" and so on. In government aided schools, the situation is a bit different: the fees are very low (especially after Primary school), but the classes are crammed with upwards of 60-80 children per division. Thus the child cannot get personal attention by the teachers.

Choosing the school:

As a parent, you have to choose which type of schooling fits your pocket and the child's skills better – whether you will be able to meet the high demands of a private set up or be more comfortable with the rather impersonal atmosphere of an aided school. Other considerations include the proximity of the school to your residence, the quality of extra-curricular facilities available and the socio-economic mind-set of the students that usually attend such a school.

To illustrate the last point further, parents often admit their child to the most snobbish school, thinking that if their child hobnobs with the rich and famous, she will also become "sophisticated". Nothing could be further from the truth.

The child will be more comfortable if she is in a school that is near her residence, has good outdoor activities and has a proper infrastructure for all-round development. She will save time commuting. You save on bus-fees. She can have an intelligent mix of studies, sports and cultural activities. Finally, she becomes a better, all round person.

Children who study in co-ed schools (i.e. where both boys and girls are admitted) get a better exposure to members of the opposite sex; while this may slightly increase the chance of "distractions" (and teen-dating is also becoming more and more common), by and large, these children learn to handle relationships with the members of the opposite sex much better than those who study in unisex schools.

<u>Boarding schools</u>:

These schools have their own charm, but there are some difficulties as well. The positives lie in the fact that the child learns to handle herself and her possessions at a much earlier age than a "normal" child; also, the child becomes more responsible, less flippant, better groomed (because of strict dress discipline, eating hours, sleeping hours and so on) and a good sportsman too. This last is because of facilities like horse-riding, swimming, football etc. which are offered in boarding schools.

The children most likely to join boarding schools are those whose (i) parents are in the armed forces and get transferred a lot; (ii) parents who are unable to control their ill-mannered, naughty and often violent or delinquent child; (iii) parents who have separated from or have divorced each other; (iv) and parents who are a little self-centred with busy social lives – and care not what their children do as long as they are studying.

It is immediately obvious that using a boarding school to reject or reform the child is patently wrong and should never be resorted to. In unavoidable circumstances, send the child after she has completed an age of at least 10-11 years and is somewhat completely independent.

Class-work, Home-work and Studying:

Children enjoy class-work and dread home-work. Period. This fact is universal, and parents have to put in an effort to encourage their child to complete their home-work before going to play with friends. In addition to the home-work supplied by the teachers, which the children will do willy-nilly, you should inculcate a discipline of studying for at least one hour everyday. This is the only way to keep abreast of the curriculum. A "sprint" of reading in the last 15 days before an exam just won't help, especially in high school. You should allocate time for home-work, time for study, time for the television and time for playing in advance, so that children do each of these things and not feel "cheated" of fun at the end of the day.

When they are doing their home-work or studying for exams, be around to provide guidance or help *if they ask for it.* Do not do their work for them. It may be all right to supplement their effort with things like arranging their books for them, sharpening their pencils, doing an inventory of the things that they might need in school the next day, preparing the next day's "timetable", providing them with health drinks or snacks in between and so on. Further, you may switch off the door-bell and the clock chimer, pull out the phone plug in their room, see that proper room-lighting is available, monitor their "relaxation intervals" so that they resume studying after the agreed breaks and prevent unwanted visitors at the door. While making the **atmosphere conducive to studying**, it may happen that your child needs soft instrumental music or a rubber ball to grasp and ungrasp so as to be able to maintain the tempo of her study. If this is so, you might have to oblige her by buying her earphones and a Walkman or a Discman. However, see that these are not misused by the child.

Tuitions:

With the advent of the modern age has come the bane of private tuitions. Returning under the guise of "personalized teaching" like the *rishis* of ancient times, the culture of private tuitions has made a paradigm shift in the thinking of people at large and parents in particular. Prohibitively high fees, cramped teaching rooms, a rigorous schedule of classes and tests and pressurization of the children's minds characterises this culture.

While it is sometimes unavoidable to "coach" a weak child, most parents now put even their very bright children in tuition classes to get them to score just "that bit more" since admission to professional courses has become so competitive. I pity the poor children who have to study for six to eight hours in school, then go to tuition classes for another two to three hours and then return home to do their home-work and study for yet another hour or two.

Are we turning our children into robots or what? They have no time to pursue hobbies, play with friends or cultivate any other interests. Success is measured only by the marks they obtain in their exams, and a difference of just one mark may lose them their chance of getting a seat in a coveted medical or engineering college/course.

Which brings me to the other point. Why are parents insisting on their children going in only for these limited courses? Is becoming a doctor or an engineer the be-all and end-all of all things? There are so many different new vocations available today. Some of them are traditional in nature while others are in keeping with the changing times. These include computer-related jobs, event management, salon-ownership, business entrepreneurship, a career in the armed forces, arts and crafts, fashion designing and so on.

Children today have become dreadfully competitive because of the faulty educational policies being pursued by the Indian Educational System. Personally, I am against the current emphasis on marks and ranks, and would much rather see no exams till the seventh standard, with promotions based only on year-round internal assessment, and only grading in the higher classes. It seems that hope is on the horizon, and by the time this book is in your hands, Delhi's CBSE would have put a Grading System in place in Standards VIII and above. However, till such a policy is implemented, I request you, as responsible parents, to NOT insist on "standing at least third in the class" or any such arbitrary level for the child, but allow the child to appear for exams in a friendly and supportive home environment.

We, as parents and elders must begin to think differently and transform the society by taking our children away from the pressure of marks-driven academics to a world where job-liking and satisfaction takes priority over our own pre-conceived ideas. We should let the children choose their careers for themselves.

Academic excellence alone is **not** the measure of the strength of an individual in life. Rather, you should try and inculcate other good skills and qualities in the child such as a wholesome personality, good character, sportsmanship, strong determination and the ability to improvise and adapt to changed circumstances, to bear a loss or a failure with dignity and equanimity and to make lifelong friends.

"Climb every mountain,
Cross every stream,
Follow every rainbow,
Till your dream comes true!"

This should be the spirit that you inculcate in your child. She should strike out at any challenge, develop an outgoing nature and have the flame of adventure glowing in her heart.

One thing that you should know: **there are no medicines, elixirs or compounds that can make a child brighter, more intelligent or more capable. Hard work and true grit and determination to succeed are the only mantras of success in today's fast and cut throat environment.**

Use of Computers at Home (see Chapter 22):

With the advent of computers, many families are giving the "digital" experience to their children by purchasing home computers. This is a real positive change, because children are naturally adept at handling the computer. Their creative energy can be effectively channelled by having them spend time on the computer instead of the "idiot box" that is the television set. Children love to play games, so it is prudent for you to buy them interactive CD ROM's with games loaded on them. There are many genres of games such as strategy, spelling, calculating, speed and logical thinking. CD ROM's of Quizzes, Encyclopaedias, puzzle-solving and so on are also available. In the last few years, the entire school syllabi are available as "Educational" CD's. Parents who can afford these would do well to remember that exclusive learning on the computer may not be good as the child will continue to use real stationery in school. Hence, I suggest you go "slow" on the last-mentioned items and buy only science and Maths CD's, and that too only in the higher classes.

Excursions and Outings:

Different schools have different policies with regard to excursions and outings. Some schools collect money for educational trips with the term and school fees, while others ask for the "damages" on a trip to trip basis. Most trips within the city entail your leaving the child at school and picking her back from there in the afternoon. When the outing is an overnight one, schools will usually buy a "package tour" so that all the responsibilities like tour, food, accommodation etc. becomes the work of the tour operator.

Trips and tours are definitely advisable for the child, for the child not only becomes independent, but also learns much more when she travels with her school teachers and in the company of her school friends. The only thing you must remember is to advise the child about her limits (like whether she can take a horse ride or not, whether she can swim or not and so on). At the same time, schools usually take a signed undertaking from the parents stating that while the tour operators and the school will take all possible precautions to avoid any mishap, they will not be responsible if anything untoward happens to your child.

Open Day and other parent-teacher interactions:

An "Open day" is a day when parents are summoned to the school, usually after a Unit test, to discuss the child's performance in the test and to exchange information regarding the academic and other activities of the child in school. Parents must make full use of this opportunity to discuss their child's performance, strengths and weaknesses with their teachers. At the same time, you should use the chance to make suggestions for the improvement of the overall working of the school. For example, you might want to bring to the notice of the Principal the rude behaviour of the bus driver who ferries your child to and from the school; or you might want to compliment the child's science teacher's new method of interactive teaching.

Apart from open days, you should also take part in other Parent-Teacher Association activities like felicitating a retiring teacher, or presenting a gift of gratitude to all teachers on teacher's day.

Extra-curricular activities and sports:

It goes without saying that a child's all round development includes her full participation in each and every non-academic activity that is available for her enjoyment. You should keep your eyes and ears open for announcements on forthcoming competitions, athletic or aquatic sports, drama and elocution activities and so on. Sometimes, the child may have to actually learn a new skill so as to do justice to the role that she is going to play/activity she is going to be a part of. Some activities may even be compulsory in nature, like "Road Safety Patrol" or "Guiding/Scouting" from the VIIIth standard onwards.

Participating in annual day concerts and dramas makes the child that much richer in experience; it makes her more confident, adds to her poise and carriage and it makes her happy from within, thereby making her more attentive in the academic field as well.

Sports and aquatics are also important: the child must be allowed to take part in both these so as to make her face competition squarely and honestly.

Problems in Regular school:

First out, let me say that the days of teachers whipping or cruelly punishing their pupils are over, at least in most cities of the nation. Such horrible stuff is still happening in some rural areas, but thankfully, in such cases too, the atrocities are reducing with each passing year.

Disciplinary actions:

Teachers resort to various forms of disciplinary actions when children misbehave. As I mentioned earlier, the days when teachers beat their pupils with a cane or a ruler are gone, but teachers and ultimately, the higher school authorities, may resort to:

a) Time-outs
b) Standing on the bench
c) Slapping the child
d) Writing tasks – e.g. to write all the questions and answers of a particular lesson three times
e) After-school task class - where the child stays back after school hours to complete her unfinished task, or writes some prescribed task from her school books
f) Taking the child to the principal for an admonition
g) Suspending the child for a few days
h) Rusticating the child from school

It is necessary to understand the genesis of any punishment because once this is explained to the child, he/she will be better able to come to terms with his/her failings/errors/misbehaviour. If the child is taught the correct way of doing a certain thing, he/she will not commit the same error again. As a parent, you should cooperate with the school authorities in helping the child learn and/or adopt correct behaviour.

Tiffs and Fights:

Internal rivalries among class-mates, bullying, ragging and physical fisticuffs (among boys) and hair pulling and nail scratching (among girls) are the main problems that we all have experienced as children, and which we all face with our children. As parents, you should try and strike a balance between being totally unconcerned about what happens to your child at school and being over-protective about her welfare. "**Neither a hen** (who minds her brood with an unforgiving attention) **nor a cuckoo** (who lays her eggs in the nests of other birds) **be**." In case your child brings home a festering complaint against some other child or children, then by all means, approach the school authorities to resolve the issue. Never say things like "you should have slapped her back" or "if she shouted at you, why didn't you hit her". At the same time, administer to her hurt (which is often more to the ego than to the body) by being compassionate and calm about the whole matter. Advise her to approach the school teacher or principal and complain to them about that child/those children.

Uneaten tiffins and Tuck-shop food:

Many children enjoy eating samosas, wadas and cakes from the canteen or tuck shop in the school. They partake of these delicacies (I'd rather call them horrors and not delicacies, but that is what they are to the children) during the short break, and then eat meagerly from their tiffin box at lunch. The lunch is brought back home, uneaten. This is a genuine problem that many parents face.

What to do? The best suggestions include (i) curtailing her pocket money so that she cannot buy the canteen items without seriously compromising her compulsory spends like bus fare; (ii) giving a limited amount of lunch in the tiffin and offering a meal on her *return* from school; (iii) asking the school canteen contractor to stock healthy snack options and (iv) speaking to the Principal of the school about it.

Injuries and illness at school:

Most schools have a first-aid box to attend to minor cuts and scratches. Some schools call a nearby doctor in case a child faints or falls sick, while most immediately call the parents to school to take charge of their wards. In any case, the primary responsibility of the school is to see that immediate help and first aid is provided. Thereafter, the final responsibility devolves on the parents. They are usually instructed "not to send the child to school until she is completely fit to resume school".

Such a compulsory absence is also imposed when your child suffers from **chicken pox**. She is liable to infect other children, and is therefore asked to remain away till the very last of her blisters have completely healed. This is called "quarantine". Unfortunately, the child has become infective about 3 – 4 days *before* she develops the classical rash, so usually, she would have *already* infected other children before her quarantine is imposed!

Difficulties in Learning:

At times, some children are unable to excel in academics. The causes may be legion. They include the following:

a) The child may be underage for a given standard.
b) The child may have a hearing handicap (so far undetected) as a result of which she is unable to hear the teacher when the latter is explaining the lesson.

c) The child may have a refractive error or may be suffering from some other eye problem, so that she is unable to read from the black board.
d) The child is under mental stress due to known or unknown fears and anxieties (parental conflicts, sibling rivalry, peer pressure, strict teacher, etc.).
e) The child is "doing drugs" (see Chapters 18 and 19)
f) The child has suffered personal grief (death of a loved one, loss of a parent).

In many of the above cases, the learning disability is of a temporary nature, and tends to resolve once the situation is improved.

Learning Disabilities:

Learning disabilities are specific problems in learning shown by discrepancy between the child's learning ability as predicted by her IQ. It is a disorder of one or more of the basic processes involved in understanding or using language, written or spoken, which may manifest itself as an imperfect ability to listen, think, understand, speak, write, spell, calculate or reason.

This term includes "minimal brain dysfunction", "developmental aphasia" and "dyslexia". It **excludes** children whose learning difficulties are due to hearing or visual difficulties, a physical handicap, a social or environmental cause like a marital conflict or death of a loved one or a noisy neighborhood, mental retardation or an emotional disturbance.

The range of problems includes:
a) Academic skills disorders – such as a reading/writing disorder (dyslexia), an expressive writing disorder (dysgraphia) and an arithmetical calculation disorder (dyscalculia).
b) Language and Speech disorders – articulation disorder, expressive language disorder and receptive language disorder and

c) Motor Skills disorder – a coordination disorder.

There are **seven areas** of specific learning disabilities:

1. Basic reading
2. Reading comprehension
3. Oral expression
4. Listening comprehension
5. Written expression.
6. Mathematical calculation.
7. Logical/mathematical reasoning.

At the same time, children may have associated problems like "attention deficit hyperactivity disorder (ADD-H), memory deficits, etc.

While basic reading and writing disorders may present in Nursery or Kindergarten, parents may not realise until a little later, because they might feel that the child may be a slow learner. Spelling errors, illegible handwriting, mathematical errors and errors of identifying correct shapes or drawing geometrical figures will become apparent in Primary school. Children with a learning disability continue to make errors and avoid reading/writing etc even as they grow older, and right into adulthood.

The **management** of a learning disability includes long-term *educational counselling, behavioural therapy* and *certifying the child as having the disability* so that she gets the benefit of doubt while performing in an exam. For board exams, the Board may allow a "writing partner" to sit with the child, much like a runner in a cricket match. Children with dyscalculia will be allowed to bring a calculator, while children who have difficulty spelling words may either be allowed to get a dictionary or be pardoned their errors while being marked.

The prodigy or the gifted child:

About 3-5 out of 100 children have an unusually high level of intelligence. They are termed "gifted" or called "child prodigies" or "geniuses". They demonstrate their talent right at an early age and it takes the skill of parents to discover their unusual nature. The child will often master the alphabet before the age of two, will learn two-digit calculations by four, and will participate in family debates with logical thinking that is normally beyond the capacity of children from her age-group. At times, the child may be gifted in computing and mathematics, or in a non-academic sphere like music, dance or singing. It is therefore recommended that the 'average' child is exposed to as many activities as possible so as to "discover" her hidden talent. You should take your child to attend plays, operas, concerts, recitals, cultural fests, drama, dance competitions and other talent shows. This will increase her interest in these activities and may "unmask" her own talent in a given field.

Once a talent is discovered, it is up to you, the parent, to nurture it by encouragement, enrolment in special classes, participation in competitions etc. At the same time, a genius should not necessarily be "advanced" to a higher class; this is because, although she is more capable academically, she needs the social and cultural support of her own-age children. At the same time, you should see that she remains emotionally balanced and not become egoistic or arrogant, for then, she will cease to be valuable to your family or to the school and may become a rule-breaker in both situations.

Ch 18
Problems and Challenges
(Age 6 – 12 years)

Nowadays, there is a pervasive tendency to treat children as adults, and adults as children. The options of children are thus steadily expanded, while those of adults are progressively constricted. The result is unruly children and childish adults

– Author unknown.

As we go along this chapter, we will discover that much of what we read in the previous chapters about problems in children between the age of 0-6 (Chapters 14 and 15) is valid for older children as well. I urge the reader to go back to these chapters for more details and to get an overview of what I am talking about.

Growth:

The major problems are:

1. A child who is not growing well
2. A child who is growing disproportionately
3. A child who is growing at more than the usual rate

An Under-growing child:

For a child who is growing at less than the normal rate, the parents are usually worried that she will remain short. However, that is not the case. A girl starts showing good linear growth from the age of 9-10 years. A boy shoots up a bit later, say after 12. So, if one sees a 10 year old girl with a 12 year old boy, one might perceive that the girl is older and looks more "mature". The boy's parent might get worried that his boy is stunted. The girl's parent might feel superior or start chiding the "sissy boy". These are inappropriate responses! As we know, after 13, the boy is going to grow at a much faster clip, and by 15-16 years of age, he is more than likely to have overshot the girl who will have achieved her full height potential (or nearly so) by 16.

At the same time, one should get worried if the pre-pubertal burst of height has NOT occurred in a girl even till 12, and in a boy till 15. This is because the spurt in height is a sort of prelude and a marker to the correct onset of puberty (see Chapter 19).

The commonest cause of a child not growing well is under-nutrition. By this, I do not mean an actual under nutrition, but a "false under-nutrition" caused by food fads and a poor dietary regimen. Some children are so fussy about eating their afternoon meal in school that their tiffin arrives home uneaten, or at best, partly eaten (see Chapter 17). Although most children will compensate for this by taking an evening meal or demand more food at dinner, some of them don't compensate adequately, and end up looking thin and "lanky".

In other children, the root cause may be genetic or what we call "constitutional". This implies a stunting or lankiness not due to under-eating but due to the child's inherent genetic make-up. In most such cases, the parents may also be a bit short, say about 5' or so in height. In rare instances, the parents may have a normal height.

Disproportionate growth:

Any child who is growing disproportionately needs medical attention, and make no mistake about this. So, a child with a small or a large head, a child with small limbs or a child with excessively long fingers – all should be seen by a Pediatrician. A normal child has no reason to grow in a haphazard manner.

Obese/Fast-growing child (see Chapter 12):

A child who goes beyond the heights of his parents may actually be emulating his grand-parents. A stocky disposition too may be normal in some families. However, a height in excess of 6 ½ feet or a definitely obese child is certainly abnormal, and must be shown to a Pediatrician.

The commonest causes of an excessively tall child are "acromegaly" or hyper-functioning of the pituitary gland (increased secretion of Growth Hormone) and the Marfan syndrome.

Obesity (see Chapter 12), on the other hand, is a result of over-eating and faulty eating habits. An obese child is frequently a couch-potato addicted to TV surfing. He/she is used to high calorie snacking, and is a frequent customer of Pizza delivery outfits. He/she enjoys fried foods, processed cheese, burgers and rolls, chips and wafers, *wadas* and *samosas* and so on. Physical exercise is anathema to him/her. Most often, he/she has been a fat infant and a fat toddler ... and all things being equal, he/she is most likely to remain a fat individual throughout most of adult life. This is a sad state of affairs indeed, for childhood obesity is a clear precursor of so many adulthood diseases like hypertension, diabetes mellitus etc. Also, it is a condition that makes the affected person feel so shy and uncertain.

This is the reason why we should prefer a HEALTHY and not a CHUBBY child!

What to do? The remedy for obesity lies in a different, more active lifestyle, regular exercise and eating sensibly and regularly. Some children may need professional help from a dietitian, a fitness trainer and sometimes, an endocrinologist.

Development:

Apart from *scholastic backwardness*, there are hardly any other developmental issues. These are discussed in Chapter 17.

Challenges:

Again, I refer you to Chapters 15 and 16 for these issues. A few pertinent questions are taken up here. Some school related challenges are discussed in Chapter 17.

<u>Relationships with parents:</u>

Parents usually always want to love their children, and be loved back. So do children. Then why is it that children resent the presence of their parents? Why do children talk secretively to their friends? Why do children want their parents to "not" interfere when they get into trouble? Part of this is because the 6-12 year old finally tastes independence from her parents for the first time in this age group. He/she is busy making new friends (and new enemies too) and finding her feet in an increasingly friendless world. Her peers are also experiencing similar challenges and facing them in the same confused manner. They tend to gravitate towards each other and find solace within their own group.

What to do? Parents must continue to remain supportive of their children throughout this period, and even beyond, during adolescence. They should allow some independence but at the same time, continue to keep some control over them.

Awareness of sexuality:

By ten to eleven years, today's generation of youngsters is already aware of their sexuality, particularly those who study in co-educational schools and those who are in metropolitan cities. For the vast majority of the children, however, this awareness will only come after 12 years of age. For more details, go to Chapters 19 and 20.

For matters like cheating, stealing, lying, abuse, etc, please refer to Chapter 15.

Part VI

Adolescence, Teenage and Puberty

If I had my child to raise all over again,
I'd build self-esteem first, and the house later.
I'd finger-paint more, and point the finger less.
I would do less correcting and more connecting.
I'd take my eyes off my watch, and watch with my eyes.
I'd take more hikes and fly more kites.
I'd stop playing serious, and seriously play.
I would run through more fields and gaze at more stars.
I'd do more hugging and less tugging.

– Diane Loomans, from
"If I Had My Child To Raise Over Again"

Ch 19
What is Adolescence?

Having a thirteen-year-old in the family is like having a general-admission ticket to the movies, radio and TV. You get to understand that the glittering new arts of our civilization are directed to the teen-agers, and by their suffrage they stand or fall.
- Max Lerner, (1902-), American Columnist.

Adolescence is the time period that covers the age group between 10 and 15 in both boys and girls. It is a time for physical, biological and mental changes. There is a growth spurt, a change in mental maturity and the onset of puberty. Thus, quality-wise, adolescence is the time of very rapid and very major changes. Most young adolescents are still grappling with the changes taking place within and without when they finally leave high school and embark on college life.

Physical and Sexual Growth:

Girls have an earlier *growth spurt* as compared to boys – they start their linear growth by 9-10 years of age, and begin to menstruate by 12. Boys begin their growth spurt by 12, and as they have no obvious "start" or "end" point, we cannot demarcate the onset of "puberty" in them as effectively. Besides growing in height, adolescents put on almost 15-20 kg weight in their years of rapid growth. While boys gain 6-7 kg/yr, girls put on 4-5 kg/yr during these crucial years.

Sexual development occurs along with growth. In girls, breast enlargement begins first, and about six to eight months after the breasts begin to enlarge, menarche occurs. During the first few years after the onset of menstruation, periods are scanty or profuse, irregular and sometimes accompanied by pain of varying severity. As the girl becomes a woman, her sexual development continues to advance. By the age of 14-15, her sexual development is usually complete. In boys, the development of facial hair, chest hair and body hair accompanies the change in voice and darkening and enlargement of the external genitalia (penis and scrotum). The boy struts around with a rudimentary beard and a thin moustache. Along with this, muscular development is also seen, and boys develop stronger and more well-defined muscles. The changes begin by 12 years of age, and are usually complete by 16-17 years of age.

Along with the growth of the body, there comes a growing interest in physical activities and sport. Boys and girls alike begin to participate in races, tug-of-war games, throwing games like javelin, discus and shot-putt, outdoor team sports like basketball, volleyball and cricket, and so on. Boys "show-off" their muscles while girls walk with an exaggerated swaying of the hips and thrust their chests forward in an attempt to "enhance" their busts. These behaviours are all a part of the golden age of adolescence, where childhood innocence is being slowly overcome by adult cunning and craftiness.

Psychological and Emotional Changes:

Don't throw away your friendship with your teenager over behavior that has no great moral significance. There will be plenty of real issues that require you to stand like a rock. Save your big guns for those crucial confrontations. - Dr. James C. Dobson, American Psychiatrist and Author

The adolescent boy or girl wants, at the same time, the independence of an adult and the dependence of a child. While he/she wants to stay out late, for example, to attend a *dandiya* program, he/she wants to be able to come home to a warm, supportive family, who can guide him/her to take his/her dinner and go to sleep in a ready bed.

The first challenge they face is the unfamiliar changes that begin to take place in their bodies. While they do not mind the height and weight gain, they are alarmed at the growth of axillary and pubic hair; they do not understand why their bodies stink so much (actually, this new smell is due to the secretion of a sweat that is chemically different from the usual body-sweat; this new sweat is formed by the special "apocrine" glands located in the armpits). Secondly, boys are thrilled and annoyed when their first facial hair makes an appearance. Initially, they are happy because the appearance of the hair is an announcement to the world that the boy is finally beginning to turn into an adult.

Adolescents are much aware of their sex and begin thinking about their future role in society; they start worrying about what they plan to pursue to fulfill their aims and social, moral and financial obligations to society. They will take risks and try and do something better than anyone else they know/ anyone else in the entire neighbourhood/ anyone else in the whole town/any other human being – because they know that this will enhance their self-esteem and image in society.

At all these steps, parents are required to give moral support as well as help their children financially or socially so that they can really do what they have set their minds on doing. They should provide them the wherewithal to pursue their ambition and interests. If your son or daughter is more gifted with words and numbers, why, encourage him/her to be an academician or a scholar; but if she is better with his/her hands and adept at mechanical tasks then do not suppress his/her desire to excel in that field. This will make him/her emotionally happier and more self-confident.

During adolescence, children often take to drugs, alcohol, smoking and other addictions, and are also experimenting with their sexual prowess, so they are vulnerable to many illnesses and may even resort to violence or suicide during one of these "misadventures". This is mainly because the adolescent wants to be "accepted" in a group of "dare-devils" in every possible way, so what if he/she has to hurt himself/herself/others in the process. Peer pressure must be countered not with parental pressure; you must not attempt to "talk down" to the child, but rather try and communicate with him/her as a friend, or as an equal. Teach him/her to say "NO" to those things that he/she finds repugnant, incompatible with his/her values or inaccessible. Remember that proper communication includes the ability and the willingness not just to talk, but also to listen to the child. Often, a distressed teen wants his/her parent to lend him/her a patient ear: say that he (the boy) feels ignored by the girl of his dreams; he is utterly "devastated" by her "rejection"; he has tried all the tricks he knows to catch her attention but they haven't worked; now, after all this, his eyes are "far away", he does not eat at dinner, he stops listening to his favourite music, etc. He won't tell you that he is "inadequate". *You* should be able to detect this by your observation skills, then confront him in privacy and ask him to tell you what is bothering him. Even then he may not tell you his innermost thoughts the first time. You should remain patient and caring and persist in your endeavour. Then one fine day (or not so fine day, depending on his point of view), he will tell you everything and put his head on your shoulder and cry. Let him. This experience will bring him closer to you (and vice versa). You may "discuss" the "affair" with him and perhaps make some constructive suggestions as well. However, you should remind him that all actions he takes are his and his responsibility alone; and that, whatever happens, he should remember that the world is not coming to an end if that girl does not reciprocate; this must be said with sensitivity though, or else the bridges between you can even get burnt at one go!

Teenagers *love* privacy and all its trappings. On no condition are you to invade her privacy: this means, you should ask for permission before entering her room; you should *never, ever take out her diary and read it;* you should never search her drawers or room, even if it is for *your* things, and you must never ask her friends about her in secrecy (such as *Did she go for her classes or not last Tuesday?* or *Does she have any boy-friends or what?*)

Confusion about the physical changes which are occurring in their bodies drives adolescents to worry about even slight blemishes that occur on their faces and acne (pimples) are one of them. They run from pillar to post to find remedies for their problem, and it is up to you, the parent, to provide them with reassurance (of the pimples being a "normal" thing at her age), confidence (you look as pretty as ever, my dear) and guidance (don't burst those with your nails, or eat less oily food). At the same time, your child may start feeling a bit "lonely" because she can neither play with younger children nor participate in "adult" things such as home discussions etc. She may then "stick" to her own girl-friends, or find someone from the opposite sex to talk and be intimate to. His looks may attract her so much that an infatuation with him may be the result of this; she may mistake it for "love at first sight", and get carried away by the reciprocation that the boy gives. This is, at once, a very lovely feeling and a dangerous one too! The teen often does not understand that her hormones are causing these feelings inside her and will often end up by offering more than just friendship to the boy of her dreams. Thus, sexual experimentation results, with necking, kissing, and hugging. The girl's mother should anticipate that her daughter *will, at one time or another, involve herself with some boy or the other, and must therefore teach her child about how she must protect herself from a sexual misadventure.*

The Adolescent's Lifestyle:

An adolescent, particularly one who has finished high school and entered college, lives a lifestyle that is completely different from her earlier life (and later life as an adult). On the one hand, there is the urge to do well in the academic sphere, and the life of a student of Std. XII is an endless round of studies, college, extra classes and tuition classes and reading of guides, solved papers etc. She is often found delving into books at late nights or early in the mornings. All recreational activities come to an end, and the student is so lost in studies that there is no time for fun, games or any form of relaxation. It is rare to see her at any family function or celebration because "she is busy studying" or "she has classes". On the other hand, there is the innate urge to do things that are "unsanctioned" by parents, teachers and other pillars of civilization. So, you will find the teen participating in endurance competitions, going to "college socials", going out for "dandiya" late into the night, taking part in all types of music and dance festivals and in general, going all out to enjoy herself. Striking a balance between these two urges is not only difficult, but well nigh impossible for some youngsters. If they pay too much attention to the cultural scene, they will not be able to do well in studies; if they keep studying all the time, why, they will miss out on the greatest years of personal freedom.

As a parent, it is your duty to rein in their innate urges and to help them balance the dose of academics and extra-curricular activities for them. They will thank you for it later.

Ordering their lives:

How teenagers resent any interference by parents is a fact too well-known to merit repetition here. Yet, it is essential for parents to understand that in her innermost thoughts, a teenager feels bewildered and helpless by the so many new things going on within her body, within her mind and around her in the social milieu she is living in. Therefore, she *wants*, maybe in her subconscious mind, for you to actually set her "house" in order for her. Fixed routines may sound like poison to her, but she will try and conform to reasonable routines so that she remains your pet and can continue to "draw" on your goodwill. If, for example, a subtle connection is made between a rule that requires her to return from her "party" by, say, 11 p.m. and the fact that you will lend her the fees for the extra class only if she asks for it at night, she will, in all likelihood, return within the deadline set by you.

She must tell you where she is going, who her other friends will be, and what number she may be reached on if you need her and so on; at the same time, she would be *required* to call you up in case she is likely to get delayed. Similarly, you should tell her how she can contact *you* in case of an emergency when you are out with your wife/friends.

You should be a good role model too. For example, if you were to go out with your spouse, and return by 11 p.m., you would have given a very important lesson to your child, namely, that you have made a rule not just for her, but also for your own self.

Children in the adolescent age group need to be given simple rules for eating, for maintaining respect and decorum in the house when you are entertaining your guests or relatives, for showing the proper regard for elders and youngsters alike, for helping in household chores, for wearing acceptable dresses and so on. Such rules should not be "handed down" but must be "discussed" freely with them, so that they feel as if their opinion is also important. At the same time, when she makes an unacceptable request, it is well within your rights to reject it outright (for example, she wants to go out with a boy who you do not approve of).

Learn to communicate with your teenage child:

This is the sum and substance of what I have been telling you in the last few pages. Be her friend. Respond to her as you would respond to an adult. Do not nag or demean her by repeatedly criticising her.

Let her contribute actively to the running of the house by offering her to join you, the parents, in formulating rules, in deciding where to place the new sofa, in suggesting the colour for the new window curtains, in deciding the menu for the grand dinner you will be hosting the next week, in helping you out with the monthly budget, in thanking her for so kindly going to the post office/grocer/chemist to get whatever you needed and in general, in keeping a healthy respect for her moods, opinions and demands.

Non-verbal communication is also important, and it would be futile for you to expect her to vocalise all her thoughts to you. If you find her distraught, try and be sympathetic and responsive to her by sitting with her and gently prodding her to tell you about what is troubling her. Remember, empathy is a solvent that can dissolve any resentment or disappointment your child may be having inside her. Learn to communicate by holding her hand, by wiping her tear, by sitting silently with her while she cries, and by commiserating with her when she needs your support. Listen to her rant and rave. Enjoy her kind of music. Join in her kind of games. Eat her choice of food the next time you dine out as a family. All this and more will make you her pet and she, your pet too. And you will never have trouble with your teen.

Health Concerns:

We've already discussed some of the special health concerns of adolescents. It is time now to discuss the rest of them. As we have seen earlier, adolescents are prone to pimples (acne), bad body odour and problems related to sexual development.

Acne is a result of hormonal changes that take place in the body. It can be simple or complicated with development of pus-filled follicles. The pimples may heal without or with some scarring. The itching induced by a pimple can cause the affected child to scratch and burst it, thereby causing new pimples to appear on the body in surrounding skin.

What to do: Acne is a normal skin problem of teens and one should, as a parent, be supportive of the child. Explain to her the harmlessness of these blemishes, and also guide her about the do's and don'ts of managing pimples. Encourage her to eat more greens, less oily foods, exercise regularly, take a bath with gentle soaps and wash her face frequently with plain water; at the same time, discourage her from breaking the pimples, from applying too many cosmetics and from trying out the myriad creams and lotions available in the market for the "treatment" of pimples.

A bad body odour should be easily masked with the use of deodorants. Hair-related problems in teenagers are no different from these problems in any age group; only, teens are aggressively worried about dry hair, dandruff, lice and so on. Teens must be taught to take care of their own hair and to never use any treatments without consulting a qualified hair expert or a skin doctor first. Dysmenorrhoea refers to the spasmodic, colicky lower abdominal pain that accompanies menstruation in a teenaged girl during the first few years after the cycles have started. This can be normal. However, relief should be provided with the intake of medicines that reduce spasm in the uterus. Poor genital hygiene and staining of underwear could also occur because of inexperience with menstruation and use of inappropriate sanitary napkins. Both these problems should be anticipated and corrected. Pain in the region of the nipple presages the development of breast tissue in both boys and girls, and often presents to the doctor as "chest pain". You should explain to the child that this pain is completely normal and needs no treatment except for a hot fomentation, and perhaps, Paracetamol. During menstruation, use of internal "tampons" should be strictly avoided, as a forgotten tampon may get infected with a life threatening germ called the staphylococcus.

One important thing to remember is that in their attempt to demonstrate their physical or mental prowess, especially to their peers or to members of the opposite sex, adolescents often injure themselves, sometimes seriously. Vehicular accidents and speeding injuries are quite common.

Adolescents have sexual misadventures of all kinds. They can either control their urge or go all the way if sufficiently misled by a more experienced partner. Infections can get transmitted, including the dreaded sexually transmitted diseases (S.T.D.) like gonorrhoea, syphilis or AIDS, hepatitis B, or ascending pelvic infection leading to Pelvic Inflammatory Disease (PID). Apart from all these infections, an unwanted pregnancy may result. **Teens should be told about protected sex, condoms, and other such things beforehand, so that they will not land up with any such complications.**

Sexual Abuse: This is a real risk, mainly for girls but occasionally also for boys. The common offenders are adult relatives of the child, elder school mates or hostel mates and occasionally, visitors to the household or complete strangers. You should never leave your child alone with someone whom you do not trust completely. You should teach your child to stay away and be wary of someone who, on the pretext of an innocent friendship, tries to physically hug or cuddle her to touch her intimately.

General disorders include Tension headaches before and during examinations and tests (for which painkillers and counselling are both required), disorders of the Thyroid gland (both hypo- and hyperthyroidism can occur in this age group), disorders of the cardiovascular system (particularly, the onset of hypertension or high blood pressure, and the occurrence of heart problems like a Mitral Valve Prolapse) are all seen in adolescence.

Trial of prohibited substances is very commonly seen in adolescence. It may be a symptom of a mental disturbance, or merely an attempt by the child to "mingle" with the more daring friends in his/her social circle. The child may try out a cigarette, or drink alcohol or even smoke a "joint". Children also try out all kinds of substances like "pot" (marijuana), "crack" (cocaine). The trials may instigate the child to try more and more substances and even experiment with mixtures of substances. A child who is addicted to drugs will show many symptoms of this at home, and it is up to the intelligent parent to pick up the clues.

Common symptoms of <u>substance abuse and addiction</u> include a recent change in the friends with whom the child associates, a recent deterioration in academic performance, poor eating and sleeping at home, a lethargic appearance, with ungroomed hair and unironed clothes, bloodshot eyes and pinpoint pupils, preference to go away from home often, preference to "be alone" and not participate in domestic activities like parties and picnics, a daily after-dinner "walk" that the child wants to take, occurrence of a "cold" and a "running nose" most of the time, darkening of lips, late night staying up and late morning sleeping, and mood changes like irritability, depression and easy excitability.

<u>Psychological illnesses</u> are also seen in this age group as in all other age groups. Adolescents are very prone to *depression*, and may even try to commit *suicide* when they feel down and out. This need not mean earth-shaking events; rather, teens have a "different" sense of proportion about events that may seem churlish or childish to you! She will, for example, be in a total state of panic if she cannot find the right bracelet to go with the new dress, but be unaffected by the rather gross event of, say, the death of your best friend. This means that you have to deal with the child/teen much more sensitively than you would deal with a younger or older child. Teens are also prone to *schizophrenia* (a major psychotic disorder), obsessive-compulsive disorders (*OCD*) and *anorexia nervosa* (AN). In AN, the teen starts believing that she is growing fat; she then starts refusing meals and becomes obsessed with her weight and appearance. She will often put her fingers inside the back of her throat and vomit out a meal that she ate just a half-hour ago (known as *bulimia*). In this manner, she keeps her weight in control, but quickly begins to lose weight till only "her bones are showing". However, the severe nutritional deficiencies alter the thinking processes and the working of the child's brain so that the child is unable to take rational decisions. It is a condition that needs major psychiatric therapy.

Lastly, a word about <u>nutritional problems</u>. Because adolescents are fast growing, and also finicky eaters, they are prone to develop nutritional deficiencies from time to time. Girls who menstruate regularly also develop iron deficiency and so they should receive extra *iron and folic acid tablets* on a regular basis.

Vaccinations: Adolescents too need certain vaccines. At 10, they would have been immunised against the Tetanus vaccine. Thereafter, a tetanus toxoid injection should be given every five to ten years to ensure life-long protection against tetanus. All girls must receive the MMR vaccine, or more correctly, the Rubella vaccine (if available) at 12 years of age, as if an unprotected girl/woman becomes pregnant and gets Rubella (German Measles) during the pregnancy, her unborn baby may be born with multiple congenital malformations. Lastly, unvaccinated children who have never had natural infections should also receive Hepatitis A vaccine and Chicken pox vaccine at this age. Remember that in case of the chicken pox vaccine, a child *above* the age of 12 years needs 2 doses of the vaccine, 4 weeks apart.

Ch 20
Family Life and Sex Education

Parents are often so busy with the physical rearing of children that they miss the glory of parenthood, just as the grandeur of the trees is lost when raking leaves.

- Marcelene Cox

Whenever someone talks of sex, one thinks of it as a four-letter word, because of the cultural influences that are steeped in tradition in our country. However, in olden times, sex was not taboo; in fact, it was celebrated back then. Rishi Vatsayana's treatise on sex, the *Kamasutra,* is even now considered to be an authoritative tome on sexual matters.

Sex is not all about the physical attraction or the act of making love; it is an appreciation of the finer qualities of life with someone who is, once you have met him/her, a part of your own self. This is the message that you have to get across to your growing child when she confronts you with uncomfortable questions concerning sexual matters.

Children imbibe knowledge about sexual matters right from childhood; they do this by observing their parents and other adult relatives; in addition, the exploding cable television and internet have brought sex right into our homes, and books and newspapers also do not shy from displaying half-clad models on their pages. With all this information available to the children, is it surprising that today's adolescent is far more knowledgeable about sex than we were a generation ago? However, the one-sided information that is seen by them may make them think that sex is all about genital organs, the act of making love and making babies and about the physical aspects alone. This assessment would definitely be wrong, because a caring and warm upbringing, coupled with the love and concern that you, the parents, show towards each other, can make their knowledge of sex a better-rounded one.

Early childhood and sex education:

By three, a normal child would know the differences between her and the opposite sex. She would then approach you with innocent queries like "where did I come from?" or, "why has Mrs. Shanbaug's tummy bloated up?" or, "what were you and Daddy doing the other night when I woke up to use the toilet?" Such questions may sound embarrassing or even irritating, and you may be tempted to shut her up and not ask them. Please do NOT do so. It is better that you reply to her with simple answers like, "You came from my stomach" or, "She is carrying a baby inside her tummy" or, "We were cuddling each other, darling". Never ever tell lies or explain sexual matters with an elaborate fairy tale like "A stork brought you" etc. Even when she asks you to tell her how the baby came to be *inside* your tummy, tell her only that she grew out of a *seed*, just like a plant grows in a pot.

Later childhood and sex education:

By seven or eight years of age, the natural curiosity for knowing about sex has got sharpened and children are keen to know why men and women do what they do. They want to know how babies are made (is it the *kiss*? is it the *hug*? is it the *marriage*?). A simple explanation of a man's *sperm* uniting with a woman's *egg* may be enough for now. In addition, one must make an effort to expand on the spiritual aspect of love and sex, and teach the child to learn to follow the path of love with her life partner, or with her friends, or with humanity in general. Teach her also about caring for her life partner. Explain to her about why marriages take place, and why one should respect loyalty and fidelity for one's life partner. Show her why married people should not have more than 1-2 children, and introduce her into family life by seeking her help in looking after her younger brother/sister.

Adolescence and Sex Education:

At twelve, your child probably already knows that physical *external* contact alone is not enough to make a woman pregnant, and since he/she has already stepped into puberty, he may have already experienced erections and even ejaculations, while she is menstruating and knows the warm feeling she gets when she gazes at her favourite hero in school or in a movie. At this stage, therefore, nothing short of the complete unvarnished truth will do. No embellishments and no lies will work. Do teach him/her not only about *how* a baby can be conceived, but also *what pregnancy is* and *how to have protected sex.* If your child develops night-time emissions or you catch him masturbating, do not whip him or spurn him; do not even think of ridiculing him in front of others. The best thing is to handle the matter factually and privately. Emissions in dreams can be normal, as is masturbation. Advise him to do such things in proper privacy.

Hygiene of the sexual organs:

Boys who are circumcised have no foreskin. In uncircumcised boys, the foreskin should be pulled back to wash away the cheesy yellow *smegma* everyday. In girls, the urethral, vaginal and anal openings are located close to each other, and they should be asked to keep all the three orifices clean; in fact, they should already know that they must wash from front to back so that the intestinal bad germs are not brought forward to contaminate the genital and urinary tracts. Once they begin menstruating, they should be shown how to keep their private parts clean, how to wear pads and told that they should keep the parts clean and dry, and change the sanitary napkins frequently.

Even otherwise, children must change their underwear after every bath, and use powder to keep the genital and buttock areas clean and dry.

Conceiving and carrying a child from error or from abuse:

Of course, pre-marital sex, rape and all forms of sexual crimes are on the rise, and one would be like an ostrich burying its head in sand if one did not accept this hard but unpalatable fact of life! Hence, parents must teach their child to stay away from strangers, friends who are doing wrong things, friends who smoke or take alcohol and friends who are too steeped in the "pub and disco" culture; they should also be told that they should stay within pre-designated limits when they interact publicly or privately with members of the opposite sex.

The truth is, however, that any menstruating, adolescent girl can become pregnant if she indulges in sexual intercourse, willingly or otherwise, between the 10th to 20th days of her menstrual cycle. This is the *ovulation period* and a baby may be conceived if she has unprotected sex. To detect when ovulation occurs, one of the simplest methods is to closely follow the morning body temperature from the first day of a menstrual period; after about 10-15 days, there is a noticeable slight rise in the temperature, which continues up until the next menstrual cycle. A missed menstrual period in a girl/woman who had regular menstrual periods for at least a year or two before is a sure symptom of pregnancy. This can be confirmed by a simple instant urine pregnancy test (UPT) within 3-4 days of the date of the missed period.

Parents must accept it if their unmarried daughter is pregnant and take remedial steps immediately. If she is too young and unlikely to be capable of carrying the child, abortion is an acceptable option. If she is past eighteen (the legally acceptable age for marriage) and the purported father is willing to accept her, an early marriage is the best option. Carrying a pregnancy alone without the biological father's or family's support is a very difficult option to consider, but it is ultimately the mother's choice and parental support should be given if she intends to give birth to the child. You should take your daughter for psychological counselling also. Lastly, legal and criminal proceedings should be initiated in case of abuse or rape.

Contraception:

The best way to avoid a pregnancy is to abstain from a sexual intercourse. Even an incomplete penetration and removal of the penis *before* ejaculation (coitus interruptus) **can** cause a pregnancy. The best results are seen with a combined use of condom by the male and the oral contraceptive pill by the female. If adolescents are taught about contraceptives, they can make an informed choice about whether they wish to indulge in a sexual intercourse; besides this, they can have protected sex (with prevention of STD's like AIDS) and also prevent conception and pregnancy.

There are many methods of preventing a conception; some are physical, some chemical, and some biological too.

1. Rhythm method: This is based on timing ovulation. Having an intercourse during the ovulation period is likely to cause pregnancy (risky) while having it just before the next menstrual cycle or just after the previous one is safe.

2. Coitus interruptus (premature withdrawal): See above. In addition, this is a difficult thing to practice at the height of a sexual orgasm.

3. Condom: This device, made from latex rubber, is worn over the erect penis by the male just before he begins penetration. By far the most used, a condom is simple, cheap and very effective. Variations on a simple condom are now available that do not reduce the pleasure and yet provide safe protection.

4. Spermicidal jelly/cream: This is applied into the vagina by the female. It is a chemical that kills the sperms. Used with a condom, it can enhance protection considerably. Used alone, it is not too effective.

5. Diaphragm/Cervical cap: These are capping devices that should have been pre-inserted less than six hours before the sexual act; they should not be removed for at least eight hours after sex. They are best used in conjunction with a condom or/and a spermicidal cream or jelly.

6. OC Pills: These are hormonal pills that prevent ovulation and regulate a woman's menstrual cycles. They are effective only if taken *everyday*. However, these pills cannot provide any barrier to STD's and must be used with a condom for safe and effective contraception. Low dose pills are reasonably free from side effects.

7. Intra-uterine Device (IUD): A T-shaped device made from copper is inserted into the uterus through the vagina in a woman who has had an active sexual life earlier. It is not appropriate for a teenaged girl who is going to initiate her sex life.

8. Injections of hormones: Injections that work for 90 days and even five years are available.

9. Post-coital pill: This is a high dose hormonal preparation that can be used by the girl in case she is not too sure of the method she used during the act and in cases of abuse or rape. The pills should be swallowed (2 initially and 2 after 12 hours) as soon as possible after the act.

Here are some useful links:

- ✔ http://science.howstuffworks.com/human reproduction.htm (reproduction)
- ✔ http://www.plannedparenthood.org/bc/ (contraception)
- ✔ http://www.noah-health.org/english/sexuality/sexuality.html (sexuality and sex education)

Part VII

Modern Age of Convenience – Challenges for Parents

. . . in all our efforts to provide "advantages"
we have actually produced the busiest, most competitive,
highly pressured and over-organized generation
of youngsters in our history and possibly the unhappiest.

– Eda LeShan, US writer,
The Conspiracy Against Childhood

Ch 21
Traditional Means of Recreation

Ye daulat bhi le lo, ye shohrat bhi le lo,
Bhale cheen lo mujhse meri jawaani,
Magar mujhko lautaa doe bachpan ka saawan,
Wo kaagaz ki kashti, wo baarish ka paani,
Wo kaagaz ki kashti, wo baarish ka paani.

- Hindi ghazal

Most readers of this book will agree with me when I reminisce about the beautiful days of our childhood. In the days gone by, we had a much simpler childhood, with simpler lifestyles, fewer Do's and Don'ts and we thoroughly enjoyed ourselves. That is not to say that children of today do not enjoy themselves. Far from it for me to suggest that we should return our children to older times! And yet, I can assure you that what we now label as "traditional" is, in fact, a very desirable method of providing recreation to today's children, and you will soon see why.

The benefits of traditional means of recreation:

In the traditional system, there are no high-tech devices to play with. Thus, hand-held video games, computers, palm-tops, tablet-PC's, mobile phone games, television sets, cable TV, portable CD players, Walkman, VCD players, etc. are all *out!*

The child plays with her other friends, using traditional toys, such as those made from wood, metal, strings, bells and so on. Often, toys are *fabricated* by parents to meet some specific requirement of play. Sometimes, children will themselves play with material to fashion toys for themselves. There is magic in making one's own toy and then playing with friends with that toy. Believe-me, I know, for I've "been there, done that". Toys provide not just amusement; by making the toy, one is introduced to rudimentary skills of engineering; one learns the properties of the material one is working with – so that you know that, for example, if I try to bend plastic in *this* direction, it will break, or if I chisel any more chalk in *that* way, it will cut through. By delicately crafting small toys, one improves hand-hand co-ordination, hand-eye co-ordination, fine motor movements and also skills of abstract thinking, spatial orientation and logical thinking.

Amazing, isn't it? But that's not all. A child who has crafted her own toy is filled with a sense of accomplishment and joy that has to be seen to be believed. Undoubtedly, the toy will have defects; it may not be a patch on the sleek, factory-made toys of today, but because the child has made it herself out of the limited resources of material and tools available to her, it is "perfect" for her. When she meets her friends and *shows off* her creation, one can imagine how confident and important she is going to feel! She is declaring her capabilities and at the same time, challenging her friends to match her skills. At the same time, she feels self-important because her friends are going to play *collectively* with a toy that she has fabricated.

Sometimes, some traditional toys are large, or are complicated enough to need the help of other friends or parents as well. For example, imagine designing a doll-house: it will need wooden planks, nails and hammer, perhaps some other tools of carpentry, chemical adhesives, paint, varnish, polishing tools, small items of toy furniture, sticking of fixtures like toy fans, tube-lights and mixers and stoves, arranging of tiny bits of crockery and utensils in the kitchen, making small dolls representing "father", "mother" and "children" and finally, creating space within the house to "lodge" the doll house so that your child as well as other friends of hers can play with this toy for days on end. Such a mammoth task will need supervision from a parent, procurement of several items from the market, planning of the construction of the house, floor plans for each floor of the house, teach the child basic carpentry skills so that the house is sturdy and at the same time aesthetically appealing and lastly, it will mean financing the purchases from the parent's till.

The child who grows up with such toys and such methods of play will no doubt be a much more developed and accomplished person as compared to the one who sits and plays with ready-made, battery-driven gizmos.

Outdoor activities:

With the advent of the modern age, children are maturing faster, or so it would seem, as we look at 9-year old boys writing poetry or 12-year old girls becoming mothers! At the same time, however, they are losing out on the pleasures of childhood. While they become "scholars" at school, they are big zeroes in the school of life: they are book-worms or so studious that their idea of a great school holiday means chatting with their next-door neighbour *through an internet relay chat*! Is it any surprise that today's children just do not get enough of the sun and the great experience of the outdoors? Let me, the author, ask you when was the last time you took your child outdoors not for a dinner, a wedding reception or a movie, but simply outdoors for some clean fun?

Taking one's child outdoors to Nature's lap is one of the most pleasurable activities for a child. It unleashes joy and a sense of freedom that not even your absence from the house can. Let the child have 1-2 hours of outdoor activity *every day*. This means letting her play games like catching, *langdi*, *kho-kho, nigochia* and other group games. In addition to this unstructured, unsupervised activity, also try and take the child to some open space at least once, or preferably, more times each week. This may be a garden, a beach, a stadium (to watch or participate in sports) or just about any open ground where the child can run around without any inhibition.

Once in two or three months, the child should be taken out of town on a small 2 or 3 day trip, while once in a year, your family should take a longer vacation to some place farther, such as a hill station, a cultural festival, a wild-life sanctuary, a trek or an adventure holiday. You can make the plans in accordance with your budget – there is no gainsaying that – but you must try to take at least one long holiday each year.

The table below lists the traditional toys and activities discussed so far in this chapter. As is obvious, the list is only indicative and not complete. It is dependent on your imagination, and that of your child, to devise newer and newer activities to spend those long, boring days of vacation together with fun and pleasure.

Table: Traditional Means of Recreation

Toys	Activities
Wood-carved toys	Playing in building premises
Rattles, wooden blocks and squeeze toys	Going to beach or garden on weekends
Push and pull string toys	Hikes and treks
Play house/doll house	Adventure holidays
Comic books, story books etc.	Long trips to hill-stations
Musical instruments and drums	Religious excursions
Cardboard containers of all sizes	Cultural holidays or heritage outings
Stuffed toys	Tent holidays and camps
Picture books	Visit to sanctuaries, parks or reserves
Art and craft set with project work	Treasure hunts and other outdoor sports
Bicycles and Toy-scooters	Sports-related activities

Here are a few lines that I have penned about the importance of traditional and natural ways of recreation. The words are spoken by the child.

CHILD'S LAMENT

My parents, please do listen, to words of mine today:
I weep not for the things you do, but for the things you don't.

You give me such nice toys, you give me clothes so cute,
You go and buy all these things with such a lot of money.

You bring me food so lovely, I can hardly eat that much;
You take me so many places, all the world is now my home.

How can I then tell you, what I really crave for?
Are all these things enough for my pretty little soul?

You bring me not the sun, you fetch me not the smile,
You give me not the caring, for you have so little time.

You never sit and hug me, you don't read or sing to me,
You hardly ever talk to me or tell me any good tales.

You do not teach me values, nor ever tell me morals,
You do not "buy" me time for us to spend together.

You have so much work and I have so many needs,
Money can come tomorrow, but my past never will.

Get me no more toys or gizmos – I am sick of them already,
Just bring me your magic love and make me feel wanted.

I am your little rose-bud – unopened – as yet,
Help me bloom to glory – or else I won't be complete.

I need the "sprinkle" of your care, and the "nurture" of your love,
So that one day you will look with wonder at me.

Make my dream come true, O Almighty up there,
Make ma and pa realise that I want their hugs and kisses.

Ch 22
Modern Gadgets and Gizmos

Recommend to your children virtue;
that alone can make them happy, not gold.

- Ludwig van Beethoven,
German Romantic composer (1770 - 1827)

In the previous chapter, we have touched upon the fetish for today's children to run after gadgets and electronic gizmos. In this chapter, we will discuss this further, and I shall try and provide pointers about how to go about disciplining them vis-à-vis these devices. You, dear reader, may choose to either agree or disagree with my point of view. I appreciate that both the viewpoints may have merit.

Radio:

There was a time when radio was the only device available to us. Today, it is considered "infra-dig" by the gizmo-guzzling children. Yet, I have observed that the radio is still universally liked by all classes of society. Recently, radio has undergone a revolutionary revival, thanks to the launch of FM channels in major metropolitan cities in India. These channels are extremely popular with the youth of the country. They have the potential to transmit key educational messages with entertainment, and some beginning has been made with creation of awareness on AIDS and its prevention with condoms. However, by and large, these channels continue to be popular and threaten to divert the youth away from the traditional culture to the broad Western culture.

Radio continues to be available through the Internet and through Blue-tooth technology on mobiles, PDA's, palm tops and the like. Advances in electronic devices have enabled people to access radio from anywhere and anyplace. Radio receivers are so small that they can fit inside the ear of the recipient. With all this portability, there have been increased incidences of accidents while driving, especially when the user drives a two-wheeler and is listening to radio with earphones. There is a law against this, but it is seldom enforced. Hence, parents must absolutely prohibit the child from using earphones while driving two-wheelers. This will apply not only to radio, but to all portable music systems such as cassette players and ACD/MP 3 players.

On the radio, there are several informative channels too, and if parents wish, they can screen these channels and choose those that impart more material that is educational.

Television:

If there is one device that has changed the paradigm of home-based entertainment, it is the boob-tube or the television set. From its early days to the present, it has transformed the way people spend their evenings, the things they eat, the way they exercise, the way they look and the illnesses they succumb to. No wonder, people addicted to the TV are called "*coach potatoes*" and the TV set referred to as the "*idiot box*".

Benefits: As the TV is an audio-visual medium, it is very attractive to children. I have personally seen how children run to grab the remote as soon as they arrive home from school. The habit is certainly addictive, what with the rise of cable-TV and the Direct-to-home (DTH) services.

There are many educational TV channels that entertain while educating. To name a few, they include National Geographic, Discovery, History Channel, Animal Planet, etc. If the child is exposed everyday to selected programmes on one or more of these channels, she can learn a lot about the world while staying in her own home. At the same time, watching TV can help her to relax and unwind.

Risks: There is a real risk of spoiling children's way of thinking by exposing them to bloodshed and violence that is shown on the TV nowadays. The so-called family soaps (serials) also preach wrong, unacceptable moral values and make a sham of age-old traditions and controls that are steeped in our culture. Infidelity, premarital sex, polygamy, etc. are all shown as if they are the "norm". Other risks include sleep disturbances because of late night viewing, digestive disturbances caused by eating junk food while viewing nail-biting shows, deteriorating school performance due to addictive watching of TV, warped view of the world as a result of watching fantasy shows and fictional programmes, advertising-induced "brain wash", and a cultural wash-down – that is, child goes away from the conservative culture of India and towards the permissive culture of the West. Obesity is also a real risk; that is why T.V. addicts are called "*couch potatoes*".

By the way, I wish to clarify that watching TV cannot spoil a child's vision in the way you think. It may, however, increase the strain on the muscles that move the eyeball and that help shrink and expand the lens and the pupil – a task we call accommodation – and thereby cause eye fatigue and general tiredness.

In rare cases, the flicker of the TV signal may precipitate a fit in a child who is vulnerable to this problem (light-triggered epilepsy).

Precautions: The child's TV time should not exceed 1-2 hours daily. She should be made to watch from a safe distance (approximately from 15-20 ft. away from a 21" screen). If she has glasses, she should wear them while watching TV. A child-lock should be applied on the channels which beam material that is unsuitable for viewing by children. This facility is available in selected models of TV sets and you should buy a model that has this facility in it. There should be "switch-off" timings that are strictly applied, regardless of which program is being aired. Generally, this switch-off is done between 10 and 11 p.m. on weekdays, and at about 11 p.m. on weekends in large cities, though earlier sleep schedules in some households may not allow such timings. You should choose a time that is right for your house, and then apply it regularly. During TV viewing, as a parent, you should prevent junk food consumption. Also, after you have all watched a program, please sit with your children and discuss the story and its merits and demerits with them. This helps them to get the corrected view of the world. It is good to keep reminding them that they are watching a *make-believe world* so that they do not take the events unfolding on the screen too personally. During "breaks", the sound should be muted or the set switched off. This will prevent the bad effect that advertisements of all kinds have on our child (-ren).

Mobile Phones:

At the time of writing this, I have just read that cell phone subscribers now exceed land-line users in Mumbai city by a whopping 10 million! Since mobile phones invaded our lives, they have been a boon and a curse to our children (and to us as well).

Benefits: Of course, the major important benefit of mobiles is easy connectivity and quick decision-making in difficult situations. With the mobile, it is now possible for the family to keep in touch with each other, for parents to be contacted by children and vice-versa in an emergency and vice versa and for official as well as recreational purposes. Now, one need not wait for a busy land-line to clear before contacting someone when time is running out.

In addition to this basic functionality, mobiles today offer so many other features such as reminder service, telephone book, calendar, calculator, timer, stop-watch, games, Short Messaging Services (SMS), photography and internet connectivity, etc. All these in a small portable device makes a mobile phone a very desirable gizmo, and children naturally want to have it too.

Risks: The use of mobile phones while driving is a very common cause of road-side accidents. The jury is still out regarding possible damage to the brain and higher risk of brain tumors with the use of mobile phones. Mobile phone usage can impinge on study time, and addiction to the internet or to SMS can inflate phone bills. Children who have a basic mobile phone may crave for high-end phones with camera, colour screen and WAP enabled services. This, too, can create similar problems in teens. It can drive teenagers to steal money from the cup-board, steal mobiles and make unreasonable demands on the parents for money. Using a mobile at a petrol pump may trigger off an explosion.

Suggestions: To avoid the above headaches, insist that your children cannot have mobile phones till they start college. Teach your older children who have mobiles not to hold the mobiles close to the ear or speak for long durations. Ask that they have a hands-free kit (either with or without wires). Tell them not to use the phones while driving or while filling petrol at petrol pumps. Above all, discourage the use of mobiles while in the house or in places where a land line is available.

Portable audio devices:

These include cassette players, CD players and the like; they are used to access music while outdoors. Children are familiar with "Walkman" even before they cross their 5th birthday. By the time they are eight or ten, they have tried to handle portable disc players too.

Benefits: Apart from the pleasure and convenience of listening to music that **you** like, portable audio players do not offer any specific benefits.

Risks: As with mobile phones, use of portable audio systems is not permitted while driving as its use in such a manner can cause the driver to lose control of his vehicle and crash or injure others. The other major risk is that when you hear loud music at loud amplitudes on portable systems with head-phones, you damage delicate nerves and the hearing organ inside the ears. This damage can be permanent and can lead to loss of hearing.

Suggestions: Ask the child to listen to portable devices when you need silence in the house, but insist that they hear at soft volumes, that they hear good music with them and that they do not keep them on while studying.

Computer and Multimedia:

The single most intrusive invention in the last century has been that of the computer, and children learn computers very quickly indeed. They are adept at several of its uses like sending and receiving mail, browsing the internet, playing games, making documents and so on. No doubt, this has had a tremendous impact on the way children learn, relax and entertain. With progress in the computer hardware and software industry, children are getting exposed to newer, bigger and better computers almost every day.

Benefits: The uses of computers are various and too many to list here. The Government of India realised the immense potential of this technology back in the late eighties and recommended that computer education be introduced in school curricula. Today, almost all urban schools impart computer education right from the third standard. Fees are collected, course books are given out and children are evaluated at the end of the academic year. As a result, children are very savvy when it comes to computers. If you intend to buy a Home Computer, there is no better time than NOW. Prices are down,

technologies are up and the market is very buyer-oriented, so go ahead and make that decision today.
When computer time is made routine for the child at home, you can use it to make the child learn things which cannot be learnt in a school classroom. Educational CD's are now available at fairly low prices and the child can be introduced to almost any topic under the sun through the amazing world of interactive learning. Apart from this, whole books, encyclopedias, magazines such as the National Geographic etc. are all available on CD's. The cost of Printers and Scanners is also within the budget of middle-class families, and a whole Home package with internet account, speakers, CD writer, printer and scanner can be purchased outright for less than 50000/= rupees.

Gaming is also instructive. A child who becomes adept at a game that involves speed and dexterity has, in fact, learnt much better hand-eye coordination, has engaged her mind at the speed devised for the game and besides, has honed her analytical and calculating skills too!

Risks: Use of a computer is very addictive. A child who gets her "fix" on a game will, unless physically dragged away, continue to remain on the machine even after bed-time. This can lead to sleep disturbances. Once the child has learnt to surf the internet, he will be able to see web-sites which are not suitable for him to view, such as pornographic sites (and there are literally thousands of such sites on the net). This can corrupt the child's innocence beyond repair. Gaming in excess can cause eye-strain, hand pain and the tension and anxiety produced while gaming can cause stress too. Working on a monitor that does not have an anti-glare screen can cause eye strain too. Moving the fingers on the keyboard can cause a kind of Repetitive Stress Injury (RSI), with pain and sprain involving the ligaments in and around the wrist and hand.

Access to cyber-cafes and internet relays/chat-rooms have led to the emergence of cyber-crimes like sexual solicitation, kidnapping dramas, pedophilia and cyber-romances (which have mostly come to grief). There have been incidences of heart-breaks and even suicides.

Suggestions: I have already recommended my suggestions above. Suffice it to say, do not be a laggard. Go for the computer now. Make some rules for computer usage: the child should have a certain fixed time to sit before the computer; she must surf the net only in your presence. You should supervise her internet usage. Fix an anti-glare screen on the monitor. While using the computer, the child must periodically close her eyes and rest her fingers so that strain in these can be avoided.

Personal digital assistants (PDA's), Palm-tops and other hand-held devices:

All these devices are also available. PDA's are like a "Personal assistant". They are useful for keeping telephone numbers and addresses, reminders, schedulers and such other information. A teenager might well want a PDA for maintaining her data. Digital Palm-tops are now available with many other functions like touch-screen operations, camera, internet access and mobile telephony. Tablet PC's are just becoming available and will transform classrooms of tomorrow where a child may directly "record" a lecture into her hand-held tablet computer and listen to it at home later on. So many advances are taking place in this area that the information given in this book will already be outdated by the time it is in your hands.

Robot toys, Game box and other gaming devices:

Companies like Sony, Nintendo and others are working at the cutting edge of technology to deliver several gaming devices like Game Boy, X-Box and the like. These are advanced gaming toys that are costly (as of now) and available only to the privileged few who decide to go in for them. Robotic toys such as humanoid figures, dogs, kittens etc are also available at hefty prices for the recreation of those who can afford them.

Conclusion:

There is a complete world out there of gizmos that cost the earth and that have functions that you never dreamt of in the past. How much of this you will give to yourself and to your children will ultimately be dictated by your comfortability with its features and its cost structure.

We should encourage a home environment where the child enjoys these gizmos but does not become a slave to them.

Links:

Useful sites to read for modern technologies:

- ✔ http://www.aarp.org/computers-features/Articles/a2002-07-02-computers_features_aggravations.html
- ✔ http://www.sony.com
- ✔ http://www.ibm.com
- ✔ http://www.apple.com
- ✔ http://www.sonyericsson.com
- ✔ http://www.nokia.com

Useful sites to get programmes to filter pornographic material that can be seen while browsing the net:

- ✔ http://www.classbrain.com/artfamily/publish/article_137.shtml
- ✔ http://www.netnanny.com/index.html
- ✔ http://www.cyberpatrol.com/
- ✔ http://www.kidsnet.com/index.asp?=M

Part VIII
Special Issues

If children grew up according to early indications,
we should have nothing but geniuses.

–J.W. Von Goethe, 1749 - 1832,
German Poet and Novelist

Ch 23
Accidents, Bites and Poisoning

The more people have studied different methods of bringing up children
the more they have come to the conclusion that
what good mother and fathers instinctively feel
like doing for their babies is the best after all.
- Benjamin Spock, 1903 -, American Pediatrician.

Every time an infant trips on an obstacle, she learns how to avoid a similar accident in future. This means that an accident is also an experience. However, the problem with the child is that we never know when a given accident will turn out to be a major one and when it will not. Hence, we should always e on guard to see that the child does not get unduly hurt by, what seems to us at first glance, to be a minor accident.

Why children are so vulnerable to accidents and mishaps:

By nature, children are fickle-minded and have improper coordination; they are curious, wild and often stubborn. They are explorers of the environment around them. Short of putting them in shackles, there is nothing one can do to prevent them from nosing around. They are eager to touch every new object they see; if is small enough, they will try to hold it; if it has a hole in it, they will put their fingers inside it; if it looks attractive, they will put it in their mouths; if a vertical surface looks challenging, they want to climb up or down it; if there is something they can tug, like a rope, they will want to pull at it. In this manner, and more, they put themselves at immense risk of hurt or injury – some of which can cause serious consequences.

By the time the child has grown up to adolescence, there is an inherent element of challenge in every task they perform: they want to climb higher, go faster and dare to do impossible things to impress members of the opposite sex or their own peers. Motorbike accidents, sometimes leading to a fatal outcome, are most common at this age.

Injuries:

Cuts, lacerations, bumps and bruises are very common in toddlers and somewhat older children as well. Sometimes, falls may lead to fractures, internal bleeding and serious head injuries.

<u>Cuts and lacerations:</u> When children play with sharp items and toys with sharp edges, they land up having cuts and lacerations.

What to do? Clean the wound with an antiseptic solution. If the wound is small, you may immediately apply water-proof Band-aid®. If the wound is actively bleeding, try and apply gentle pressure with a clean cloth or a bandage. If the wound looks big or if the bleeding does not stop within 5 minutes or so, take her to the doctor, who will evaluate the wound and decide whether it needs immediate suturing (stitching). Keep the child nil-by-mouth if you suspect that she will need to be anaesthetised for the suturing. Home remedies like applying *chuna* or *haldi* on the wound is not recommended.

For roadside injuries, wash the wound with soap and take the child to her doctor to take advice on preventing wound infection and tetanus.

<u>Bumps and bruises:</u> When children learn to crawl, they put themselves at risk of falling, stumbling, tripping and hurting themselves. It is important to prevent such injuries by securing the home environment of the child in such a way that injury is minimised. For this, see that low-height furniture has rounded corners and padded edges, balconies have sturdy railings, stairs have firm balustrades, the floor of the house has a soft carpet, the child's cot has a proper railing and there are 2 foot high partitions between the living room and the kitchen and between the living room and the main entrance of the house. Avoid leaving skates, pillows, clothes and other objects in the middle of the floor.

When your child has already hurt herself and is crying loudly, do not panic. Apply ice over the bump or bruise for at least 10-15 minutes. Give her Paracetamol to reduce pain. Above all, reassure her that she will be all right by hugging her and rocking her to silence. Apply ice or hot fomentations to relieve the pain. Both work equally well; use the one you and the child are more comfortable with. Offer a chocolate or a sweet after about half an hour. Remember that a bruise looks very bad, but is practically harmless. All it does is to cause pain, limping (if on the legs) and some limitation of movement of the involved part. It will take about a week to completely heal. If the bump is on the head, then you should be a little more careful to rule out any internal injury to the child's brain.

<u>Head Injury:</u> Bouncing the child up and down can lead to tossing of the brain inside the skull back and forth and up and down, thereby precipitating internal bleeding (whiplash injury). Falls on to the head can also cause internal bleeds. This complication is a rare event; most head injuries cause no internal harm or a temporary swelling of the brain (a concussion). In such cases, there will be a bump and/ or a bruise, with irritability, vomiting (repeatedly) and occasionally, an incomplete loss of consciousness from which the child recovers in less than 24 hours. In the rare event of a major injury, there may be harbingers of it such as bleeding from the ears or nostrils, loss of consciousness and convulsion (s) (fits). Recovery may not occur in

24 hours and the child may need further evaluation as a hospitalised in-patient.

As it takes some time for blood to collect and clot within the skull, either outside or inside the brain tissue, sometimes, you may think that the child is all right, but she may develop symptoms later (lucid interval). Thus, the child must be kept under close watch for at least 12-24 hours after any head injury. In suspected cases of internal injury, hospitalisation is compulsory on medico-legal grounds to rule out the possibility of foul play. In such cases, a CT scan or a MRI may also be asked for (see Chapter 33).

<ins>Fractures:</ins> If you find that the child, after a fall, keeps one or more limbs in a bizarre position, or is scared if anyone touches her on a certain part of the body, or if you see a large swelling with bruising on a particular limb, or if the child is breathing shallow and crying with each breath and has had a fall on to her side, you should suspect a fracture of some bone or the other. As soon as you see and suspect a fracture, you must:

-call a doctor and fix up an urgent appointment to see him;
-try and minimise the movements of the affected limb by putting it in a sling or splinting it with a wooden stick (if possible);
-not move her neck till the doctor or a trained person has given the all-clear sign and ruled out fractures or injuries of the spine; and
-keep the child nil-by-mouth in case the child will need fracture reduction/surgery.

Skull fractures, when they occur with the bumps of the head region, do not need any surgery *unless the skull bones are deformed or displaced widely.*

Burns and Scalds:

Scalds are extremely common and occur when the child and her caretaker sit with food and hot liquids to feed the former. Hot water, dals, soups, tea and coffee are the usual culprits. The child may cause the accident by tipping the glass of hot milk on to herself or pull the table-cloth from under the hot glass, thereby upsetting all the items on the table.

To prevent scalding and burns, keep all hot things out of the reach of children. Check the temperature of the bath before pouring it on her; do the same with tea or soup before offering them to her. Never let hot utensils, clothes iron or other similar items sit where the child can reach them and touch them; do not allow the crawling or toddling child to enter the kitchen (see above). Take all necessary measures to prevent a fire in the house (the details of this are outside the scope of this book). It is very important to keep the stove at a height that is safe from the reach of the child.

Diwali and lighting of fire-crackers is a major cause of burns all over the nation and in all age groups of people. Exploding crackers can affect important body parts like the eye and may even cause blindness.

The most important first aid in case of a burn (whether dry or wet) is **to put the burnt part under cold running water for at least 5-10 minutes**. If that is not possible, take cold water in a large jug and pour it on the burnt area, *regardless of the child's protestations.* Once you have finished with this step, remove the child from the water source, gently allow the area to dry up and then apply an antibiotic salve to the burnt area.

Go to the doctor thereafter to seek help regarding the adequacy of your treatment and to dress the burnt area professionally. The doctor will also advise whether a visit to a specialist or plastic surgeon is needed or not, and if so, when.

In some cases, burns need more careful handling; these include:

- burns of the palms, hands and feet
- burns of the face or genital area

- burns involving a large portion of the body (more than 10%)
- burns that are deep (third degree)
- burns affecting the internal membranes of the mouth, the food-pipe, the wind-pipe or other structures and
- burns caused by industrial fluids or chemicals.
- electrical burns

In the last-mentioned case, burns can be prevented in the following ways: (i) avoid keeping any sockets where they can be reached by the child (ii) do not leave any electrical appliances with long snaking wires lying here and there (iii) ensure that all appliances are connected to the main DP switch through MCB's only, so that there is less risk of electrical malfunction or short-circuiting of wires (iv) cover all sockets with plastic dummies that will close all the holes (or use sockets that come with self-closing flaps) (v)arrange buttons and circuitry near the bathroom and wash-basins in such a way that no one has to touch any electrical points with their wet hands and (vi) remove all plugs of appliances from the sockets and roll them up and keep them safely when not in use.

If the child has put her finger inside a live socket or has got stuck to a live wire, immediately switch off the supply to that socket/wire or put off the main DP switch. Use a wooden stick, magazine or newspaper to disconnect the child/victim from the source of electric current. The victim who does not die from electric shock may still end up with deep burns at both, the entry and exit points, or with internal damage to the heart or the brain.

Choking on something/suffocation by blockage of breathing:

Infants as well as older children may sometimes choke suddenly either while eating or while playing with food or other small objects. When the child chokes on something, you should immediately rush to her side. Do not try to give her water to drink. Do not ever attempt to sweep your finger inside her throat, as this may push the object even deeper inside the throat and impact it inside. The best thing to do is to lift up the child in your left hand and lay her astride your forearm, head down and back up; next, thump her with the palm of your right hand 4-5 times between the shoulder blades – and check whether the object has been dislodged or whether it has already been removed from the throat. If the child is older, sit on a stool and lay the child down in your lap in much the same way: with the legs up and the head down. Thump her in the same way on her back till the foreign body is dislodged and drops out of the child's mouth.

If the above method fails to remove the object and/or the child starts turning blue, perform the **Heimlich manouvre** to remove the object. In case of a toddler, make her sit on a table or bed in the knee-chest position with the head down and the hips a little up; then place both your hands around her abdomen: now press towards the child's head (i.e. upwards) with the fingers of both the hands and keep thrusting in the same direction till the object is expelled. In case of an older child, you may ask her to remain standing. You should stand behind her and repeat the same manouvre with your hands. The thrusting action has to be stronger and deeper for the older child.

If the above method is also ineffective or if your child continues to experience a choking effect, becomes more and more blue or becomes unconscious, she will need immediate resuscitation by CPR. In the meantime, call an ambulance to transport her to an intensive care unit.

Note: You can teach your older child to perform a Heimlich manouvre on *herself* by putting her own hands just below the rib cage and pressing upwards with the hands repeatedly till she is able to remove the offending object.

Prevention of choking accidents:

1. Do not allow small children to play with/eat/handle small items like peanuts, chickpeas, buttons, small parts of toys,

maize grains, kernels of apricots, seeds of melons, confetti balls etc.

2. Do not bring toys with small detachable parts and small decorative items like tea-cups, screws etc.
3. Do not let the child play or talk while eating and encourage her to eat slowly and chew the food thoroughly. If you are giving fish, clean the fish properly (by removing bones) prior to feeding it.
4. Don't allow the child to hide inside cupboards or *almirahs* while playing hide-and-seek games.

Other foreign objects put elsewhere:

Children have a habit of exploring their body openings like the nose, the mouth (see above), the ears and in girls, the vagina, with their fingers, or more often, with other objects like pencils, peas, buttons, safety pins, rubber bands, marbles, small sweets and other small objects.

If the object is inserted into these orifices with force, it may lead to crying, pain, bleeding or injury. The object may get impacted in the cavities inside, such as the nose or the external ear canal. Sometimes, insects may go inside the ear canal and cause a peculiar buzzing sensation due to their wing-flapping. The child will be restless; she will keep scratching the ear and cry. Most people heat some oil and drop it into the ear. This will usually kill the insect and relieve the child almost instantly. Ear-drops of any sort may be used instead of oil – with almost the same result.

Depending upon the orifice involved, you should take remedial steps immediately. If the object is in the nose, do not try to remove it with your fingers, as it will go further in. The best action will be to go to an ENT doctor who will remove it with professional tools at his disposal. If the object is in the ear canal, again, the best remedy is to submit it to the ENT specialist for necessary action. A vaginal foreign body may be removable directly if it is superficial, but if it is inside and beyond the hymen, special instruments will be needed to remove it.

If the child has eaten a coin or a smooth object such as an eraser or a marble, you should not worry; the object will not cause any internal harm in over 99% of cases. Just wait for it to be excreted in the stool of the child within 24-48 hours. You may feed the child bananas and mashed rice or potatoes to get such objects out.

Poisoning:

Children commonly ingest household cleaning and disinfecting liquids, rat poison, cockroach poison, kerosene or naphthalene balls in cities, and seeds and poisonous fruit or leaves in villages. They may even accidentally drink medicines or swallow or chew tablets used by the adults in the house.

The first step is to suspect accidental poisoning: do so if you see your child sitting and playing next to a half-filled bottle of medicine or household liquid; the cap will be open, or the bottle broken and the liquid partly or fully spilled out; the same liquid may be visible on the dress, the mouth or the hand of your child and the smell of the liquid may be present on and around the child and within her mouth. Alternatively, she may be already symptomatic and may be vomiting, retching or be lying amidst the liquid and bottles either drowsy, blue, or having fits.

Unless the child is already drowsy, or is suspected of having ingested kerosene, other aromatic liquids (such as thinners and insecticide sprays, furniture polish or petroleum products), *immediately try and induce the child to vomit by either putting your finger inside her throat and tickling her throat, or giving her a glass of highly salted water to drink.*

If the child successfully vomits, she will feel very sick thereafter, so reassure her, and give her some cold milk to drink. If she does not vomit, do not try to make her retch again. It will be preferable to take her to a doctor for further treatment.

Never take any suspected case of poisoning lightly, because the effect of the poison may start later, and an apparently well-looking child may suddenly take a turn for the worse as the poison takes effect. The most prudent thing to do is to rush her to a nearby hospital. Do remember to take the half-empty bottle and/or any item that will give a clue to the nature of the poison and guide the doctor to deciding how much poison the child may have ingested. If you were not present at the time when the child apparently ingested the poison, do ask around for any eye-witnesses who will be of tremendous help to the treating doctor.

For food poisoning, refer to Chapter 39.

Bites and Stings:

<u>Bee and wasp stings:</u>

The usual reaction to stings by bees and wasps is redness, itching and pain at the site of the sting. The insect's sting will often be visible in the puncture – a hallmark of bee and wasp stings. In fact, the insect itself will die after stinging a victim, a sort of herd defense.

Rarely, a sting may trigger off a life-threatening generalized reaction with breathing difficulty, swelling of the whole body, generalized rash and so on.

The child must be consoled. She must be exhorted to cooperate with your further treatment. Look for the sting: if visible, remove it with tweezers or a blunt, clean knife or blade. Apply a soothing lotion such as calamine lotion or a cold cream over the site. Some traditional methods include applying a preparation having baking soda dissolved in a few drops of water, vinegar or onion juice. If the itching is severe, the child may need an anti-allergic medication and perhaps paracetamol (for pain) and a sedative (to make her sleep). In case of a severe allergic reaction, rush the child to the hospital.

Ants, cockroaches, bed-bugs and other insects:

Usually, other insects do not produce any serious reactions, but sometimes, cockroaches may produce small abrasions and peeled off skin on the tips of the fingers or toes. In some children, insect bites trigger a more generalized but harmless skin reaction that may appear as small raised reddish black papules all over the body. This is likely to remain for many days and needs only symptomatic treatment.

Dog-bites:

Dogs are vectors of a 100% fatal disease called rabies; when a rabid dog bites a human being, the rabies virus can get transmitted to the victim. In India, rabies is also transmitted by bites from cats, mongoose, cattle, monkeys etc. However, rabies is not transmitted by bites from rats, mice, bandicoots or rabbits. Bites that are given by stray dogs or by dogs whose vaccination status is not known are more likely to cause rabies in the victim. Since the virus is absorbed from the skin and must reach nervous tissue (nerves), there is a variable period after a dog bite when the victim is normal. After this variable *incubation period*, the victim exhibits symptoms of the disease, and ultimately succumbs to it.

Bites on the following areas are considered dangerous: face, palms, soles, head and neck; also included in the danger category are bites with opening up of the flesh and exposure of nervous tissue, bites by unvaccinated or stray dogs and bites in small children.

The immediate steps to be taken include the following:

1. Wash the wound thoroughly with soap and water.

2. Do not apply turmeric powder, chilli powder or *chuna* over the wound.
3. Immediately rush to the doctor for post-exposure vaccination (see Chapter 30).

Children must be taught never to disturb sleeping or resting dogs. They must never hit dogs with sticks or stones, and never try to touch or pet stray dogs. Never trouble a bitch which is nursing its puppies. Ignore a growling dog and do not try to stare it down or act "brave" and approach it and "tell it to 'sit'" or to obey your commands. Pet dogs should be regularly taken for rabies shots. They should be kept clean and trained to be friendly and calm.

<u>Snake bites:</u>

Of the thousands of species of snakes in the world, about 200 or so are poisonous and of these, around 40-50 are found in India. However, not every bite by a poisonous snake is fatal; in fact, over 75% have little or no symptoms of poisoning as the bite may have been non-penetrative or the snake's poison glands may have been empty at the time of biting and injecting the victim. As the child has a smaller weight, a given bite is likely to be more dangerous than in an adult.

The first step in treating a snake-bite victim is to reassure him/her that help is on the way and that he/she should not panic. Reduce the movement of the affected limb by splinting or immobilising it. Then tie a tight bandage/dupatta/dhoti-cloth or long neck-tie on the same limb over the thigh or the upper arm proximal to the site of the bite. The pressure should be sufficient to cut off the venous return of dirty blood (mixed with poison); the arterial pulse should not get cut off. After this, examine the bites to see how deep they are. If a person trained in handling first aid is available, ask that person to help you make a cruciate (X-shaped) cut which will open up the bite site and allow the wound to bleed; the poison will come back out with the blood. Do not waste further time and proceed to a hospital or treatment facility which has the expertise to treat snake-bite victims. Loosen the tourniquet for a few minutes after every 15 minutes so that the supply of fresh, arterial blood is not permanently occluded. If you have managed to kill the snake, take it to the hospital for identification.

The Kiss-of-Life:

Cardio-pulmonary resuscitation (CPR) is something every adult person must learn as it can save a life in case of an emergency. CPR can be learnt online at: http://www.cprtoday.com (a paying course) or at http://depts.washington.edu/learncpr/ (free leaning).

Arrest of breathing can damage the child's brain irreparably within 2-5 minutes and can kill her if she is not resuscitated (revived) immediately. Such a situation may occur with inhalation of a foreign body (see above), near-drowning, electric shock, poisoning, snake-bite (by cobra) or in a fire (by smothering). Hence, a CPR-trained person can save the child's life if he is available at that time. Hence my insistence that all adults MUST learn CPR.

The <u>steps</u> in CPR are as under:

1. Determine if the child is breathing: see if the chest is rising or falling with a rhythm.
2. See if she is conscious: shake or tap her vigorously to check for response.
3. Try and ensure that the airway is clear and there is nothing in the mouth or airway such as an impacted foreign body.
4. If anything is found, attempt to remove it with the methods described above. Do not proceed to the next step till the foreign body is dislodged and out of the way.
5. Once the impediment is removed, check the breathing again: bring your face sideways near the child's mouth and nose and feel for the air being breathed out by the child; at the same time, see if the chest is moving. If the child is breathing

on her own, no further treatment is needed. Call the doctor immediately.

6. If there is no breathing to start with or after the foreign body has been removed, proceed to give 2 mouth-to-mouth breaths (the kiss of life) (Fig 23-1). Breathe out with a force that is sufficient to displace the child's rib cage by at least ½ to 1" or so.

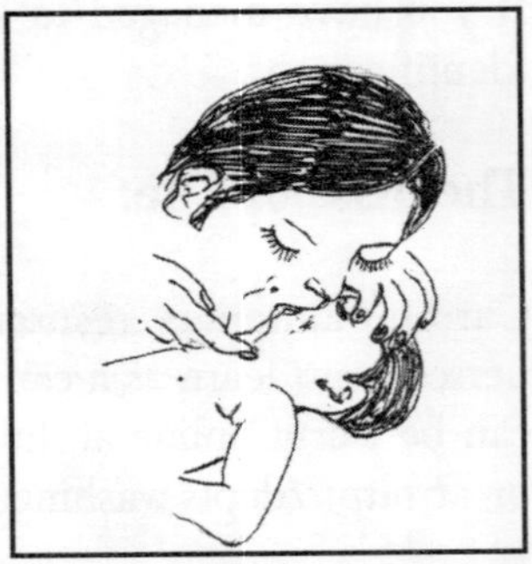

Fig 23-1

7. After 2 breaths, put your palm on the child's chest just to the left of the breast-bone and feel for the heart beat. If the heart is beating well, continue mouth-to-mouth breathing till medical help arrives or till the child begins to breathe on her own. The rate of breathing should be 26-32 breaths per minute.
8. If there is no heart beat, begin to give heart massage (external cardiac massage or ECM). For this lay the child on a firm surface. Kneel beside her and compress her chest with the open heel of the palm of your hand perpendicular to the ground. Your shoulders should be level with the breast bone and your arm should be straight at the elbow and at right angles to the wrist. The chest should be pushed down at least 1 ½ to 2 inches. The rate should be 80-100 compressions/minute.
9. After every 5 compressions, switch to give one mouth-to-mouth breath. Continue till medical help arrives, heart beat is restored or the child begins to breathe.

In infants, the method is slightly different; the ratio of heart massage to chest compression is not 5:1 but 6:1; the heart massage is delivered by the first two fingers placed over the centre of the breast-bone (Fig 23-2); the chest is pressed only 1" downwards; and the mouth-to-mouth breathing includes the *nose* of the child, which is taken into the care-giver's mouth *along* with the mouth of the baby.

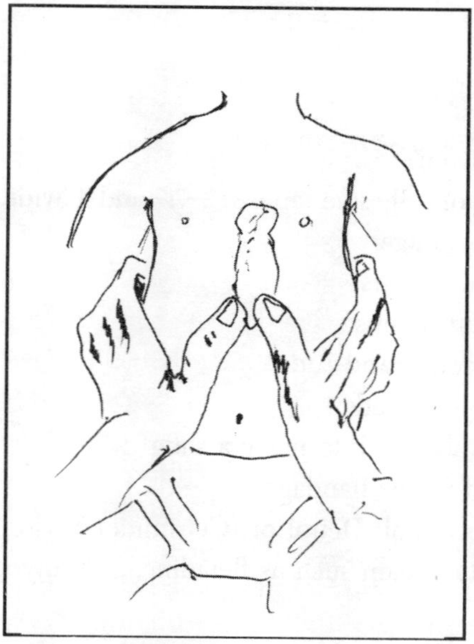

Fig 23-2

The First-aid Box:

Keep the following items in the first-aid box at home and learn to use them by approaching your family doctor or a friendly compounder or nurse at a nearby clinic.

a) Medicines:

- Paracetamol
- Anti-allergic – Promethazine syrup, Cetirizine syrup
- Anti-inflammatory – Combiflam
- Vomiting – Domperidone syrup
- Loose stools – W.H.O. approved Oral Rehydration Salts powder

b) Dressing material:

- Cotton wool
- Surgical or adhesive tape, ½", ¾" and 1"wide
- Roller bandage
- A pair of scissors
- Tweezers/forceps
- Water-proof Band-Aid
- Sterile gauze-pads
- A triangular cloth to make a sling
- A roll of Crepe bandage
- (Chloroxylenol) Dettol or (Cetrimide) Savlon solution
- Antibiotic cream such as Betadine, Soframycin or Nadoxin

c) Miscellaneous Items:

- Soothing solutions like Calamine
- Cloth strips for dunking in cold water for mopping the head in fever
- A clinical thermometer
- Hard cardboard listing all emergency telephone numbers

All the above items must be stored in an air-tight plastic box and kept out of the reach of children but at a prominent, easy to access location in the house

Ch 24
The Handicapped (Challenged) Child

Do not handicap your children by making their lives easy.

- Lazarus Long

A handicapped child is one who cannot live a normal productive life due to some disability of her body or mind. About 1/10th of individuals in the world have some handicap or the other. Broadly, handicaps can be divided into the following categories:

1. Visually challenged (blind).
2. Hearing challenged (Deaf or hearing-impaired).
3. Lame (limb defects or deformities causing difficulty in gait).
4. Mentally challenged (mentally handicapped or retarded).
5. Spastic (cerebral palsy).
6. Congenital organ or system malformations (heart, lung, kidney, liver, etc).
7. Chromosomal disorders (Mongolism) (see also Chapter 30).
8. Miscellaneous disorders.

Causes of Handicap:

It is obvious that it is impossible to totally avoid disabilities, although that is the goal of all health authorities. The causes can be genetic, environmental or a combination of both.

Genetic factors include abnormalities that come up due to marriages between close cousins and the higher incidence of chromosomal disorders like Mongolism in mothers with an advanced age, among others. Environmental agents include intake of alcohol, cigarette smoking, exposure to X-rays, exposure to radio-active compounds (used in certain advanced tests and in treatment of cancer), ingestion of potentially harmful drugs to abort an unwanted foetus, etc. See also Chapter 30.

After birth, handicaps can occur due to injuries, occurrence of illnesses like poliomyelitis, hearing loss due to repeated middle ear infections, mental retardation secondary to uncontrolled epilepsy or pyogenic meningitis, poisoning by certain drugs and toxins and many other causes. At times, a genetic disease may have a later onset; for example, patients with certain inherited diseases get blindness or spasticity at a later age.

I am devastated. *What will I do*?

Most parents get the above feeling when they are confronted for the first time with the news that their child is abnormal in some way. They pass through different moods such as denial, anger, rejection, frustration, depression and guilt; with proper guidance, however, they will *accept* the handicapped child with dignity and forbearance. The parents (and their families) blame each other (and each other's families) for the handicap. They feel it is the bad seed of their spouse which led to the handicap manifesting in their child. This may be correct in the rare case. Usually, however, the fault does not lie in any one parent; it is just their bad fortune. Parents must accept the handicap as a will of the Almighty.

It is important to understand the nature and the severity of the handicap too. Parents do not always comprehend these two facets of the handicap, unless there is an obvious handicap like total blindness or absence of both hands. They must consult their family practitioner, their pediatrician and the specialist whose domain the handicap belongs to. This, plus some reading on the topics of how to deal with a handicap and how to manage their child's *particular* problem will go a long way. There is a selection of books and web-sites at the end of this chapter for those who desire to read more about handicaps in children.

Once the parents have accepted the child (and not just the handicap), they must begin the task of rehabilitating the child so that he/she grows up into an individual who has adjusted well to his/her limitations and is an active contributing member of the society. The parents must provide tender loving care in infancy and throughout the dependent years; they should encourage the child to be confident and courageous and face all difficulties with fortitude; they should allow the child to interact with the neighbours, the relatives and the other members of the society; they should consult the primary care provider, the counsellor, the pediatrician, the physiotherapist and all other necessary professionals to ensure that the best possible care reaches the child at all times; they should meet parents of other children with a similar handicap in Parent Support Groups; finally, they must plan the child's future in consultation with the educators who are looking after the child.

If you are a parent to more than one child with the same handicap, you should seek expert genetic counselling before planning the next child. In a case where it is thought safe to go for the next baby, or where the parents wish to take the risk, a minimum gap of three to four years must be allowed between the handicapped child and the yet to arrive baby.

Rehabilitative treatment:

There are so many conflicts that arise while looking after a handicapped child. Economic conflicts can threaten the very integrity of the family. A perception may start doing the rounds in the house that more money is being "thrown down the drain" after that "imbecile" or "lame" fellow at the cost of the "normal" siblings who have to forfeit some of their demands because money is not available for them. This can prove to be unfortunate and perhaps even dangerous for the disadvantaged child whose advocacy role the parents will have to continue to play. The harried mother can become rebellious if she finds that she just cannot cope with the simultaneous duties of being a house-wife, a mother to normal children, a wife to an unhelpful father and a provider to the handicapped child as well.

Thus, rehabilitation of the child must be accompanied by a continuous process of adjustment for the whole family. For example, a fixed portion of the income of the family should be kept aside for the other normal members who should be allowed to pursue their own dreams; a house-maid who stays in the house for all the 24 hours can relieve the mother's burden considerably; the father must take out time to interact with his other children, and also to help his wife handle the various house jobs that keep cropping up; and so on.

While services are improving with every passing year, India still has a long way to go in providing optimum services for the rehabilitation of the handicapped. The aim of the rehabilitation is to provide the handicapped child with the best possible opportunities to best optimise her available faculties. Every effort must be made by the parents to:

- get information about the child's disease
- find out who are the right professionals who will provide the necessary medical and rehabilitative care
- enroll themselves in Support Groups

- continue to provide education, if possible, in a normal school, but if not, then in a special school
- leave no stone unturned in seeing to it that the child becomes self-sufficient in daily activities like feeding, changing clothes, visiting the toilet, climbing up and down stairs, etc
- try and teach the child an activity that can become his/her vocation and
- uncover hidden talents and untapped potential in other areas of development. (For example, it is well-known that Mongol babies have a very good sense of music.)

As the handicapped child continues to get proper guidance and training, he/she learns more and more skills and improves in all spheres of life; however, he/she is unlikely to ever become a completely normal individual.

Mental Retardation (MR):

Children with mental retardation are slow in achieving all the milestones of development. Thus, they may not smile till much after 3 months, the normal age of achieving a social smile; or, they may not turn over till they are over a year old – normal babies do it by the age of 4-5 months of age. In addition to such major milestones, they may be found to lack fine motor skills, cognition and language appropriate for age. They may also suffer from other associated handicaps like spasticity (see below), blindness, deafness, convulsions etc. Physical abnormalities like a small head (Microcephaly), growth retardation (due to poor feeding and poor psychological stimulation) and abnormal facies may also be found.

Mental retardation can arise due to many causes, before, during and after birth as well as during later childhood. Causes include birth asphyxia (failure of the newborn baby to breathe at birth), head trauma (at birth or later, due to falls from a height), meningitis and encephalitis (swelling and infection of the meninges or the brain), genetic factors (Mongolism) and endocrine problems (cretinism or hypothyroidism).

Management of a child with M.R. requires a multidisciplinary approach. The pediatrician is the central care provider; he takes backing from the genetician, the psychologist, the psychiatrist, the endocrinologist, the physiotherapist, the occupational therapist, the neurologist and the special educator. Sometimes, other professionals are also involved. If the cause is treatable, such as hypothyroidism, it should be treated. Once treatable causes are looked after or ruled out, the child must be rehabilitated in the manner described above. One must remember this: **there are no medicines that can actually increase intelligence**. Thus, parents must not unnecessarily spend money on such unrealistic remedies.

If you need more information on MR, read the following link:
http://www.thearc.org/faqs/mrqa.html

Cerebral Palsy (CP):

Unlike a child with M.R., the palsied child has little or no mental deficit; rather, she suffers from a *motor control disorder* with tight muscles that do not move under their control. This is best summed up as: "A sound mind in a disobedient body". As a result, the child has an inability to speak well, sit, walk or do any volitional activities properly. The condition may arise due to a genetic problem or due to prematurity or other birth-related insults (like severe neonatal jaundice, neonatal meningitis, etc.). Because birth conditions have a role to play, children with C.P. also sometimes have M.R., hearing impairment, visual impairment, fits or involuntary body tremors.

A very highly competent physiotherapist team is needed to properly rehabilitate a victim of C.P. Every positive step must be complimented: the child is gradually taught to speak (with better enunciation of consonants), to feed, bathe and clothe herself, to participate in play activities and to learn special stuff like painting, playing instrumental music, etc. Spasticity is the term used to describe the tightness of the muscles of the body; it can be relieved with a combination of medicines, Botox* injections and surgery. Children with a lesser handicap can be prescribed special shoes or splints to enable them to sit erect or to stand with proper stability.

Obesity is a real possibility in spastic and/or paralytic children because of reduced physical activity. Hence, these children should not be given heavy meals, and the food that is selected for them should be rich in nutrients and not in calories.

Look up the following links if you need help for a child with CP:

- ✔ http://www.iicpindia.com: This is the web-site of the Indian Institute of Cerebral Palsy
- ✔ http://www.nrcissi.org: This is the web-site of The Spastics Society of India
- ✔ http://www.webhealthcentre.com/general/cp_index.asp: This is an excellent Indian site on CP. You need to have a free membership to consult online, but no log-in is needed to read the text that is easy to understand.

Attention Deficit Disorder (with Hyperactivity) (ADD-H):

This not uncommon neurological disorder is more common among boys than girls. It is believed to be a disorder of chemical neurotransmitter function of the brain. Earlier, it was called Minimal Brain Dysfunction (MBD). The essential components of this disorder are the presence of restlessness and attention deficit, a near normal to completely normal intelligence, impulsive behaviour, aggressiveness and hyperactivity – semi-purposeful, excessive and uncontrollable activity that provokes the parents and care-takers to "shout" at the child and "put him down". Due to the low attention span, the child is unable to complete a given task at hand: for example, he will not eat his meal properly, but rush through it; he will often suffer from constipation or encopresis as he does not sit through the bowel movement; he has scholastic backwardness as he cannot listen attentively in class and cannot complete his studies in time; and so on. Due to the hyperactivity, he may end up fidgeting and squirming when he is required to stay still; he will not make lasting friendships, disobey elders, often appear to be "anti-social", carry out tasks with inefficiency and at times, break things that are his responsibility or even set fire to things and be destructive without any provocation.

The hyperactivity is sometimes spontaneous, while at other times, it may be precipitated by intake of tea, coffee, food preservatives, food-dyes and vitamin C-rich foods.

Not every clumsy child is a child with ADD; not every energetic, ebullient brat a case of ADD-H. This must be kept in mind that unless the child has been seen over a period of time by child psychiatrists and developmental psychologists, a label of "Attention Deficit Disorder" must not be applied to every child who has attention deficit and hyperactivity.

Rehabilitation of children with ADD-H is difficult since they need continuous guidance, handling patience and expert counselling; they should be assigned tasks under supervision so that they can carry out these tasks and gain confidence in themselves. They should be encouraged to participate in meditation, yoga and other brain calming activities at all times. If you help them when they are trying to complete a task, they will frequently do the task with 100% efficiency. A percentage of these children need medicines to control their hyperactivity. In spite of this, they may not improve completely.

Autism and Autism Spectrum Disorder (ASD):

Like ADD-H, autism is also believed to result from a dysfunction of chemical neurotransmitters in the brain. It is a scarcely properly recognised disorder and its diagnosis is missed even by pediatricians in their busy office practice.

These children are normal in their first one or two years; after this, they begin to show regression of social behaviour and communication skills. They "live in their own world', that is, they do not interact with others in the family or around them. They have shifty eyes even when they are talking to you; they do not like to be held or cuddled either. They lack emotional warmth. You will often find them enjoying television, looking crazily at strobe lights or staring at moving lights and rotating fans. They will "enjoy" toe-walking, sniffing or licking objects around them.

They may not speak or speak repetitive clauses or gibberish; they may even have "echolalia", that is they repeat what has been told to them with little meaning. They hate when somebody tries to rearrange things around them; they are often attached to a favourite toy or article, which they always keep beside them, awake or asleep.

The way to suspect autism is to look for the above signs and symptoms in an otherwise bright child. Since it is non-verbal communication that is faulty, the autistic child is often unable to understand the "implied meaning of something spoken to them". They cannot interpret like a normal child can, the meaning of body language, of gestures and of inflections of the voice of a person speaking to them.

Autistic children often have mental retardation, epilepsy and other neurological problems.

There is no specific therapy for autism. The child needs compassionate care and psychological counselling.

<u>Autistic Spectrum Disorder (ASD)</u> includes any disorder where there is a problem in understanding or articulating non-verbal communication. To know more about autism and ASD, look up the following link: http://www.pediatricneurology.com/autism.htm

Education of a Handicapped Child:

All handicapped children have a right to get educated. The educational process must be appropriate for their intellectual level, the nature of their physical limitations (if any), their age, their socio-cultural milieu and their individual and particular needs.

By this is also meant the *parental responsibility* of ensuring that their handicapped child gets such education. As far as is possible, handicapped children should be taught in *schools for normal children.* Exceptions include children with major mental handicap, Down syndrome and children with multiple anomalies. Even when the child is enrolled in a *special school,* parents must continue to be involved in the educational process throughout the duration. This means getting information about the child's progress from time to time, informing the educators about any changes in the child's medical condition, learning how to teach the child special skills of daily life like untying a shoe lace or eating with cutlery etc.

As a parent, you would do well to organise or join a "Parent Support Group" for all handicapped children in general, or of those children who have the particular handicap that your child does. To give an example, the Spastics Society of India was formed by the parent of a spastic child.

The Persons with Disabilities Act 1995 of the Government of India:

To provide equal opportunities to handicapped people, the Government of India passed the Person with Disabilities Act in 1995. According to this act, the following seven categories were included for the sake of defining a handicapped person:

- blind person
- visually impaired person
- deaf person or hearing impaired

- person with a locomotor disability (that is defect of movement of body and/or limbs
- leprosy cured person
- mentally retarded person
- mentally sick person

Under this act, a number of concessions and facilities are available for disabled persons for job, for travel and for tax purposes. To know more about the Act, read the following link: http://www.disabilitynet.org.in/legal/pwdact1995.htm

Useful Net Resources and Books on Handicapped Child:

✔ http://www.ericdigests.org/pre-9215/rights.htm: This website outlines in detail the rights and responsibilities of the parents of a handicapped child to secure proper, age and intellect-appropriate education for them (the children). It also lists the resources available for American parents of handicapped children.

✔ http://www.udaan.org/misc/home.html: This is a web-site of a doctor on the subject of cerebral palsy in India and has many useful web-pages for parents and care providers.

✔ http://www.nabindia.org/sited/index1.htm: This is the website of the National Association of the Blind, India.

✔ http://planningcommission.nic.in/reports/sereport/ser/stdy_ied.pdf: This site has a complete downloadable book in .PDF format for parents of handicapped children.

✔ http://disabilityindia.org/: A general website for all disabilities organizations:

- ✔ http://www.disabilitynet.org.in/legal/pwdact1995.htm: This page has the full text of the "person with Disabilities Act 1995 of the Govt. of India.

- ✔ http://www.yale.edu/ynhti/curriculum/units/1982/6/82.06.08.x.html : This web-page has many references to books available for parents on the subject of a handicapped child. I have listed a few here which look promising. You may have to order these books from the web-page directly, or search www.Amazon.com for the purchase.

Useful Books:

- Bigge, J. L. and O'Donnell, P. A. *Teaching Individuals with Physical and Multiple Disabilities.* Columbus, Ohio: Charles E. Merrill, 1976. Discusses teaching strategies and family involvement with children who have multiple disabilities. Emphasis on severely physically disabled.

- Bricker, D. and Casuso, V. "Family Involvement: A Critical Component of Early Intervention." *Exceptional Children,* 1979, 46, 108-115. Emphasizes the necessity of habilitation of the disabled infant from birth.

- Farber, B., and Jenné, W. C. "Family Organization and Parent-Child Communication: Parents and Siblings of a Retarded Child. *Monograph Soc. Res. Child Develpm.,* 1963, 28, Whole No. 91. Discusses relationships between family members having a retarded child at home.

- Finnie, Nancie R. *Handling the Young Cerebral Palsied Child at Home.* New York: E. P. Dutton, 1975. Detailed book describing family life with a cerebral palsied child. Emphasis on the physical needs of the child feeding, positioning, etc.

- Grebler, A. M. "Parental Attitudes Toward Mentally Retarded Children." *American J. on Mental Deficiency;* 1952,

56, 475-483. Discusses parental feelings toward their mentally retarded children.

- Greer, Bobby G. "On Being the Parent of a Handicapped Child." *Exceptional Children*, 1975, 41, 519. Mr. Greer discusses his personal feelings regarding being the parent of a handicapped child.

- Heisler, V. A Handicapped Child in the Family. New York: Grune and Stratton, 1972. Describes the effects of a handicapped child on the family.

- Robinson, H. and Robinson, N. M. *The Mentally Retarded Child.* New York: McGraw Hill, 1965. Comprehensive textbook detailing all aspects of a mentally retarded individual's life and needs.

- Strom, R. and Johnson, A. "The Parent as a Teacher." *Education*, 1974, 95, 40-43. Tells how parents can help their child learn at home.

Ch 25
The Child with Birth Defects

"You are the bows from which your children as living arrows are sent forth."

- Kahlil Gibran

Broadly speaking, a birth defect is defined as any defect of a system or organ of the newborn present since birth. Birth defects may either be due to genetic factors, environmental causes or both.

As such, one must remember that Nature has so designed the process of "selection" that abnormally developing foetuses are naturally aborted within the first three months (the so called "blighted" ovum). In fact, it has been determined that almost half of all first trimester abortions are due to an abnormality in the foetus. In most cases, these abnormalities have been major and not compatible with life.

Causes of birth defects:

1. Genetic factors: In some cases, birth defects or congenital abnormalities are due to genetic or hereditary causes. These causes may have arisen in previous generations or they may have appeared for the first time in this generation. Examples include Mongolism,

extra fingers on all four limbs (polydactyly), hereditary causes of mental retardation and others. In all these cases, either a single gene may be defective or there may be an entire extra chromosome that causes the defects. Owing to the impact of genetics in the occurrence of birth defects, the incidence of these defects is higher in the progeny of cousin marriages.

2. Exposure of mother to various external agents: During pregnancy, the mother may, either advertently or otherwise, be exposed to a host of agents that can produce birth defects. These include X-rays, drugs, medicines, infective agents and addictive substances like alcohol. The defects are most likely to occur if the exposure is during the first trimester, as this is the crucial period when the organs and external features of the foetus are being formed. Repeated X-rays can produce foetal abnormalities. So can viral infections like German measles, bacterial infections like syphilis and protozoan infections like toxoplasmosis. Excessive alcohol intake can produce a mentally retarded, grossly abnormal child.

3. Maternal nutrient deficiency: A peri-conceptional* deficiency of *folic acid*, a water-soluble B-vitamin, is responsible for defects of the brain and spinal cord. Hence, young married women who are planning for a child should start taking folic acid pills regularly.

4. Multi-factorial causes: In most cases, such as a heart defect or a cleft palate (hare lip), it is believed that a combination of the above factors may be responsible.

Types of birth defects:

Birth defects may be classified into life-threatening, major, minor or inconsequential.

**peri-conceptional = six weeks before and six weeks after the baby has been conceived.*

Life-threatening defects include defects of the heart, lungs, brain and other vital organs. Gastroschisis is one such defect where most of the front-side abdominal wall is absent. The abdominal organs are exposed outside (Fig 25-1). Defects in this category may be incompatible with survival, e.g. absence of both kidneys. In other cases, though, such defects can allow for a normal life if they are identified and corrected as soon as possible after birth.

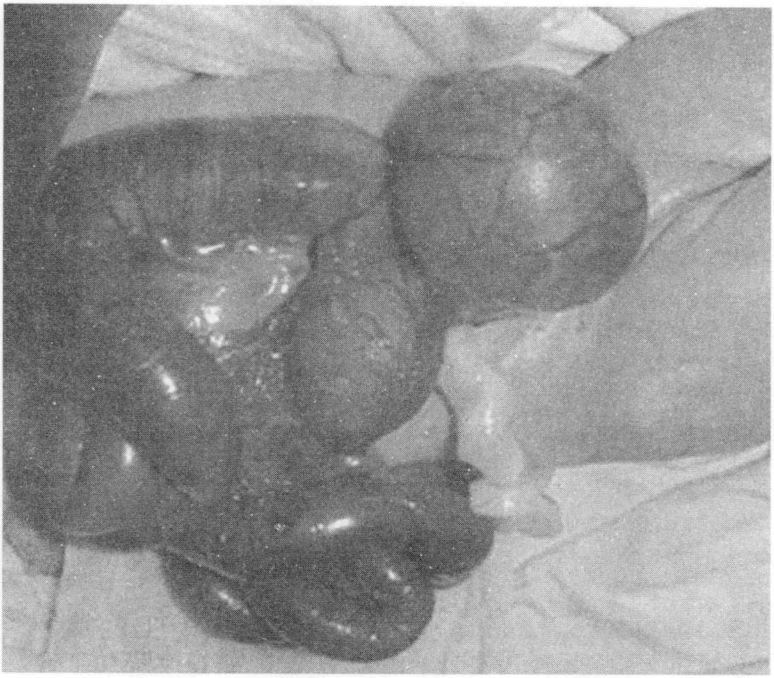

Fig 25-1

Examples include congenital intestinal obstruction due to a poorly developed section of the intestine and an abnormal connection between the food pipe and the wind pipe that prevents the baby from breathing normally unless surgical correction is done within a few hours after birth.

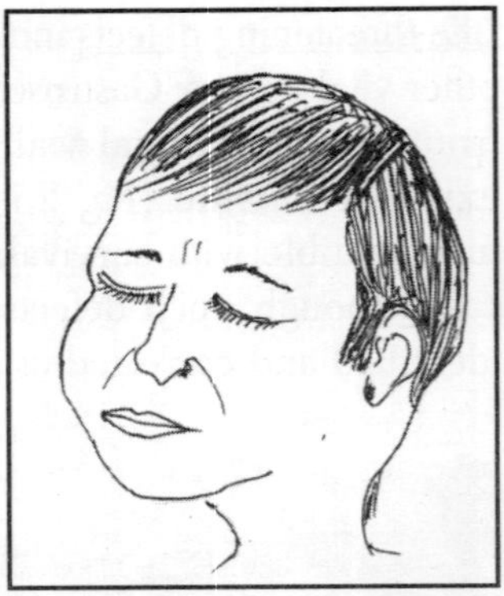

Fig 25-2

Major congenital anomalies include absence of an entire limb, absence of an eye, a hole in the heart that is not life-threatening, absent single lung, absent single kidney, a small (Fig 25-2) or a large skull, or mental retardation with minor congenital defects (of the external ear, fingers, etc.). In such cases, the defect is a major one, but there is no urgency to treat it at birth. The mental trauma of seeing a child with one of the above abnormalities is sometimes worse than with a life-threatening abnormality, because in this case, the child (and also the parents) will have to live with the defect (s) throughout life (unless they are surgically treatable).

Minor congenital anomalies include large birth marks, extra fingers, cleft lip, bony deformities, borderline mental handicap, club foot (Fig 25-4), umbilical hernia, short height (dwarfism) and others. In these cases, there is no dread of loss of life or a life-long disadvantage as the child can have a well-rounded, full life; however, some of these can lead to a social disadvantage, such as a large red stain on the face or a height of less than 4 feet in adulthood. The social cost of such handicaps is higher than the medical cost.

Inconsequential anomalies are aberrations that have no perceptible impact on the appearance or life style of the affected person. Examples include small birth marks, excessive body hair on a covered portion of the body (such as the lower back), a single bony defect that can be hidden within clothes and so on. The child will often live with the defect and no one will ever think of submitting her to a surgeon to correct the defect.

Bones and Muscles:

Extra finger (s) and toe(s) are very common minor defects; they may be on only one, two or all four limbs. The extra digit may be a small, incomplete digit attached to the hand or foot by a skin tag only, or it may be a completely well-formed, functioning digit with bones and all. Extra digit (s) may be all that the child has, or they may be a part of many other defects in the child. In some communities, an extra digit is considered a "good omen", while in others, it is looked down upon as an undesirable appendage. If so desired, extra digits can be removed surgically. If the digit is attached to the hand by a skin tag only, one can choke off its blood supply (which comes through the tag) by tying off the tag with a linen or nylon string; the appendage will fall off on its own within a few days without any further complications.

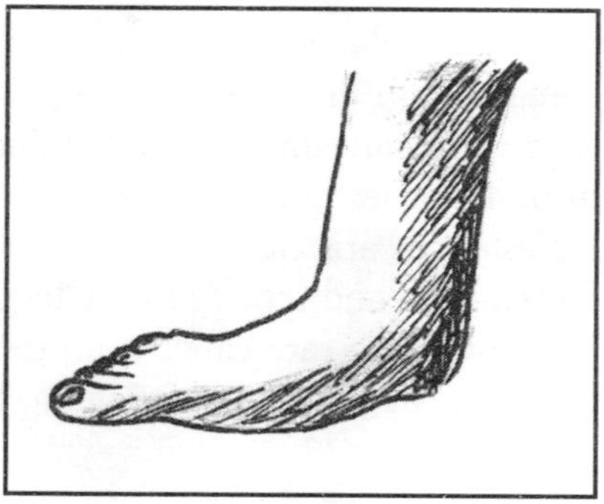

Fig 25-3

Flat feet (Fig 25-3) are normal in infancy; as the child starts walking, the arches of the feet develop. After 1 ½ to 2 years, the wet foot of a normal child leaves an adult type of impression on a glass or cardboard surface. In case of a child with flat feet, however, the impression is that of a "complete" foot with the inner side of the foot also visible on the surface. The parents may find that the inner edge of the child's shoes wears off as fast as the outer edge, or that the child doesn't want to walk most of the times. The child may not be able to run properly. Once diagnosed, flat feet are correctable with specially designed shoes and physiotherapy.

Club foot (Fig 25-4) is a foot which is turned downwards and inwards or upwards and outwards. It may be seen on one or both sides and is attributed to the abnormal position of the foot/feet in the womb

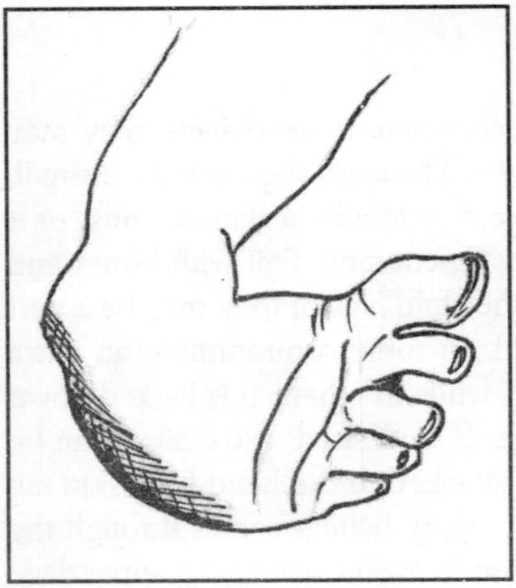

Fig 25-4

before birth; the foot/feet get pressed in an abnormal direction by the womb pressing inwards from outside. If the deformity is slight and not accompanied by too much spasm of the "pulling muscles", it can be corrected by a regimen of repeated re-positioning of the affected limb from its abnormal position to its NORMAL position. The action of pushing the foot to its normal position must be done at least 20-30 times a day (with rest periods in between). This may correct the defect completely within 2-3 weeks. When the defect is major, and the spasm of the pulling muscles cannot be reversed by manual movement, the re-positioning is carried out under sedation or under anaesthesia; after this, the foot position is maintained with a plaster of Paris cast. As the baby grows fast, the cast may need to be removed and replaced by a bigger cast repeatedly over the next 3-4 months. In rare cases, if no treatment is done in early infancy, the child has to be operated upon. Even then, the result may not be perfect.

Dislocated hips are a common congenital defect; they occur in 1 in 600-800 newborn babies. The child presents with a waddling gait, abnormal stance and unequal limb length after infancy. A plaster cast or surgery is needed.

Contractures are joint deformities caused by abnormal shortening of the musculature around the affected joint. They are a rare congenital defect and very difficult to treat.

Bow legs and *Knock knees* are common abnormalities of the knee and lower leg. Bow legs are legs that curve outwards below the knee, while knock-knees refer to knees that touch each other with the lower legs diverting outwards. Bowing of legs is normal up to the end of the 2nd year of life; knock knees at birth point to a bone defect (which has no treatment). In older children, rickets is a common cause of bow legs.

Abnormal walking includes walking with a waddle (duck-like gait), walking with the toes placed inwards (pigeon-gait) and toe-walking. Some of these defective gaits can be corrected by training and physiotherapy; in other cases, no treatment is possible except by drastic orthopaedic surgery.

Head, Brain and Spine defects:

Hydrocephalus: A large head is usually due to abnormal fluid formation and collection within the brain inside the "ventricles" (the fluid sacs within). The gaps in between the skull bones will be very large, and the window on top of the skull is very large and bulges out with tension. The eyeballs may be pushed downward by the pressure of the fluid inside the brain. The child will have bulging skull veins visible on the head. Treatment is by surgery; it should be offered early to prevent mental retardation.

Microcephaly (Fig 25-2): This is a term for a "small" head. It is usually, but not always, associated with mental retardation. In some cases, the problem arises due to a premature fusion between the various skull bones due to an unknown factor (*craniosynostosis*). In these latter cases, a release of the bones is needed to allow the brain to grow further; otherwise, the child will remain mentally arrested and ultimately retarded.

Spina bifida means a "split" spinal bone; this can occur at any level, but it is most commonly seen in the lower back. When the spinal bones do not fuse in the midline, the spinal cord and the nerves can develop poorly and "come out" of the normal place and be seen as a midline swelling at birth (*meningomyelocele).* The normal brain fluid (cerebrospinal fluid or CSF) may be leaking out of the opening. The child may be paralysed below the level of the split, so that the child has dribbling urine and stools and absence of normal movements of both the lower limbs. The condition is thought to occur due to a peri-conceptional deficiency of folic acid in the mother (see above). Spina bifida imposes a heavy life-long social and financial burden on the family. At times, it is associated with hydrocephalus.

Abdomen and Genitals:

We have already mentioned about intestinal obstruction. In fact, absence of an anal opening or *imperforate anus* is a fairly common problem. The anus is NOT SEEN at birth itself. This condition requires urgent surgery.

An *umbilical hernia* is an outpocketing of the umbilical skin usually from birth or from the age of a few months. In cases where the hernia develops later, excessive crying may have a role to play in "unmasking" the disorder. The umbilical region swells up when the child cries or strains, and it returns to normal when the child goes to sleep. Gentle pressure with your index finger will also successfully push the swelling inside when the child is quiet or sleeping. The content of the swelling is the child's own intestinal loop (s). It is useless to tie a cloth strap or fix coins over the swelling; over 90% of umbilical hernias disappear within 1-2 years *without* surgery. The rest will need surgery.

An *inguinal hernia* is seen in the groin; it is less common, but it has less chance of spontaneous cure and surgery is indicated immediately upon diagnosis, because there is a risk that the bowel loop that is present inside the outpouching will stay out and get strangulated by the ring through which it came out. This can become a life-threatening surgical emergency.

Fig 25-5

Undescended testis (Fig 25-5) is another common birth defect seen in boys. It means a testis that is not found in the scrotum. As the testis is formed inside the abdomen and it descends into the scrotum through the groin area, any arrest of this normal developmental descent will mean that the testis will stay in the abdomen, in the inguinal passage or just above the scrotum, depending upon when the arrest took place. One can wait for 6-12 months of life to see if the testis descends on its own. If it does not descend by 1 year of age, surgery will be necessary.

Hydrocele is the term used for collection of fluid in the scrotum around the testis; it can be normal in a newborn baby, but it disappears on its own by three to four months.

Cleft lip and cleft palate:

In this condition, the child is born with a cleft lip, a cleft palate or both. There may be a one-sided cleft in the lip and palate or the clefts may be present on both sides. The defects may be partial or complete, that is, extending all the way back to the end of the hard palate. The nose is also malformed. The child will find difficulty in sucking milk at the breast and will have to be fed with a dropper or a small spoon. If there is a cleft lip alone, it can be repaired early, even within the first few weeks; results are better if the repair is carried out early. If there is a cleft palate also, the child will face even more difficulties in feeding and will have speech difficulties and nasal speech in later life. It is possible to construct a temporary "prosthesis" which will close off the palatal opening and allow feeding and speech development to occur unhindered. Final surgical repair is done at the age of 1 ½ to 2 years, depending on the skill and experience of the plastic surgeon.

Mongolism (Down syndrome):

This is the commonest chromosomal abnormality. It is seen in 1:400 deliveries. The condition is caused by extra chromosomal material involving Chromosome No. 21. Either there are *three* of these chromosomes instead of the customary two, or the extra material is transferred on to one of the other chromosomes such as the 14th or the 15th pair of chromosomes. The child has *Mongolian* features, with a smaller than normal head, small, low-set ears, slanted eyes, a large, protruding tongue and a "dull" look which is characteristic. The child is usually mentally retarded and may have other congenital defects too, the commonest being a heart defect.

Mongolism is associated with advanced maternal age; women who are over 30 and who become pregnant must approach a genetic counselling service to rule out mongolism in their unborn baby.

Children with mongolism are borderline retarded, but they are happy, pleasant and cheerful by nature. They love art and music and can be made to learn activities of daily living to make themselves independent of their parents. Some can even learn easy skills like basket-weaving, handicraft etc and these will be self-sustaining in the future. Children with mongolism are educated in special schools and usually are unable to marry and bear children.

Skin problems:

These include birth marks or naevi. These may be flat or raised and may be differently coloured from the rest of the skin. Some examples include the *strawberry naevus,* the *port wine stain* and the *salmon patches.* While the first two are distinctly abnormal, salmon patches are dull pink areas found in up to 40% of all newborns on the upper eyelids, forehead, nape of the neck and occasionally, elsewhere on the face. They tend to disappear on their own within 3-6 months of age.

Some children have lighter-than normal (*hypopigmented*) or darker-than-normal (*hyperpigmented*) marks on their bodies. Each of these may be present on its own, or be a part of some clinical condition that needs further evaluation.

How to prevent birth defects?

- Avoid cousin marriages
- Women to get married and have children before they cross the age of 25.
- Pregnant women should not smoke or drink.
- Around the time of conception, or when you begin to plan for a child, start supplements of Folic acid.
- Eat a nutritious diet and take vitamin, mineral and iron pills regularly during pregnancy.
- Avoid exposure to X-rays, drugs, unnecessary medicines or other external agents, esp. during the first trimester of pregnancy.
- Do not try to abort a baby by using unlicensed abortifacients.
- All girls must take a dose of Rubella (German measles) vaccine before they become sexually active/marry (in the Indian context).
- When both partners have relatives with genetic defects, they should visit a genetic counsellor before contemplating marriage.

Ch 26
Two Parents or One?

A Single Parent Rearing

We never know the love of the parent till we become parents ourselves.

- Henry W Beecher 1813 - 1887,
American Preacher and Writer.

It is not every child's fortune to grow up in the midst of both his/her parents. There are many reasons why the child loses the support of one of his/her two parents. The commonest cause by far, in Indian circumstances, is death of one of the two parents. In the West, separation, with or without a divorce, is the commonest cause. Whatever the cause, the child has to then grow up with just one parent. At least until that parent chooses to tie the knot again, when the child will automatically get a second parent again.

This chapter will explore the problems of a single parent in brief.

Death of a spouse or the break-up of a successful marriage due to an emotional upheaval can devastate the family unit; it can cause the remaining parent to experience grief that is colossal, even if the separation was a very sordid affair, as the absence of a life-partner can effectively diminish the individual to a struggling, unhappy person. Most such parents will pass through the five stages of grief in the same or different order from the one given here:

1. Denial: This cannot happen to me
2. Anger: Why is this happening? Where did I go wrong?
3. Bargaining: To get the partner back if possible.
4. Depression: The stage where you begin to accept the situation and mope in the privacy of your home.
5. Acceptance: You accept the truth and begin to move forward in life.

Difficulties of single parent rearing:

It is certainly not a "piece of cake" when it comes to single parenting, and I have no doubt that most single parents have to rough it out before they see peace and achievement on their home front. Joint families in India and other South Asian countries are perhaps enabling single parents to be more successful at handling the problem, but remember that a joint family might have *prevented* the other spouse from seeking a divorce in the first place.

Social development does not prepare adults to be successful single parents, so that almost in every case, the single parent is at an early disadvantage *vis-à-vis* taking good care of his/her children. The single parent must expand his/her own abilities, devise peaceful means of interacting with the other parent and juggle the home finances optimally to ensure the best possible rearing for his/her children.

Home-making and cooking are the major challenges for the single father and most of them are able to pick up the requisite skills and get by successfully; however, some single parents just cannot do so and they remain frustrated and mentally stunted.

Children who live with a single parent are also more stressed about routines, schedules and such, but when it comes to special situations, they will find that their single parent will often consult *them* before taking any important decisions. This can weigh heavily on their mind, though most children will take this very positively and emerge as better, more accountable individuals.

Suggestions to make the living enjoyable:

This section attempts to explain what you, as a single parent, must do to make single parent rearing an acceptable and enjoyable task:

- Be the best parent that you can be: Do not try and do something that is beyond your capabilities, but at the same time, give of yourself one hundred per cent.
- You can't be both Dad and Mom, so stop trying: Up to a point, you may succeed in being the ideal parent and juggle the responsibilities of being a father and a mother together on your shoulders, but forget it; most of the times, this will *not* work out to your satisfaction. However, do realise what your strengths are and work to develop those properly. Seek help in areas where you just cannot do it: for example, if you cannot cook, you cannot cook. It will be a better idea to appoint a house cook, or arrange for a year-round tiffin or something else that works well for you.
- Forgive, even if you can't forget: It is essential to forgive the other parent of your child if you are to foster a healthy, joyous atmosphere in the house. If you won't do so, the child will "sense" the bitterness and be unable to adjust without his/her other parent.
- Make the most of everything you have: Even if you don't have a lot of money, you still have your child, your house and your "family". Remember that a child will enjoy any activity as long as you participate in it, even if it is free. So indulge with him/her and have painting, dancing, walking and singing sessions everyday.
- Integrate with your larger family and your neighbourhood: The child will thank you immensely if you integrate, mingle

and interrelate with other relatives, neighbours and other well-wishers. This will also help you be a better parent. Do not hesitate to join Single Parent support groups if there are any in your city.

- Take responsibility for your own life: If you are fat, slim down; if you have diabetes, visit the doctor immediately. Remember that an innocent person (your child) depends upon YOU to live a healthy, complete life. Thus, take charge of yourself as early as possible after becoming a single parent.
- Set up daily routines:
- Be consistent and dependable: You are the only friend, philosopher and guide for your parents. If you lead a stress-free, consistent and dependable lifestyle, your child will feel safe with you and trust you completely. Even if you are tired when you return home, cook a good family meal, sit with your kid and enjoy his/her company as he/she enjoys yours. Do not betray him/her.
- Take the issue of re-marriage very seriously but go slow with it till your own child (ren) begin(s) to accept the idea: Arrival of a step-parent in the house is an idea that needs to be "cautiously welcomed". It is quite possible for you to get someone to agree to be your new spouse, but it is very difficult for that *same someone to be your child's new parent.*

Single parenting can be successful too:

It is common to talk about the problems that can happen if one of the parents is not there to look after the child. Not all children growing up in single-parent families experience negative consequences, just as not all overweight people have a heart attack.

Dr. Stephen Duncan, a Parenting specialist has written that there are several important characteristics that mark a successful single parent:

- They accept the fact that it will be a difficult thing to manage the child/children single-handedly.

- They are not on a self-pity or ego trip; rather, they know their own shortcomings and are always trying to improve their parenting skills.
- They are committed to their family 100%. They will often sacrifice their own leisure activities and be after their child/ children.
- They encourage open communications and foster individual expression. The parent is more often willing to listen to his/ her child and less likely to enforce his/her version of discipline on the offspring.
- They are successful organizers of the home and the hearth. They are better time managers too.
- They take good care of themselves, whether through diet control, exercises, yoga or anything else.
- They maintain rituals, traditions and relationships properly. Thus prayers, bedtime story-telling, sitting together at meal-times, going out on Sunday evenings etc. all play an important role in cultivating happiness among the children. In a disturbed environment, a fixed routine and maintenance of tradition can be very soothing
- Successful single parents allow the other non-residential parent to visit the child and the child to go and visit the other parent (if divorce or separation was the cause and the other parent is alive).
- They continue to maintain a positive outlook toward single parenting and toward life in general.

Benefits of single parenting:

This might sound a bit contradictory, as conventional thought dictates that single-parent reared children are "inadequate" in some way or the other. However, here are some distinct benefits that could accrue from single parenting:

- If an acrimonious divorce was the reason for a parent to leave the house, single parenting will bring with it a reduction of hostilities and tension and a return to a more peaceful, serene household with no devastating conflict.
- A single parent will have more flexibility in planning quality time with his/her child as there is no demand for his/her time from the other adult in the house. Not only is planning easier, the parent and child get *more* time to spend with each other.
- As the single parent has no one else to turn to to resolve difficulties, he/she often involves the children in the decision-making process. This has the advantage of increasing the children's self-confidence as also of bringing the family members closer.
- Single parents often have to learn new skills like cooking (for fathers) and balancing the cheque-book (for mothers); this makes them better, stronger individuals.
- Children also become better, more broad-minded individuals as they are exposed to two different spheres of influence in their lives – that of the father's family, and that of the mother's family too.

Tips for Single Parents:

Here are some ideas for single fathers/mothers that may come in useful for them:

- Find ways to keep in touch with your child (-ren) regularly. Letters, e-mails, gifts, jokes etc. may all come in handy if you cannot see the child (-ren) every single day.
- Never talk negatively about the child (-ren)'s mother or her family in front of the child (-ren).
- Be predictable and consistent in your dealing with the child, the other parent and with the society in general.

- Remember holidays and birthdays and celebrate them so that the child (-ren) will have sweet memories of those events for a lifetime.
- Help the child (-ren) to express her/their feelings by being supportive and encouraging; do behave nicely with her/them as they will gain confidence from you.
- Find and spend quality time with each of your child (-ren) separately and individually.
- Take the kids out for walks, hikes, outings and camps; enjoy games like football or badminton; swim or dance with her/them.
- Keep praising the child (-ren) five times more than criticising her/them.
- Find books that tell about child (-ren)'s feelings through stories and read these stories to her/them. This will help them face her/their problems, vocalise them and seek your opinion and guidance without fear.

<u>Suggested links for further reading:</u>

✔ http://singleparents.about.com/
✔ http://singleparentscentral.com

B. Working Mothers

In the present day economic scenario, many house-wives are electing to supplement their husband's income by going to work. I am not talking about Professional women like doctors or beauticians, but about the average working woman who has a pleasing manner, average looks, some training in secretarial practice, typing and computer operations, and the courage to "go out" and do the additional work, *besides also handling household work and looking after the child (-ren)*. This part of the chapter is for those women who are considering work along with their child-rearing activity. In some respects, some of the information in the previous section applies also to the working mother, although here there is a vital difference: the husband **is around** to help.

Why some women work:

Some women are ambitious and career oriented. Not for them the drudgery of raising child (-ren), pressing the feet of their husbands and cooking for three hours everyday. This chapter will obliquely address them as well, but is not really meant for them.

The larger majority of working women are in this because they wish to become financially independent as well as supplement their husband's income and usher in a better, more liberated and luxurious lifestyle. They feel important as well - and this adds to their self-confidence and empowers them to achieve more and more in life.

It appears like an impossibility to effectively do three things simultaneously: managing the home, going for the job and looking after the kids; and yet, many thousands of mothers do just this day in and day out throughout the year.

Of course, if the mother is also a single parent, she will *have* to work to look after her child's and her own financial needs.

What, how and when should mothers work?

<u>Double Income No Kids (DINKS):</u> Ideally, if possible, young couples should plan not to have a child for at least 4-5 years after marriage if they are both professionals, or working in any capacity. They would both contribute to the family's kitty, and this "double income" can serve them well when they plan to raise a family and have child (-ren). At the same time, couples who marry in their late twenties should NOT delay having child (-ren) for 4-5 years as the chance of a genetic

handicap or malformation increases as parental age (esp. maternal age) advances (see Chapter 30).

When? Once there is a new member in the family, ideally, the mother should NOT work for at least 2-3 years, so that she can provide uninterrupted breast feeding, 24-hours undivided attention and effective mothering till the toddler begins school. If this is not feasible, she must avail of the full permissible *maternity leave;* she should start the leave at or just before the time of delivery so that she gets the maximum possible days after delivery to look after the baby. She may also utilise sick leave and earned leave (if these are available). In this manner, she can, with some effort and some adjustment, manage to exclusively breast feed her baby for six months.

What? The preferable option for a mother of a small baby is to choose a job or profession that permits flexible hours of working, working from home and part-time work. Nowadays, with the software sector opening up, computer-based jobs can be easily done from the home or at flexible hours, including evening hours, when the nursing baby is often asleep, and allows the mother some free time to work. In the same manner, jobs such as a receptionist for a consultant doctor, private tuitions, embroidery work, tailoring, small-time catering, cookery classes, etc. are all adaptable to flexible timings, working from home and part-time work. As far as possible, the mother should look for such jobs till her life settles down.

How to work and breast feed at the same time:

I have come across several inspirational accounts of working mothers who have successfully exclusively breast fed their babies for six to seven months after birth. Here are some excerpts from one such woman. She writes:

- My son never had a drop of artificial baby milk and was exclusively breastfed until he began trying solid foods at about 8 months old.

- Combining working and breastfeeding was not always easy, but it has been worth every second of effort. Of all the things I've done as a parent, I have to admit this is one of my proudest accomplishments.

The way to go about doing this is to **pump** breast milk before going to work; the mother should either use a manual method of expression and use her hands or a manual breast pump or use an electrical breast pump (available for about 2500 to 3000 rupees in big cities). The first time you pump the milk, leave it at home for some caretaker to feed it to the baby at about 12 noon. In the afternoon, if you can come home, well and good. Feed the baby directly at the breast once or twice as the time permits. Go back to work. At 4 p.m. or so, during the coffee break, pump some more breast milk in the office and collect it in a clean container. Bring that home and give it to someone to feed it to the baby while you unwind from the day's tiring schedule. By 7 p.m., you would be free to directly feed the baby again.

Role of a crèche:

If your workplace has a crèche, and you have no one to lean to, you can always take the baby with you at work; in this case, pumping may not be needed at all if you can go and feed the baby every three hours or so.

Role of a house-maid:

If possible, hire a trustworthy, clean, young house-maid about 1-2 months before you go in for the delivery. She will be immensely useful to both you and the baby in many respects. I know that getting a good house-maid is a tough job as they don't come cheap, at least in big metros, but by and large, you should be able to get them to stay from 8 a.m. to 8 p.m. for about 1000 rupees a month. The lunch and teas would be also at your expense. It is highly advisable to photograph the maid, get her medically checked and investigated to rule out TB, HIV, etc. and to take her to the local police station for a quick check of the criminal records of her that may exist. If you find everything to your satisfaction, you can appoint her.

She would be expected to feed the baby your milk/top milk or weaning foods in your absence (apart from doing other household work).

Role of grandparents and other extended family members:

Nobody can do for little children what grandparents do.
Grandparents sort of sprinkle stardust
over the lives of little children.

- Alex Haley (1919)
US novelist, short-story writer.

This is valid only where there are still joint families. Grandparents of the child can be a real boon. However, many ungrateful parents of small babies do not appoint a maid and live a relaxed lifestyle while the grandparents are doing all the baby-related household work. I am totally against this outright shirking of one's responsibilities. Parents may request their own parents to help them in looking after the baby in their absence; however, they must not use this as an excuse to not appoint a maid, to go out to movies and late night parties and to various "functions". They must also not give "hard to perform" household tasks like cooking, washing child's nappies etc. to their parents.

On the other hand, grandparents may, if they wish, do whatever they can to relieve the parents' burden; for example, they may want to keep the folded clothes back in the almirahs, prepare the dining table, play with their grandchild when the latter appears to be cranky or bored (and also read to her stories), feed the baby the breast milk stored in the refrigerator, and such other soft jobs.

Grandparents can be a source of immense pleasure to the baby, just as the baby can rejuvenate her old grandpa and grandma. You, as understanding parents, should try and see that a homely, happy environment prevails in the house.

Role of the father:

Times have changed, and the father is no longer the newspaper-reading, tea-guzzling, mustachioed armchair-lolling tyrant that 19th century fathers once were. (I am not casting aspersions on my grandparents, but rather, lightening your mood just to explain the stereotyped image of the father about a century ago!)Today's modern father is fully expected to share with his working wife all the responsibilities of rearing the child. He should not hesitate to look after the baby while his wife is cooking, to change the baby's diapers, to feed her mother's milk when the mother is away and so on.

<u>Further Reading:</u>

- ✔ http://www.kjsl.com/~cee/working.htm
- ✔ http://www.breastfeeding.com/workingmom.shtml\
- ✔ http://www.suite101.com/articles.cfm/working_mothers

Ch 27
The Adopted Child

I have included this small chapter on the adopted child to explain to those who have an adopted child as to how they should go about parenting this child. The chapter has been designed to address the commonly asked questions on the topic.

What is adoption?

Adoption is a process of taking a son or a daughter who is not your own, but of someone else, but whose custody is being willingly given to you. The adoptee child may or may not be related to the adoptive parents. While there is a state law on Adoption by Hindu parents, (The Hindu Adoption and Maintenance Act, HAMA, 1956), minority communities follow The Guardians and Wards Act, GAWA, 1890 or their own Personal Law for the purpose of adoption. A simple act where the donor parents hand over a child to the adoptive parents without due process of law is an illegal adoption; it does not confer any rights on the child or the parents; the biological parents may return to claim the child in future. To see the full text of HAMA, see the following link:

- ✔ http://www.vakilno1.com/bareacts/hinduadoptionsact/hinduadoptionsact.htm

Is there any difference between the above two laws?

Yes, there is. The HAMA is applicable to Hindus, Sikhs, Jains and Buddhists. The adoption is irrevocable and biological parents forfeit all claims to the child once they give away the child to the adoptive family. Only one child of each sex can be adopted, provided that the parents do not already have a child of either sex. The GAWA is applicable to Christians, Muslims, Parsis and Jews. In this act, the adoptive adults are labelled "guardians" and the child is called a "Ward". The "adoption" is NOT irrevocable and the biological parents can re-claim the child later.

Who are eligible to adopt a child?

Well-settled single persons or childless married couples are all eligible to adopt a child. They are screened by the court to see if they are mentally capable of looking after the child, whether they are financially secure and whether they have an environmentally adequate residence.

Indian laws also permit similarly eligible foreigners to adopt Indian children.

What is the procedure for adopting a child?

In brief, the procedure is as follows:

The adoptive couple has to first register with an Adoption Agency, fill out forms and pay some registration fees. They will have to furnish various documents that support their age, marital status, infertility status report, photographs, community references and recommendations, statement of net worth and property owned, employment or tax related documents, bank reference, and an undertaking by a relative who will agree to look after the child in case the adoptive parents die.

After this is completed, individual and joint interviews of the parents are taken by the social worker and a Home Study Report is prepared. The Indian Council for Child Welfare (ICCW) and the Indian Council for Social Welfare (ICSW) are the main agencies involved in the scrutiny procedures. A suitable child is identified and the child's medical records are handed to the parents for scrutiny. The parents can arrange for the adoptive child to be examined by their own Pediatrician.

The legal process gets under way, and as soon as a petition is filed on behalf of the couple, the child's custody is given to the couple. A court hearing is held within a month from the filing date, where the court may ask the couple to deposit a considerable amount in the child's name for financial security. Once this is done, most of the hurdles are removed and the court order is soon released which legalises the custody into an official adoption.

The court will usually ask the social worker to periodically visit the adoptive home to verify that the child is being looked after properly.

Care of the adopted child:

If you have adopted a baby who is less than three months old, you will have to look after her feeding, immunisation, check to see if she sees and hears normally, whether she is growing normally and whether her development is normal or not. If you are a mother who just lost her baby, it is likely that you will be able to breast-feed the adopted child; otherwise, the baby will have to be started on top milk or formula milk. If the centre that cared for the baby before you got custody of her has been timely in giving the baby its vaccine shots, you have nothing to worry about; in all other cases, the baby may have to "catch-up" with her vaccines.

If the child adopted by you is between 3-9 months old, again the aims will remain the same; the extra work you will need to do is to make the child "like" you (over 75% of babies over 6 months old have stranger anxiety). The other thing you need to do is to initiate weaning, catch-up on vaccines and check the child carefully for normal sight and hearing and the pace and quality of physical and mental development.

If the adopted child is over a year but less than 3 years old, you will have to work somewhat harder to win the love and confidence of the child. Excursions, picnics with the family, treats when you return home and spending quality time with the child will go a long way in familiarising you with the child and vice-versa.

It is usually not a tough task to get an older, recently adopted child to be nice and civil to you externally, but it is indeed a tough task to get her to love you unreservedly, because she will be able to see you for what you are: a caretaker and not a biological parent; she will be critical of every small error that you make in the house or elsewhere and will secretly keep measuring you against her mental image of the "ideal" parent. I am not trying to scare anyone here, but prepare yourself to face some degree of belligerence and reservation from her in the initial few months as she assesses you. Acceptance will come, but it may take time.

In general, the overall care of the adopted child is no different from that of a biological child.

Disclosing that the child is an adopted one:

Most authorities are agreed that it is advisable to inform the child that you have adopted her and that she belongs to you but is not born from you. The disclosure, however, is an ongoing process, and is explained to the child in a way that she can comprehend – that is, how you tell her depends on her stage of development. Parents are advised to use picture books, stories and such other material to impassionately reveal the facts to the child.

Resources for Adoption:

Please contact the following:

National Association of Adoptive Families
Rm. No. 7, 1st fl.,
Sanyas Ashram Municipal School,
Vithalbhai Rd.,
Vile Parle (W), Mumbai 400066
Tel: (022)26703838
Web-site: http://www.naaf-india.org
E-mail: naaf@rediffmail.com

Further reading:

- ✔ http://www.sitagita.com/article.asp?cyberspace=38-2-0-0&leafId=8659
- ✔ http://newstodaynet.com/2003cd/250703.htm
- ✔ http://www.familynyou.com/channels/atpdindex.php3?idtitle=55&channel_sub_id=118
- ✔ http://www.naaf-india.org/faqs.htm
- ✔ http://persmin.nic.in/arpg/adopt.htm

Ch 28
Child Abuse and Neglect

What is a neglected child? He is a child not planned for, not wanted. Neglect begins, therefore, before he is born.
-Pearl S. Buck, 1892-1973, American Novelist.

Many parents believe that discipline means taking the rod to the child. In their misguided enthusiasm to "improve" their offspring, they beat the child regularly. Beatings can range from a single slap on the bottom, to hitting the child with a stick, burning her with a hot iron, or even using a sharp instrument like a knife or a pointed item and stabbing her with it. Starving the child, locking her up in a room, shutting up the child in a dark environment, chaining the child to a piece of furniture – all these are examples of unreasonable punishment.

<u>Corporal punishment</u> almost always fails in reforming the child and instead, it creates resentment in her mind against the parent. While corporal punishment was considered a norm in the past, modern thinking coupled with decades of research has shown this type of punishment to be completely misguided. Not only that, it can be positively harmful to both the child as well as the parent. While the child actually ends up with physical injuries, the parent keeps feeling

guilty from within, and may even hurt himself/herself for having hit his/her child so badly.

Spare the rod and ... save the child:

Indeed, it was once said that sparing the rod "spoilt the child". Hindi movies have "celebrated" this type of thinking by showing how a rigid, rod-wielding father proudly declaims that it is only because of his beatings that his children have all grown up to be models of society. It is then shown that he is completely misinformed: his sons are drunks, womanisers, gamblers or plain evil people, but outside of his knowledge.

In general, withdrawal of parental love and nurturance is a much better alternative to corporal punishment. In this method, the child is given "time-outs"; she is told "not to talk with her mother or father"; she is not allowed to see her most favourite programmes on TV; she is asked to get up from the table and go away only when dessert is served. The child who has misbehaved knows her error. The moment she is punished by the "withdrawal of love and nurturance" method, the message has hit home, and hit hard, despite there being no physical violence involved. The parents can always "recall" the punishment at the end of a certain pre-decided duration and claim back the love of their child. Nobody is hurt.

What is abuse?

Child abuse and neglect refers to the situation where a child is hurt ritually and regularly, or he/she is neglected all the time. This can happen if:

a) the child is unwanted
b) one (or both) of the parents is (are) not the biological parent (s) of the child
c) the abusing parent is a chronic alcoholic or a drug-addict and irresponsible
d) in the Indian context – the child is a girl child

e) the abusing parent suffers from a psychiatric disorder

In all the above circumstances, the parent (we will assume that it is the father, just to simplify the language here, but it could well be the mother, step-parent, foster parent or both parents) just does not feel any sympathy or empathy for the child when he sets out to punish his child.

He will exhibit "civil behaviour" only to show the child, the other off-springs and the other parent that he is being "reasonable and nice" about it. In reality, however, he has already resolved to "teach the brat a lesson he will never forget". He may begin the assault with a gradually rising voice; as the child has previously already experienced his father's anger, he will immediately try and move away from his father and try and hide behind his mother, or run out of the room and go and hide in some other part of the house. Little does he realise that his father is out to have his hide, come what may, and by these evasive manoeuvres, he is merely delaying the inevitable. Thus, physical punishment soon descends on the child: he may have to face slapping, pummeling, pounding, thrashing, pinching, etc. Alternatively, his father may decide to hurl things at him, or push him violently so that he goes and hits the wall or cupboard. The father may use a weapon, if only so that "I don't get hurt, you twerp!" The weapon may be a blunt item like a small stick, a *danda*, a cricket bat or any handy item that lies next to him, even a long broom. Sometimes, the father may use a sharp item like a pointed pencil, a knife or a pointed tool from the tool box: in both the cases, there is a real danger that the child may get hurt badly.

Feelings of remorse may take a back-seat if the abuse leads to an injury that needs immediate medical attention. The abusing parent will then threaten the child not to spill the beans at the doctor's clinic, and then take the child to the doctor, where he will fabricate a story about an accident that caused the injury. If, on the other hand, there is no immediate need to visit a doctor, the father will just go back to whatever he was doing earlier, completely ignoring the looks of the other family members.

This kind of behaviour, occurring day in and day out, constitutes child abuse.

What is neglect?

Neglect is the other side of the Abuse-Neglect coin. In this type of abuse, there are no beatings or burnings and hence no external evidence of abuse; however, the child is neglected: when he is hungry, she is not fed; if fed, she is given substandard, diluted food; when she is sick, she is not given medicines and medical attention is not sought; when she asks for money for school, she is not obliged, so that her education suffers. An extra-ebullient child might be tied up to the cupboard and left there crying. This type of negligence is extremely difficult for others to pick up and even after it is picked up, it is quite difficult to rectify.

The Law in India:

The laws on child-care are virtually non-existent in India. A parent has carte blanche to do what he likes with his own child (-ren). There is no compulsion on the parent to seek early medical care etc. However, in case of the problem becoming serious enough to force the parents to admit the child to a hospital, the doctors will usually call in the social welfare officials to look into the matter and take remedial action if possible.

Sexual Abuse:

This is a particularly heinous form of abuse that is believed to be occurring fairly commonly in urban metros nowadays. It can take the form of sodomy, fellatio, vaginal penetration, fondling, caressing, molesting and so on. The perpetrators may be adults in the family, older siblings, servants, teachers, goons, etc. In most cases, the stories never see the light of day due to fear of social ostracism.

What can you do to stem the tide?

As discussed in the beginning of the chapter, be humane while meting out punishments to your own children. If you detect someone among your acquaintances who is abusing or neglecting the children under his care, report him/her to the nearest social welfare centre. Protect your own children from abuse by keeping a close watch over them when they meet with friends and relatives whom you do not know personally. Especially if these friends or relatives are of the sex opposite to your child.

Further Reading:

- ✔ http://www.womenexcel.com/law/childabuse.htm
- ✔ http://www.darshandentalcollege.com/newsletter/abuse.htm
- ✔ http://nccanch.acf.hhs.gov/

Part IX
Medical Care

There's something like a line of gold thread
running through a man's words
when he talks to his daughter,
and gradually over the years it gets to be long enough
for you to pick up in your hands and
weave into a cloth that feels like love itself.

– Author Unknown.

Ch. 29
Consulting A Specialist

He who cures a disease may be the "skillfullest",
but he that prevents it is the safest physician.

- Thomas Fuller, 1608-1661,
British Clergyman, Author.

It is a sign of the times that more and more parents prefer to visit a Pediatrician each time they need to see a doctor for their child's problems. It is also heartening to see that many parents do not mind going that extra distance or paying that little extra to get their babies' shots (immunisations) and advice directly from a Pediatrician.

There are several reasons why this is a better state of affairs. The first reason is, simply, that a Pediatrician is better equipped to handle your child's medical, psychological and sometimes, even social problems. I am not trying to say that your family doctor cannot be a good guide to you – in fact as a child, I received my routine care from a very empathetic, knowledgeable and concerned family practitioner. At the same time, the field of Pediatrics has expanded very fast – there are so many new disease entities, so many new concerns, so many new vaccines – that every child must be shown to a Pediatrician at least once in a fortnight in the first three months, once a month till one year, once in three months from one till two, once in six months from then till 5 years, and once a year thereafter till she is eighteen.

Once you have selected your home where you are going to raise your family, do make enquiries and check local newsletters to see which Pediatricians and what hospitals are available nearby. Nowadays, it is possible to get such information online, by looking up www.pediatriconcall.com. Telephonic yellow pages, like Hello Midday at +912223510000 will give the information on phone. So will other help-lines like Times of India Info line at +912226005555 or Just Dial Service at +912224444444. These are the numbers for Mumbai. One can seek such information from other yellow pages too, like those of MTNL or Tata Donnelly.

Many a times, your family's Pediatrician may not be easily accessible, so keep a locally available doctor too, who you can approach in an emergency. Check out the doctor's qualifications, the hospitals he/she visits, the patronage he/she gets from the people around him/her, and so on. Also make preliminary enquiries regarding his/her experience, charges and fees, special knowledge in newborn care and so on. These answers will help you find the right doctor for your yet-to-be-born baby.

Put up the doctor's name and number on a ready to see card in front of the telephone, so that you may be able to find it quickly in an emergency. Also keep the child's medical papers in a file and keep this easily accessible so that when you go for a consultation, you do not forget to take her file with you.

Preparing for the Visit to the Pediatrician:

The following information should be readily available to the doctor when you see him/her for the first time:

a) Child's birth details
b) Child's blood group and other neonatal test reports

c) His previous illness reports and X-rays
d) Treatment details
e) List of drugs or food-items that the child is allergic to

At the same time carry with you the following <u>things</u>:

a) List of questions that you wish to ask the doctor
b) Some favourite toys of the child that she can play with
c) Extra napkins and loose clothes in case the child soils or spoils the clothes worn by her
d) Some water or milk in a beaker/plastic glass with lid
e) Some quick snacks like biscuits/mashed fruit/mashed rice and curd
f) Her medical file and any relevant medical reports like scans, X-rays etc.
g) Sufficient cash to cover the doctor's fees, traveling, cost of urgent investigations (if ordered by the doctor) and cost of snacking out (if planned beforehand, this can be a very pleasant diversion from the sad task of the doctor's visit)

<u>Keep enough time</u> for expected and unexpected delays. These include –

a) Travelling delays caused by traffic jams, *morchas* and processions
b) Doctor's absence because of an emergency visit by him/her to see another patient
c) Queue of patients due to an increase in the illnesses in the community
d) Sudden arrival of a serious patient into the clinic
e) Time inside the doctor's cabin for your own child

As such, one should provide for at least 25-30% extra time when planning a consultation.

Dress of the baby: Dress her up in loose clothes which can be easily removed. Avoid tight-fitting *baba suits* with buttons on the insides of the thighs and genital region. Frilly clothes are also a no-no.

Other tips: Carry your mobile phone with you. If the child is seriously ill, ask whether you can take her directly to a hospital, where emergency treatment can be begun quickly. Always take a prior appointment for the consultation if possible. If you anticipate that the child will need costly tests or hospitalization, carry more cash or your credit card if you have one, so that you may access an ATM machine to withdraw cash in an emergency situation.

The Actual Consultation:

Barring the first one or two visits, the alert child recognizes the environs of the Pediatrician's clinic even before setting foot inside the building where the clinic is located. There is a natural anxiety and it is unavoidable. It is therefore the combined skill of you as parents, the doctor's receptionist and the Pediatrician himself that eases the child's anxiety and allows you to relate the child's story and the doctor to examine her unhurriedly and to then delineate the line of treatment. He also has to explain how the medicines must be given, and counsel you regarding other steps to be taken to heal your child as quickly as possible.

Hence, the need for toys, distracting items and milk-feeds in smaller babies. Do remember that the doctor may have limited time at his disposal, so prepare a list of all the important questions you need to ask before you come for the consultation. Write down the advice that he gives you so that you do not forget it. If he has ordered any investigations, ask where they are to be done, when they are to be done, and if any prior preparation of the child is needed before taking her for the test.

Remember to ask how the medicines are to be given – whether on an empty stomach or after a meal. Understand what the doctor means when he says half a teaspoon, full teaspoon, etc. in exact milliliters, as it is imperative that you feed the proper dose of the medicines to your child. Ask how the medicines are to be stored, whether in the refrigerator or outside.

Follow-up telephone call and visits:

Having started the treatment suggested by the doctor, you may follow-up on this by telephoning the doctor when your baby fails to respond to treatment, when she develops new symptoms, when you cannot procure a certain medicine from the pharmacy and when the doctor has himself asked you to call him up.

A repeat visit is also warranted halfway during a prescribed course of treatment when your child's response is less than satisfactory. It is definitely needed at the end of treatment for an acute disease, and at intermittent intervals during treatment for a prolonged or chronic illness.

<u>Telephonic Consultation Etiquette</u>:

In case of an emergency, it is perfectly reasonable for you to call up the doctor at any time of the day or night on any number, including his mobile number or residential line. In all other cases, you should remember that doctors are also human, and need rest and need to spend time with their family, friends and social circle. Hence, take care to avoid calling him during early mornings, late nights, meal times, and when he has just left his clinic and is probably commuting in heavy traffic to reach home.

Doctors are frequently irritated when patients or their care-takers call up at odd hours to ask about some routine or inconsequential matter(s). There is some truth to the adage that patients cannot really say if their legitimate concern is actually mediocre or something serious in medical terms. At the same time, calling up the doctor on his mobile to simply ask if you can see him today at the clinic (when you could have done so by calling up the receptionist at the clinic) is really unforgivable.

Before you dial the number of your doctor, keep a paper and a pen handy by your side to take down the names of any medicines that he may dictate on the phone. Keep the child's most recent doctor's prescription also nearby. This will save your time as well as the doctor's.

Other Useful Tips:

- If the doctor has prescribed you some medicine on the phone for an emergency during the night, it is your responsibility to visit him the next day to show your child to him.
- Re-confirm the spellings of all the medicines that he has dictated to you over the phone before hanging up.
- When your child seems very sick, it is always a better option to take him/her first to a hospital that your doctor is attached to, and let the child receive emergency medication, while the resident doctor alerts your pediatrician to come over and see the child.

Giving medicines properly:

Children are fussy about taking medicines and everyone knows that! Hence, I am going to briefly outline how they should be given medicines.

Infants less than three months old: Try to use a dropper to give the medicine. Many medicines are available in a drop formulation for use in this age group. Carefully open the baby's mouth and feed her the medicine drop by drop, taking care to see that the exact quantity is given.

Infants three to twelve months old: In this age group, both dropper-based medicines and syrups are all right. To give syrups in quantities less than 2.0 ml, use a dropper or a small, disposable plastic syringe (without the needle); for larger quantities, use the plastic cup that is placed on top of the lids of most medicine bottles. If the baby is uncooperative, open her mouth by pressing on the cheeks between both her jaws, and gently pour the medicine inside her mouth in the space between her teeth and the inside of her cheeks. Pinching of the nose is rarely needed.

<u>Some General Points:</u> Dispersible tablets, chewable tablets and flavoured granules are other possible pediatric drug formulations available for selected medicines. Antibiotics are usually available as dry syrups, in which clean water must be added up to a certain mark found on either the label or the bottle itself. Hot water must NOT be added. These reconstituted medicines are stable for just a few days, and that too if stored in a refrigerator. Recently, many antibiotic formulations have become available in ready-to-use liquid forms. This has made administration of these medicines much easier.

After the child has taken the medicine, wipe her face, give her some water to sip and then leave her be.

Conclusion:

In conclusion, I must reiterate that when you consult a pediatrician, you are in fact entering into an unwritten "contract" with him. While you naturally expect him to cure or relieve your child in reasonable time and without many investigations and procedures, he also expects you to follow his instructions religiously. If he asks you to give a certain medicine to your baby for, say, five days, do not stop the medicine because the child has improved at a faster pace, or because the "bottle got over". If you do wish to truncate the child's treatment, try and speak to the Pediatrician before doing so. If, on the other hand, some symptoms of the child do linger after the prescribed course is over, ask him again if the medicines can be continued for a longer time.

It is your bounden duty to obey the doctor's instructions, as long as they are bona fide and reasonable. If you wish to see another doctor for a second opinion, why, you are free to do so; it would be better if you took your first doctor's permission and/or letter – but even if you did not seek his permission, do take all his papers to the second doctor, so that that doctor is able to help your child better.

Ch.30
Vaccines and Immunisations

Children are our most valuable natural resource.
- Herbert C. Hoover, 1874 - 1964,
31st American President.

Vaccines are preparations that are used to prevent diseases. They may be oral preparations or injections. The science of Vaccinology is continuously evolving. Timely administration of these agents has prevented many thousands of children from succumbing to the plethora of life-threatening illnesses that have plagued mankind since ages. Vaccines continue to save lives everyday. Even when they fail to prevent a disease, they mitigate the dangerous consequences of those diseases, so that even in a failed case, the illness is shorter and milder than if it had occurred in an unvaccinated individual.

Indeed, it would not be an exaggeration to say that *no other scientific advance has been so fruitful and satisfying in the entire history of mankind.* Today, small pox has been consigned to history as it has got eradicated from our planet only because of global vaccination. Polio is also on the way out, with only a handful of countries still reporting active poliomyelitis in 2003. India, unfortunately, still has some way to go before we bid goodbye to this dreadful disease. However, it is only fair to say that there has been a 95% reduction in the incidence of new cases in India. The death rates due to other vaccine preventable diseases have also declined, e.g. measles, diphtheria, tetanus and whooping cough. Most of these diseases have completely disappeared from developed countries. Successful elimination of some of these potentially lethal illnesses has encouraged vaccine manufacturers to make vaccines against diseases that do not usually kill their sufferers, but cause loss of health, loss of work and pay, deformities, scarring, chronic debility or a future susceptibility to cancer. Some of these diseases are Hepatitis B, Hepatitis A, Chicken Pox and Typhoid fever. These newer vaccines are now being gradually accepted by patients and their care takers, since avoidance of morbidity (sickness) is also considered important.

There is a contrary opinion prevalent among some medical practitioners, especially some homoeopaths, that vaccines are NOT to be used – that homoeopathic methods forbid their use, or make them unnecessary. To all such doctors I have only to show the past successes of vaccination as an effective promoter of healthy childhood and a nasty deterrent to disease causing bugs.

What is Immunisation?

Controlled administration of modified microbes (either killed, or made less virulent) with the intention to provoke a protective antibody or immune response by the individual is called immunisation. The agent used to immunize the individual is called a **vaccine**. Vaccines are manufactured in sophisticated factories. They are made from disease-causing germs which are either killed or suitably modified so that they retain their power to provoke antibodies against them; however, they cannot cause disease. Some germs secrete poisons or "toxins", which cause the individual to have disease; for such cases (e.g. tetanus), a "toxoid" is prepared from the toxins, and this becomes the "vaccine". **Table 1** shows the types of vaccines available today.

As can be seen, vaccines may contain live but "attenuated" germs, they may have components of killed germs, they may be simply modified toxins or they may be prepared from the antigenic component of the bacteria. Of the list, Hepatitis B vaccine is now also "manufactured" by genetic engineering. Unlimited stocks of this vaccine can thus be generated.

Table 1: Vaccines currently available in India for routine immunisation

Live germ vaccines	Killed germ vaccines	Toxoids	Antigenic vaccines
B.C.G. (against T.B.)	Pertussis (whooping cough)	Diphtheria	Hepatitis B vaccine
Oral Polio vaccine	Typhoid Vaccine	Tetanus	Typhoid (Vi antigen)
Measles	Cholera		H. influenza b vaccine
Mumps			Hepatitis A vaccine
Rubella			
Chicken pox			

Let us now examine the vaccine preventable diseases in brief.

1. Tuberculosis (B.C.G. vaccine):

Tuberculosis is a major public health problem in India and many other countries, despite widespread use of the B.C.G. vaccine. Infection occurs by inhalation of the germs from the cough droplets of an "open" case of lung T.B. (usually an adult). The commonest organs to be affected are the lungs, though lymph glands of the neck, abdominal organs like intestines, liver and kidneys, eyes, bones, brain and the meningeal coverings of the brain, joints and even the heart can get affected if the disease is not diagnosed early in its course and treated effectively. Occasionally, T.B. may be transmitted vertically from an infected mother to her unborn child.

The symptoms (Chapter 40) include fever with an evening rise, loss of weight, loss of appetite, cough, enlarged lymph glands in the neck and weakness. The illness is more severe if the affected person has a reduced immunity, for example, a child with measles or AIDS.

Untreated T.B. can cause death in just 4-6 weeks, depending upon the organ (s) affected.

<u>The vaccine</u>: B.C.G. (Bacille Calmette Guerin) is a live injectable vaccine that is shown to reduce the risk of the dangerous, potentially lethal forms of tuberculosis (such as T.B. meningitis) in immunised persons. It is given at birth or within the first few months to every child by intradermal injection on the left shoulder. It does not prevent primary infection.

After vaccination, a reddish nodule appears within 2-3 weeks; it enlarges over the next few weeks, and may soften, with yellowish pus-like substance visible within it. It may then ulcerate; the pus is expelled and the site heals with a thin, papery scar. This entire sequence needs no treatment. While appearance of a whitish small scar indicates successful vaccination, absence of a scar does not always mean that the vaccine did not "take"..

2. Hepatitis B (Hepatitis B Vaccine, or HBV):

There are many viruses as well as bacteria and other microbes which can produce an inflammation of the liver (or hepatitis). Of these, some of them are called the Hepatitis viruses; Hepatitis B is one such virus that can produce both acute and chronic jaundice; it may also lead to liver cancer in a small percentage of cases. This virus is extremely communicable, through infected needles, transfusion with Hepatitis-B contaminated blood, sharing of syringes by drug addicts and through child-to-child contamination with blood or saliva (spit). Vertical transmission is also known, and occurs from the infected mother to her newborn.

After a relatively long waiting period (incubation period) of 1-3 months, the virus produces the characteristic symptoms of jaundice, dragging right-sided abdominal pain, vomiting, fever, loss of appetite and rapid loss of weight. The urine is high-coloured, and at times, the stool becomes light coloured and pasty in consistency. The illness may wax and wane in intensity for weeks to months before abating. Rarely, it may progress to chronicity.

The vaccine: Hepatitis B vaccine is given at birth, at one month and at six months of age. Alternative schedules are also recommended by some authorities (see Appendix b). The vaccine is given by intramuscular injection into the thigh. In an older child too, the 0, 1, 6-month schedule can be followed. No additional doses are needed afterwards.

There is an increasing trend in our society to immunise adults against Hepatitis B. This is NOT recommended unless the adult works in a health-care related field (e.g. doctor, nurse, blood-bank worker, laboratory technician, etc.), or in the armed forces, or emergency forces (such as fire-fighting, ward boys, home guards, etc.). Routine Hepatitis B immunisation of all adults is NOT NECESSARY.

Apart from the genetically engineered vaccine that has now gained almost universal acceptance, some countries still use vaccine prepared from the serum (blood) of patients who recovered from a past episode of Hepatitis B and have good levels of protective antibodies in their system. Both the types of vaccine have similar protective levels. There are no major side effects of these two vaccines.

3. Diphtheria (D. of D.P.T. vaccine):

Diphtheria is a serious infection of the upper airway passages that can rapidly produce obstruction to breathing that is serious enough to cause death. The illness is transmitted by droplets from coughing by an infected person. The characteristic symptoms are fever, soreness of throat, swelling of the neck, progressive difficulty in breathing, noisy breathing and breathlessness. Toxins produced by the diphtheria germs cause the illness. A thick, impermeable membrane of pus and dead tissue is seen on the tonsils and in the areas surrounding the throat and the voice box (larynx). The toxin may even produce swelling of the heart and paralysis of the swallowing apparatus *after* the acute illness has subsided.

<u>The vaccine:</u> See below (under D.P.T.)

4. Pertussis (Whooping Cough) (P. of D.P.T. vaccine):

This is also an acute infectious respiratory illness that spreads through droplets from the cough of an infected person. Fever, sore throat and running nose presage a progressively worsening cough that is intense, spasmodic and debilitatingly severe. The cough is so severe that it can cause bleeding in the eyes, facial tissues, in the breathing muscles and occasionally inside the brain too. At the end of a typical bout of cough, the child takes in a deep breath to compensate for the lack of oxygen in the body. This is heard as a "whoop" by the family members. The cough may last for weeks or even months and cause weakness and fatigue in the child.

<u>The vaccine:</u> See below (under D.P.T.)

5. Tetanus (T. of D.P.T. vaccine):

The germ that causes tetanus can survive in a dormant state in the soil and excreta of animals. Tetanus in the newborn can occur when the baby's umbilical cord is cut with a dirty knife or blade or its cut end is covered with cow dung to stanch the bleeding. In the older child, tetanus can occur if the child is involved in a roadside injury, especially if he has major open wounds and contamination of the wound with soil. Cuts with sharp objects and middle ear infection can also precipitate tetanus in the older child.

The symptoms of tetanus include irritability, lock jaw (inability to open the jaw), difficulty in swallowing, tightening spasms of the whole body with arching of the back (especially when the child is touched or stimulated in any way, or when a loud noise is made in the vicinity of the child). In the neonate, these symptoms can prove lethal in a matter of days, while the older child may suffer for many days despite treatment. The illness is caused by secretion of toxins by the tetanus bacteria. The death rate from tetanus can approach 25% in older children and even 50-60 % in neonates.

<u>The vaccine:</u> See below (under D.P.T.)

<u>The D.P.T. vaccine (Injection Triple Antigen):</u>

The D.P.T. vaccine is a combined vaccine that offers protection against diphtheria, pertussis and tetanus. While the "D" and "T" components are "toxoids", the "P" component of this traditional vaccine comprises the killed pertussis bacillus (germ).

Three injections of D.P.T. vaccine are given to all infants at 1 ½, 2 ½ and 3 ½ months of age. This is followed by a repeat dose (1st booster) at 18 months and at five years (2nd booster). This schedule gives more than 95 % protection against all the three diseases discussed above. The vaccine produces side-effects like fever, excessive pain, swelling and redness at the injection site, crying and occasionally, a thigh abscess (pus collection).

To prevent these side effects, a new <u>DTaP vaccine (with *acellular* Pertussis component)</u> has been developed. It has been used successfully in developed countries, but it is very costly and is unlikely to find universal acceptance in third world countries.

<u>The Dual Antigen vaccine (D.T.):</u>

A separate D.T. vaccine is available for use as an optional third booster to all children at 7 years of age. This does not have the pertussis component. Also, a *Tetanus Toxoid vaccine* (Injection T.T.) is also used freely to immunise older children after injury etc. to prevent tetanus. Three injections of this vaccine, taken a month apart each are sufficient to protect the child against tetanus for five years. Thereafter, a single dose may be taken every five years to maintain the protective status for life.

6. Poliomyelitis (Oral Polio Vaccine):

Fever and loose motions mark the onset of this dreaded illness that is, hopefully, on its way to eradication, thanks to the Global Polio Eradication Campaign of the WHO. The illness spreads by ingestion of food or water contaminated by fecal matter from infected children. *Pain and soreness of the muscles follows next, and many children recover without any further deterioration from this back to normal.* However, in some cases, there is a development of a stiff neck and back, and finally, onset of weakness of various muscles of the body. The muscles become loose, flabby and cannot be used for voluntary action. The weakness can progress to a paralysis that is remarkably asymmetrical, that is, affecting one side more than the other and one group of muscles more than the other. At times, muscles of the breathing apparatus are affected, and this may lead to a life- threatening respiratory failure and even death. However, we must remember that not all polio-infected cases develop paralysis; 99 % resolve without the above progression. One of the strange things that may occur in such cases is the development of paralytic polio if they are administered an intramuscular injection at this stage. Hence, *intramuscular injections should never be given to an unimmunised child when she is brought for fever, vomiting or loose motions of less than 7 days' duration.*

<u>The vaccine:</u> The oral polio vaccine (O.P.V.) contains attenuated strains of all the three types of polio viruses that may cause the disease. Two drops of the vaccine are given orally to all babies at birth or soon thereafter, and then at 6, 10 and 14 weeks; this is then followed up by doses at 18 months and 5 years. Additional doses may be given during National Immunisation Days and during other

epidemiological interventions. There is no "boosting" effect and each dose is, in fact, a revaccination.

In developed countries, such as the U.S.A. and most of Western Europe, where the wild polio virus is not "in circulation", an Injectable polio vaccine (I.P.V.) is given instead of the oral vaccine. In fact, the Oral Polio Vaccine is NOT BEING USED there at all.

7. Measles (*Khasra, gobri, maata*) (Measles Vaccine, M.M.R. vaccine):

Measles is a well-known disease that spreads from the oral-nasal route. It is characterised by high fever, gradually worsening cough and cold, redness of eyes and a flat-to-raised red rash that begins just behind the ears, and spreads to the face, neck, shoulders, chest, abdomen, arms, hands, thighs and legs over the next two to three days. The rash then resolves in the same sequence, while at the same time, the fever also gradually abates. Some children develop complications like pneumonia, middle ear infection, brain inflammation (encephalitis) or a hemorrhagic rash; these carry a poor prognosis. A lowered general immune status can precipitate secondary bacterial pneumonia or even tuberculosis in a measles-affected child.

In the past, measles was a dreaded infectious disease since there was no vaccine against it. It killed thousands of infants every year. It caused the survivors to suffer from tuberculosis and severe malnutrition. With the advent of measles vaccine, these stories are relegated to history. Although measles still affects a lot of children, and causes considerable morbidity, it is no longer the serious public health problem it once used to be.

<u>The vaccine:</u> Measles vaccine is part of the Immunisation programme of the Government of India. It is injected subcutaneously in the thigh or gluteal region. It gives reasonable protection against measles, though a lot of measles-vaccinated children get measles *after 4-5 years*

of vaccination. This may be occurring due to declining antibody protection in vaccinees. The attack of infection in these older children is much milder. This may be due to the presence in their blood of some anti-measles antibodies.

A way to prevent such break-through attacks of measles is to give the M.M.R. vaccine to 15-month old babies. This vaccine, which is a triple vaccine against Measles, Mumps and Rubella, acts like a "booster" for the measles component. The general experience is that a child who has received both measles and M.M.R. vaccines is at very low risk of developing even attenuated measles.

In some children, both the measles and the M.M.R. vaccine may cause a rash and fever about 7 -8 days after vaccination. The rash resembles that of natural measles, but it is very minor and sparsely scattered and disappears in 2-3 days. The fever, too, is transient and minor in intensity.

8. Mumps (*gaalgonda, kaanpedey*) (M.M.R. vaccine):

Mumps is an extremely common childhood infectious disease that spreads by droplets from a sneezing/coughing person who has already acquired the virus. After an initial period of fever, cough and a running nose, the affected child develops swellings of one or both parotid salivary glands. These glands are located just below and behind both the ears. The swollen glands are very painful, and make the child irritable and sick very soon. Additionally, the child is unable to open her mouth to eat, and finds it difficult to swallow anything, including water and her own saliva. After a period of 4-7 days, the glands subside and the child recovers without any residual problems.

Rarely, the course of the disease becomes complicated with development of complications like encephalitis, orchitis (inflammation of the testes) or pancreatitis (inflammation of the pancreas).

The vaccine: See M.M.R. vaccine below.

9. Rubella (German measles) (M.M.R. vaccine):

This is a milder illness than measles. It is caused by the rubella virus and spreads by droplets from an infected person. There is fever, cough and a runny nose with pain in the back of the head due to enlargement of lymph glands behind the ear and in the back of the child's neck. A mild skin rash may also develop; it lasts for 2-3 days after which all symptoms abate over the next 2 days and there is full recovery.

The real problem with rubella is that if it occurs in a pregnant woman, it can cause the baby to have malformations (congenital abnormalities) like a small head, cataracts in the eyes, heart defects and mental retardation. This is why Rubella prevention is essential.

The vaccine: See M.M.R. vaccine below. A separate Rubella vaccine is also available, and may be given to an adolescent girl or an older woman if she has no recall of rubella infection and if she has never taken the M.M.R. vaccine in childhood.

The vaccine is injected subcutaneously like the Measles vaccine. It may produce a transient rash but has no major side effects.

Both the Rubella vaccine and M.M.R. vaccine should NOT be given to a pregnant woman, a woman LIKELY to become pregnant soon afterwards, or to a woman or girl in whose house a pregnant woman is present.

The M.M.R. Vaccine: As detailed above, this is a combination triple vaccine containing protection against Measles, Mumps and Rubella. It is given subcutaneously to all affording children at the age of 15-18 months. To a child who already had Measles vaccine at 9 months, the M.M.R. acts like a Measles booster. Such children hardly develop breakthrough measles at an older age.

The vaccine itself is free from any major side-effects.

Some authorities recommend a M.M.R. revaccination between 10-15 years of age so that even if they become sexually active, their unborn child will not be malformed – should they become pregnant and get natural infection in the interim.

10. Hepatitis A (*kaamil, kaavil, kamlaa*) (Hepatitis A Vaccine):

The common term "Jaundice" often means Hepatitis A viral jaundice. It spreads by the oro-fecal route, and its incidence is seen the year around, with peak in the monsoon season in our country. The illness starts with fever, malaise (a sense of ill-being), loss of appetite, severe nausea and incessant vomiting. The patient starts having pain in the right side of her abdomen and passes dark brown coloured urine by the fourth or fifth day of the illness. A yellowish discolouration of the whites of the eyes marks the main symptom of the disease. The jaundice deepens over the next several days; the child passes pasty, whitish stools and the urine continues to be dark yellow in colour. After this, the child begins recovering and the symptoms abate over the next 7-10 days. Full biochemical / laboratory recovery may take longer, but the child's appetite returns to normal even as the deep jaundice has just begun to fall. During the deep jaundice phase, the child may have intense itching of the skin.

While over 95 % of the cases make a complete recovery within a month, about 1 % die from an acute massive liver failure, and the rest improve after a longer period of time. It is useful to remember that while the illness is relatively mild in younger children, its intensity is much more as the child's age increases. The other important point is that as the mainstay of treatment is complete rest for almost a fortnight, the illness can cause the older child to miss school or college and suffer academically. If the illness occurs at the time of the child's final exams, he/she may even lose a full academic year!

The vaccine: Hepatitis A vaccine is given as a single injection to any child over the age of one year. To impart life-long immunity, a booster must be given 6-12 months after the first dose. The vaccine is relatively free from side effects. A smaller dose is needed for infants and children up to the age of 12 years; thereafter, an "adult" dose equivalent to twice the pediatric dose is given. This vaccine costs a lot, and it is not included as a compulsory childhood vaccine at present. If one can afford it, one should give it to their child (-ren).

Nowadays, even many adults are opting for a Hep-A vaccine. It should be remembered that most Indians acquire the wild virus in childhood, and most are already *naturally immune* before they reach adulthood. I strongly advise anyone desiring to take this vaccine to first check out the blood levels of protective antibodies; if these are positive, they won't need the vaccine at all.

11. H. influenzae type b infections (pneumonia, meningitis) (H. influenzae type b or Hib):

H influenzae infections generally occur during the first few years of life. The germ has many sub-types, of which the 'b' subtype causes the most severe illnesses. The three chief illnesses caused are pneumonia, meningitis and middle-ear infection. At times, the infection is very acute and may claim the child's life. As the child grows older, the threat from this infection declines, so that by the age of three or four, the risk is down to a non-significant level.

The vaccine: The Hib Vaccine is given to infants along with the D.P.T. vaccine, that is, at 1 ½, 2 ½, and 3 ½ months of age, followed by a booster at 18-24 months. The vaccine has no known side effects. This is a costly vaccine, and is offered as an "additional vaccine" to those parents who can afford it. If the infant is older than 6 months at the time of first contact for this vaccine, fewer doses are needed. You should ask your pediatrician about the details.

12. Chicken pox (*choti maata*) (Chicken pox vaccine):

Like its older "cousin" (small pox), chicken pox too is an acute communicable disease characterised by the onset of fever, cough and cold, followed, within 3-4 days by the appearance of a typical rash all over the body. The rash is marked more on the trunk, thighs and arms, but can spread all over the body, and is also seen on the face. It is just a reddish boil to start with, but soon shows watery content within it (a vesicle). New boils continue to erupt over the next few days, so that the child will have all types of boils at the same time on different regions of the body. The boils itch a lot. After a few days, the boils heal with scab formation, and the scabs soon fall off, leaving behind a scar of variable depth.

Chicken pox is highly contagious, and children can pass on the virus to other children *even before they themselves develop the rash.* As a result, outbreaks spread rapidly in classrooms and day-care crèches.
The course of the illness is benign in smaller children, but more severe in older children and even worse in adults. Complications include bacterial infection of the rashes (which will then need antibiotic treatment), encephalitis, a body imbalance disorder that may take weeks to resolve (post chicken pox cerebellar ataxia) and pneumonia in older persons.

The main problem is the compulsory quarantine from school or place of work that causes academic or monetary loss to the individual.

<u>The vaccine:</u> Chicken pox vaccine is given as a single dose to all children above the age of one and below the age of thirteen; above 12 year-old children and adults need two doses of the vaccine to get complete protection. The injection is given subcutaneously in the upper, outer thigh. Its effect begins in about 14 days, and it offers life-long immunity thereafter. Side effects include pain and mild fever with or without a vesicular rash 7-8 days after the vaccination. These symptoms disappear after 24-48 hours.

Like Hepatitis A vaccine and Hib vaccine, this too is an additional vaccine and is offered only to those who can afford it, on account of its very high cost.

13. Typhoid fever (Enteric fever) (Typhoid vaccine):

Typhoid fever is a bacterial infection caused by ingestion of water or food contaminated by typhoid germs. It is a common infection in India, and is usually seen in children above the age of 1 ½ years. The main feature is a prolonged, high-grade fever, accompanied by headache, abdominal pain, vomiting and loose stools and loss of appetite. Bloating of the abdomen, development of jaundice and drowsiness herald very severe typhoid illness which can advance to gastro-intestinal bleeding, unconsciousness and even shock.

Indiscriminate treatment has led to the development of typhoid germs which are resistant to usual antibiotic therapy. These multi-resistant germs are hard to eradicate and often necessitate hospitalization, institution of intravenous antibiotics and other inconveniences, besides increasing the cost of treatment.

As a result of these facts, we now recommend Typhoid vaccination to all children 2 years and above; the vaccine needs to be given periodically (every six months for the whole-cell vaccine and every three years for the antigenic Typhoid Vi vaccine and Typhoid oral vaccine). An individual who wishes to protect himself or his children against typhoid should consider taking/giving the vaccine every time it becomes due again.

The vaccine: As discussed above, there are three forms of Typhoid vaccines , of which the whole-cell vaccine and the oral vaccine are not available at present. Hence, the injectable Typhoid Vi vaccine is used. A single dose, given intramuscularly in the thigh or the arm, is sufficient to give immunity for up to three years in about 85-90 % of vaccinees.

The vaccine may cause mild to moderate fever for up to a day. No other major side effects are known.

14. Rabies (Mad-dog bite) (Rabies Vaccine):

A bite by a rabid animal like a dog, a cat, a jackal or a monkey can transmit rabies to a human being. As you probably know, rabies or hydrophobia is a 100 % fatal disease. After a variable period of 20-100 days after the bite, the victim evinces symptoms of rabies, chiefly fever, muscular pains, change in emotions and mood, agitation, excessive salivation and fear of water (hydrophobia) and fear of a draught of air (aerophobia). Death invariably occurs after a variable period of 5-10 days after the full blown illness has manifested.

The only way to prevent the occurrence of rabies after a bite by a known rabid animal (or a bite by an animal whose status is unknown) is to meticulously clean the bitten part with soap and water and to administer the anti-rabies vaccine as soon as possible.

The vaccine: Earlier, neural vaccines were the mainstay of rabies vaccination programmes in our country. They have been almost totally abandoned as the incidence of potentially serious side effects is unacceptable. These neural vaccines were prepared from the brain of killed rabid sheep.

The modern rabies vaccines are all tissue culture vaccines and free from the hazards of the neural vaccine. Usually, following a bite, the vaccine is given on the same day (day 0), and after 3, 7, 14, 28 and 90 days. The last dose is optional and may be avoided.

If the child has an open wound or a wound on the face or the hand or has multiple bites, a Human Rabies Immunoglobulin is also used. Half of the calculated dose is injected in and around the wound(s), while the other half is given intramuscularly on the limb opposite to the one in which the vaccine was given.

Other Vaccines:

Several other vaccines have been available in the past, are available today or are under development. They include the small pox vaccine (no longer available to all; only used by the U.S. armed forces at the present time), the meningitis vaccine (against some types of Meningitis germs – usually given when there is an outbreak of this disease), the rota virus vaccine (against a common diarrhoeal germ – given up because of possible deaths associated with the vaccine), the yellow fever vaccine (which is mandatory for travel to advanced countries), the Cholera vaccine (available on request from some governmental centres only during an epidemic of cholera) and the Tetanus vaccine (which is given after wounds or injuries, see above).

The Immunisation Schedule:

The schedule is shown in Appendix (b) on page 527.
Some relevant comments on the schedule are included here.

i) The exact schedule may change from one doctor to another only in minor respects, but the overall emphasis will continue to remain on maximizing immunisation coverage with minimal visits to the doctor's clinic.

ii) Before the doctor actually injects the vaccine, do try and ask him whatever you need to know about the vaccine, such as its cost, efficacy or safety. The doctor is also duty-bound to give you this information.

iii) Learn about how to prevent or treat the side effects that can occur following the vaccination. Do this before the vaccine is given.

iv) The oral polio vaccine may be given even to a child who already has polio, since the type of virus she had may be just one of the three types that the vaccine has.

v) If your child has any immunity-suppressing condition like leukemia, AIDS, malnutrition, etc, do inform the doctor about this. Such a child may not be able to get vaccinated against live vaccines like the Oral polio vaccine, chicken pox vaccine etc. An injectable polio vaccine (available abroad) can be used.

vi) If a mother of a baby has active tuberculosis, the baby should not be given the B.C.G. vaccine, but must be started on anti-tubercle medicine in a preventive dose. The B.C.G. vaccine is then delayed for 3-6 months and is given after the medication to the baby is completed.

vii) In a baby whose mother has Hepatitis B virus (HBsAg) in her blood, the baby MUST receive not just the Hepatitis B vaccine but also Hepatitis B immune globulin within 12-24 hours after birth.

viii) Jaundice may still occur in a child who has received both Hepatitis A and B vaccines, because there are many more viruses (such as Hepatitis E or enteroviruses) that can cause jaundice.

ix) Similarly, while the Hib vaccine protects against Hib-induced pneumonia and meningitis, these latter two infections can still occur as many other bacteria, viruses and other germs may cause them.

x) No vaccine has a protective efficacy of 100 %, and sometimes, the vaccine may fail in a given individual due to reasons that cannot be controlled or understood fully.

xi) The above chapter is not an exhaustive discussion on the entire subject of vaccinations and I invite readers to read the following additional resources for a more in-depth study of the topic.

Suggested Reading:

- ✔ http://www.cdc.gov/nip/recs/child-schedule.PDF
- ✔ http://www.aafp.org/x7666.xml
- ✔ www.immunization-and-vaccinations.com/ html/childhood-immunizations
- ✔ The Vaccine Guide: Risks and Benefits for Children and Adults by Randall Neustaedter

Ch 31
Home care of a sick child

A. General Care

Your children need your presence more than your presents

- Jesse Jackson

When a child becomes ill, a sort of pall descends on the whole family. A single sneeze can drive a loved one's mother right up the wall! It is not surprising that once a child is ill, and I mean really ill, the entire household is up and about. Grandpa is busy on the telephone, while grandma is in the kitchen, busy making a soup; the father decides to call in sick at his office and the mother frets and worries over which medicine should be given in what quantity at what time and with what accompaniments. This is a very natural sequence of events; even the siblings are not spared ... the younger ones are not sent to the school, while the older ones may have to shoulder some of the outdoor responsibilities.

The most common illnesses that cause the above scenario to be created include severe sore throat, gastroenteritis, wheezy respiratory illness, food poisoning, typhoid, injury or post-vaccination illness.

As children's illnesses are brief and usually followed by complete recovery, the "anxious" phase of the family is also short-lasting.

Common Concerns:

The major parental concerns include the following:

a) What is my child suffering from?
b) How quickly should I consult the doctor?
c) Is there any home treatment that I can initiate before I take her to the doctor?
d) How do I give her medicines?
e) What should her diet be like?
f) Does she need rest? How do I enforce it?
g) What happens to her studies?
h) Should I let her go down to the compound/ground to play?
i) Should I let her friends visit her?

Let us explore these questions one by one. It is difficult to give a generalized advice that will work for all children, all illnesses and all social situations, but the discussion below will try and achieve just that.

What she is suffering from/ how quickly I should see her doctor:

Naturally, each illness has its own onset, progression and recovery characteristics, and parents cannot always determine what illness their children are having. However, it is vital to at least determine if the illness your child is having is a serious one or just a minor one. Parents who see their child fretful, restless and not eating anything might think that her illness is a major one, when actually their child may be having simply a common cold. On the other hand, a child who just fell off a cot might look lucid and normal, but may soon develop fits or paralysis due to an expanding internal hemorrhage. Thus, sometimes it is very difficult to decide if an urgent visit to/by the doctor is necessary.

The usual rule is: if in doubt, go to the doctor. Even in routine cases, one should at least call up the child's doctor and discuss the case with him as early as possible, so that he can advise you accordingly.

Danger signals that need immediate consultation with a doctor include:

- Headache following a fall on to the head and/or accompanied by vomiting/blurring of vision/fever
- Vomiting uncontrolled by one or two doses of a suitable medication
- Loose stools, particularly if large, watery, foul-smelling, accompanied by blood/mucus/high fever or if occurring more than once every hour
- Cough that is spasmodic, with bouts lasting more than 30 seconds, or accompanied by vomiting, or causing the child to turn red/blue in the face
- A nose-block that significantly interferes with a small baby's sleep, breathing or feeding
- Any difficulty or lethargy in feeding
- Swelling of the abdomen, especially if accompanied by constipation, vomiting, lethargy or high fever
- High fever with shivering
- Bite by a street-dog/cat/rat
- Fall on to the head with/without bleeding from the nose/ear(s)/mouth
- Loss of consciousness due to any reason
- Occurrence of fits
- Jaundice/high-coloured urine
- Sudden development of weakness in any part of the body
- Pain that does not resolve with one or two doses of a pain killer

- A rash that develops on the body
- Any symptom that develops soon after ingestion of a medicine or drug or a newly tried food item
- Difficulty in breathing/fast breathing or deep, sighing respiration

In addition, there may be individual circumstances in individual cases. A sudden change in the habits of a child may be enough ground to seek a consultation. When an epidemic of, say, chicken-pox is raging in the building, and your child gets a typical rash of chicken-pox, it may be all right to wait until the next morning; but if the same child develops increasingly worsening rash or a bad cough (suggesting pneumonia), you will *have* to go to see her doctor urgently.

In many cases, you might decide to first speak with her doctor on the telephone. You should clearly describe the symptoms, their order of appearance and progression and seek advice on immediate measures that you need to take before going in to visit the doctor. *A telephonic consultation not followed by an actual visit is dangerous, and can lead to perilous events that may endanger your child's life.*

Home treatment to be initiated before the doctor is contacted:

With most illnesses, there will be some way(s) to reduce the child's pain/discomfort or any other major symptom. For example, giving Paracetamol to a child burning up with fever is perfectly right; in fact, the doctor will compliment you for your foresight if you do so. Many parents feel that giving Paracetamol and bringing down the fever will "alter" the child's symptom to an extent where the doctor will not be able to correctly "gauge" the severity of the illness. I feel, however, that reducing the chances of a fever-induced fit is *far more important* than masking the symptom of fever. In a similar vein, a dose of a vomiting medicine or a cough medicine that you already have in the house, an attempt to stanch the blood in a case of injury, a trial of Oral Rehydration Solution in a case of diarrhoea and a simple splinting of a fractured hand with a stick and a handkerchief are all acceptable home remedies that one can initiate before rushing to the doctor.

One should remember to check the expiry date of any medicine that is retrieved from the cupboard after a long duration. Also, one must make it a point to mention any home treatment that you may have given when you actually go to the doctor.

How do I give her medicines?

This is discussed in Chapter 29. The doctor's instructions should be followed to the letter. If necessary, call him back if you need to clarify any doubts in your mind.

What should her diet be like?

When the child is ill, she will eat almost nothing, and it is foolish for parents to expect her to eat heartily. She may even lose up to a kilogram or so in weight owing to the rigours of the illness, combined with her poor appetite. Remember that in viral illness, loss of appetite is often the first presenting symptom, and it may even *precede* the development of all other symptoms; also, it is the *last* symptom to go away, so that even when the cough and cold have more or less settled down and there is no fever, the child refuses to eat well for almost 2-3 more days at the end of the illness.

It is prudent to ask the doctor about the items that need to be restricted, the items that need to be given in greater quantities and the items that can be given normally. In general, **starving** the child is never recommended in any illness, and the doctor would normally advise admitting the child to hospital if she has to be starved for any reason. Most illnesses allow a **light diet**, that is, an intake of simple home-made juices, soups, gravies, curries, rice and *chappatis* and so on. A greater allowance is made for **liquids** in children with fever, loose motions, vomiting and respiratory illnesses. In such cases, water,

water containing salt and sugar, water containing *gur* (jaggery) and lime juice, water containing ORS powder, buttermilk, citrus juices, clear soups and milk are all adequate.

In some illnesses, like stomach upsets and diarrhoea, the doctor may recommend a **soft diet**. This consists of pulp fruits like banana, rice with curds, bread and butter, *khichri, idli, upma, poha,* etc. Finally, in the vast majority of minor illnesses, no restrictions are imposed and the child may continue to eat a **full diet**. This includes children with the 'flu, children with a simple cough and cold, children with dysentery, children with injuries and children with any other illness not heretofore specified.

During the phase of recovery, a high carbohydrate diet with plenty of fruits and vegetables is to be provided to the child so that she makes a quick physical recovery from the illness.

Does she need rest? How do I enforce it?

It is very easy for a doctor to advise rest, but very difficult for parents to enforce rest in the sick child. By rest, a Pediatrician means simply that the child may be allowed to move about within the house, and even go down to the compound of the building to sit and watch others play in the garden. By rest is meant staying away from school, physically demanding sport like running, cycling, jumping and so on. It is impossible to ask the child to "remain lying in bed"!

Most common illnesses do not require a mandatory period of rest; in fact, the earlier the child is sent back to school, the faster is her recovery. In some case, however, rest has to be ensured for recovery. The best example of this is Hepatitis or jaundice. Other instances include children with large injuries, fractures, severe typhoid or malaria and a child with muscular or joint pains – the last instance being an example where the child herself will prefer not to move about.

If at all it becomes necessary for you to "enforce" rest, you may involve the child in interesting activities which can be carried on from bed, or while sitting on a chair next to the bed. These include reading stories to the child, playing games like carrom and chess, sitting and watching cartoons or wild life series on the television, singing songs, decorating items like pots, vases and other stuff with paint or beads and indulging in other art and craft activities. Telephoning friends, playing games on the computer and encouraging the child to get an afternoon nap are other interesting ideas.

What happens to her studies?

In general, a short absence of two or three days is needed, so there is not much loss of studies or class work. Either the parent or the child herself can retrieve the work done in school when the child was absent. The problem occurs when the child remains absent for a longer duration of, say, one or two weeks, and more particularly so when she is in a higher class (Std. VII or above).

While teaching establishments usually honour a medical certificate and excuse the child's absence, the onus is upon you, the parents, to periodically contact one of the class-mates/friends of your child and bring back home their books for you to copy the class-work from; also, you need to contact her teacher(s) and get information about what is being taught at school. During the child's enforced absence, if she is able, you may give her some of her school books to read and study. However, she should not be under pressure to study.

In the rare event of the child remaining absent for periods of months, the school may be forced to keep her back for the next academic year.

During the convalescent phase, many parents insist on feeding their children almonds and other herbal preparations which are thought to improve cerebration. There is no concrete evidence that these food items or herbs actually improve mental skills.

Permitted and banned activities:

Once the acute phase of illness is over, the child may be allowed increasing freedom to play. She may be allowed to go out of the house and meet her friends. Initially, she should be asked to sit in the shade of a tree and sit and talk to her friends or watch them play; once her physical strength returns, she may be allowed to gradually participate in the games herself.

During the illness, friends may be allowed to visit her in your home only if the disease is non-contagious – for example, if the child has chicken pox or measles, the friends are not permitted to visit.

Conclusion:

Looking after a sick child is usually a matter of common-sense, but specific instructions for particular illnesses should be followed properly. Children tend to recover more rapidly than adults, so that your more conservative approach to adult illnesses may not be justified while looking after children. During the acute phase, the child should not be force-fed; at the same time, during the recovery phase, attention should be paid to providing the child with easy to assimilate high carbohydrate foods with a generous helping of fruits and fresh vegetables. All through the illness, parents must keep track of the studies that are going on in the school during the child's absence and get the books home for copying and for the child to read from.

B. Fever and its management

A child is a beam of sunlight from the Infinite and Eternal, with possibilities of virtue and vice – but as yet unstained.

- Lyman Abbott (1835 - 1922)
US religious leader

Fever is the commonest symptom of disease, and is also the most misunderstood one among all. Human beings are warm-blooded animals and they have the ability to maintain their internal body temperature at around 36.8°C +/- 0.4°C (98.2 +/- 0.7°F). There are minor fluctuations in the temperature during the 24 hours of each day, with the lower temperatures seen in the morning and the upper ones in the evening. The range of fluctuations is between 98°F to 99.5°F (in the mouth). This maintenance of temperature occurs through the function of a special "thermostat" located inside a deep area of the brain. The thermostat is not so effective in a small child, and hence temperature fluctuations are wider and more common in them, especially in very hot or very cold weather. They need closer attention so that they do not rapidly become hot or cold.

How does fever occur? Is it a friend or an enemy?

Fever occurs in response to a wide variety of insults and aberrations that take place in the body. Germs that cause infection also provoke formation of antibodies against them by the host's immune system. This flare-up of immunity causes collection of inflammatory cells at the site of entry of the germs. The additional activity of this system creates heat energy; to this is added chemicals released by dead host cells as well as dead bacteria; the net result is fever.

As this is the cause of the fever, it is obvious that occurrence of fever indicates that the body's defence mechanism is *fighting the invasion of germs*. At the same time, the rise of body temperature also affects the survival chances of germs adversely; this is because, like us, germs too have a "comfort" zone of temperatures at which they can multiply fast and thrive. When the temperature climbs up, the germs die. This is, in fact, one of the mechanisms of a "self-cure" of minor illnesses. (Remember the last time you had fever and cough, and you did NOT go to the doctor and STILL got well? That's what I mean.) As a Pediatrician, I am more worried when a patient under my care shows evidence of infection and *yet, does not have fever or a raised WBC count in the body*. (See Ch. 25 for the significance of raised counts.) This means that his immune mechanisms are depressed or they are overwhelmed by a serious infection.

Fever has some negative consequences too: a very high fever may produce a "febrile convulsion" (*fever fit)* in a vulnerable child. This is particularly seen in children between the ages of 6 months to five years (see Chapter 43). Fever can trigger a fit in an already epileptic child too. Fever increases the fluid and calorie requirement of the body, and if these are not recognised by parents or care-takers, the child can end up with dehydration or lose weight. During fever, the child's heart beats faster and his breathing also becomes more and more "restless". Although these are not harmful *per se*, a child with a pre-existing heart or lung condition may find the going tough.

Measuring a child's temperature:

With the advent of modern technology, it is now easy to record a child's temperature. In the old days, we used a simple glass thermometer. It had to be shaken vigorously before being applied to the patient. Sometimes, it slipped and broke while shaking the mercury down! At times, children bit off the mercury bulb in anxiety and swallowed a heavy dose of mercury. Now we have many other temperature measuring devices at our disposal. They include:

1. An electronic thermometer: this is a digital device that runs on button cells. The mercury bulb is replaced by heat sensitive metal that needs to be kept in the child's armpit/ mouth/anus. A digital L.C.D. reads off the rising temperature. An in-built alarm sounds when the reading is completed. No more looking at a watch to count off the 120 seconds!
2. A forehead strip: this is less sensitive to minor fluctuations, but it has been calibrated to reflect the *core* temperature. You just wipe the child's forehead (meant for small babies and infants up to 1-2 years only), and put the strip and see the LED glow green as the strip records the heat change. The last green rectangle on the strip (the reading area is divided into rectangles sitting side by side) corresponds to a temperature value that is written by its side on the strip.
3. Ear-canal thermometer: this expensive device (costing near about Rs. 2500-3000) is also a digital device that has a conical ear-piece which is placed inside the ear canal of a child (older than 2 years). A button is pushed, which activates the sensor in the ear-piece. A visible L.C.D. display directly shows the temperature in just 1 second! The temperature corresponds to the child's *core* temperature.
4. A Pacifier thermometer is also available! The baby sucks on the pacifier while the nipple senses the oral temperature and displays it on a L.C.D.!

Of course, an experienced parent will often be able to guess her child's temperature merely by putting her hand on the child's stomach or neck! This is reliable only after you have nursed the child through (God forbid!) many illnesses. Use the back of the hand to sense the temperature. When the doctor has advised you to give a fever medicine only if the temperature reaches a *particular value*, you may check the temperature with a thermometer, and then follow up the first recording by frequently touching the child on her tummy with the back of your hand.

Remember that core temperature is highest, mouth temperature 0.5° C lower, and armpit temperature, 1.0° C lower even normally.

Managing the fever:

As I have said before, mild fever is a useful thing as it helps the child to fight the germs and at the same time, forces her to rest so that the body's energy can be directed to combating the illness. Hence, one should not instantly give fever medicines for a temperature that is less than 100° F in the armpit.

Good supportive care, nutritious food and increased intake of fluids is all that is needed up to this point. See Part A of this chapter for further details on general care. It is wrong to forcibly cover the child with blankets, switch off the fans and close all the windows when a child has fever. Also, some parents erroneously starve the child. The febrile child should be allowed to "throw away" the blankets if she wants to; she should be allowed to sit under a fan or even in an air-conditioned room and allowed to eat whatever she wants – if she has no problems with these things. A febrile child can eat curds, bananas or even ice-cream under the cover of treatment.

Anti-pyretic therapy: Paracetamol is a time-tested fever medicine. It is reasonably safe and may be used up to 5-6 times in a day if required. The dose is about ½ a teaspoon for every 5 kg weight of a standard preparation containing 120-125 mg per teaspoon of paracetamol. Some preparations have 250 mg in each teaspoon, so be sure to check the fine print before giving a dose of one of these preparations.

Other anti-pyretics are also available, such as combinations of Paracetamol with other drugs, Nimesulide and Mefenamic Acid, to name a few. Recent reports suggest and recommend that Nimesulide (about the use of which there was a big controversy in 2003) is as safe or unsafe as paracetamol when used in the febrile child in the correct dose, which is about ½ teaspoon per 25 kg body weight 2-3 times a day.

Sponging and Ice-packs: At times, when the body temperature climbs rapidly to levels more than 101°F, you should begin sponging the child. For this, you will need a large bowl of tap water, a small vessel filled with boiled water, some hand towels, a small vessel filled with ice water, small mops and some amount of cotton.

First, add the boiled water to the tap water to make the latter luke-warm. Now undress the child so that she is wearing just underwear (shorts or panties). Begin wiping her body with a towel dipped in this warm water – this must be done from the chest down to the knees. Keep sponging repeatedly. At the same time, dip some cotton into the smaller, cold-water vessel; squeeze the cotton dry, and put it into one of the two arm-pits of the child. Leave the other side empty for taking temperatures with the thermometer. Use similar cotton wads to pack the groin areas. Once this is done, you may put small strips of cloth dipped in the ice water on the forehead. *It is not necessary to add salt or eau-de-Cologne to the water.* Some children feel uncomfortable with ice-cold sponges and may do all right with just the luke-warm sponges. Others want an ice-bag on the top of the head. There is no harm in this. One more point: when the child is being sponged, check the body temperature periodically (say every ten minutes) by using the empty arm-pit to keep the thermometer; alternatively, keep your finger inside the child's mouth and see how hot the oral cavity is (or you may put a small baby to the breast, if you are the mother – your nipple will feel the heat instantly).

Note: Many parents erroneously begin sponging the whole body with cold water. I do not recommend this for more than one reason. Firstly, cold water feels very uncomfortable to the child. Secondly, the skin rapidly turns cold, while the core temperature continues to remain high. This is a dangerous situation as the unwary parent may touch the skin and get falsely reassured that the fever has come down. The child continues to burn from within, and may throw a fit before the parent has thrown away the water.

Home treatment in some specific fever-causing diseases:

To understand how to manage fever in specific diseases, first read general home care of a sick child in section A above and management of fever above. Then proceed to the following passage:

Malaria: Malaria is an acute infection caused by *Plasmodium* species, a form of one-celled living organisms. These parasites gain entry into humans through the bites of mosquitoes. The illness is characterised by an acute onset of high, intermittent fever with chills and rigors (shivering). The fever and rigors are due to a sudden breakdown of red blood cells and release of the parasites into the blood stream in large numbers. Although there are four different species of Plasmodium, the most serious type of malaria is caused by *P. falciparum,* which causes cerebral malaria and many other types of serious complications. Besides the specific treatment of malaria, one should also do the following: Include plenty of fluids, nutritious diet, rest, anti-pyretics, sponging and ice-mopping under general care. Let the child decide if she wants to put blankets on herself or not.

Viral Fever: See "Coryza" management in Chapter 36. Nurse the child in a cool, well-ventilated room. Make her wear light cotton clothes. Give plenty of fluids, nourishing diet, fresh salad and greens, and anti-pyretics as needed. Salt water gargles and steam inhalations provide good temporary relief to the sore throat and the blocked nose respectively in a case of the 'flu. Antibiotics are useless in clear viral infections and must not be used indiscriminately. Beware the doctor who says that your child has a "virus" and goes on to prescribe an antibiotic because he has no better drug to offer.

Heat Stroke: On occasion, a child who is standing for long in the sun may suddenly feel hot and fall to the ground. This often happens in scout camps, parades, march past etc. The temperature climbs rapidly above 105°F and the child becomes delirious or stuporous. Fits may ensue. There is no sweating at all. Such a high temperature may cause a threat to life if not immediately rectified.

What to do: Remove the child to the shade. Loosen her clothing and preferably wrap her in a wet cloth sheet. If an air-conditioner is available, put it on, start cold sponging (justified in this case) and call for the doctor immediately. If the child is conscious, give her cold fluids to drink. Anti-pyretics are not of much use.

<u>Heat Exhaustion:</u> Prolonged exercise or exertion can cause the child to sweat profusely and lose vital fluids and salts from her body. She will feel weak and crumple or run to a corner and sit dazedly, feeling giddy (if she is an older child) and confused (ditto). There is no fever. Vomiting and headache may occur.

What to do: Make her sit in a cool, well-ventilated room, under a fan, or in an air-conditioned room. Give her lemon juice with sugar and salt or just any electrolyte spiked drink and ask her to drink it sip by sip. Soon, the child will feel relieved.

Ch 32
Hospitalisation: When and How

Children are living jewels dropped … from heaven.
- Robert Pollok, 1798-1827,
Scottish Religious Poet

As a parent, if there is one thing I have dreaded, not just for my own children, but also for my patients, it is the need, on the rarest of rare occasions, for hospitalising a sick child. Illnesses in children come in all shapes and sizes; while the majority of them are acute and short-lasting, some are chronic and debilitating. Both acute and chronic illnesses may need hospitalisation, if not to cure, then at least to manage them more effectively.

Reasons for hospitalisation:

The doctor aims at curing a child completely. To this end, he may either elect to prescribe medications and other remedies to be taken at the child's home, or he may choose to hospitalise the child.

Some of the reasons for hospitalisation include:

- a serious illness that will need expert care to save the child's life or the use of all her abilities

- an undiagnosed illness that is causing increasing sickness in the child and that needs proper observation and investigation for diagnosis and management
- the administration of drugs into the veins round the clock for more predictable response
- medico-legal purposes

Goals of hospitalisation:

The goal of hospitalisation is to cure an illness where a cure is possible; when a cure is not immediately possible, the aim of hospitalisation is to ameliorate the discomfort of the child in whatever way possible. To carry out his goals, the doctor will, according to the indication, give the child all forms of therapy that are available with him. Whether he succeeds in his endeavour depends not only on his skills and the facilities available with him, but also upon the cooperation extended by you to him.

What parents can do to extend cooperation:

Once the doctor advises hospitalisation, parents are bound to have several questions about this. They may ask the doctor as to why the hospitalisation is necessary; whether it can be avoided; whether it can be delayed till say, the next morning or the weekend; what will the chance of recovery be; what will the duration of hospitalisation be; whether the same treatment can be given at home; what the cost of the hospitalisation will be; will the same doctor continue to treat the child or some other doctor will take over – and so on.

Once the doctor has answered all the questions, it is the duty of parents to proceed to the suggested hospital forthwith and without any further delay. While packing things to take to the hospital, the parents MUST remember to take all old reports, medical papers, X-rays etc. of the child with them. They should also carry all the medicines that are already being given to the child.

They will be required to deposit some cash or register the admission under an insurance policy (if they have one). They should then write down the telephone numbers of the hospital in their diaries, note down the ward number, floor, bed number etc. with a clear hand and then take the child to the assigned bed for further care.

Parents should never hide any details of the child's illness from the resident doctors who are stationed in that particular ward. They should arrange for the purchase of whatever stuff is required for their child's care. They should not bring valuables and should remove jewellery from their child's body.

If the child is going to stay for more than a few days, the parents must write a note to her school to inform the teacher about the child's absence from school and meet with the teacher or principal to discuss the illness and the enforced absence from school.

During the hospitalisation, parents should be ready to pay more money if needed, arrange to be present when the doctor comes for his visit and cooperate with the resident doctors and nurses in every manner possible so as to optimise the outcome of the illness.

General Hospital vs. Private Hospital vs. Nursing Home:

Whether to treat a sick child in a general hospital, a private hospital or a nursing home is mostly dictated by the financial wherewithal of the patient's family. At times, some or the other necessary facility may not be available at one of these three places, and the child will HAVE to be taken to a place where such a treatment modality is available. Sometimes, the attending pediatrician may recommend admission to a hospital and not a nursing home because the child needs round the clock intensive care, investigations and monitoring or expert nursing care not available in a nursing home.

Treatment in a general hospital is mostly free of cost, or heavily subsidized, while treatment in a private hospital is costly; for example, treating a 2-year old child who is on artificial respiration in an intensive care unit of a private hospital in a big Indian city may cost over 3000 rupees per day! On the other hand, intravenous fluid therapy and routine injection treatment of a child with loose motions in a similar hospital may cost just Rs. 600-700 per day. Costs in a nursing home depend on the type of nursing home. An average nursing home's bill may be in between that of a private and a general hospital, but more towards the former than the latter. A posh nursing home may cost much more than an average private hospital. Doctor's professional charges also have to be taken into account. Many charitable private hospitals have fixed doctors' charges, so you can easily predict how much the doctor's fees will total up to.

Concluding Remarks:

In conclusion, hospitalisation is often unavoidable in many illnesses. As a parent, it is your responsibility to assess the doctor's explanations and to enquire thoroughly about costs before taking the child to the hospital.

Ch 33
Role of Laboratory and Radiological Investigations in Child Care

Injections are the best thing ever invented for feeding doctors.
- Gabriel Garcia Marquez, 1928- , Colombian Writer.

Children fall ill from time to time, and it may not even be necessary to see a doctor each time: for example, if your son hurts himself while playing and has a slight cut on his knee, I am sure you will be able to clean the wound and apply an antiseptic all by yourself. You may even dress the wound with a medicated plaster dressing and you won't be faulted. However, when an illness is a serious one or one with which you are unfamiliar, you will have to see a doctor. You will find that on many occasions, even a doctor may not understand what is wrong with the child. Rather than berating him, you should appreciate that the field of medicine is vast, that doctors deal every single day with life and death, and that in recent times, if the doctor misses a diagnosis, he may be hauled to the consumer court. He has therefore no choice but to order tests, some of which may be unnecessary and superfluous.

In this chapter, we shall try and find out the importance of the laboratory (in Section A) and the radiological department (in Section

B) in managing a child's illness. I have chosen the Q and A format to keep the discussion lucid and brief.

A. LABORATORY INVESTIGATIONS

What are the commonest tests ordered by the doctor when a sick child is seen by him?

There are literally thousands of "tests" which may be done on a sample of the child's blood, urine, stool or any other body secretion or tissue. Of these, about 20-25 tests are done most often in an acutely sick child. The rarer tests are done when the child's illness is non-responsive to treatment, a rare malady or a rare manifestation of a common illness.

The commonly done tests include a Complete Hemogram (or C.B.C.), tests for malaria/typhoid/jaundice or urinary tract infection, tests for tuberculosis, dysentery or diarrhoea, blood group test, biochemical tests (glucose, electrolytes, calcium) and clotting tests (bleeding and clotting times).

Less commonly, hormone levels, thyroid tests and kidney function, liver function or immunity-function studies are done. The rare tests include organ-biopsies (liver, kidney), bone-marrow tests and others.

Is it "usual" for doctors to test all patients?

No, this is certainly not true. In fact, tests are generally never done on the first consultation unless the doctor apprehends a fast-progressing disease or a major problem that could get out of hand if not rapidly controlled. This is because:

- Most diseases are self-limiting, resolving within 7-10 days. These include sore-throat, cold, sprains and minor injuries, skin boils, gastric upsets and so on.

- Many simple diseases are easily diagnosable by clinical history and physical examination and tests are unnecessary.
- Tests of some diseases become positive after some days, for example, a creatinine test in renal failure, or a Widal test in typhoid.
- Unneeded tests increase the overall cost of medical care and doctors are only too aware of this fact.
- Unwarranted tests cause pain and suffering in the child.

What, then, are the indications for tests to be done?

In the outdoor clinic, tests are done for the following common reasons:

a) To clarify the diagnosis – e.g. in a case of fever, where there are no "pointing" symptoms and time is of the essence.
b) To estimate disease severity – e.g. creatinine level in renal failure, and bilirubin level in jaundice.
c) To eliminate the possibility of common symptoms being caused by a rarer, more serious disease – e.g. a raised white blood cell (W.B.C.) count not due to infection, but blood cancer.
d) To establish the child's baseline values before starting a treatment – e.g. a blood glucose level in a child diabetic.
e) Before a planned procedure or surgery, some tests are mandatory – e.g. a bleeding time and clotting time and blood group before surgery.
f) Rarely, doctors may ask for tests even though there is no real medical need just to alleviate the anxiety of the parents and other relatives.

What are the reasons for "repeat" testing in the same child during the same illness?

It is very agonising for patients (and parents) to be told that more samples need to be taken from them/ their wards. However, it is unavoidable in the following circumstances:

a) Previous tests not done in a standardised laboratory, or ambiguous results reported;
b) Results are at variance with clinically predicted profile, or do not match the progress level of the disease of the child;
c) The child develops further symptoms not consistent with earlier thinking;
d) The therapy is titrated with the help of some parameter on investigations – e.g. white-cell count in infections, pus cells in the urine in urinary tract infection and blood glucose level in diabetes; This is called *monitoring* a disease;
e) To confirm that the child's illness is not responding to the current line of treatment;
f) Where tests determine if hospitalization, surgery or transfer into or out of the Intensive Care Unit is needed;
g) Where normalizing of an abnormality is used to determine the end of an illness, the resumption of normal schooling, or the reduction or alteration of some medication – e.g. bilirubin and liver enzymes in jaundice, normalization of a W.B.C count for stopping antibiotics in an infection, etc; and
h) Where a negative test is inexplicable, in light of strong clinical suspicion of the same disease – e.g. a blood smear for Malarial Parasites – which may sometimes be negative, even if the person has malaria.

Why do results of tests vary from one laboratory to another or from one child to another with the same disease?

It is true that the results of tests may vary in the above circumstances. There are many reasons for this:

a) The child is not in the same clinical condition;
b) The state of fasting is not the same;
c) The child may have been in a different state of rest/physical exercise before the tests;
d) Medicines taken by the child in the interim may have altered the values;
e) The technician collects the sample with a different technique, uses different standards of normal, or performs the same test with a different laboratory method or different brand of chemicals;
f) Erroneous procedure of testing or use of date-expired chemicals may be responsible;
g) Wrong calculations by the technician before reporting the result; and
h) Typing errors by the typist who prepares the final report.

Is there any risk to the child during or after a blood test?

Most children experience pain when the needle is inserted. The pain is momentary, although the anxiety may last longer and make the child cry for a longer period. You should follow the instructions of the pathologist to avoid any untoward effects. The amount of blood removed is usually inconsequential to the general health of the child. This is because new blood is being constantly formed inside the body. Even after repeated testing, one need not worry on this account.

Sometimes, the site of insertion of the needle may develop a bluish bruise, which pains for 3-4 days.

Remember the following:

1. Laboratory tests are frequently needed in sicknesses.
2. One should insist on the tests being done in standardised laboratories.
3. The instructions of the doctor and the pathologists should be followed to the letter.
4. Repeat tests are not always a pointer to the inefficiency of the doctor.
5. Usually, the child who undergoes testing suffers from no long – lasting side – effects.

I hope the above account addresses most of the important issues that you as a parent face while taking your child to a laboratory for a test.

B. RADIOLOGICAL TESTS

Are X-rays a harmful type of radiation?

Used by doctors since the early decades of the twentieth century, radiographs, or X-rays as they are called popularly, are a boon to modern clinical medicine. X-rays are a part of the spectrum of waves around us. They cannot be seen or felt by us. X-rays may be harmful to the developing embryo of a mother-to-be. Hence, X-rays should be avoided in pregnancy. An average human can easily undergo up to 15-20 X-rays in a year's timeframe.

When do doctors ask for X-rays (Radiographs)?

An X-ray of the chest is asked when illnesses of the heart, lungs, rib-cage or the spine (of this region) are suspected. An abdominal X-ray is asked to diagnose suspected kidney stones, intestinal blockages, and lower spine disease and so on. Skull X-rays are asked for in cases of headaches, head injuries, ear or sinus diseases and in children with convulsions or mental handicap. In case of accidents and skeletal diseases, more than one X-ray is requested.

Repeat X-rays of the same region are taken to monitor the course of an illness, e.g. T.B. or rickets.

What is Ultrasonography (USG)?

USG is a technique where special sound waves, which can neither be seen nor heard, are directed through the human skin on to internal organs, which then partly absorb the energy and partly reflect it back to the probe. The "echo" is seen on the USG machine as an image of the organ under study. Like conventional radiography, USG too depends upon the examiner on interpretation.

When is a USG exam requested?

Head USG is possible only in newborns and small babies, as the probe can direct the sound waves into the skull through the open fontanelle; in older children, once the fontanelle has closed, head USG cannot be done. Head USG in newborns and small babies is done for problems like water collection in the brain, brain swelling, birth asphyxia, infection and bleeding. Heart USG is invaluable in the diagnosis of congenital heart disease and in cases of suspected acquired heart disease such as Rheumatic heart disease. This USG requires a special machine and the procedure is called an "Echocardiography". Abdominal USG is the commonest study in Pediatrics, and is done for children with acute abdominal pain, jaundice, swelling of abdomen, prolonged fever of unknown origin, urinary tract infection, lump in the abdomen and stool problems.

Is Ultrasound harmful?

USG is totally harmless, even in a baby. It is safe throughout pregnancy. One can repeat the study as often as desired.

Why is USG costly?

The machine costs anywhere between 6-40 lakhs of rupees. Hence USG is a bit costly in private practice.

What are scans?

There are many different types of scans, such as the C.T. scan, the M.R.I., the radionuclide scans etc. While the C.T. (Computed tomography) and M.R.I. (Magnetic Resonance Imaging) scans are chiefly designed to study the internal body *anatomy,* the Radionuclide scan is a scan devised to study *function* within a particular organ or system.

When are scans indicated?

All the above-mentioned scans are costly; their use must be limited to genuinely difficult-to-manage cases only. Examples include:

C.T.: Head injury, suspected brain tumour, unexplained convulsions, etc.

M.R.I.: Small lesions inside the brain, study of the spinal cord, structural delineation of lung and chest tumours, etc.

Radionuclide scans: Thyroid swelling, suspected hypothyroidism, kidney function study, etc.

Are there any complications of scanning?

Generally, scans are absolutely safe.

Part X
The Sick Child

I think the biggest disease this world suffers from…
is people feeling unloved.

– - Lady Diana,
Princess of Wales, 1961-1997

Ch 34
Aches and Pains

All pain is either severe or slight, if slight, it is easily endured; if severe, it will without doubt be brief.

- Marcus T. Cicero, c. 106-43 B.C., Roman Orator and Politician.

It is believed that even a newborn is capable of feeling pain! Considering this, and taking into account the fact that smaller children are unable to express themselves apart from crying, is it surprising that pains and aches are the commonest complaint (after fever) brought before the Pediatrician? Also, parents get immediately anxious when their little one complains of pain, especially if it is in a relatively important part of the body such as the head, the chest or the abdomen. It hurts the child (and the parent) even more if the pain occurs again and again, day after day, in a recurrent fashion.

Pain is actually the "cry" of a diseased organ. Disease itself means "dis" "ease" or discomfort. When there is some alteration in a tissue, the organ sends "pain" signals through chemicals to pain nerve fibres. These fibres transmit the signal to the conscious-aware centres of the brain. This makes the child aware of the pain. When she cries, she draws *your* attention to her discomfort, and you then try and find out what is wrong with her. If you can find out what is causing her to cry, well and good. Otherwise, I can bet my last rupee that you will soon consult a doctor. Such is the power of pain as a protective agent. In addition, pain acts like a self-protector too. A child who has sprained his ankle while running will wince and stop in his tracks almost immediately; he will refuse to allow anyone to move his ankle joint this way and that; he will not stand up on that ankle due to the agony it will cause. If he has no prior idea of this, he may attempt to stand, but the severe shooting pain up his ankle and leg will force him to crumple back to the ground. In this way, further injury to the ankle ligaments is effectively prevented.

Accompanying the pain will be other symptoms that suggest anxiety, such as a rapid pulse, palpitation, sweating, rapid breathing (often with a catch in breath as the pain becomes unbearable) and crying. All these symptoms suggest an overworking sympathetic nervous system. In addition, there may be other symptoms that suggest either the cause of the pain (such as fever or swelling suggesting inflammation) or the other consequences of the primary disease (such as reduced vision in the affected eye where a ball hit the child).

Some children can bear pain more effectively than others. This is because the pain threshold is different in different people. Those who have recurrent pain are more sensitive to the onset of pain, but may bear it better once they realise that the pain will soon subside. Those with chronic pain may bear it better, but are more fearful of the eventual outcome and hence complain more about it.

Children whose parents often scare them about the "painful" injections that the doctor will give if they do not eat well will be frightened to visit the Pediatrician. This policy must never be followed by parents.

Headache:

Children may have a headache due to myriad causes, some of which are listed below:

1. Febrile illnesses like malaria, typhoid, the 'flu, etc.
2. Dehydration due to any cause
3. Inflammations of the eye, ENT organs, sinuses, teeth and the meninges (the covering membranes around the brain)
4. Eye strain in school (refractive errors)
5. Tension before and during exams
6. Heat exhaustion
7. Migraine

The headache in case of febrile illnesses is generalised, while in case of sickness of specific organs, the pain is either unilateral or more localized. Tension headache usually occurs on both the sides of the head, while headache due to meningeal inflammation is usually generalised or at the back of the head and in the neck too. Headaches resulting from eye strain and heat exhaustion occur at the end of a school day or end of an outing in the sun. Migraine in children is rare, but may occur in children in whose families migraine is common; the headache is precipitated (brought on) by stress, bright lights or noise; it is unilateral (occurring on one side) or generalised, moderately severe to very severe and lasts for many hours. Such attacks may repeat themselves every few months.

Migraine is diagnosed when there are at least 5 attacks fulfilling the following:

- Headache attack lasting *1* to 48 hours
- Headache has at least 2 of the following:
    1. Either bilateral or unilateral (*frontal/temporal*) location
    2. Pulsating quality
    3. Moderate to severe intensity
    4. Aggravation by routine physical activity
- During headache, at least 1 of the following:
    1. Nausea and/or vomiting
    2. Photophobia and/or phonophobia (fear or avoidance of bright light and/or loud sounds)

What to do: Headache is usually due to an underlying cause; hence, you should attempt to discover the cause and treat it. *When headache is accompanied by forceful vomiting, blurring of vision or any other visual disturbances, it may indicate a medical emergency; you should take the child immediately to a hospital for admission.* In all other cases, the simplest way to relieve the child is to give her paracetamol. If required, up to 3-4 doses of paracetamol may be given in a 24-hour timeframe. In a case where the cause cannot be found, you should consult her pediatrician. Where the cause lies in some other organ(s), the respective specialist must be consulted (such as Ophthalmologist, ENT surgeon, Dentist, Psychiatrist, etc). Migraine needs specific treatment to abort the acute attack as well as to prevent further attacks.

Many hospitals have "Headache Clinics" and "Pain Clinics". These provide comprehensive diagnostic and therapeutic services under "one roof".

"Stomach-ache" or Abdominal Pain:

This is the commonest pain symptom in children. It may be of acute onset or it may occur recurrently for many weeks or months. At times, the child suffers from chronic pain. **Acute pain** starts over minutes to hours, and may indicate either a medical or surgical illness: when accompanied by urinary or bowel symptoms, it may point to a urinary tract infection or a gastroenteritis or dysentery; when it follows a high coloured urine and vomiting, it points to Jaundice; when it is localized in the right lower part of the "stomach" and accompanied by high fever and vomiting, appendicitis is a possibility.

Recurrent abdominal pain means pain occurring repeatedly for a few days over the past 3-6 months. It may be due to intestinal infections, worms, chronic appendicitis, peptic ulcer or amoebic colitis, to list a few causes. However, by far the most common cause is *psychological or "functional" pain*: in this, the child complains of non-specific central (umbilical) area pain that comes and goes on its own, is not associated with any other symptoms and is brought on by the prospect of being asked to eat, or go to school or the fear of being punished for a mistake not yet discovered by the parent at home or the teacher at school. The child may mimic the pain she has seen her mother or grandmother complain of at an earlier date; if you ask her more questions, she may be unable to describe the characteristics of the pain clearly. The child may complain of vague pains in other parts of her body. She is otherwise active and playful and the pain "disappears as if by magic" as soon as the conflict is either resolved or "successfully averted".

Chronic abdominal pain is usually organic, that is, it points to some medical disorder; it may represent an unresolved acute situation like appendicitis or it may point to some other disorder. A pediatrician must be consulted.

A word about **Peptic Ulcer**. You might have the impression that peptic ulcer disease only occurs in stressed adults. This is generally true; however, a small number of older children and adolescents suffer from peptic ulcers due to a faulty lifestyle and too much stress. These children worry too much and eat a lot of spicy food, pickles, tea, coffee etc. They have bloating of the stomach, pain after eating food, water-brash (pain and acidic liquid upsurge from the abdomen into the chest just behind the breast bone) and symptoms of indigestion. As a part of the treatment, the children should be asked to eat simple, bland foods, stop having fried foods and allowed to have milk and curds. Antacids and antibiotics will be prescribed by the doctor, whose advice you must follow religiously.

Acute appendicitis is also a common medical condition that can threaten the child's life. It presents with high fever, pain in the lower right side of the abdomen and vomiting that worsens over the next 12 hours. The child should be immediately taken to the hospital.

Growing pains:

In this condition, the child experiences moderate to severe dull aching pain in the calves of both legs especially at night. The pain occurs almost every night following a particularly hectic, playful day, and it is seen in almost 5-10% of children between 2-12 years of age. The pain does not imply anything serious, and all you need to do is to reassure the child that she will be okay, and give her a massage or a hot water bag to place over the legs. If the pain is severe, you may want to give a pain-killer like paracetamol or Combiflam*. Some children respond to blood-building tonics (hematinics). Vitamin E and Calcium supplements have also been tried with variable success.

Dysmenorrhoea:

Dysmenorrhoea means painful menstruation. It is a common problem in teenaged girls, particularly during the early years of menstruation. Paracetamol, antispasmodics and hot water bags are advised. After a few years, the pain goes away.

Toothache:

This is usually due to tooth cavities or infection in the root of a tooth. The pain is excruciating, and may spread over the full jaw, the head or the overlying cheeks. The child will be in agony. You may try putting a cotton wad dipped in clove oil for temporary relief; you may also give her pain killers like paracetamol or a combination of this medicine with Ibuprofen (e.g. Combiflam*), but the right thing to do would be to take her to the dentist as soon as possible. Sometimes, there is no toothache, but the headache is due to tooth trouble. This can make the diagnosis a bit tricky.

It is recommended that the child be shown the correct way of brushing teeth, be given food and sweets in a way that caries is not encouraged, and be taken to a dentist once every six months for a check-up.

Conclusion:

Aches and pains are going to come and go, regardless of what precautions you take or don't take. Hence, you must make an attempt to make light of small pains and to avoid fussing over them in a way that the child keeps crying and reminding you of the pain. Overprotecting the child can also be harmful as it prevents learning by the child. Allow her to be free; if she falls or hurts herself, administer first aid (cleaning the wound with running water and antiseptic, stopping the bleeding (if any), applying an antibiotic ointment for an open wound and dressing up the wound). After this, do not fuss and fret too much. Take her to a doctor only if she has a big injury or some other complication. Offer her your closeness and your tender loving care (T.L.C.) instead of accosting her with allegations and screaming at her "for climbing the cupboard" at the time of injury. Recriminations should be left until later.

Practicality should be the guiding principle and not blind love and unlimited moping over the small ailments of a sprightly child such as yours!

Ch. 35
Worms and Intestinal Parasites

Which came first--the intestine or the tapeworm?
- William S. Burroughs 1914-1997,
American Writer.

What is the relevance of worms in child health?

A majority of children in developing countries and tropical nations have infestations with worms at some point or the other in their childhood. Sometimes, they continue to "harbour" these worms even in adulthood. However, the problem is, to a large extent, preventable with good personal and environmental hygiene and sanitation. To this end, widespread education of the people is the only solution. The government, on its own, can do a lot for the problem too.

How do infestations occur?

Different worms have different methods of entering the human host. The most common route is the fecal-oral route: here, the eggs of adult worms are passed in the stool of the previous host (may be another human or animal), and this enters the food/water through either the unhygienic storage of cooked food, through water-supply pipes, or through house-flies. These eggs are then ingested by the child/subsequent host and develop into adult worms in his/her intestines. Pin worms and round worms spread in this manner.

If the partly uncooked flesh of some animals is eaten by humans, tape-worms can enter the human host. For example, the beef tape worm and the fish tape worm enter in this way.

Larvae of hookworms enter the human body by piercing the skin of the feet of children who walk bare-footed in soil or water puddles. Guinea worms may also enter in this way.

Drinking contaminated water or food also leads to amoebic and giardial infections. We shall talk about these later in the chapter.

Remember this: Eating sweet food does not cause worms.

What are the symptoms of worm infestation?

The commonest symptoms are pain in the abdomen, anal-area itching or burning, urinary infection, episodes of diarrhoea, increased appetite, paleness of the skin and eyes, easy tiredness, bloating of the abdomen and vomiting of a worm through the mouth.

Pin-worm females lay their eggs around the child's anal orifice, and may even become visible under bright light at night when the child wakes up scratching her anal area and complains to you. If the worm migrates forward into the vagina or near the urinary orifice, she may experience burning and wake up screaming, holding her genital area, or, alternatively, complain of burning while passing urine, or increased frequency of passing urine.

Round-worms may either cause no symptoms, or cause abdominal pain, vomiting, constipation, loose stools or even respiratory symptoms like cough and throwing out sputum when their larvae pass through the lungs. Sheer high numbers of round worms may, at times, choke up the entire small intestine and present as an acute medical emergency. Round worms move when irritated, and worms have been seen to come out of the mouth, the nose, and rarely, even the child's ears. Increase in appetite is also due to the large number of worms competing with the child for the food. In spite of an increased appetite, the child will seem not to grow well, and have a rather large, bloated abdomen.

Hookworms can produce irritation and rash at the point of entry on the feet. Once lodged in the child's intestines, they suck blood and other nutrients from the child's body. Infested children develop anemia, a condition characterised by paleness of the eyes, tongue and skin, easy tiredness and pica – a condition where the child is seen to eat mud, chalk, plaster from the walls and other such things (Chapter 44). The ensuing deficiency of iron may cause long-term problems such as growth failure, or even a mental slowdown.

Tape-worm infestations are usually harmless, but the pig tape worm may cause the larvae to settle in the child's brain or the muscles, and produce painful muscle swellings, or even convulsions (fits).

Guinea-worms cause a red, visible line of inflammation to appear on the trunk of the child, and this line will be seen to move as the worm moves from one part of the body to another just under the skin.

Remember this: Worms do not cause white spots on the face. They do not cause teeth – grinding either.

How can one prevent worm infestations?

We have already seen some of these measures above. Scrupulous food hygiene is the name of the game. Proper hand-washing before and after visiting the toilet and before and after eating any food is the single most useful advice I can give. Ensure this in your child, and in yourself, and you can say good-bye to worms. To prevent infestations by hook-worms and guinea-worms, encourage the child to always wear long-legged trousers or night-suits and protective closed shoes while taking outdoor walks in soily or soft-ground areas. The child should not step into a well to collect water without covering his feet. Water for drinking should be filtered, and if possible, boiled for 10 minutes to kill off all worms and their eggs. In fact amoebic and giardial parasites also perish with boiling water.

Green leafy vegetables and salad items should be washed thoroughly before they are diced and cooked.

In addition, auto-infection occurs with pin-worm eggs; children with long finger-nails who scratch their bottoms where the pin-worm eggs are deposited just outside the anus carry these eggs back into their mouths and infect themselves. Hence, careful attention must be paid to keeping the finger-nails trimmed and free of dirt.

How are worm infestations diagnosed and how are they treated?

Most worm infestations can be diagnosed by careful history taking accompanied by a proper stool test. Pin worms can be seen emerging out of the anus at night. The eggs may be picked up by sticking a Scotch-tape to the child's bottom. The eggs can then be seen under a microscope. Round worms and in tape-worm infestations, segments of the tape-worm may also be seen in the stool.

The blood counts may show anemia (hook-worm), or elevation of *eosinophil count* (a type of white blood cell). Their presence indicates an active allergic response to the worms in the body.

There are effective single-dose and multi-dose de-worming agents that are used by doctors to treat worms. For tape worms which infest the brain, longer treatments are required, and sometimes the child may also need surgery if he has recurrent non-responsive fits.

Amoebiasis and Giardiasis:

While amoebiasis occurs with ingestion of contaminated water or food. giardiasis is the result of ingesting contaminated water. Amoebic infection can either produce an acute painful diarrhoea with passage of blood and mucus in stools, or a chronic illness with abdominal pain, constipation and diarrhoea. Sometimes, acute amoebic infection can produce pus-filled abscesses in the liver, lungs and other sites of the body.

Giardiasis causes a chronic illness characterised by recurrent abdominal pain and flatulence with passage of bulky, foul-smelling frothy stools. Loss of weight and reduced appetite are also important clinical features. There is no acute illness like amoebiasis.

Diagnosis of both these illnesses is made by history of typical symptoms, examination of the child and a stool test. Treatment is with readily available medicines, although the abscesses may need to be treated by a surgical method.

Ch 36
ENT Problems in Children

Half of us are blind, few of us feel, and we are all deaf.

-Sir William Osler, 1849-1919,
Canadian Physician

The ears, nose and throat of a person are interlinked to each other through various structures. It is for this reason that their study falls into one medical speciality known as "otorhinolaryngology" or, simply, ENT. This chapter is dedicated to the explanation of the management of various ENT problems in children. To know the meaning of the various medical terms that are scattered in this chapter, please take a look at the Glossary on page xxx.

The Common Cold (Coryza):

The common cold is one of the most common illnesses to afflict children all over the world. Its incidence is higher in the tropical countries as the warm, humid climates in these countries allows the cold viruses to thrive. There are over 200 different viruses that cause cold. They cause infections throughout the year, but more so in the winter and when the weather changes. Cold is the commonest cause of absenteeism in school.

Epidemiology: Infection with one of the cold viruses begins with the entry of the virus into the child's ENT organs. The entry is facilitated if the child is weak, just recovering from another illness or if her immunity is depressed due to any reason. She catches the infection from one of her contacts who is also suffering from coryza. This may be one of her family members, a friend from the nursery or school or a casual contact. Once she is infected, she will continue to spread the virus directly while coughing and sneezing and indirectly through infected clothing like towels, handkerchiefs etc. She will remain infective from one or two days before she develops symptoms to 1-2 days after her symptoms have abated.

Symptoms: The illness begins with a fever that is accompanied by cold, running nose, sneezing and blockage of nose. Cough, sore throat and general symptoms like headache, body ache and pain in the legs also ensue. The child becomes miserable, cranky and fidgety as she finds it difficult to breathe, eat, sleep or rest. Loss of appetite is an early symptom and it persists for a few days after recovery from the respiratory symptoms. Smaller children often have vomiting with their bouts of cough. The virus may involve other unrelated organs such as the eyes (conjunctivitis), the bowel (gastroenteritis), the brain (encephalitis) and so on.

Complications: A common-cold by itself is a self limiting disease which recovers in 5-7 days. However, the virus may spread to affect other organs as described above. Of these, gastroenteritis, pneumonia and encephalitis are the most dangerous. Secondly, there may be a secondary bacterial infection over the viral infection: this may involve the tonsils, the middle ear, the sinuses, the pharynx (back of the throat) or other ENT structures. The infection may even spread to more remote structures such as the meninges (meningitis). Thirdly, an attack of coryza can act as a trigger for an acute attack of wheezing in an asthmatic child or a child prone to develop asthma. Lastly, a cold-like illness may not represent coryza but the start of some other viral infection like measles, poliomyelitis, chicken pox, mumps etc.

<u>Treatment:</u> There is no specific treatment for coryza. We often say that if left untreated, cold lasts for a week, while with treatment, it abates in 7 days! Treatment thus consists of remedies to- a) keep the nostrils of the baby open b) reduce pain in the affected parts of the body c) control fever and d) control the running nose and the cough. e) At the same time, we attempt to "cure" the illness with nourishing food and general support.

a) Keep the nostrils open: The best solution for this is nasal instillation of *Normal Saline* nose drops. These can be prepared afresh everyday by adding a pinch of salt to a glass of water; alternatively, one can use ready saline nose drops that are available in the market. You should lay the child in your lap with the head hanging backwards and then put 1-2 drops of saline in each nostril about 5-10 minutes before feeding time. After putting the drops, gently turn the tip of the nose in a circular movement to enable the drops to penetrate into the deeper channels of the nose. Next, if available, "suck" out the secretions with a soft nasal suction bulb. If this is not available, you may use the twisted corner of a handkerchief or a soft cotton bud to tease out the secretions manually. Other methods include *inhalation of steam,* encouraging the older child to *"sniff"* out the blocking secretions, and using inhalants like *Vicks®* or *Inhalade®*.

b) Reduce pain: The child may have pain in the throat, headache, bodyache or leg pains. All these, as well as the fever, can be controlled with timely doses of Paracetamol, Combiflam®, Nimesulide or similar anti-inflammatory analgesic. Dosing can be frequent with paracetamol, but with Combiflam, one must not exceed three doses, and with Nimesulide, two doses in a day (i.e., 24 hours).

c) Control fever: This can be done with repeated dosing of one of the drugs mentioned above. To this, one may add the benefits of sponging (see Chapter 31).

d) Control the running nose and the cough: This can be done with one of the readily available cough and cold remedies. For this, you may have to visit your doctor from time to time.

e) Food and general support: This is provided in the form of nourishing food, rest, intake of plenty of warm liquids and home remedies. Food must be light, easy to digest and low in throat irritants like spices, oil and lime. However, ginger and lime together are thought to be beneficial, and their extract, when added in honey makes for a nice home remedy for a sore throat. Warm liquids like water, tea, milk, soup etc. are very useful as they soothe the throat, improve the clearance of secretions from the nose and throat and help in expectoration of sputum. Vicks® contains eucalyptus oil, peppermint oil and menthol. Rubbing this on to the chest and back of the child helps to relieve nasal blockage. Putting the child onto her stomach also helps her to breathe better. So does a steam inhalation. All these measures may be tried singly or jointly in an effort to help the child. However, do not force them on the child if *she does not want it.*

Antibiotics are not usually needed in simple coryza, but when there are complications like pharyngitis, tonsillitis, otitis media, etc. their use is warranted. In cases where you suspect any of the above complications, or where the symptoms do not subside within a week, please consult her Pediatrician.

<u>Important:</u> Common cold should not be confused with *allergic rhinitis*, an allergic condition characterised by either seasonal or perennial running of the nose due to allergy to dust, pollen grains (of flowers), insects or some other foreign substance (s). Here, sneezing is a marked symptom and there is no cough. Itching sensation in the eyes and nose, and an increased preponderance of allergic wheezing illness is also a clue to the diagnosis.

The second condition that resembles a common cold is *Acute Strep throat*: this is a more serious illness characterised by redness of the throat, enlargement of lymph glands in the neck, enlargement of tonsillar glands inside the throat and hardly any cough. There is an increased risk of prolongation of symptoms if the child is not rapidly diagnosed and treated with antibiotics. In some cases, children who have acute strep throats go on to develop a serious cardiac illness called *acute rheumatic fever* (see Chapter 41); in others, the sore throat may be followed by a not uncommon kidney problem known as *acute glomerulonephritis* (in which there is passage of blood in the urine along with high blood pressure and swelling of the body; the illness usually gets cured on its own, but some children need extended therapy under the care of a nephrologist).

Prevention: It is impossible to completely prevent attacks of common cold; however, exclusive breast feeding for at least 4-6 months is definitely helpful in reducing the frequency of the attacks that would otherwise occur. The child must be kept clean and be encouraged to wash her face and hands often. She must be kept away from crowds and from people known to be suffering from the cold; care-givers must remember not to sneeze or cough at the child when *they* have a cough and cold; they should not be exposed to cold drafts of air (such as when you take them out on a bike); their play environment should be free from pollutants and allow good cross ventilation; they should be encouraged to avoid refrigerated items too often, and to shun unhygienically prepared/stored/sold food, such as is available on roadsides from hawkers; finally, they should continue to receive unlimited parental love and nourishing food so that they do not fall prey to this "common" illness. No vaccine is as yet available against the common cold.

For more info, go here:

- ✔ http://www.medicdirect.co.uk/PDF/Commoncold.pdf
- ✔ http://www.niaid.nih.gov/factsheets/cold.htm

Nose-bleed (Epistaxis):

This is a common condition in children. It may occur without any obvious fall or injury and it may occur suddenly in hot weather and in dry climate. Occasionally, it may follow injury to the delicate blood vessels inside the nostrils due to nose-picking or putting sharp objects like a pencil point into the nose.

What to do: Do not get alarmed or panicky when you see a child bleeding from her nose. Just go up to her and re-assure her that she'll soon be all right. Ask her to sit in the shade or under a fan or in an air-conditioned room on a comfortable chair, with her head bent a little forwards. Next, ask someone to pinch her nostrils tight between the thumb and the first finger and ask the child to breathe through her mouth. The bleeding will stop within 8-10 minutes. You may apply ice over the bridge of the nose and the middle of the forehead to hasten the stoppage of bleeding.

If there is profuse bleeding, visible injury or wound or if the bleeding has not stopped in about 10 minutes, you should show the child to an ENT specialist.

Ear pain:

Around the age of 5-7 months, many babies are brought to the Pediatrician with the complaint that the baby keeps scratching or rubbing her ears. They are keen to rule out earache as a cause. Remember that at that age, many children normally rub their ears because of boredom or because of the experience of a novel sensation. Once this "normal" rubbing has been ruled out, the other causes include an insect or some other foreign body in the ear, impacted wax, boils or some other infection of the external ear canal, swelling of the ear drum or otitis media (see below). Rarely, ear ache may be due to tooth ache, mumps and inflammation of the joint of the lower jaw that is located just in front of the ear.

Earache causes the child to become cranky and irritable, or to scream intermittently.

What to do: Shine a torch inside the ear canal and see if you can spot anything unusual. If nothing is seen, the safe course will be to see her Pediatrician or ENT doctor. In the meantime, DO NOT PUT WARM OIL OR COTTON BUDS INSIDE HER EARS. If you have pain-killer ear drops, consult the doctor on the phone before using them. Some children may also need a pain-killer medicine by mouth. Wax is a normal secretion of the ear canal and its purpose is to protect the ear drum against floating objects like dust particles or insects. DO NOT TRY TO REMOVE IT WITH BUDS OR ANY SHARP INSTRUMENT LIKE MATCH-STICKS, HAIR PIN, SAFETY PIN ETC. Use a pair of blunt tweezers to pick out a loose object like a moving wax plug or a dead insect. If you see something that you don't understand, seek an urgent appointment with the ENT specialist.

Tongue-tie:

The tip of the tongue is attached to the floor of the mouth by a small fold of mucous membrane known as the "frenulum". The frenulum in a normal person is thin and just long enough to allow the tongue to move freely enough to be able to be protruded outside the lips and to be touched on the roof of the palate.

Occasionally, the frenulum is short and thick; the child may be unable to carry out the above tasks; the tip of the tongue may show a visible notch when the child attempts to protrude her tongue. Many people then blame this condition, known as a tongue-tie, for abnormal speech or difficulties in feeding. While a true tongue-tie may cause difficulty in pronouncing the sounds of the letters D, TH, L, N and T, a tongue-tie is never a cause of difficulties in feeding. In spite of this, many parents opt for a surgical cutting of the frenulum even where there is no true tongue-tie only on a presumption that cutting the frenulum will make their child start talking or utter clear speech. This is wrong. Consult an oral surgeon before scheduling this surgery on your child.

Middle Ear Infection (Acute otitis media):

Before I discuss this topic, I must explain how the ear is intimately connected to the nose and the throat. Have a look at the figure below. (Fig. 36-1)

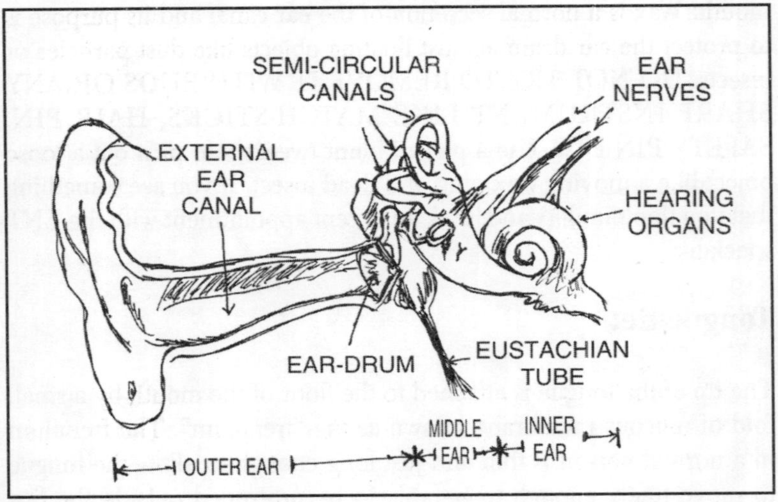

Fig 36-1

As you can see, there is a tiny fragile tube that joins the middle ear (the part of the ear that is behind the ear drum but in front of the hearing organ) to the back of the throat (or *pharynx*) just behind the rear openings of the nasal canals on either side (just about a few millimeters away from the *internal* nostrils).This tube is called the Eustachian tube. Its function is to help adjust the pressure of air within the middle ear in such a way as to optimise the hearing and sound-amplifying ability of the middle ear. It also helps to keep the middle ear dry and clean as it "drains" any fluid that might otherwise collect – into the mouth.

Middle ear infections occur when this tube gets blocked as a result of inflammation within it or at its mouth-end where the *Adenoid glands* (see below) are located. Such inflammation of the adenoids (adenoiditis) and blockage of the tube can occur in any child, but more so in children who are fed milk from a *propped-up feeding bottle* while they are left to feed all by themselves in the supine position. Parents who put oil in the ears and nose of their babies are also liable to "gift" an attack of otitis media to them.

Symptoms: Suspect this illness if, during the course of an uncomplicated cold or cough, the baby suddenly becomes irritable, cries intermittently, screams out of pain and starts putting her finger repeatedly into her ears. If the ear drum is intact, the crying may get worse. If the pressure within the middle ear becomes too much, the ear drum may get perforated and a thick, yellowish pus mixed with a slight quantity of blood may come out of the ear. Once the ear drains out, the pain disappears; the perforation will get sealed off and the ear may heal completely with appropriate treatment; otherwise, the infection may linger, or heal and then recur once or more than once, each time damaging the delicate structures in the middle and inner ear, finally leading to hearing loss that may be permanent. Hence, you should immediately take the child to a specialist.

Prevention: Since blockage of the nose and infection of the adenoid glands commonly precede otitis media, one should remember to keep the nostrils open with normal saline nose drops. Never put oil in the nose and ears right from the newborn period.

See this link for more information on Otitis media:

- ✔ http://unthscdl.slis.ua.edu/patientinfo/otorhinolaryngology/ear/middle-ear/otitis-media.htm

Tonsillitis and Adenoiditis:

Every human being is born with a pair of tonsils that are located just behind the tongue on either side of the mouth. These glands normally act like sentinels, in that they prevent the entry into the body, through the oral orifice of germs and other matter. As children are more prone to ingest or inhale germs, the tonsils are normally very "active" in childhood, esp. between 2-10 years of age. They may become enlarged from time to time, and occasionally even show acute infection in the form of yellowish red pus points on their surface. These points of infection are called "follicles". This is therefore called "Acute Follicular Tonsillitis". It is commonly also referred to as "strep" throat and needs 7-10 days of strong antibiotic therapy (see above).

Adenoid glands are located just behind the internal openings of the nasal canals. (See figure). They cannot be normally seen by opening the mouth. Like the tonsils, the adenoids also act as sentinels for dust and germs entering through the nose; they too get enlarged from time to time. The problem is that when they get enlarged, they block the nostrils from the back end and cause difficulty in breathing, noisy breathing, running of the nose and snoring in sleep. The child keeps her mouth open, gets inadequate sleep at night (due to the breathing difficulty and the discomfort/ pain at the back of the throat) and develops a nasal twang to her voice. As discussed above, enlarged adenoids can block the Eustachian tube and lead to repeated attacks of acute otitis media.

Recurrent or chronic adenoiditis can change the child's face completely, imparting it a "dull" look on account of the drooling saliva, the open mouth with a protruding tongue and a sleepy demeanour (the so-called *adenoid facies*).

Removal of tonsils and adenoids: In the past, it was considered prudent to remove the child's tonsillar and adenoid glands as a precaution once a loose interpretation was made that the child had "many" respiratory illnesses in the recent past. Nowadays, indiscriminate surgery is abhorred since more and more people have realised the value of these glands; one should order surgery only if all other options have proved unsuccessful.

Acute Sinusitis:

There are three pairs of air-filled sacs or sinuses that outpouch from the nose cavity into the surrounding cheek and forehead bones. Inflammation and infection of these sinuses is called sinusitis. Sinusitis is commonly a complication of the common cold, and causes headache, running of the nose and acute discomfort when the child turns his head in a direction that fills up the sinus with secretions and pus. Commonly, this happens when the child bends down to pick up something.

Cough and cold medicines that have decongestants in them, along with antibiotics help improve the infection. Along with this, the child may also be given steam inhalations.

When sinusitis becomes a chronic condition, surgery becomes essential to drain the infected material and to prevent repeat attacks of sinusitis.

Miscellaneous problems:

Thrush: Thrush is a thick, spotty white coating of the tongue, oral mucosa and gums due to infection by a fungus called *Candida*. Candidial infection occurs by contamination from infected teats of feeding bottles or infected nipples of the mother's breast, infected fingers of an adult who puts them in the baby's mouth without any real reason and occasionally right at the time of delivery by contamination from the mother's vagina. The child gets pain while feeding and swallowing. Regular application of a local anti-fungal lotion before feeding will quickly cause the patches to disappear.

The mother should be checked to see if she has similar patches in her vagina or on her breast; if so, she should also be treated.

Drooling: Drooling may be normal in some infants. On the other hand, parents feel that a drool always means mental retardation! Nothing can be more wrong. In fact, over 99.5% of droolers are mentally just fine, and only 20-30% of all mentally retarded children actually drool. The other causes of drooling include thrush, oral ulcers, teething, gum pain and children with mouth breathing due to nose block or adenoid disease (see above).

Aphthous ulcers: Extremely painful small ulcers that develop on the tongue, inner sides of the lips and gums and other areas of the oral cavity are called aphthous ulcers. They occur in some families, in both adults and children, without any preceding factor or cause. Local applications of antiseptic anaesthetic mouth creams/gels and use of mouth-washes in older children are, to some extent, able to relieve the pain and discomfort. The ulcers tend to heal on their own after a few days to a week.

Further Reading:

- ✔ http://www.sinuscarecenter.com/: This is an exhaustive site for many ENT illnesses.
- ✔ http://www.entnet.org/kidsent/: ENT discussed from the Pediatric perspective.

Ch 37
Common Eye Problems of Childhood

Of all the senses, sight must be the most delightful.
- Helen Keller, American Blind/Deaf Author and Lecturer.

The eyes are the mirror of our souls and their sparkle and charm is what makes even the most ill-bred, hard-hearted person fall in love with a child, no matter what colour, race or religion the child may belong to. Eyes are our special sense to see the world around us. To know how the eyes and their capacities improve as the child grows up, go to Chapter 13.

Throughout childhood, parents are worried about anything happening to their child's eyes. They take the utmost pains to take care of their child's vision by giving them carrots to eat, by making them watch the T.V. from a distance and so on. However, some eye problems are unavoidable since they are genetic in nature. Others like infection, traumas etc. are avoidable, but often children do develop these and worry their parents. This chapter is not a treatise on Ophthalmology. I have supplied links to some of the best Patient Information sites available on the Internet. Do take a look at those if you need more information.

Watering from the eyes:

There is a tiny tube that connects the conjunctival sac (or the visible front part of the eye) to the internal cavity of the nose. This tube is called the *naso-lacrimal duct*. It normally helps to drain the tears (that are continuously being secreted by the tear glands) into the nose cavity. Occasionally, the eye-end opening of this tube gets blocked by dirt or dead cells. This may even be present from the newborn period. The blockage stops the normal drainage of the tears, so that they start "overflowing" on to the cheeks all the time. Parents get worried and the child is then taken to the pediatrician or the ophthalmologist for opinion. Remember that the block may disappear on its own as the baby grows. In most cases, we can help the recovery process by gently rubbing our thumbs or index fingers just on the inside of both eyes over the bridge of the nose. This exercise must be done three to four times a day for 5-10 minutes each time for about 7-8 days. If the blockage persists, please see an eye surgeon, who will probe the opening with a soft, blunt wire to open the duct.

Stye:

A stye is an inflammation/infection of one of the oil-glands or follicles of the eye-lashes. Styes are common in some children, particularly those with generalised weakness or those who have some refractive errors. In such children, styes may recur from time to time. A small bump is seen which is inflamed and causes pain and sensation of heaviness on the eyelid. The pain and discomfort may subside with hot fomentations, but most children will need antibiotic eye-drops, ointment or/and oral antibiotics.

Children should be encouraged to never rub their eyes with dirty fingers and to keep them clean with splashing water into open eyes and the hands clean with frequent hand washing with soap and water. This will prevent such infections.

Refractive errors:

Children with normal vision can see things clearly. The lenses of their eyes change shape to focus on objects. They change to different shapes depending on how close or far away the objects are. Children with refractive errors do not have normal vision. They may not be able to see things that are far away (near-sighted) or see things that that are close (far-sighted). Figs. 37-1, 37-2 and 37-3 show the structure of the eye and the formation of the image in the normal eye, the *hyperopic* eye and the *myopic* eye respectively. In children with hyperopia (far-sightedness), the image of distant objects forms behind the retina, while in children with myopia (near-sightedness), the image

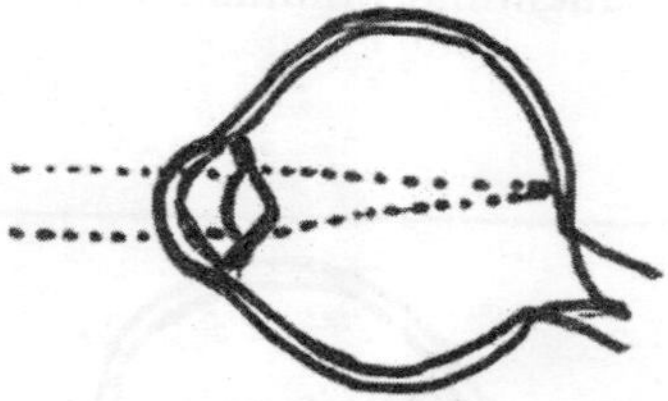

Fig 37-1

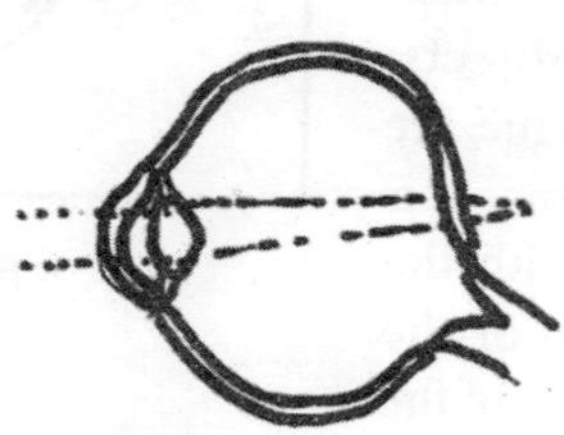

Fig 37-2

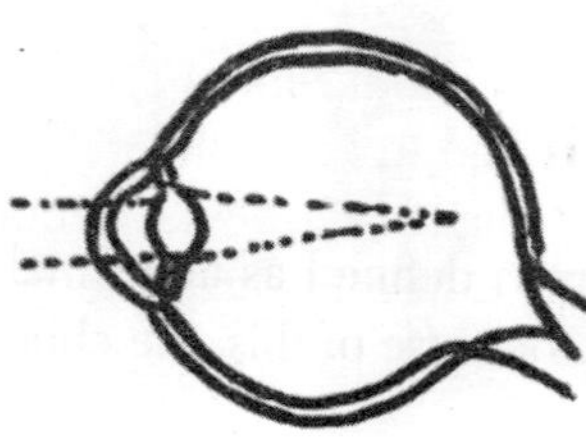

Fig 37-3

of objects forms in front of the retina. The errors can only be corrected when lenses are used to re-direct the image on the retina.

Hyperopia is less common than myopia in childhood. Both may run in families. As the child grows, the myopia may become worse and the child may need higher-numbered glasses. **It is essential that the child continually wears the glasses that she has been prescribed, otherwise the error may increase**, or if her vision is blurred, she may not do well in her studies. To read more about refractive errors, look up one of the following links:

- ✔ http://www.vh.org/pediatric/patient/pediatrics/cqqa/visualprob.html
- ✔ http://unthsc-dl.slis.ua.edu/patientinfo/ophthalmology/refractive-errors.htm

Astigmatism (Fig 37-4):

Astigmatism is suspected when the child complains of distorted vision, blurring of vision and is found squinting her eyes while looking at small objects. Headache and eye fatigue are also associated symptoms. It is caused by problems with the curvature of the cover of the front portion (the cornea) of the eye. This type of problem is solved by using cylindrical lenses.

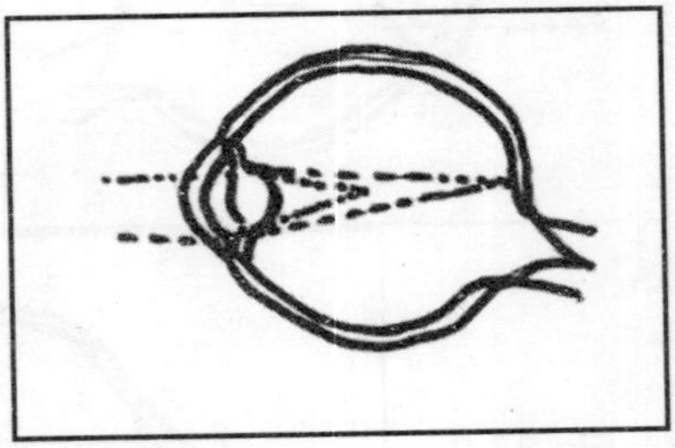

Fig 37-4

Squint:

Squint is defined as abnormal alignment of vision between the two eyes. Because of this, the child appears to be simultaneously looking in two different directions. Almost all infants have a transient squint in the first 6-8 months of life. This is because of impending development of fixation of vision which in turn is dependent on the maturation of the brain. True squint is more common in preterm and small-for-dates babies. When squint persists beyond 6-8 months, or develops afresh after this age, one should consult an ophthalmologist.

Colour Blindness:

This is a genetically transmitted condition seen only in boys. It is a rare disorder of the retina in which the child is unable to see the red and green colours correctly; instead, he sees them as shades of gray. This condition has no treatment. It is suspected only when the child tells his parents about how he cannot see things like traffic signals properly.

Conjunctivitis:

This means inflammation or infection of the thin membrane that overlies the visible portion of our eye at all places except over the cornea. Infection mostly occurs in infants at the time of birth, or soon thereafter, if the child's eyes are exposed to germs, as for example when dirty *kajal* is rubbed into the eyes, or when dirty fingers or handkerchiefs are inserted into the corners of the eye with intention to clean accumulated eye- discharge or muck that is lodged inside.

In epidemic conjunctivitis, it is a virus that attacks the eyes. It affects many individuals at the same time. In both cases, the eyes become red and swollen and there is a discharge which is initially clear but later turns sticky and yellow like pus. There is pain, itching and some degree of discomfort when the child tries to look at bright light.

The infected eyes should be washed liberally with water containing boric acid; after this, antibiotic eye-drops or ointment should be applied into the eyes repeatedly and daily, till the child recovers completely. Drops may be used in the day-time while ointment is applied at night or whenever the baby goes to sleep. It might be the right place to tell readers here that the practice of wearing dark sunglasses during epidemics of conjunctivitis is only to prevent dust and other dirty stuff from entering the inflamed eye, and NOT TO PREVENT PASSING ON THE INFECTION TO OTHERS, as you might have thought.

Anomalies of the eye:

These are rare congenital anomalies and include cataracts, small eyes, pigmentation disorders, blindness, absence of eyeballs, anomalies of the eye-lids, etc. Every child with a congenital eye anomaly must be shown to the Ophthalmologist.

Lazy-Eye:

Normal children see equally well with both eyes. When one eye sees better than the other due to some disease or deformity in the weaker eye, the brain "learns" to prefer the good eye; this leads to a peculiar situation where the brains "ignores" the weak eye and that eye gradually begins to turn "blind". It may begin to go cross-eyed or just rove "lazily" in its socket while the good eye is used to focus on the objects around the child. Lazy eye can result if the child has a squint in one eye, a cataract, or any other defect in the eye. The doctor will initially treat the defect (if it is treatable) and then "train" the weak eye to begin "seeing" again by *closing off the good eye with a patch*. If this is done early in life, the weak eye may be restored; otherwise, the outcome is poor.

Suspect a lazy eye if your child squints, if she tilts her head to one side to look at something, if she covers one eye while looking at things, or you see her eyeball roving about in the eye-socket aimlessly. Take her to the eye specialist immediately.

<u>Useful link:</u>

- ✔ http://www.mic.ki.se/Diseases/C11.html#C11.338.133 ... gives an overview of most ophthalmic conditions.

Ch 38
Skin Problems in Childhood

There is no way in which to understand the world without first detecting it through the radar-net of our senses.

- Diane Ackerman, 1948,
American Writer, Poet and Naturalist.

The skin is the largest organ of the body. People all over the world spend billions of dollars to keep the skin looking young and glowing ... like that of a baby. However, even babies may suffer from all sorts of skin problems. All through their childhood, and later, in teens, children get skin afflictions of all kinds – from congenital problems to allergies, infections, infestations and injuries, to acne, dark patches, light patches, and so on. A complete discussion on all skin problems is outside the scope of this book, but a few excellent links provided at the end of this chapter, as well as at other places throughout the chapter, will give the reader an opportunity to look up more information if he/she should so desire.

Dandruff (*roosi*) and Seborrhoeic dermatitis:

Dandruff manifests in an infant as a cradle cap (Fig 38-1), a condition in which a brownish scaly area develops on the top of the infant's skull right in the first few months of life. It is a kind of dandruff, and the evidence that it is so is provided by the fact that a dry scaliness may be seen simultaneously on the cheeks and on the side of the face where the ear meets the jaw-line. Cradle cap persists for several weeks to a few months. It can be eased off by the parents after some days of coconut oil application when it will become loose and be easy to remove. One may use Savlon® solution and a soft brush to remove it once it has loosened up.

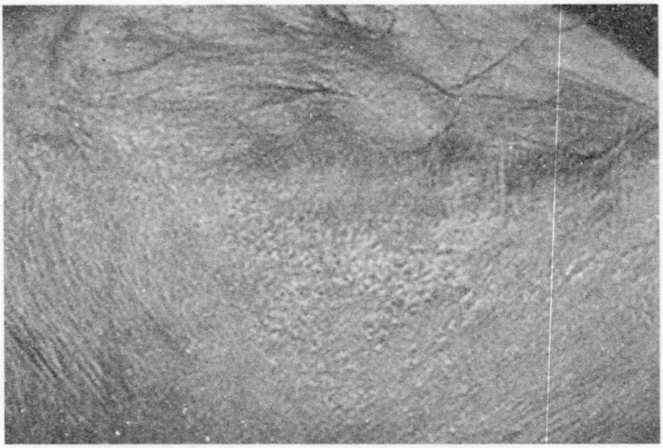

Fig 38-1

Excessive secretion of oil by the glands at the roots of the hair follicles produces whitish flakes on the scalp, the classical dandruff or "seborrhoea". The flaky discharge by the skin may also be seen over the eye-lashes and eye-brows. There is itchiness over the scalp. At times, reddish rashes may develop on the scalp, sides of the nose, eyebrows, eyelids, skin behind the ears, and middle of the chest. Other areas, such as the navel (belly button), buttocks, skin folds under the arms, axillary regions, breasts, and groin (Fig 38-2), may also be involved.

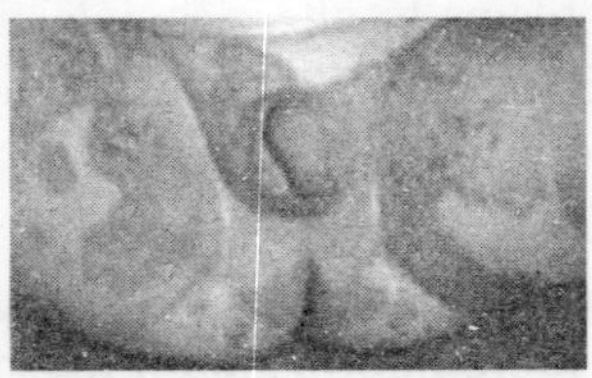

Fig 38-2

When scaling and redness are both seen, we call the condition seborrhoeic dermatitis. In this condition, a yeast-like organism is also involved. Hence, to prevent spread, you should keep the hair-combing implements clean and not share them with other members of the family.

For dandruff in the hair, special medicated shampoos containing Cetrimide, antifungal agents like Zinc Pyrithrone (ZPTO) etc. are used. These need to be applied almost daily in the beginning, and then periodically for a long time to ensure that the dandruff does not return.

Eczema (atopic dermatitis) (Fig 38-3 and 38-4):

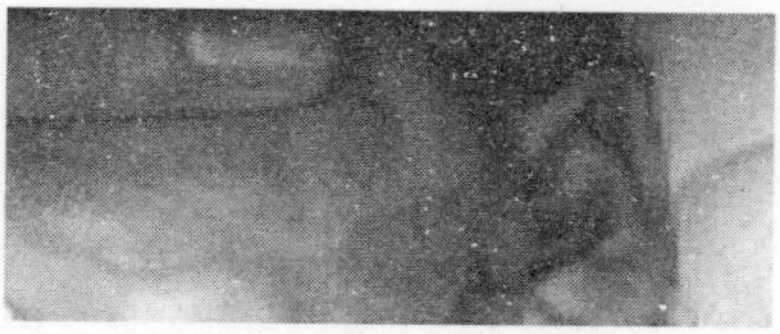

Fig 38-3

Fig 38-4

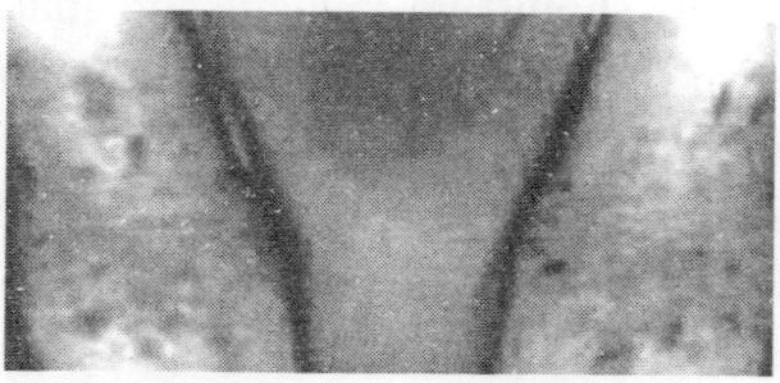

A hereditary predisposition for allergies in some families leads to the development of one of the many allergic conditions in the body. These include hay fever, allergic rhinitis, allergic conjunctivitis, atopic dermatitis and asthma. Eczema is the common name given to the skin problem. It is a condition that frequently begins in infancy, and is marked by phases when the illness is "active" (relapse) and when it is "inactive" (remission). A *relapse* may be brought on after exposure of the child to some antigen (allergic substance) e.g. foods like milk, eggs, nuts, soya beans, wheat items like chapattis; skin irritants like soaps, shampoos, detergent, woollen clothes, nylon; skin infections; emotional triggers like anger, anxiety, frustration; and inhalants like pollen grain, dust mites, insect excreta, etc.

The cheeks and the forehead are often the starting points for the eczema lesions. There is redness and formation of tiny, fluid-filled boils (*vesicles*) on the affected skin. As some vesicles rupture, the whole area has a wet or a "weeping" appearance. When the fluid dries, it forms "scabs" that itch tremendously. Secondary bacterial infection may occur on the primary eczematous lesions in some cases. As the area heals, the child starts feeling better, but the skin heals with thickening and later, with some bit of scarring. After a variable duration of *remission*, the next wave of skin lesions erupts, to remit again later. New relapses may involve new areas of the body such as the knees, the ankles, the neck, the elbows and the wrists and other flexural areas of the body.

What to do?

Identification of the allergic antigens will prevent relapses! Thus, parents should be vigilant and make a food intake diary, and note down the items that the child took in the preceding one or two days before the onset of a relapse. In this manner, one can, like a detective, discover what agent (s) is/are causing re-activation of the disease. Give a daily bath very gently and with just warm water. Dab the baby dry with a soft towel, taking care not to break the delicate vesicles or cause pain. Apply a moisturizer or emollient over the skin after the bath as well as at bed-time. Corticosteroid creams may be used to control the eczema from time to time; they should be used very sparingly, one or two times a day as per the advice of the dermatologist. Itching is sometimes very severe and the child may damage her skin if her nails are not trimmed; hence, keep the nails very short.

Diaper rashes:

Prolonged contact with a wet and/or soiled diaper (nappy) produces a characteristic redness and thickening of the skin on the bottom area of the baby. This is known as a nappy rash or a diaper rash. Tight-fitting panties or nappies that keep the moistness in are held responsible. Use of rubber or plastic liners may also precipitate a diaper rash. Nappy rashes that remain for more than a few days get super-infected with the fungus *candida albicans.* When that happens, the child will show a central, large area surrounded by smaller areas of redness and raised boils all over the bottom area and the lower back (the so-called satellite lesions).

What to do:

<u>Prevent</u> usage of plastic or rubber liners, tight diapers, diapers made from synthetic material and panties. Be on the lookout for passage of urine or stool by the baby and immediately change her diaper after she has done so. Before putting on the new diaper, apply a <u>barrier skin cream</u> containing zinc oxide. Next, sprinkle some talcum powder, or preferably <u>anti-fungal powder</u>, over the cream. If there is fungal infection, an <u>antifungal ointment</u> must be applied before sprinkling the powder. Wash and disinfect the nappies thoroughly, removing all soapiness and stool remnants off them, and dry them till they are crisp. If possible, keep the bottom uncovered and let the baby lie *prone with the bottom sticking out.* This will dry up the skin fast and help the healing process.

Redness around the anus:

Many children develop redness around the anal orifice, especially when the mother or the care-taker wipes her anal skin too energetically, or uses a rough cloth to dry that area, and even more when the child has active diarrhoea, or when she has just recovered from a bout of that illness. I have seen anal regions that are so "angry-red" that I have felt sympathy for the baby, whose pain and anguish can only be imagined.

What to do:

When cleaning the anal area, use a wet cotton swab or wash directly under a stream of warm water to prevent such redness from occurring. In infants prone to develop such redness repeatedly, the routine use of a barrier skin cream containing Zinc oxide is recommended. When fungal super-infection has occurred, proceed as for nappy rashes described above.

Prickly heat (*ghamori*) (Fig 38-5):

Fig 38-5

This condition, called *ghamoriyan* in Hindi, is so common in children during the summer months that parents often do nothing about it, other than to use one of the commercially available anti-prickly heat powders. What happens is that the openings of the sweat glands of the skin get blocked by debris. The sweat gland ducts then rupture, and the sweat accumulates under the skin, causing the appearance of an itchy, red rash. The rash is usually seen over the neck, chest and back and it gradually spreads over the whole body. The itchiness makes the child scratch all the time, leading to development of scratch marks on all parts of the body.

What to do:

Employ all possible measures to reduce heat around the child and in your home. Allow the child to take frequent cold water baths. Do not dry the child with a towel after the bath. Use the fan /cooler/air-conditioner as needed in the child's playing/sleeping area. Anti-prickly heat powders, calamine lotions and other soothing remedies may also be tried.

Urticaria (hives) (Fig 38-6):

Urticaria is the skin manifestation of an allergy to something that has been introduced in the body by some or the other route of entry. The allergen may be a food substance, a food additive or dye, an insect bite, intestinal worms, medications consumed or the effect of allergy to soaps, detergents, etc. In some cases, exposing the child to hot or cold water may also cause wheals/ hives/ urticaria. Children from allergy prone families have this problem more often than those from non-allergy prone families. The child herself may have/have had eczema, wheezing or allergic rhinitis or conjunctivitis – or his family members may report such an occurrence among them.

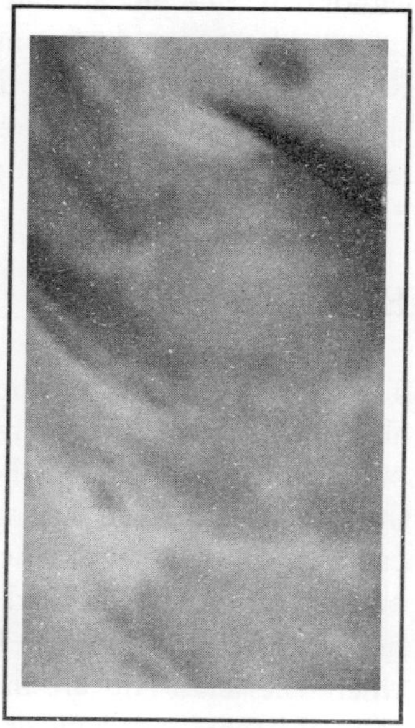

Fig 38-6

The blotchy large patches develop suddenly over the body. They may be transient, that is, they may appear and as suddenly, disappear; or, they may stay at one spot for hours or even days. They itch very much, and cause the child to stay awake despite sleep, or continuously cry for relief or shun food and water as long as the rash causes irritation.

Occasionally, the urticaria may be the starting manifestation of a generalised allergic response to some allergen, and the child may develop breathlessness, a fast and thready pulse or a deadly swelling of the voice-box and the airways (*anaphylaxis*).

What to do:

If possible, the offending food/drug/application must be removed/ withdrawn. The wheals and itching respond to a combination of calamine lotion, anti-histamine medication and steroids (in rare cases). Relapses can be avoided if the common allergens are avoided, the child given a medicine for removing intestinal worms and the anti-histamine and/steroid are stopped gradually over a period of several days.

Head lice (*joon-ay*):

The presence of nits and lice in the hair of a child who is found always scratching her head reflects on the personal and hair hygiene of the whole family. As the lice spread from one member to another through close contact, sharing of combs and so on, the spread of lice can only be thwarted if strict hygiene is implemented immediately on discovering that the child has head lice, probably picked up from her mother, sister or close friend at the school or in the building where she stays. Nits are the eggs of the louse, and she lays them along the roots and shafts of the hair; they are seen as shiny, pearly-white small dots along the hair shafts; the lice themselves hide very "professionally" and are seen only when a diligent parent (usually the mother of the infested child) begins to search for them. When a lice comb is used, the lice can be brought out expertly, along with most of the nits.

What to do:

Daily care of the hair should include shampooing and careful combing of the child's hair, as also those of the other family members. Anyone found scratching her head almost continuously should be considered a potentially lice-infested patient, and he/she should be "combed" to bring out the lice or the nits if no other cause of scratching is evident.

Scabies (*khujli*):

Scabies is caused by a mite: the infestation is caused through intimate contact with an afflicted person. The male mite dies after fertilizing the eggs of the female; the female lives inside a specially created burrow within the dead top layers of the skin in certain areas of the body such as the inside of the wrists, in the neck, the groin and genitalia, in the armpits and occasionally, elsewhere on the body. New hatchlings crawl out of the burrow and cause new lesions to appear. The face is usually spared.

The symptoms include a rash and intense itching, which is worse at night. The rashes may get infected with bacteria. There are scratch marks on the body too. The infestation may spread from one member of the family to another. Soon, almost all members get infected.

What to do:

There are a number of local medicines, both creams and lotions, to kill the scabies mite. The lotions are better, as they can be applied in all affected areas very easily. The general recommendation is to apply the lotion over the whole body *except the head and the face* after a scrub bath with a plastic wire –sponge or a pumice stone. The scrub helps to open up the burrows and lets the medicine reach the female mite residing within the depths. The child will need this treatment on 5-7 successive nights. Along with this, the child may also need anti-itching medicines, antibiotics for the bacterial infection and attention to nail trimming to prevent scratching injuries.

Along with the child, the other family members should also be treated.

Boils (furuncles, impetigo):

Superficial infection of the skin is common in the months of summer and monsoon. Excessive sweating, overcrowding, poor general hygiene and manual bursting of previous boils leads to development of fresh boils (furuncles) or a more diffuse skin infection (impetigo). Initially, a boil is just a red pimple, but it soon enlarges and gets filled with pus. Some boils rupture (break) on their own, leaving behind a scab that starts itching. Boils are most common on the forehead, the scalp, the upper lip, nose, the rest of the face, the armpits, the groins, the buttocks and the shin and backs of the legs.

What to do:

Boils can be prevented by attention to cleanliness, moderation in intake of mangoes (with the season of which the season for boils coincides), use of an antiseptic soap for washing the areas of skin prone to develop boils, twice daily bath with lukewarm or tap water and educating the child to not break open the boils which have already occurred. Nails should not be allowed to grow long, and the child should keep her towels, clothes and undergarments separate from those of the others.

Once boils have already occurred, smaller ones can be handled with a local solution of an antibacterial compound like 1% gentian violet or a tube of "triple cream". Pus-filled boils in a newborn may need to be evacuated with a sterile needle. Larger or more numerous boils need usage of a systemic antibiotic. The child may need medicines to treat pain and fever.

Acne (pimples, *muhase*):

Excessive secretion of the sebaceous glands of the skin due to a hormonal surge that takes place around adolescence leads to the development of classical acne or pimples. Oily-skinned people have a greater chance of developing acne. Eating of a fat-rich diet, too much of refined carbohydrates like chocolates and sweets and the high environmental humidity are all contributors of acne.

Initially, acne begins like a red pimple, which goes on to develop black-heads, white-heads, comedones, pustules and, in advanced cases, nodules. Beginning with the face, acne can go on to affect the upper back, shoulders and buttock areas too, more commonly in boys.

What to do:

The face should be washed repeatedly with water and soap. No cosmetics or moisturizers are to be used. Do not touch or squeeze the skin lesions, as this will lead to more and more acne lesions and also more scarring. The affected teenager must partake of a healthy diet rich in greens and fruits. Several treatments are available for the care of acne, but they should only be taken under medical supervision.

Further links:

- ✔ http://www.skinsite.com/index-dermatology-diseases.htm
- ✔ http://www.vh.org/Pediatric/patient/dermatology/faq/index.html

Ch 39
Diarrhoea, Dysentery and other G.I. problems

A child eats to live, while a glutton lives to eat.

- Author unknown.

A. Diarrhoea, Dysentery and Acute Gastroenteritis:

What is diarrhoea?

Diarrhoea is defined as the passage of *three or more liquid stools* in a child in a 24-hour period. It is one of the most common ailments of childhood, and its high incidence is a major cause of pediatric morbidity (illness) and mortality (death). An illness that begins with vomiting and proceeds downward to lead to diarrhoea is called *gastroenteritis*. To call an episode of loose stool as diarrhoea, it is important to verify that this is a *recent change from the child's normal stool pattern*. The threat to life occurs because of the loss of water and electrolytes from the body – a condition labelled as dehydration. The other major consequence of diarrhoea is malnutrition (or under-nutrition, to be more precise), that results from faulty management of a diarrhoeal episode.

What is dysentery?

Dysentery (*pechis, marda)* is defined as the passage of semi-formed stools with mucus and or blood in a sick-looking child. The child experiences pain *(tenesmus)* and fever along with the dysenteric stools. The main problem here is not dehydration but the other symptoms, some of which can cause misery and sickness.

What is not diarrhoea?

In the following situations, the passage of loose stools can be normal and the condition is not called diarrhoea.

- A 3-4 day old newborn often passes 5-8 loose, green stools. These are called transitional stools and it is normal. It subsides in 24 hours without any specific treatment.

- A breast-fed baby's stools are frequent, pasty and pale yellow. At times, they are golden yellow and have a slight amount of liquid too. This, too, is not diarrhoea.

- During teething, the child may have an increased frequency of stools for a day or two, coinciding with the date of appearance of the tooth. The stool is never too liquid, however, and the "problem" settles within two days.

- When mothers take antibiotics or other medicines, the baby may have some loose stools if they are feeding at their mothers' breast. This is because the medicines are passed into breast-milk.

- When some babies are given iron drops, they tend to have dark brown to black, sticky and semi-loose stools three to five times a day. This also does not need treatment.

Causes of diarrhoea:

To a large extent, breast-fed babies do not get infective diarrhoea because breast milk is sterile, hygienically available and always fresh. It also contains many useful anti-infective substances in it. Babies fed with top milk using a cup and spoon or a bondla also have a relatively lower risk of diarrhoea. Bottle-fed babies, however, have a high risk *even if the feeds are given with near-perfect precautions to prevent contamination*. This is because near-perfect situations *cannot* be perfected further in the home. Most infants get diarrhoea once their weaning process has begun. They are exposed to newer foods and offered water to drink after being fed. Hence, there are ample opportunities to catch bugs from either the water or the food or as a result of unhygienic feeding procedures.

In older children, diarrhoea is caused by the ingestion of contaminated water or food. As bacteria thrive in hot, humid climes, diarrhoeas are much more common in the summer and the monsoon seasons. Viral diarrhoeas are caused by the gastrointestinal spread of a respiratory virus or by the direct air-borne spread of a G.I. virus. As viruses proliferate during the colder months of the year, these diarrhoeas are commoner between October to March as compared to bacterial episodes which occur between April and September. Apart from bacteria and viruses, infections caused by protozoa such as Amoeba (amoebiasis) and Giardia (giardiasis) and by fungi (e.g. candidiasis) also produce loose stools and/or dysentery.

Non-infective causes of diarrhoea include diarrhoea due to ingestion of certain medicines, diarrhoea due to chronic intestinal diseases and diarrhoea due to food poisoning and poisoning by other substances.

Symptoms and course of illness:

Acute gastroenteritis (gastro) (AGE) is a clinical illness caused by the above-mentioned microbes. It starts as repeated episodes of vomiting which gradually progresses into diarrhoea. Stools are passed effortlessly and with great force, so that the nappy becomes all wet within a few seconds. The stools are usually yellow, watery to semi-loose and may have lots of mucus in them. When the diarrhoea is due to bacterial infection, the stools are foul-smelling and greenish to dirty yellow due to presence of infective material in them, and they may contain blood. As the child continues to purge and vomit, she develops dehydration, as a result of which she becomes cranky and irritable, and keeps asking for water to drink. Over the next few days, the vomits subside and the stool starts turning green and more solid. With time and proper treatment, the diarrhoea subsides in about three to seven days. The child may develop rashes and fungal infections in the nappy area; these will need treatment too.

In dysentery, too, the symptoms and course of illness are similar; however, vomiting is not a major symptom of dysentery. The stools are frankly infected with both blood and mucus in them; the child is obviously sick and has high, intermittent fever, severe colicky, griping pain in the stomach before and during the passage of the stools (tenesmus, see above) and looks very tired because of the effort of passing the stools.

The main danger of diarrhoea is the development of dehydration. If the child with diarrhoea is not given adequate replacements of water and salts, she goes on to develop all the symptoms and signs of dehydration. To wit, these are as follows: In the early stages (*mild dehydration*), the child has no signs. She just has an increased thirst, and to quench it, she keeps drinking or demanding water. This also causes her to become irritable and cranky. As dehydration progresses (*moderate dehydration*), the child develops drowsiness; she loses interest in the surroundings and goes to sleep. She may wake up crying after passing a stool or after vomiting. Her eyeballs seem to be "sunken" inwards; she has a dry mouth and a coated tongue (unless she is vomiting repeatedly, in which case the mouth may remain falsely moist); her eyes stop tearing (she cries, but there are no tears); her urine output falls and the urine becomes dark yellow and reduced in quantity. The skin becomes dry and loses its bounce and elasticity. If you lift up the skin over her abdomen by pinching it between your thumb and first finger and then release it, it will take some time (less than 2 seconds in moderate dehydration, and more than that in severe dehydration) before the wrinkle that you made disappears. With *severe dehydration*, the child becomes unconscious; her breathing becomes deep and rapid due to collection of "acids" in the body (*acidosis*); all the earlier signs are now more prominent; the window at the top of an infant's skull has gone in and does not pulsate. The hands and feet become cold, bluish and numb. Without treatment, the stools decrease in quantity as there is no fluid in the body to pass stools. The eyes become glazed and there is no urination for hours. If the child is not treated immediately, she may die of *shock*.

The second major danger is the danger of <u>malnutrition</u>. This is not a natural consequence of diarrhoea but a result of faulty management by the care-takers of the child who falsely believe that starvation is the right treatment of diarrhoea! As a result, the parents stop breast-feeding as well as solids, and keep giving *sabudana* (arrowroot powder) *kanji* and other worthless foods. In addition, the child's appetite is reduced and there is a decreased absorption of nutrients from the lining of the inflamed bowel. Thus, there is a real risk of the child falling prey to a downward spiral of bad nourishment, reduced immunity, further diarrhoea and so on.

Home treatment of acute diarrhoea:

Since diarrhoea is a self-limiting illness in over 75% of all cases, the thrust of management is on preventing dehydration and malnutrition by a) ensuring that the child keeps drinking water enriched with salts (Oral Rehydration) and b) allowing the child to continue feeding at her mother's breast.

A. <u>Correction of Dehydration:</u> To meet the first objective, the child must be given Oral Rehydration Therapy (ORT) with World Health Organisation (WHO) approved *Oral Rehydration Salts (ORS) solution.* ORS is the ideal solution for preventing as well as correcting dehydration. It can be prepared in the home either with salt and sugar or with ready-made ORS powder available commercially.

Home-made ORS: To prepare ORS with salt and sugar, do the following:

a) For a glassful of ORS: Take 200 ml clean water in a large glass. Add a 2-finger pinch of salt to this water. The pinch should have just enough salt to fill the pinch, with no salt stuck on the outside of the pinch. Stir the water. Taste it. Its saltiness should be just as much as the *saltiness of tears.* If the saltiness is more, throw away this water and start afresh. If the salt is less, add a bit more till the taste is properly adjusted. Now add one teaspoon of sugar (or as much sugar as fits into the hollow of the palm of a hand). Stir further. Add a few drops of lemon juice for taste.

b) For a litre of ORS: Take one litre of clean water. To it, add a teaspoon of salt and taste the water after stirring it. It should have the taste of tears (see above). Next, add 8 teaspoons of sugar, stir, and add the juice of one lemon. The ORS is ready for consumption.

Ready-made ORS Powder:

Use a small sachet of ready-made WHO ORS powder to prepare a glass of ORS solution, and a large sachet to prepare a litre of ORS solution. Some of the WHO approved ORS powder brands include: Punarjal, Walyte-P, Peditral CP, Electrobion, Cerelyte and Ricetral.

ORS Substitutes:

A variety of home-made ORS solutions may be used if the child does not like the standard sugar-salt solution. These include rice *kanji*, weak tea, salted diluted curd (*chaas*), coconut water and moong-dal soup. They are all equally effective in preventing dehydration. However, to correct dehydration, one must rely only on the WHO formula.

Use of ORS:

ORS solution, once prepared, should be used liberally on the child. The best way to give ORS is to give it sip by sip with a spoon. This is because allowing the thirsty child to drink it in big gulps directly from a glass is apt to lead to vomiting. If the child is already dehydrated, stop all feeds and breast feeding for the first 3-4 hours and feed her only with ORS to correct dehydration. She will need about 1 glass of ORS per 4 kg body weight – therefore, a 1 year old child will need approximately 2 glasses and a 3 year old will need 2 ½ to 3 glasses; a five year old will require 4 glasses in these 4 hours. Additionally, give her as much extra ORS as she is losing through the stools and vomit: this adds up to about quarter to half glass for each loose stool passed by the child and about the same for each time the child vomits. At the end of this phase of rapid rehydration, the child's thirst should be under control and she should show no signs of dehydration.

As soon as this phase is over, the child's feeds and food must be re-started. In this, the maintenance phase, the child's regular requirement should be given to her as ORS or as other liquids; the ongoing losses should be replaced with ORS as described in the previous paragraph above. In this manner, the child must be fed ORS till she recovers from her illness.

Refusal to accept ORS: If the child refuses ORS because of its salty taste, you can go in for the abovementioned substitutes if there isn't any dehydration; but if she is already dehydrated and also vomiting anything that is being given, it will be preferable to take her to hospital for further treatment.

B. Continuance of Nutrition: This is the second objective of home treatment. After the initial 3-4 hours of rapid rehydration, the breast-fed infant should be put back on her mother's breast; the older child should be allowed to drink rice kanji, *chaas* etc, and be made to eat "safe" foods like *moong khichri*, soft, cooked rice with curd or dal, soft, cooked vegetables with chapati or bread, soft, overripe bananas, grated apples and other fruits etc. If the doctor discovers that the child has a digestive problem and is unable to digest *lactose,* he may prescribe a soya-based milk powder which can be digested easily as it is a lactose-free formula. Return to normal nutrition should be effected in about 5-6 days in usual cases, and about two weeks in children with lactose intolerance.

C. Other Treatment: Anti-vomiting medicines are given if the child has too much vomiting, but as vomits subside on their own, such treatment needs to be given for just 2-3 days. Antibiotics and anti-diarrhoeal medicines are generally not needed as the diarrhoea is self-limiting, but they may be needed if the signs and stool reports suggest an active bacterial infection of the gut. It is advisable not to use antibiotics indiscriminately as this may lead to a) resistant infection b) antibiotic induced diarrhoea and c) occasionally, drug fever.

Anti-motility agents and anti-spasmodics are not indicated either, as their use may slow down intestinal peristalsis and cause bloating of the stomach, with disastrous consequences.

Recently, a new class of drugs has been introduced. These are called probiotics. Their purpose is to encourage the growth of human gut-friendly organisms in the intestine of the victim, and throw out the bad germs. They also stimulate intestinal (local or gut) immunity. These drugs do not have a role in the initial few days, but they may be used without any untoward effects if the diarrhoea gets prolonged into the second week.

Other supportive treatments include treatment of fever with paracetamol, treatment of rashes in the bottom area with anti-fungal creams and powders and so on.

Need for hospitalisation in a child with diarrhoea or AGE:

The following are the danger signals that warrant urgent hospitalisation in a child with AGE:

1. A baby less than 3 months of age or one who is severely malnourished. 2. Presence of high fever, frank blood in stool or severe tenesmus. 3. Persistent uncontrolled vomiting. 4. Inability to take ORS or feeds. 5. Loss of consciousness or extreme irritability. 6. Severe dehydration, cold hands and feet or skin elasticity spring-back time of more than 2 seconds. 7. No urine passed for more than 4 hours. 8. Severe abdominal distension. 9. Large watery stools at a frequency higher than 1 per hour. 10. Diarrhea of more than 14 days' duration. 11. Worsening dehydration despite adequate intake of ORS. 12. Investigations show abnormal blood electrolyte patterns. 13. Deep, sighing respirations suggesting acidosis.

Keep your child free from diarrhoea:

Do these things:

- Exclusively breast-feed for six months, and continue breast-feeding for as long as possible, but at least till one year of age.

- Avoid using feeding bottles, pacifiers and other sucking devices that can transfer germs to the baby.

- Give clean and safe water all the year around to everyone in the family. Use a water purifier if possible, or boil the water for at least 10 minutes before using it.

- Ensure strict hand washing before and after meals and after toilet; a liquid soap is preferred to a soap bar; antiseptic soap is preferred over beauty soap.

- Keep all toys of the child clean by washing them frequently with soap and hot water.
- Observe proper food preparation hygiene.
- Keep the child's (and your) nails trimmed and clean.
- Protect cooked food from house-flies and cockroaches.
- Consult the child's doctor if she passes more than a few stools with an episode of teething.
- Consult the doctor before using any medicines other than ORS.
- Learn how to assess the level of dehydration and how to prepare home-made ORS.

B. Other Gastrointestinal Disorders:

Vomiting:

Vomiting can either be due to common, harmless illnesses or due to some serious illnesses. In the *benign* category are causes like normal regurgitation of curdled milk in an infant, vomiting due to over-eating, forced eating or a bout of cough, vomits caused by intake of bitter medicines and an attack of mild viral gastritis (*stomach flu*). Some stubborn children will vomit during their intractable crying and screaming spell to evoke sympathy among onlookers.

In all these cases, there is no need to panic. Either the vomits will decline on their own or be controlled with simple medicines like Domperidone. If a supposedly benign cause does not abate within 48-72 hours despite proper medication, one must initiate a diligent search for the more serious causes.

The *serious* causes include an acute gastroenteritis, a gastro-esophageal reflux (GER), systemic or lung infection (e.g. pneumonia) and inflammation and/or swelling of the brain and its surrounding membranes. Lastly, persistently dark green vomits suggest obstruction to the small intestine or the large intestine below the level of the opening of the common bile duct. These last few causes warrant urgent referral to a specialist. In GER, the child repeatedly brings up previously swallowed milk or other fluids. This happens because the valve between the food-pipe and the stomach does not function properly. Some degree of GER is normal in small infants; reflux persisting beyond the age of 1 year is, however, abnormal. Most children respond to a regimen of thickened feeds, upright posture and some medicines; the rest may need surgery too. In pneumonia, vomiting is a reflex phenomenon that may occur following a bout of cough. It may also occur due to the large amounts of lung secretions that the child swallows all the time. With brain infections and raised internal pressure due to infection or tumors, the vomits are uncontrolled, forceful and projectile.

What to do?

The correct thing to do would be to take her directly to the doctor if you suspect that the vomits are NOT benign in nature: that is, if they are forceful, too frequent, green coloured, tinged with blood, or accompanied by abdominal symptoms or severe headache.

Food Poisoning:

There are several ways in which food poisoning may take place:

1. Food that is stale may have toxins in it that are formed by bacteria that have multiplied inside it.
2. Stale food may have mold or fungus growing in it which is not detected.
3. Some foods are themselves toxic, such as some types of mushrooms, berries etc.

While heating food that has been left outside a storage device like a refrigerator may kill the germs in it, it will not affect the toxins already secreted by the germs; hence, it is always better to either quickly refrigerate left-over food or to discard it or to pass it on to some unprivileged person.

Usually, food poisoning is suspected when all the people who have consumed a particular food are affected more or less simultaneously, e.g. all the invitees at a marriage function, or the entire family in case of a private family meal at home or in a restaurant. There are cramps in the abdomen, vomiting and loose stools, which may be so severe as to need hospitalisation within a matter of hours. In less severe cases, ORS and some hours of starving for older children and adults will lead to quick recovery. Younger infants should not be starved.

Constipation:

Constipation means passage of hard stools, usually less frequently than is the accepted normal for a given age. Passing one stool every fifth day is *not* constipation for a three-month old if the stool is well-formed and if the child does not have any abdominal discomfort in the days between; passing one hard stool *every*day *is* constipation if the child has pain and griping while passing it.

A child who is on top milk (cow or buffalo) may have constipation as the milk from these animals is rich in casein. Such a child will be helped by an allowance of honey, extra sugar and fruit juice.

Intake of iron-containing pills or syrups, high grade fever, poor intake of insoluble fibre and occurrence of cuts or rashes in and around the anal orifice are all common causes of constipation in older children. *Fibre-containing foods* include green leafy vegetables, germinated pulses and legumes, sweet potatoes, radish, carrots, lady's finger (okra), tomatoes, apples, figs, raw bananas (in the form of cooked preparation), papayas, etc. Children and the whole family should be encouraged to use less refined flour items like biscuits, white bread and so on and eat more whole wheat chapattis, brown bread, soya flour chapattis, red rice etc. As can be seen, most of these items are *not* liked by the vast majority of children. Hence, constipation is fairly common in children.

A *benign episode of diarrhoea* often causes *cuts or rashes* in the anal region; as these cuts take some time to heal, the child gets scared to pass a stool. Constipation is then unavoidable as the child continues to suppress the stooling urge. This leads to a vicious spiral of pain-fear-hardening of stool that is inside-passing a very hard stool-further pain-further cuts-etc. At times, a psychological aberration makes the child stand against walls and "keep back the stools within". This can cause constipation to such an extent that the child's tummy bloats up; she may have a choked up bowel and may begin to pass a liquid stool that slips out by the side of the hard stool lodged inside the full rectum. This may soil her panties (*encopresis*). The parent must not misinterpret the loose stool as diarrhoea but must realise it for what it is.

Rare but more serious causes of constipation include a congenital narrow large bowel (*Hirschsprung's disease*) and a low thyroid hormone condition (*cretinism* or *hypothyroidism*) (see Chapter 45).

What to do:

Apart from the dietary modifications already discussed above, you may try laxatives like Milk of Magnesia, Osmotic agents like Lactulose and other medications to relieve the constipation. Emotional and psychological treatment will be needed for children who willfully retain stools and end up with encopresis.

Ch 40
Respiratory Problems

There are two kinds of people; those who are always well
and those who are always sick.
Most of the evils of the world come from the first sort
and most of the achievement from the second.

- Louis Dudek

Cough is the most striking symptom after fever and vomiting in any sick child. When a child coughs, parents immediately become alarmed. As the intensity and frequency of cough increases, morbid thoughts of deadly infections and sicknesses race through the minds of the parents, who might begin to think that their child will definitely NOT be able to withstand this onslaught.

And yet, cough is a protective thing. By coughing, the child can hastily remove whatever it is that has entered her respiratory passages, most notably, a foreign body, phlegm or a mucus plug. In the event, she may end up turning red in the face; in severe cases, the child may actually become breathless and show cyanosis, a bluish discolouration of the mucous membranes and the nail beds due to reduced oxygen levels in the blood; she might, if the bout is prolonged and accompanied by heaving sensations, vomit; rarely, the child's cough may provoke bleeding within the skin, the conjunctival membrane in the eyes and elsewhere. There are frightening reports where the effort has caused the diaphragm, the large breathing muscle between the chest and the contents of the abdomen, to tear.

Anecdotal memories of such catastrophies have therefore made parents wary of cough, and rightly so. If your child has asthma, or has suffered from whooping cough, laryngitis, or bronchitis, you will know what I mean. This chapter will dwell chiefly on asthma, but I shall briefly discuss a few other respiratory problems. For descriptions on the common cold, sinusitis, otitis media, pharyngitis and tonsillitis, please go to Chapter 36.

Stridor vs. Wheezing:

When the child's airway passages become narrowed due to any obstruction from outside (such as a large lymph gland or an abnormal growth) or from within (due to secretions as in bronchitis or spasm of the muscles of the airways as in asthma), there is a difficulty in the intake of breath or its expulsion (inspiration and expiration). Difficulty in inspiring air occurs when the largest air passages such as the larynx, the trachea and the main bronchi are obstructed. It results in a curious musical sound which is called *stridor.* On the other hand, blockage of the smallest air passages out there in the lungs leads to another musical sound that is called a *wheeze.* In the latter case, as the air can go into the lungs but cannot come out, the lung becomes "over-inflated" over time, and the child acquires a "barrel-shaped" chest.

Wheezy bronchitis of childhood:

As the child's airways are smaller, the tendency for her to get a wheeze is much higher than in an adult; this is because *the narrowing effect is multiplied 4 times* the actual reduction in the diameter of the airway (a physical property of tubes in general). The commonest cause of wheezing in a small infant is **Acute Bronchiolitis**. This is an inflammation of the small "bronchioles" just before they expand to form air sacs where the exchange of carbon-dioxide for oxygen is to occur. The inflammation causes secretions to accumulate in the tubes and the tubes to get "choked up", much like the choking of the drainage pipe in your kitchen sink. The cause of such inflammation is infection by a rogue virus called the **RSV** virus. The effect is breathlessness and wheezing very similar to that seen in childhood asthma. Once a child has had an attack of acute RSV Bronchiolitis, she is more prone to repeated episodes of wheezing; internal damage to the lining of the air passages is responsible for this, and in fact, the child can very well progress to development of an illness that is indistinguishable from asthma. There is, at present, no way to prevent such a progression, other than rapid diagnosis and vigorous treatment of any child with acute bronchiolitis with oxygen, intravenous fluids and perhaps, other special medicines.

Apart from the above cause, wheezing can occur due to inhalation of smoke, poisonous fumes and foreign body etc. Lastly, as I said above, the bronchi may be obstructed from outside by enlarged glands, abnormal growths and abnormal blood vessels. **Thus, all wheezing is not asthma.**

Bronchial asthma:

When continued airway inflammation leads to "jumpy" airways that go into spasm whenever they are exposed to an allergen or some other trigger factor, in a child with a past or family history of atopic eczema, atopic dermatitis or asthma itself, we are mostly dealing with asthma. The two characteristics of childhood asthma are *episodic wheezing* and *hyperreactive airways*. Common allergens that induce "bronchial spasm" include dust, dust mites, pollen grain of flowers, hair or dander of animals, cockroaches, etc. Food additives like food colours and preservatives may also cause asthma, as may mould (fungus), nuts and dry fruit.

Triggers are agents that cause an acute attack to begin. The commonest trigger is a common cold or coryza (Ch. 36); other triggers include heavy physical exercise, smoke inhalation, medications like aspirin or ibuprofen, pollen season, pest-control activity in the house, dusting the carpet, inhalation of cigarette smoke, auto-pollution etc. Use of *agarbattis, dhoop,* incense sticks, soaps, cosmetics, air fresheners and the coil-type of mosquito repellants may all bring on an attack in a susceptible child.

Symptoms and characteristics of asthma:

The commonest presentation is of a child who gives either a past history or a family history of asthma, allergic dermatitis, eczema or urticaria; she comes with a short history of sneezing, cold, redness and watering of the eyes, and goes on to become progressively more and more short of breath. Cough and wheezing occur in different proportions, depending upon the age and individual characteristics of the child. Inspiration is normal, but expiration is prolonged, laboured and accompanied by a wheeze, which may be audible with the naked ear in the advanced case. Some children present only with nocturnal (nightly) cough with just a minimal breathlessness (*cough variant asthma*).This means that **asthma can occur without a wheeze.**

While some children have infrequent episodes of asthma, and are well in between, others have more frequent attacks, with loss of school days, academic deterioration and need for occasional hospitalisation. On the most severe end of this spectrum are children whose breathing is well controlled only with round the year medication, that too at the safest tolerable doses. It is very clear therefore, that asthma symptoms form a continuum from a well child with no cough or wheeze to a sick child in an emergency setting who needs urgent hospitalisation. We call the former as mild, intermittent asthma, and the latter as severe persistent asthma. Excluding the first category, almost every asthma child will require *preventive asthma medication* (see below).

Over the years, 30-40% of pre-school asthma patients will be free of the disease by 5 years, another 10-15% by 8 years and another 40-

45% by the age of 18 years. Only 10-15% of childhood asthmatics will persist having attacks after reaching adulthood. The problem is that we cannot identify which child will be among the 90% who will outgrow asthma, and which one will be among the remaining 10% who will continue to suffer throughout their lives.

Owing to the fact that nearly nine out of ten childhood asthmatics will outgrow the illness, there have been many claims by people of miraculous cures achieved through alternative medicine systems like ayurveda, homeopathy, aromatherapy, swallowing herbal medicines put inside a specific variety of fish which must be eaten "live", and so on. Live-fish treatment is so popular in India that there are long queues for it when the treatment is disbursed by a close-knit family in Hyderabad; the treatment is supposedly *free of cost* to the patient. Many a times, so-called "Ayurvedic" or "unani" medicines have contained corticosteroids that have provided relief at the cost of the child getting the side-effects of ingesting high doses of steroids everyday without the supervision of a qualified allopathic practitioner.

How asthma is controlled and managed:

Asthma management begins with identification, **prevention and control of the trigger factors** that cause an acute attack to begin in a vulnerable child.

Prevention of trigger factors: To this end, the house is subjected to many changes. Rugs and carpets are thrown out if possible; if not, they should be vacuum-cleaned everyday. The vacuum cleaner is also used to clean nooks and crannies in the house, and to disinfest pillows, rugs and carpets with an eye to remove the microscopic but dangerous *house dust-mite*. Pillow stuffing is changed if it was originally made from bird-feathers or cotton; long curtains and other cloth material are washed weekly and vacuumed daily; no pets are allowed to be kept; adults who smoke are allowed to do so when they are outside the house; if the house is small, lacks ventilation or is too crowded, attempts are made to relocate the child to where these problems are absent; house-plants and gardens around the house are NOT encouraged.

Early treatment is sought for the most minor cold as it can trigger an acute attack of wheezing; the child is trained to use a preventer inhaler before embarking on a stint of exercise like a game of football or a race in a sports event; baths with cold water are discouraged if the child has reacted to it in the past with an attack. The child is moved away from all smoke-causing devices like incense sticks, cooking stoves, barbecue parties etc. No perfumed sprays or similar cosmetics are to be used where the child is present. During the pollen season, the child is not taken out to gardens and open spaces where he may develop an acute attack. Liquid mosquito repellants are relatively safer than coils, but their use should be permitted only if the child can withstand it. If possible, herbal methods of pest-control (which are now available commercially) should be resorted to.

Medical Treatment of Asthma:

There are many modalities for treatment of asthma, including oral medicines, inhalational medicines and injections. The first, that is oral medicines, have limited use. They are used in managing the illness in small infants, in children who are unable to learn inhalational medicine usage, and to treat associated problems such as infection in the lungs or fever.

Inhalation treatment is the mainstay of asthma management. Its chief benefits are:

1. Less of the medicine is given per inhalation: for example, while each teaspoon of an oral bronchodilator administers 1 mg of a drug (that is 1000 micrograms), an equivalent inhaler of the same drug will deliver 100 micrograms per inhalation – and that too, directly to the lungs.

2. Direct delivery to the target organ: When an oral medicine is used, it has to be circulated to the liver, heart and the rest of the body, and only 5% reaches the target organ, viz. the lungs. When inhaled mode of treatment is used, much more medication reaches the lungs and relieves the child faster.
3. Fewer side effects: Due to use of less of the active medicine *and* targeted delivery to the lungs, there are hardly any side-effects.

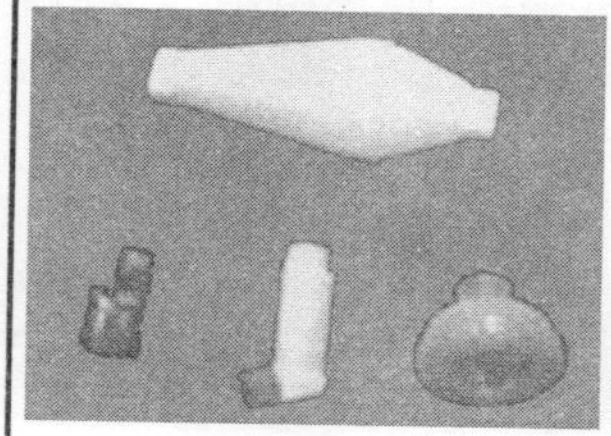

Fig 40-1

Many types of inhaler therapies are available. They include MDI's, Rotahalers and Dischalers, among the commonly used ones. Also used are ancillary items like Spacers and Baby Masks. Some of these items are shown in Fig 40-1. The bottle-shaped structure at the top is a "Spacer", while the other objects are, from left to right, a rotahaler, a MDI inhaler and a baby mask. The baby mask is attached to the spacer and used in small children with asthma. Let me explain these terms one by one.

1. *MDI Inhaler*: The Multi Dose Inhaler is either used alone or preferably with a spacer device. It must be shaken before it is put to the lips or attached to the spacer (Fig 40-2). When the medicine canister inside the MDI is pressed, one puff of medicine is delivered into the lungs. The patient must coordinate the timing of the pressing of the canister with the sharp intake of breath, otherwise the medicine gets wasted.

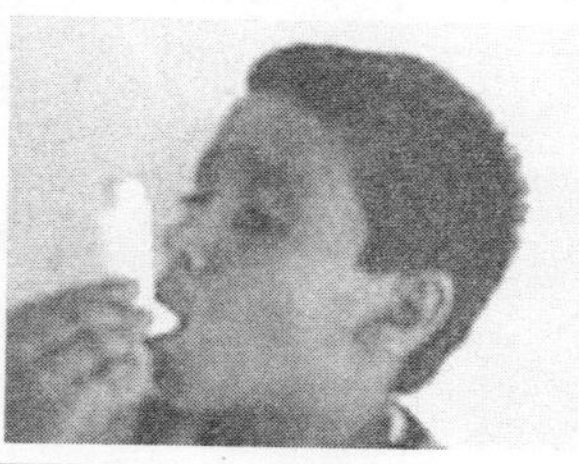

Fig 40-2

2. *Spacer*: This is a plastic bottle-shaped conical device with apertures at both ends. The MDI inhaler is inserted into one end while the

child puts the other end into her mouth and after pressing the canister, she inhales 7-10 breaths through the mouth end. After this, she should remove the spacer and MDI assembly and slowly breathe out. See the picture below for a demonstration of how the MDI and spacer are used.

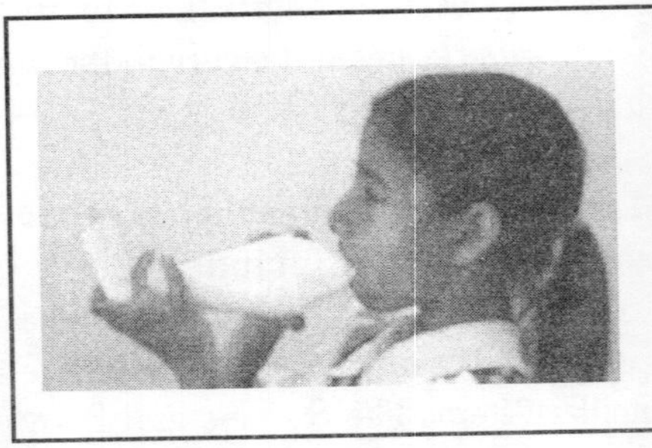

Fig 40-3

In Fig 40-3, the child is inhaling the medication that is inside the Spacer. She should be upright while inhaling. Such inhalations can be taken as often as desired. It is always better to use the MDI with a spacer than to use it directly because this increases the deposition of the medicine into the lungs and reduces wastage; at the same time, the child can inhale the medicine with regular breathing and she will not have to coordinate her inhalation with the pressing of the canister.

3. *Rotahaler*: This is a small unbreakable plastic device that can be used by children above the age of 5 years; it is very handy, can be carried to school and is very easy to use. A special medicinal capsule called a *rotacap* is inserted into the rotahaler. It contains a dry medicinal powder. The medicine is released into the lower part of the rotahaler (the receptacle) when the upper portion of the rotahaler is twisted against the rotacap. The child then puts the mouth piece of the rotahaler into her mouth and inhales deeply: the dry powder that was inside the receptacle gets inhaled by the child into the lungs (Fig

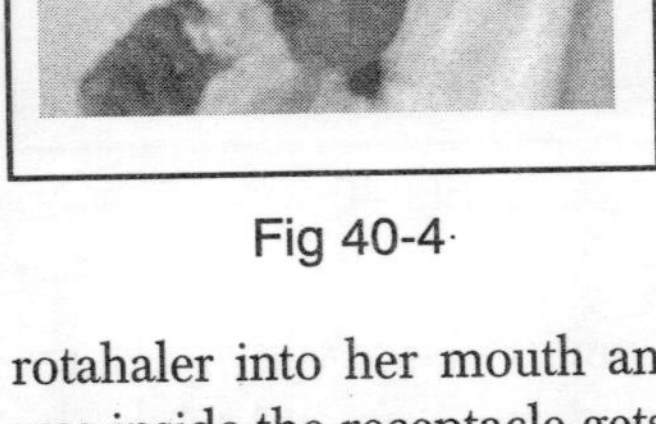

Fig 40-4

40-4). The empty capsule can then be removed from the rotahaler and discarded. The problem with the rotahaler is that inhaling the powder needs more effort than inhaling the medicine from the MDI, and therefore, it is not very useful when the child has an acute attack of severe asthma.

4. *Dischaler*: In this device, the medicine is kept in small blisters which are attached end to end to form a strip that is kept inside a disc. Compared to all the above inhalers, the dischaler needs the least inspiratory effort to inhale the medicine. However, this is a costly inhaler device.

5. *Nebulisers*: These are electrical devices that can deliver liquid medicine into the lungs. Until recently, they were used only in institutions and doctors' clinics, but when they became more affordable, patients bought them and learnt how to use them even at their own residence. On evaluation, it was found that they were only marginally better than MDI used with spacers. Hence, their popularity began to decline, and their use is now limited to hospitals for the care of the most serious patients.

Medicines used in inhalers, injections and oral medications: These are of two types. There are *relievers* or bronchodilators, and *preventers* or those medicines that aid in reducing the inflammation of the airways and ultimately help prevent acute attacks. Preventers include inhaled steroids as well. While relievers are used only when the child has an acute attack, preventers are used for a much longer duration of over two years or even more, till the child outgrows asthma (if at all she does). The use of inhaled steroids is safe as the dose used in the inhalers is very small and it is hardly absorbed into the system.

Monitoring treatment: It is recommended that the child be made to check her breathing capacity at least twice a day using a special

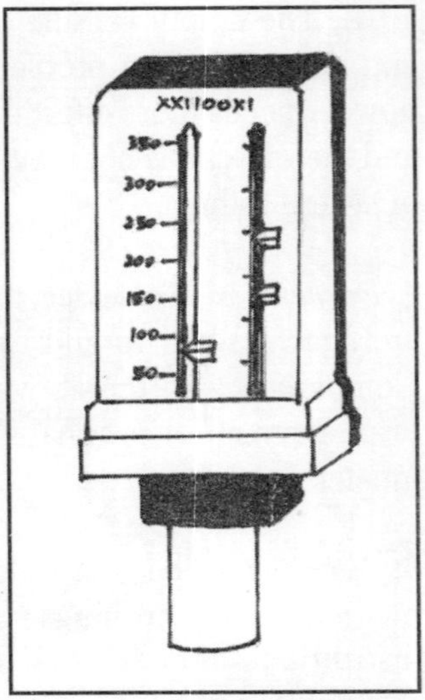

Fig 40-5

instrument called the Peak Flow Meter (PFM) (see Fig 40-5). This instrument measures the *Peak Expiratory Flow Rate (PEFR)*, or the rate of flow of expired forceful breath at a given point of time. The picture shows a Low-range PFM that is made especially for small children. A normal individual's PEFR depends on his/her age and body frame, and there can be a 10% variation from the person's average reading depending upon the time of day when the PEFR reading is taken. In an asthmatic child, a variation of up to 20% may be taken as normal, but anything above 20% on the lower side should be considered as an abnormal reading and a sign that the child may be going in for a fresh attack of bronchospasm. Medical attention should be sought urgently.

Other treatment: Antibiotics and cough expectorants are not very useful in an acute attack. Drinking warm water and steam inhalations are of some benefit when relievers are not available. Diet of an asthmatic child should be nutritious; it should be rich in antioxidants, vitamins and trace minerals. The child should be trained to learn breathing exercises and enrolled in Yoga classes to improve her lung function.

Some other questions:

1. Sports: An asthmatic can certainly participate in sports like a normal child as long as she is free from symptoms. If she has exercise-induced asthma, she must inhale a bronchodilator about 15-20 minutes before actually exerting herself. The child should cut off her activity if she starts feeling breathless. She must not go solo on a long run or cycling trip and never swim without supervision.

2. Drugs to be avoided: Pain-killers like aspirin, ibuprofen etc. can aggravate bronchospasm in an asthmatic child. Hence, such drugs are contraindicated in an asthmatic child.

3. Hospitalisation: If an acute attack does not respond to two or three doses of the inhaler, if it is so severe that the child cannot walk, speak or talk, or the child's fingernails or lips are turning blue, the child must be hospitalised immediately.

More information:

- ✔ http://www.vh.org/pediatric/patient/pediatrics/asthma/index.html
- ✔ http://www.respuleskids.com/consumer/about_asthma/index.asp

Acute Lower Respiratory Infections:

Let us now shift our attention to other respiratory problems. Among these, infections of the lower respiratory tract are the most important. They include acute bronchitis, pneumonia and tuberculosis.

Bronchitis and Pneumonia:

Both bronchitis and pneumonia are serious infections of the lower respiratory tract in small children. Both may be caused by either viruses or bacteria; in addition, pneumonia may rarely be caused by other agents such as fungi or the babies of intestinal worms as they travel through the lungs during their life cycle.

Bronchitis is characterised by a gradually worsening cough that assumes a brassy, metallic sound over a period of 3-4 days. It is dry initially, but as the lining of the main bronchi is inflammed, the cough becomes a moist one, and the older child may bring out yellowish green sputum; the younger children simply swallow the sputum as they do not know how to bring it out. The child may also have fever, vomiting and breathing difficulty as the accompanying symptoms. Vigorous treatment, sometimes accompanied by hospitalisation, administration of oxygen and IV antibiotics, is needed.

Pneumonia may follow as a complication of bronchitis or pharyngitis, or it may occur without any of these as a primary illness. Smaller infants become very sick with pneumonia and are at risk of dying if not treated with higher antibiotics. In babies, there may be no cough to indicate that the illness is in the lungs and the child may die without a diagnosis. One of the causes of a "Sudden Infant Death Syndrome (SIDS)" is pneumonia. In a child with measles, pneumonia is a common after-illness. The symptoms of pneumonia include fever sometimes accompanied by chills and shivering, a gradually worsening cough (with sputum in older children), breathlessness and excessive irritability and crying due to chest pain and difficulty in breathing and talking. The doctor will order radiographs and blood tests and sometimes advise that the child be hospitalised.

Complications of pneumonia include collection of fluid or pus inside the chest cavity in the pleural space just outside the lung. In such cases, the child will need to be hospitalised for removal of fluid from the cavity by insertion of an indwelling tube within the chest cavity. Even so, the child may be left with internal scars and other sequelae.

Foreign body (F.B.) obstruction:

Occasionally, a child may become suddenly breathless because of a foreign object inhaled into the lungs. While we've discussed this topic in Ch. 23 (page xxx), I want to remind you, the reader, that if the foreign body cannot be dislodged by Heimlich manoeuvre or other methods, but if the child can breathe somewhat easier, you might give up the urgency and forget about the matter. Then the F.B. may persist in the lung and lead to dramatic intermittent acute episodes of cough and breathlessness, which the doctor may also diagnose wrongly as recurrent pneumonia and miss the diagnosis of F.B. since you never told him about it.

Tuberculosis:

Tuberculosis (T.B.) of the lungs is the commonest chronic infection in people from India and many other developing countries. It is caused by a germ called *Mycobacterium tuberculosis.* Even though we give the B.C.G. vaccine right after birth to protect against T.B., we cannot totally prevent its occurrence.

A child usually contracts this infection from an adult with open T.B. (that is, an adult with live T.B. germs) who releases the germs in the space surrounding him whenever he coughs. The type of T.B. that an adult gets is different from the one that a child gets. Barring exceptional cases, T.B. causes a "closed" illness in children, with no T.B. germs being coughed out when a child coughs. As a result, *a child can neither pass on the infection to someone else, nor can he acquire a fresh infection from a child.*

Surprisingly, T.B. can occur in a well-to-do family as easily as it can in a poor man's house. It can affect a well-nourished child as easily as it can affect a thin, underweight urchin. Often, an illness like measles unmasks tuberculosis. The usual symptoms of childhood T.B. are fever that occurs mostly in the later part of the evening and early at night, weight loss, loss of appetite, cough, enlarged lymph glands in the neck and increased susceptibility to upper respiratory infections.

The physician must have a high index of suspicion to consider T.B. even in difficult cases. There is no harm in starting a therapeutic trial of anti- tuberculous drugs in a child who meets the clinical criteria for diagnosis but has negative results on the tests. Missing T.B. can be a costly mistake as it can progress to complications such as T.B. meningitis, brain T.B. and so on.

Treatment of childhood T.B. is easy and involves administration of a fixed dose of anti-tubercular medicines daily for six to nine months. The child must remain under the supervision of a Pediatrician as the drugs used in the treatment of T.B. may cause side-effects that need to be recognised early before the child suffers from their ill-effects.

Ch 41
Heart Problems

A Great Man is he who does not lose his childlike heart.
- Mencius (Mengzi Meng-tse, c. 370-300 B.C., Chinese Philosopher.

It is a rare but sad thing to be inflicted with a heart problem right at birth. It is rarer still for a heart problem to occur later on in childhood. Among the problems present since birth, the commonest is a congenital heart problem called a VSD – a hole in the heart. Among the acquired conditions, rheumatic fever and rheumatic heart disease are the most common. We will discuss these in brief.

Congenital heart disease:

There are literally hundreds of minor to major defects that can occur in the developing heart and circulatory system. The commonest defect is an abnormal opening between the two ventricles; in other babies, there may be an abnormal connection between the main artery, the aorta, and the main pulmonary vessel or an abnormal positioning of the great vessels; rarely, one sees even more complex cardiac malformations.

Some malformations may be so severe as to cause the baby to die before full term. On the other hand, the affected child may not have trouble until after birth because during fetal life, it does not depend on its own circulation to survive; there are connections with the mother which help it to derive oxygen and nutrients from there. After a few days following birth, however, the child begins to be symptomatic. The parents may notice that the child has a rapid pulse, a fast breathing rate, sweating, difficulty in feeding and swelling of the feet. These are symptoms of a heart under stress. Examples of defects that produce such symptoms include holes between the two atria (the two upper chambers of the heart) or the two ventricles (the larger, lower chambers).

In other children, there is a bluish discolouration of the lips, the tongue and the tips of the hands and feet. This is called c*yanosis.* It indicates a lack of circulating oxygen in the blood of the child. This happens because "pure" oxygenated blood (red in colour) is being contaminated with "impure" de-oxygenated blood (dark blue in colour). Over a period of time, the chronic lack of oxygen will lead to easy fatiguability, growth failure and thickening of the tips of the fingers and toes (*clubbing*). Cyanotic children often go into spells of deep cyanosis, a condition that may prove fatal to them unless they are shifted into an intensive cardiac care unit. Defects where cyanosis is a major issue include complex heart malformations with holes, abnormal positioning of the great vessels and sometimes even abnormal heart valves.

The even more common presentation of congenital heart defect is a completely normal child who is detected to have an abnormal sound, called a *murmur*, in his heart when she is being routinely checked with a stethoscope.

Regardless of the way the child is detected, she should be immediately put under the care of a pediatric cardiologist who will take further decisions in the matter. The child may either need urgent surgery, or she may be put on medications that will then control the problems that have occurred. However, medicines cannot "correct" the defect; they can only buy the patient time till she is suitable for surgery.

I shall end this brief discussion on a note of optimism: many of the holes in the wall between the two atria or the two ventricles close *on their own* within 2-5 years of age; no surgery may then be needed. It is also true that some heart defects are clinically non-significant and the child may continue to thrive despite not getting any medical or surgical treatment.

Rheumatic fever and heart disease:

This dreaded disorder is an acquired affliction of the heart that results from an abnormal body response to a common throat germ known as the *Group A streptococcus.* Normally, this germ causes a sore throat that abates with antibiotic therapy. However, in some individuals, especially those who receive wrong antibiotics or inadequate treatment (the optimum is 10 days treatment with Penicillin, or at least 5-7 days' treatment with higher antibiotics), the throat itself heals but the person goes on to develop an illness that is characterised by i) a short-lived, flitting inflammation and swelling of the joints of the body (particularly the joints of the wrists, knees, elbows and ankles), ii) malfunction of the valves and the muscle of the heart, iii) development of reddish swellings on both shins and other areas of the body and occasionally iv) an involuntary movement disorder of the body. Not all symptoms will be found in every individual who has this, the *Acute Rheumatic Fever.*

The cardiac involvement leads to symptoms of heart failure such as easy fatiguability, breathlessness, puffiness of the face and swelling of the feet, palpitation and pain in the right side of the abdomen (due to enlargement of the liver). The doctor will, on auscultation, discover murmurs that represent malfunctioning of one or more valves of the heart. Patients need to be urgently put on medication; some will need surgery.

Those who already have heart damage (Rheumatic heart disease) can get fresh attacks of acute rheumatic fever every time their throat has a streptococcus; hence, they should be given vigorous treatment for each such attack; they are put on a strict regimen of Injectable Penicillin every three to four weeks for life: this is to prevent the recurrence of a streptococcal throat infection; as time passes, if it is found that their cardiac condition merits surgery, they are scheduled for it; in the meantime, they must inform about their cardiac status to their dentist and when they go in for any surgery as they need special antibiotic cover to prevent a heart infection.

Palpitation:

Many children sometimes become aware of their own heart-beat. This commonly occurs in a setting of excessive physical exertion. The heart beats faster and stronger during physical exertion to meet the demands of the body for increased oxygen. In such a situation, when the child stops to pant, she may suddenly feel her heart thumping inside the rib cage. Not knowing the significance of such a feeling, she may wrongly report this as pain in the heart region. Parents have often brought their children with such a symptom. This is called palpitation. It is totally normal and no treatment is necessary.

Occasionally, however, we come across children who feel palpitation at rest, that is, without any exertion. If it is confirmed that they do have palpitation, we examine these children and subject them to an E.C.G. examination. Some such children turn out to have a heart rhythm disturbance. This is a rare but important cause of palpitation and easy tiredness. The moral of this story is that you should not neglect palpitation *at rest.*

Ch 42
Genito-urinary Problems

Laugh a little: The reason grandparents and grandchildren get along so well is that they have a common enemy.
- Sam Levenson (1911 - 1980)

Apart from the obvious functions of the genito-urinary system, namely, excretion of urine and reproduction, this system is also important for the proper psychological development of the child. Any outward abnormality in the appearance of the external genitalia can lead to a devastating impact on the mind of the child: it can lead to an inferiority complex, lack of self-esteem, doubt as to the sex of self, doubts about his/her abilities to "perform" as an adult and so on.

Hence the importance of this chapter. Apart from external abnormalities, we will also discuss a few important problems of the internal genito-urinary organs as well.

Brief anatomy of the systems:

The **urinary system** consists of a kidney on either side at the back of the abdomen, a ureter that transports the urine formed in the kidneys to the urinary bladder located at the centre of the lowermost portion of the abdomen and a urethra that conducts the urine from the bladder to the exterior. While the anatomy of this system is identical in both boys and girls up to the level of the bladder, there are differences in the length and disposition of the urethra. The urethra is short and relatively straight in the girl, but it is tortuous and relatively long in the boy, as it has to traverse the full length of the penis.

In *boys*, **the genital system** consists of a pair of testes located one on each side within the scrotal sac, a convoluted tube called the *vas* that conducts the sperms to the urethra and the urethra itself, enclosed within the penis. In *girls*, the system consists of a pair of ovaries which are located inside the abdomen and the uterus, the originator of the menstrual cycles and the repository of a future pregnancy.

External genital and urinary problems:

A. <u>The foreskin:</u> In boys, the foreskin or the "prepuce" is a single fold of skin that is located on the tip of the penis. It is tightly applied to the penis and cannot be moved back (retracted) in the first one to two years of life. Inside the prepucial skin lie the glands that secrete a light yellow cheesy material called the smegma. The exact function of smegma is not known. Its production is minimal in infancy and early childhood, but it reaches its peak between 20-40 years of age. It is believed to act as a lubricant that allows proper movement of the penis during sexual intercourse. (Read this link for a drawing and details on the functions of smegma: http://www.cirp.org/library/normal/wright1/).

When a normal infant passes urine, there may be a ballooning of the prepuce; this is normal. Do not attempt to retract the prepuce if it is tight till at least 2 years of age. After two years, you may try and pull it back during a bath. During the next few years, the child should be shown and taught how to pull the skin back and wash the penis surface, in particular, to remove the smegma from deep within the fold of the skin, as stagnant smegma begins to give off a foul smell.

As a part of religious requirement, Muslims and Jews practice removal of the foreskin or circumcision. However, it has been practiced even before this for the past over 5000 years. In medical instances, circumcision is done when there is recurrent infection of the prepucial skin, severe stricture and narrowing of the orifice through which urine is ejected and pain during erection because of scarring of the prepuce (which may be a long-term sequel of napkin rashes). While there is an intense debate as to the need or otherwise for circumcision, generally, it makes the penis a "cleaner" organ with no smegma-related problems. It is also believed that the risk of penile cancer is reduced by circumcision.

I do recommend, however, that it should never be done by an unqualified person and never without local anaesthesia.

B. Undescended Testi (e) s (Cryptorchidism):

Normally, the male gonads or the testes are formed within the abdomen in fetal life; they descend "outwards" from about the 30th week of pregnancy; they are just outside the abdominal wall at 34 weeks; halfway to the scrotum at 35 weeks and within the scrotal sac at 36 weeks of pregnancy. In a newborn child, slight stimulation of the scrotum, particularly if done gently or with cold hands, causes the testis to "jump" upwards a short distance. It will go back down in a few seconds.

When a newborn is found to have an empty scrotal sac on one or both sides, the doctor will try and determine if the testis is totally undescended (that is, within the abdomen) or if it has come down some of the distance and can be felt along its normal descent pathway. Rarely, the testis may choose a "wrong" path and be located completely elsewhere (an *ectopic testis*).

Nothing needs to be done up to the age of 6-9 months in case of a unilateral undescended testis. If the problem is bilateral (both sided), and the testes are not felt anywhere outside the abdomen, one should take the child for a trial of hormonal therapy (a 3-6 month course of monthly injections of a hormone called HCG) or directly for surgery: the surgeon will trace the testis up its track, locate it and bring it out and place and fix it in the scrotal sac. Mind you, the earlier this is done, the higher is the chance that the testicular functions of sperm formation will remain active; this is because the longer one takes in deciding, the higher the chance that the warm internal abdominal temperature will have killed off the cells that form the sperms in adolescent and later life; *it is believed that a delay of more than a year may render the testis totally sterile.*

The other reasons for quick action are: a) it may be embarrassing for the child to move about with an empty scrotum and b) once the heat has damaged the testis, there is an increased risk of cancer developing in the organ: hence, it is always better to bring the testis out so that any change in its size etc. can be picked up early.

Note: If too many years have passed before surgery, the testis will have become useless functionally. In such a case, the surgeon may advise you to have that testis removed and an artificial oval, testis shaped ball inserted for cosmetic purposes.

C. Hypospadias and Chordee:

On occasion, the penile shaft is a little bent downwards: this is called chordee. When there is a chordee, the prepucial skin is already shrunken around the base of the triangular tip of the penis. A circumcision is then thought unnecessary from the religious point of view.

Rarely, the urethra, instead of opening at the tip of the penis, opens in an abnormal position, such as at the base of the scrotum, below the shaft of the penis and occasionally, near the tip but not at the tip. A very "proximal" opening will jeopardize the acts of urination and ejaculation. It needs to be surgically corrected.

D. Female Genitalia:

Female circumcision is practiced by some Muslim communities; in this, the foreskin of the clitoris is removed in much the same way as in boys. Its purpose is to "cool the passion" of a girl and to "control" her "wayward" sexual urges, though this is garbed well in religious scriptures. I leave it to the reader to assess whether female circumcision is useful in any way. I personally do not subscribe to it.

Putting long thin objects into the vagina is a normal habit of some toddler girls. One should be on a lookout for the same as it can potentially cause injury.

Redness and rashes in and around the vulva may be an extension of napkin rashes or represent a fungal infection. Repeated rashes may lead to formation of a raw area on the edges of both the labia; sometimes, these raw areas may fuse in the midline and close off the vulva until only a small opening remains which allows the urine to come out. The *small adhesions* that are responsible for this closure can be separated gently by the doctor using only his fingers or a gauze piece, but the adhesions may re-form; therefore, after the separation has been carried out, the labial edges should be continually dabbed with a cream so that adhesions do not form again. Estrogen-based creams give the best results, but their use should be limited as they may cause darkening of the skin of the vulva.

Urinary System Diseases:

A. Infections of the Urinary Tract (UTI):

UTI's are often asymptomatic and missed. They are more common in girls owing to the short, straighter urethras that they possess (see above). Nappy rashes, intestinal pin-worms and poor genital hygiene all predispose to UTI. In children with symptomatic infections, the onset is with high grade fever with chills and shivering (rigors). The child has increased frequency and urgency of passing urine. The infection may remain a "lower" UTI involving just the urethra and the bladder (cystitis), or it may affect the "upper" organs, i.e. the kidneys too, and cause "pyelonephritis". Cystitis causes difficulty in passing urine (dysuria) and sometimes causes a spot or two of blood to be passed at the end of urination.

To diagnose and treat a UTI it is essential to do a proper mid-stream collection of urine after cleaning and washing the tip of the penis with the prepuce retracted. The samples should be sent for both, *routine examination* and *culture with antibiotic sensitivity.* Antibiotics should be preferably started *after* the samples have been sent for routine and culture studies.

Early recognition and appropriate antibiotic and ancillary treatment is vital for the health of the kidneys. Complications of an untreated or improperly treated infection of the urinary tract include development of resistant infection, flaccidity and reverse flow of urine in the ureters (*vesico-ureteric reflux*) and recurrence of infection. The last named complication can ultimately lead to scarring and reduced function of one or both kidneys, and rarely to chronic renal failure, in which case the child becomes dialysis dependant or in need of a renal transplant in future.

B. <u>Nephrotic Syndrome:</u>

Voluminous loss of protein from the body through urine is what the main problem is in Nephrotic syndrome. The illness is a chronic condition characterised by swelling of the whole body, loss of protein in urine and increased blood cholesterol; it is caused by many diseases through the mechanism of direct damage to the kidneys, or more specifically, to the *glomeruli*, the microscopic structures that are present in their millions throughout the kidneys – they do the work of filtering the urine and throwing out/rejecting the waste products. The classic Nephrosis occurs due to an unknown cause and affects children above 5 years of age, although smaller children may also be involved. The swelling is seen on the face and the eyelids to begin with. Very soon, though, the whole body gets bloated, with swelling of legs, the genital areas, and the back of hands, the back and the abdominal area. Fluid may collect in the abdomen and in the chest cavity. Urine output, body temperature and vital signs are normal. (Fig 42-1)

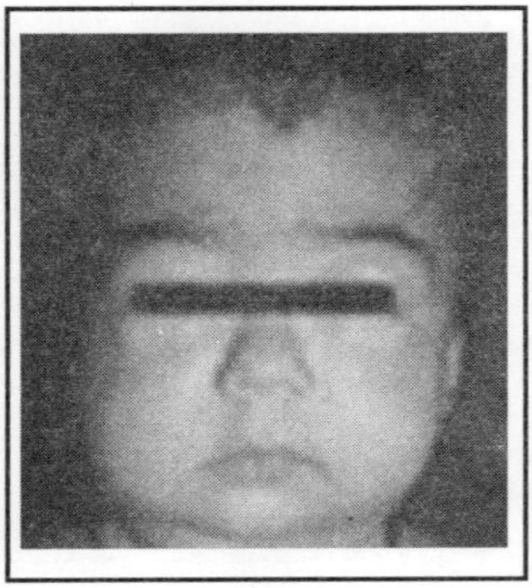

Fig 42-1

Such a child is put on a high protein, salt restricted diet, hospitalised under a pediatrician and treated with corticosteroids and diuretics (drugs that increase the urine output and thereby reduce the swellings in the body). Long term follow-up is needed as the episodes may occur repeatedly, or any one episode may fail to respond to the standard medicines and may need higher medicines. Home monitoring of urine, periodic lab tests, repeated visits to the Pediatric Nephrologist and regular follow-ups with the Pediatrician are all necessary. The incidence of relapses declines in the teens and spontaneous cure may occur between 15-18 years of age.

Ch 43
Brain and Nervous System Problems

A baby is born with a need to be loved and never outgrows it.
- Frank A. Clark

The development of the brain starts by the beginning of the second trimester of pregnancy. It continues to develop throughout the first five years. Almost 95% of the development is over by then. Thereafter, there is no increase in size of the brain, but an increase in the inter-connections and maturity of the erstwhile child's brain. By ten years or so, even that is complete. Throughout the next 10 years, the brain continues to perform at its peak, but an irreversible "dying" process of brain cells starts by the end of the second decade, and we lose our cerebral capacity every single day. In spite of this, we are able to excel in higher studies, be creative, be intelligent and be philosophical in life.

Several incidents that hurt the developing brain may in fact cause minimal effects on the brain that are missed by the child, the parents and even the pediatrician. Who is to tell whether an IQ of 140 is the optimum IQ for, say, Lalita, who hurts her head against a desk at the age of two but has no unconsciousness or any other untoward effect at the time of the incident? In a similar vein, someone with a slightly above average intelligence may have had careful nutrition and has therefore reached his optimum intelligence in adulthood.

Convulsions (fits):

A fit or convulsion is a sudden involuntary tightening or twitching of the whole body or parts of the body of an individual with or without loss of consciousness. Fits have been traditionally associated with "evil eye", "effects of a roving ghost", insanity and what have you. In reality, a fit is an intra-cerebral electrical disturbance that leads to the body movements just described.

There are associated changes in the glucose, calcium and other electrolytes in the peripheral blood. One or two convulsions during childhood, especially when occurring in an otherwise healthy child may not lead to epilepsy or mental handicap, but chronic or recurrent fits can do so over a period of time. In fact, a chronic epileptic will often be an invalid and sometimes have tight limbs like a palsied patient.

<u>Epilepsy:</u>

About 4-6% of children the world over are epileptic, that is, they suffer from recurrent fits or seizures. As stated above, the fits may be generalised or localised. *Generalised fits* tend to be familial in nature; the sight of a convulsing child is quite frightening for the uninitiated. There is an onset, sometimes with a scream or a shout, followed by rapid loss of consciousness, tightening of the whole body and rolling upwards and inwards of both eyeballs with frothing at the mouth; the "tight" phase is marked by a cessation of breathing for a variable duration; this may be so severe that there is development of bluish discolouration of the lips and nails (*cyanosis*); after a small gap, the child begins to twitch from head to toe, again for a variable period of time; finally, the fit ends with the child often passing urine and stools involuntarily; after this, the child remains limp and goes to sleep for at least a few hours. <u>*Localised fits*</u> more often than not may be due to injury to the head, specific illness like tumor or infection or a congenital malformation; they involve just one side of the body or even smaller areas like just one upper limb, or only the face, etc.

The diagnosis of epilepsy is made after doing an EEG; this is an electrical activity record of the brain that is somewhat like an ECG done for the heart. Abnormal electrical activity is studied to derive conclusions. Sometimes, doctors ask for a video record or a 24-hour sleep and EEG study to uncover mild epilepsy. Once epilepsy is diagnosed, an anti-epileptic medication is usually started. The use of such medicines imposes some restrictions on the lifestyle of the child: for example, she may not be allowed to go for swimming, and if she is taking one of those anti-epileptics that cause drowsiness, she may not be allowed to go out of the house without a companion. The medication must be taken regularly, usually for years together, and sometimes, for life.

What to do if the child has a fit: When you are by the side of an epileptic child, and the child has a generalised fit in your presence, what must you do? If you are a parent, some doctor may have already asked you to keep a dose of *rectal diazepam suppository* with you. If you have that, immediately open the pack and insert one suppository into the child's rectum. Call the doctor after this. Loosen the child's clothes and make her lie down on a flat surface. Do not attempt to open her mouth, insert a spoon or part her teeth if they are clenched: you may accidentally injure her tongue, lips, teeth or other oral structures. Turn her on her side when she begins to froth at the mouth, because in this position, the secretions will drain out and not get mistakenly aspirated into the lungs. Do not waste time in fetching a shoe or an onion for the child to smell: these age-old "remedies" are useless. If time is less or the doctor is not contactable, it is best that you pick up the child and rush to the nearest hospital for further care.

Febrile convulsions:

This is a common illness resulting from an incompletely understood effect of high fever on a small child's developing brain. Between the ages of 6 months to 5 years, infants and small children may throw a convulsion when they are suffering from high fever due to any cause – not necessarily something related to the nervous system. The problem is more common in some families, and its incidence is higher in families with epileptic patients. The convulsion occurs at the height of fever, is generalised, lasts 2-3 minutes and is followed by unconsciousness that resolves within 2-3 hours or by crying and irritability.

What to do? The general precautions mentioned in the paragraph on Epilepsy will apply here as well. The second most important thing you need to do is to take steps to bring down the fever: for this, medicines, sponging and fan/AC all should be used (see Chapter 23).

Children may have febrile convulsions repeatedly or at least more than once; such children should be advised to go for an EEG; they should be put on diazepam or similar drug along with a fever-reducing drug like paracetamol during the course of a febrile illness.

It is important not to confuse this entity with epilepsy. In febrile seizures, the outcome is excellent and the child does NOT need long-term anti-convulsant medication.

Meningitis:

Inflammation of the membranes covering the brain and the spinal cord due to infection by harmful microbes is called meningitis. Fortunately, meningitis is a rare illness. In acute meningitis, there is headache, vomiting, fever and development of fits within hours. Some microbes, such as the *meningococci*, produce a wide-spread rash that soon becomes hemorrhagic in character. Shock may result in these patients. They have a very poor prognosis.

Children who have fever, excessive irritability, a boggy, full and pulsatile anterior fontanelle and vomiting must be suspected to have meningitis and taken to the doctor immediately.

Meningitis caused by *H. influenzae* is preventable with the Hib vaccine which is given in infancy; that caused by meningococci needs a vaccine only just before and during an epidemic of meningococcal meningitis. Viral meningitis cannot be prevented. See Chapter 30 for details on vaccinations.

Ch 44
Diseases of the Blood

Blood will tell, but often it tells too much

- Don Marquis, 1878-1937,
American Humorist and Journalist.

What can one say about blood? It is the most visible, powerful and obvious symbol of life, of power and of the equality of all human beings below the surface of the skin. We associate our health with the colour of our blood. We are alarmed when our blood is taken for tests. We faint when we see blood. Tales of vampires and Dracula begin and end with blood. Is it surprising that a parent gets worried if he learns that the child may be having a blood-related illness? This chapter will discuss "Anaemia" in detail, but it will also touch on other blood-related problems like bleeding disorders, abnormal hemoglobin, etc.

Anaemia:

Anaemia is deficiency of hemoglobin in the blood. It may be caused by many things, but the commonest cause is nutritional deficiency of iron. When I say anaemia in this chapter, I mean nutritional iron deficiency anaemia. However, for the sake of completion, let me show you, through a small table, what the other causes of anaemia are:

Causes of anaemia
Nutritional: • Deficiency of iron • Deficiency of folic acid/ B12 • Severe protein deficiency Social: • Prolonged breast-feeding without weaning Intestinal Causes: • Hook-worm infestations • Bleeding from the GI tract Blood loss: • Menstrual losses in adolescents • Other types of chronic blood loss Abnormal break-down of RBC's: • Malaria • Hemolytic anaemias Chronic Diseases • Tuberculosis • AIDS Blood Cancers and other cancers • Leukemia

Let us now move on to the most important causes of anaemia in our country. Without doubt, nutritional iron deficiency anaemia is the most common of all. After this come hook-worm infestation, chronic menstrual blood loss anaemia, malaria and tuberculosis. The other causes are rarer than these five common causes.

Iron deficiency anaemia:

Infants are born with sufficient stores of iron in their bodies to have no anaemia till the age of almost 4-6 months. Add to this the fact that iron present in human breast milk is highly bio-available to the baby. Add also the fact that most Indian mothers *do* breast-feed their babies till at least six months, and you will realise that iron deficiency anaemia (IDA) is not common in the first six months of life. After six months, however, many mothers do NOT begin weaning their babies, or wean them with foods that are not rich in iron. This leads to a drop in the hemoglobin levels in infants beyond 6 months of age. Unhygienic rearing also exposes children to dysentery and worm infestations; both these cause slow, chronic blood loss and lead to further anaemia. The occurrence of malaria in an already anaemic child causes a nutritional disaster that can last life-long if not recognised and treated in time.

Symptoms and findings:

These include paleness of the palms of the hands and soles of the feet, nails, tongue and the conjunctiva (remember how the doctor pulls down the lower eye-lid and takes a look at the fold of mucosa inside it? Well, he's looking at the colour of the conjunctiva!). Along with this rather obvious symptom, the child looks weak, tires easily while playing or walking, feels short of breath while playing active games and eats less; she may want to eat dirt, chalk or the plaster that is peeling on the wall (pica, see Chapter 15); she may be more prone to infections than a healthy child; and it is now believed that a slightly off-normal intellect may also be due to iron deficiency. In fact, the general feeling is that iron sufficiency is necessary for optimum brain development in the first decade of life. The diagnosis of anaemia is made when a *hemoglobin* test is done. The normal hemoglobin of a child does vary with age. It is about 16-20 gm/dl of blood in a newborn. During the first month of life, it may be about 14-18 gm/dl, during early infancy, 12-16 gm/dl, during late infancy, 12-14 gm/dl and during the toddler stage, 11.5 – 14 gm/dl normally.

Thus, a hemoglobin (often denoted by the acronym Hb) of less than 12 gm/dl of blood is anaemia.

Prevention of iron deficiency anaemia:

Iron-rich foods should form an important part of a baby's diet right from the time weaning is begun. These foods are listed in Chapter 10. Briefly, they are whole pulses and legumes, sprouts, cereals, esp. wheat and ragi (*nachni*), dark green leafy vegetables, eggs, chicken, mutton, liver, and kidneys. Addition of Vitamin C in the form of lime juice, intake of citrus fruits and use of amla helps in the absorption of iron from the gut. Preventive use of iron preparations is also recommended in infants, adolescents and menstruating women.

Treatment of anaemia:

<u>Correction of IDA:</u> This is the main stay of treatment and easy to carry out. Along with the use of iron preparations under the supervision of a doctor, the child's diet should be modified too. Also, it is important to check what, if anything, was contributing to the development of anaemia. For example, if there is a complaint that the child has a bloated tummy and has anal area scratching everyday at night, treat her for worms (see Chapter 35).

<u>Look for other causes:</u> One should have the child checked out for other causes if an apparent IDA does not respond to the above simple measures. Search for intestinal worms, chronic disease, malaria and in extreme cases, rarer illnesses.

<u>Duration of iron therapy:</u> Normally, three months are needed to bring the Hb back to normal. After this, an additional month or two of treatment is given to build up iron stores in the body. The dietary modification plan should continue life-long, that is even after the medicines have been stopped for good.

For more information on anaemia, please check out the following links:

- ✔ http://www.who.int/nut/ida.htm
- ✔ http://www.drlockie.com/disease/anaemia.htm
- ✔ http://www.nhsdirect.nhs.uk/en.asp?TopicID=24
- ✔ http://www.vh.org/pediatric/patient/pediatrics/cqqa/anemia.html

Hemophilia:

Clotting of blood following injury or any other reason occurs due to a complex well-orchestrated chain of events requiring more than 20 different biological substances. Some of these substances are called "Clotting factors". Hemophilia is a blood disorder in which clotting of the blood does not occur properly. It is due to a hereditary deficiency of a vital clotting factor in the body, known as Factor VIII. This disorder is X-linked, that is, it is transmitted by mothers to their sons only, while daughters carry the abnormal gene to the next generation without any symptoms.

Symptoms:

The disorder is suspected when, after an injury, or a surgical cut (most commonly, at the time of circumcision done for religious purpose in small male infants), the bleeding does not stop within a few minutes (as is usual), but continues for a long time. Occasionally, in a child who never has injuries or is not circumcised, the diagnosis may be missed till he develops a spontaneous hemorrhage, such as large bruises, blood in a joint (the knee being the most commonly affected joint), or intra-cranial hemorrhage (bleeding within the skull cavity).

Recurrent bleeds may leave behind scarring, which can lead to deformities, particularly when joints are affected. Intra-cranial bleeds can be life threatening.

There is, at present, no way to cure hemophilia. However, one can take precautions to prevent bleeds in a known hemophiliac.

Precautions and Treatment:

These include protecting the child against injuries by offering a careful, sheltered lifestyle with no exposure to impact sports, an accident-free home environment, plastic "guards" to be worn all the time over the major joints such as the knees, giving the child no intramuscular injections (as is sometimes done by general practitioners in India without any warning) and having the child wear an amulet or necklace with information about his disease enclosed within it. Proper dental hygiene is also very important, and the child must be given soft tooth-brushes for his teeth. Any gum disease must not be taken lightly. At the same time, when a hemophiliac *has* to undergo surgery, he should be first given "cryoprecipitate" or "Factor VIII" before he is taken for surgery. This is replacement of the defective factor by intravenous route. The replacement is also the only known treatment available for a bleeding hemophiliac patient. Following surgery, replacement therapy must be continued for a few days till the threat of bleeding has completely disappeared.

Rehabilitation therapy will be needed for children with scarred joints (something that should NEVER occur in modern times, since Factor VIII replacement therapy is *always* available).

To read more about these, please look up the following links:

- ✔ www.vh.org/pediatric/patient/pediatrics/cqqa/hemophilia.html
- ✔ http://ghr.nlm.nih.gov/condition=hemophilia

- ✔ http://www.wfh.org

Other bleeding disorders:

Apart from hemophilia, there are other inherited bleeding disorders too. These involve deficiency of other clotting factors. The principles of treating them are the same as for Factor VIII deficiency. Replacement therapy, when available, is the mainstay of treatment of these disorders.

Non-inherited bleeding disorders may occur with chronic liver failure, platelet diseases and with snake-bite from a Russell's viper.

Thalassemia (Cooley's Anaemia):

Thalassemia, like many other blood diseases, is an inherited disorder of hemoglobin *production* that is transmitted from both parents (who are carriers) to their offspring of either sex. The basic problem is that not enough of the "adult" type of hemoglobin (Hb A) is formed; another normal hemoglobin, called the "foetal" hemoglobin (Hb F), is produced instead.

Each parent is a carrier; he/she has mild anaemia and is known as a "Thalassemia minor/trait". There is a 25% chance that each of the children of both carrier parents will inherit both the abnormal genes and have "Thalassemia major".

Symptoms:

The child with Thalassemia ("major") is normal at birth and for the first three to four months, since every normal child also has Hb F at birth; however, unlike in a thalassemia-affected child, the Hb F containing red blood cells (RBC's) are normally removed from the system of a normal child over the first three months and Hb A containing RBC's take their place, so that by three to six months, no

Hb F remains in the child's body. In the thalassemic child, however, the Hb F to Hb A switch does not take place, so that Hb F-containing RBC's persist. These RBC's do not work as efficiently as the Hb A containing normal RBC's; besides, they are fragile and break down easily. Thus, after the first three to four months, the child begins to show anaemia that gradually increases in severity over the rest of the first year. The child is taken to the doctor because of his/her pallor; the doctor may find a slight enlargement of the spleen and of the liver. A very low Hb of less than 8 gm/dl should prompt a diligent doctor to think beyond nutritional causes and send the child for further tests to rule out, among other illnesses, thalassemia major.

In fact, Thalassemia is the best known among all the so-called "Hemolytic anaemias" as it is also the most common. It was imported from the region of Macedonia when Alexander the Great invaded our country in the 4th Century B.C. In India, it is common in Sindhis, Kutchis, Lohanas, Punjabis and others from the Indo-Pak border areas. Thalassemia is now recognised all over the world.

Managing the child:

Like most hereditary diseases, at present, there is no cure for thalassemia, although a recent treatment called "Bone Marrow Transplant" (BMT) is now providing at least affluent patients with a permanent cure if it is successful (a BMT can cost anywhere between 5-15 lakhs of rupees initially and at least 1500 rupees/month throughout life afterwards in medicines).

The present treatment is a two-fold programme of repeated blood transfusions to maintain the Hb above 11 gm/dl, combined with a medication programme to remove the excess iron that is retained by the body with each transfusion. The latter is done with "iron chelators", of which both injectable and oral varieties are available. The injectable one has to be used as a 24-hr continuous sub-cutaneous infusion; it is costly but very effective; the oral one is in the form of capsules, but it is not as effective as the injectable variety and may cause some unwanted side-effects. Some hematologists call the injectable treatment as the "Gold Standard" while others are hailing the cheaper oral treatment as "revolutionary".

Over the decades, thalassemia patients are now surviving into their thirties and even early forties, and concerns about their reproductive abilities and their basic quality of life have assumed a lot of importance. Patients have a reduced fertility, but have been known to have children whether with or without help from modern treatment methods. Interested readers should contact the relevant Thalassemia Society in their country for further information. Some links are provided at the end of this discussion.

Prevention:

Prospective couples from communities where thalassemia is common should go in for pre-marital counselling to detect whether they have thalassemia minor; if both parents have the trait, they should weigh the options before them before they take the "plunge". in case one member of the pair is normal, while the other has the trait, there is no risk for their progeny, so they can safely get married. In case of both parents being cases of Thalassemia minor, they may go in for "pre-natal diagnosis" before deciding whether to continue with a pregnancy or not, as each unborn child has a 25% chance of having thalassemia major.

Further reading:

- ✔ http://www.cooleysanemia.org/index.php: This is the worldwide parent site on thalassemia.
- ✔ http://www.thalassemia.com/: Another comprehensive site from North California.
- ✔ http://www.cooleysanemia.org/bodies/body163.php: This is the story of an Indian thalassemic who is now in Texas, U.S.A.

- ✔ http://in.dir.yahoo.com/Health/Diseases_and_Conditions/Thalassemia/: lists all the societies worldwide on Thalassemia and related hemolytic anaemias.
- ✔ http://icmr.nic.in/car/bone.htm: lists details on BMT in India's premier Christian Medical College, Vellore.

Other Hemolytic anaemias:

Other inherited hemolytic anaemias include "Sickle cell anaemia" (SCA) and other forms of abnormal hemoglobin. In SCA, as in thalassemia, both parents must have the abnormal gene to transfer it to the child. The illness may cause bone, brain and other problems in infancy, but patients do not need regular transfusions as with thalassemia. Sickle cell Hb is an abnormal hemoglobin that causes the child's RBC's to deform into a sickle-shape (crescent moon) whenever there is a relatively higher demand (as after vigorous exercise) or a lack of (as with a trek to a high mountain) oxygen.

Sickle celled RBC's have an inbuilt resistance to getting infected with the malarial parasite, and according to one theory, the development of sickle cell Hb may be an adaptation of the human body against malaria infestation.

To know more about SCA, read this: http://www.scinfo.org/

Ch 45
Some More Problems

Your body is the church where Nature asks to be reverenced.
- Marquis De Sade, 1740-1814, French Author.

Acquired Immune Deficiency Syndrome (AIDS):

AIDS is a relatively new infectious disease on this planet. It is caused by the HIV viruses. *Perinatal* transmission accounts for over 75 % of the cases in children; the rest are infected via breast milk or intimate mother-child contact, by transfusions of blood that is infected, by use of infected needles for injection, and in adolescents, by unprotected sexual activity (both same sex and opposite sex).

UNAIDS estimates that as of December 2000, there were an estimated 36.1 million people living with HIV/AIDS (34.7 million adults and 1.4 million children under 15). Of these, almost 6 million need urgent anti-retroviral treatment. Unfortunately, appropriate medical treatment and AIDS medicines are currently only available to 400,000 individuals. The World Health Organisation (WHO) is committed to provide anti-retroviral therapy to at least 3 million affected persons by the year 2005 (the 3 by 5 initiative, see: http://www.who.int/3by5/en/). Since the epidemic began, an estimated 21.8 million people have died of AIDS (17.5 million adults and 4.3 million children under 15). Every year, 3 million people die of AIDS, of whom 500,000 are children below the age of 15 years.

Symptoms and Features of AIDS:

Aside from the fetal loss that occurs to a HIV positive pregnant woman, and a few physically abnormal babies born to some of them, the baby born to a HIV positive mother is essentially NORMAL. Symptoms of the illness appear by 6-24 months of age; most affected children die by the age of five if not given anti-retroviral therapy (ART).

Symptoms of AIDS are due to the effects of a generalised immune deficiency; the child cannot prevent various illnesses and infections from attacking him/her; some such infections normally do NOT occur in normal children and are called *Opportunistic* infections: they affect HIV positive children only because these children are immune deficient. These include unusual bacterial, viral, fungal, protozoan and metazoan infections and infestations. Other unusual illnesses such as rare forms of cancer and degenerative illnesses may also occur and overwhelm the child.

The AIDS-affected child is a stunted, sick child with fever, enlarged neck glands, runny nose and cough; she will also have tuberculosis that does not respond to the usual anti-T.B. medicines. There is reduced appetite, ulcers in the mouth, enlargement of the liver and spleen, a bloated stomach with a thin, emaciated body frame and a "smell" of looming death in the most advanced cases.

Diagnosis:

A blood test for HIV is usually positive in the baby of a HIV positive mother, but it may not indicate that the baby is infected, as it may just reflect the presence of HIV in the mother. These are passively transferred maternal antibodies present in the baby's blood, and they will gradually wane and disappear by 15 months. Presence of a positive test beyond 15 months indicates that the baby has active HIV infection.

Nowadays, modern technology has permitted diagnosis of active HIV infection even in the neonatal period. The newer tests are not universally available and they are costly too.

Management of a child with AIDS:

The AIDS-affected child is likely to be orphaned while still a child as she most likely acquired the disease from her own mother/father/ both parents. She will need early institution of ART. She will need a good, nourishing diet and expert care to prevent and/or treat any of the severe opportunistic infections that she may have/be likely to have. She should not get immunised with live vaccines like the B.C.G., the oral Polio vaccine, the Measles vaccine, the M.M.R. or the Chicken Pox vaccine; in addition to the routine vaccines, she will need the Injectable Polio Vaccine (IPV) which is a killed-virus vaccine. She will also need special vaccines against Pneumonia, Influenza and so on.

Prevention of AIDS:

AT present, there is no method to predict or prevent mother-to-child transmission of AIDS. No vaccine against AIDS is available. AIDS in society must be sought to be prevented on the whole by proper education, sex education and counselling, prevention of other sexually transmitted diseases, use of condom, avoidance of sexual promiscuity, avoidance of anal sex, avoidance of homosexuality, proper checking of blood and blood products to prevent transfusion-related AIDS and stopping the sharing of needles and syringes by IV drug addicts.

Further reading:

- ✔ http://www.aids.org/info/FAQs.html#numbers
- ✔ http://www.who.int/hiv/en/

Cancer in children:

Cancer is thought to be a disease of the elderly. Unfortunately, however, it may also occur in children. Even newborn infants are known to be born with cancer. The commonest type of cancer in children is blood cancer, or *leukemia.* Cancers of the brain, kidneys, lymphoid tissue and embryonic tissue are also common in children.

Symptoms of leukemia include fever, loss of weight and appetite, enlargement of lymph glands, liver and spleen (with resultant enlargement of the abdomen), bone and joint pains, easy bruising or bleeding from injuries, anaemia and increased susceptibility to opportunistic infections (see AIDS above).

The diagnosis is suspected on a complete Haemogram and confirmed by a bone marrow examination. The child should be treated by a medical oncologist. *Chemotherapy* (medicines, mostly IV, but some oral too) and *radiotherapy* (irradiation) will both be needed. During these treatments, the child will need complete support and love. Both these treatments can make the child look "different" as there is loss of hair, development of skin and internal infections, loss of weight and mental depression.

During the care of a child with cancer, it is very important that the house (the child's room in particular), is kept sanitised and visitors are limited. Fever during treatment is to be counted as an emergency and immediate medical attention with the oncologist must be sought. During travel, take the child with a face mask covering her mouth and nose; travel in a taxi with windows drawn up to prevent infectious agents from assaulting the child. At home, dehumidifiers and air-conditioners are helpful, as are air-filters that remove particulate matter from the air. These devices should be purchased if you can afford them and maintain them later on.

Attention to a nutritious diet and personal hygiene are both important. An optimistic environment must be maintained in the house at all times. Private home-based tuitions may be continued only if the child wants them so that he/she does not get left out of the academic loop later on when he/she has recovered. The cure rate for leukemias in children is more than 60% worldwide, so an air of doom and depression must be avoided at all costs. Nowadays, many cases of leukemia are offered a Bone Marrow Transplant (BMT), a procedure that, if successful, may cure the child permanently of his/her cancer.

When it is apparent that the child is unlikely to recover, or when he cannot tolerate the treatment any more, his/her life should be made as comfortable and happy as possible. His/her desires should be fulfilled. Pain medications and sedatives should be given as needed. A trip to a desired place may also be arranged so that the child meets his Maker in a happy state.

The principles discussed above are applicable to other cancers as well. Children with solid tumors like cancers of the kidney etc. will also need *Surgery* in addition to the above two modalities of therapy. However, the outcome is not as good as with leukemia.

Diabetes Mellitus:

Although traditionally, diabetes is a disease of the elderly, and is associated with the problems of obesity, hypercholesterolemia and hyperlipidemia, it can occur even in children. When diabetes mellitus occurs in kids, its symptom profile, the diagnosis and the treatment are a bit different from that in adults. This small section will help you to identify diabetes in childhood so that you can take appropriate action.

What is diabetes?

Diabetes is a disorder of the pancreas, the gland that nestles in the abdomen inside the loop formed by the C-shaped duodenum. It is the organ that manufactures "Insulin", a hormonal chemical that is responsible for the maintenance of glucose levels in the blood. Insulin permits the body to process proteins, fat and sugars in food to make body tissues, produce energy, and store energy. Glucose levels should stay between 80 and 120 mg/dl of blood in healthy individuals, including children. With a lack of insulin, the blood levels of glucose do not remain in the healthy range and tend to go up as the child's liver starts making more and more glucose from the protein and fat in the food.

Both genetic and environmental factors cause diabetes. In children, the disease is thought to have an "immune" basis: the child's body receives distorted information that its insulin forming cells are "not its own" and "must be destroyed". The body forms immune cells against the pancreas and mounts an "attack" against itself. In the process, the pancreatic secretion of insulin starts falling, and diabetes sets in.

Symptoms of childhood diabetes (Type 1 diabetes):

Diabetes that occurs in children, young adults and some older persons is also classified as Type 1, Juvenile, or Insulin dependent diabetes. Symptoms include frequent urination, white spots on the underwear (due to passage of glucose in the urine), sudden weight loss, fatigue, excessive thirst and excessive demand for water, nausea, vomiting, repeated bladder infections, skin infections, tingling of the hands and feet, etc.

The most dangerous event that occurs in a diabetic child is sudden onset of unconsciousness due to a very high blood glucose level, often more than 400 mg/dl. This emergency can cause death if not treated fast with insulin and other medicines. The problem is that this can sometimes be the *first presenting event* in a childhood diabetic, with the illness never being diagnosed before. Therefore, be vigilant to your child's early symptoms of increased thirst, vomiting or weight loss. A family history may often be missing.

Another strange phenomenon has been noted in the last few decades: an increased number of children get Type 2 diabetes because of obesity. These children respond much better to the exercise and oral drugs regimens practiced on the elderly diabetics, but may need insulin later.

Management:

In children with diabetes, management includes frequent and sometimes nightly monitoring of blood and urine glucose levels (either at the laboratory or in the home with digital home monitoring equipment), lab measurements of special parameters at periodic intervals, initial therapy with two injections of variously mixed insulin preparations (which may later go on to be three, or even four daily injections), recognition and treatment of complications like *Ketoacidosis* (the unconsciousness mentioned above), *Hypoglycemia* (a *low* blood sugar as a result of vigorous exercise soon after insulin, for example), kidney problems, eye problems, skin infections and others, and continuing patient and family education and orientation toward a life-style that is extremely difficult to be happy with.

With correct treatment, a childhood diabetic can have a normal, uncomplicated life-span. However, there is no cure to this disease, so treatment has to continue lifelong.

Further reading:

- ✔ http://www.diabetes.org/home.jsp

Hypothyroidism:

Hypo-(less)thyroidism is the commonest childhood hormonal disorder and it can be caused by many causes. The commonest cause of hypothyroidism is *iodine deficiency*; the hypothyroidism in this case is accompanied by an enlargement of the thyroid gland, or goiter. Deficiency of iodine in the ground water causes this problem and it is seen mostly in children (and adults) living in the sub-Himalayan region and in hilly terrains all over the country. While adults have large goiters, children of different ages suffer from goiters as well as varying degrees of hypothyroidism. Hypothyroid mothers give birth to hypothyroid babies, sometimes with congenital goiter.

Recognition of Hypothyroidism:

Congenitally hypothyroid babies are lethargic, feed slowly, cry little and pass no stools for days and days. They have prolonged neonatal jaundice. Their milestones are delayed. They have a typical appearance with a dull look, dry skin, increased body hair, a slightly large tongue that protrudes from in between partly open lips, hoarse voice and cry and a somewhat distended abdomen, with umbilical hernia in some. A goiter may or may not be present. As the child grows, the delay in milestones is what alarms the parents and the family. The dull look is more marked and over more time, the child remains stunted in growth. By this time, diagnosis and early treatment must be done; otherwise, the child may stay permanently mentally handicapped and physically stunted.

In late onset hypothyroidism, the illness is thought to have an immunological basis: the immune mechanism treats the child's own thyroid cells as "foreign" and mounts an antibody response against them. Here, the child develops the more generalised symptoms of lack of thyroid hormones: there is retention of fluid with swelling of the face, eyelids, abdomen, etc. along with academic deterioration, constipation, weight gain and laziness.

Treatment:

Hypothyroidism is treated by simple *Replacement therapy* with orally available thyroid hormone, thyroxine. It has to be taken lifelong.

Prevention of IDD (Iodine Deficiency Disorders):

Iodine content of foods depends on the iodine content of the ground water. However, sea-food, milk, meat and poultry are good sources of iodine; universally, salt that is commercially available usually has iodine added to it; other unknown/miscellaneous sources include iodine present in medicines, iodised oil, vitamin supplements, topical antiseptics (povidone iodine) and food colouring. The problem in India is still quite widespread as only 70-75% of the salt consumed is iodine-supplemented. Many people do not have access to iodine-supplemented salt because of its cost or because of cultural differences.

There is no other simple way to prevent IDD.

Further reading:

- ✔ www.vigyanprasar.com/comcom/feature47.htm

Teeth Problems:

In this section, we shall look at some of the common dental problems that affect children.

Avulsion of tooth:

If a tooth gets accidentally (or intentionally) knocked off the jaw of a child, it may be possible to wash it and carefully re-insert it into its original space and keep it pressed for some time to let it "meld" with the tissues around it. After this, the child should be told to avoid chewing and brushing on that side till the tooth gets "taken up" and heals. If you are unsure how to reimplant the tooth, put it in a cup of cold water or cold milk and take it to the dentist who will then do the needful. Reimplantation works only if done within ½ an hour after avulsion. After reimplantation, it takes 2-3 days for the tooth to heal.

Staining of teeth:

Brownish staining of teeth may be present at birth in babies whose mothers were given medicines called "tetracycline" (a type of antibiotic) during the first trimester of pregnancy when the dental buds were being formed in the embryo. Brownish staining of teeth in later infancy and childhood may occur because of use of tetracyclines during the first decade of life, use of oral iron preparations without rinsing and brushing of teeth afterwards, high fluoride content of drinking water and as a delayed effect of severe neonatal jaundice (where the stain represents accumulation of bilirubin).

Tartar:

This is brown mottling of teeth due to improper brushing and care. If a child brushes her teeth for less than 2 minutes, or does not rinse her teeth and mouth after consumption of sweets, snacks and meals, or does not brush the teeth in the prescribed manner (see Chapter 13), she will definitely get tartar. Additionally, children whose teeth erupt in a crooked manner (dental malalignment) also find it difficult to brush all the nooks and crannies of the teeth, and end up having tartar. Tartar is harmless, but requires to be removed by the dental surgeon with a process of scaling and cleansing.

Caries:

Teeth which are not cleaned properly will, over a period of time, develop hardened tartar that is called dental plaque. Plaque is not easy to remove with brushing. Acid-forming bacteria then "infect" these teeth. The acid dissolves the delicate dental covering called the "enamel" and exposes the dentin to the exterior. If left unchecked, the dentin will dissolve too. At this point, we will see a depression on the surface of the tooth. This is called a "*cavity*". When the child eats food, some of it may go and sink into the cavity; if the dentin has eroded, the food particles will impinge on the sensitive pain nerve fibres located in the core of the tooth. This will cause severe pain. The pain is aggravated when the child has cold or hot foods like ice cream or tea. Due to the infection, there is a swelling and pain in the gums too, which may develop pus within. This will cause bad breath. Pus collection in the gums is called a dental abscess, and it may cause systemic effects like headache, fatigue, fever and so on. A child with suspected dental illness should be rushed to the dentist.

Caries of the front upper jaw teeth (incisors) in bottle-fed babies is a special condition that needs a short paragraph here. It is called "*bottle feed caries*" or "*baby bottle tooth decay (BBTD)*". It is caused by prolonged contact with almost any liquid other than water. This can happen from putting the baby to bed with a bottle of formula, milk, juice, soft drinks, sugar water, sugared drinks, etc. Allowing her to suck on a bottle or breastfeed for longer than a mealtime, either when awake or asleep, can also cause BBTD. Use of chocolates in excess can also cause a similar decay of the primary dentition of a small child. The point to remember is this: <u>decay of primary or milk teeth can also affect the buds of the permanent teeth that are still to erupt.</u>

To prevent BBTD, the following recommendations have been given by the dentists:

1. Never use a feeding bottle to give milk or other liquids to the baby. If a bottle is used, never give it in the sleeping position or in bed.
2. Don't use a pacifier or a bottle as a pacifier; do not allow the child to keep it in her mouth or to walk around with it for extended periods.

3. Teach the baby to use a beaker or a cup as soon as possible.
4. Keep the baby's mouth clean and brush her teeth for her as soon as is possible.

For details on baby bottle tooth decay, see:

- ✔ http://www.medem.com/MedLB/article_detaillb.cfm?article_ID=ZZZKBW52R7C&sub_cat=11:

Dental Malocclusion:

This is a term used to describe children whose jaws (and hence teeth) are not shaped properly, so that the bite is crooked, overlapping or ineffective. Most such children have the defect as an inborn defect which cannot have been prevented by any possible precaution during pregnancy. In some children, though, the upper teeth begin to protrude outwards and get malaligned and maloccluded as a result of bottle feeding or aggressive thumb-sucking for years. In both cases, the help of a specialist dentist known as an "orthodontist" is sought. He will, at a suitable age, begin the process of "*orthodontia*"; this involves careful measurement of all the wrong alignments, planning a long-term schedule of removing crowded teeth, inserting braces and palatal implants and so on and so forth to give the child a 1000-watt smile before she is turned out in society as a teenager.

Part XI

Appendices

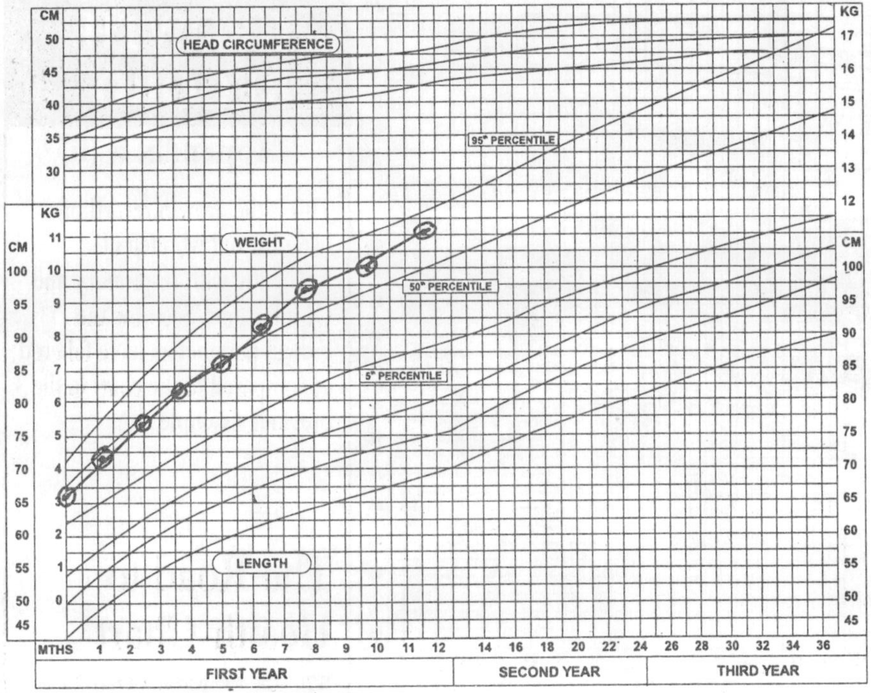

GROWTH RECORD

Appendix a (i)

This is the growth record of a normal baby aged two years. Note the secular increase in weight, head circumference and body length/height.

The Road to Health Chart

SOURCE: NATIONAL CENTRE FOR HEALTH STATISTICS (NCHS)

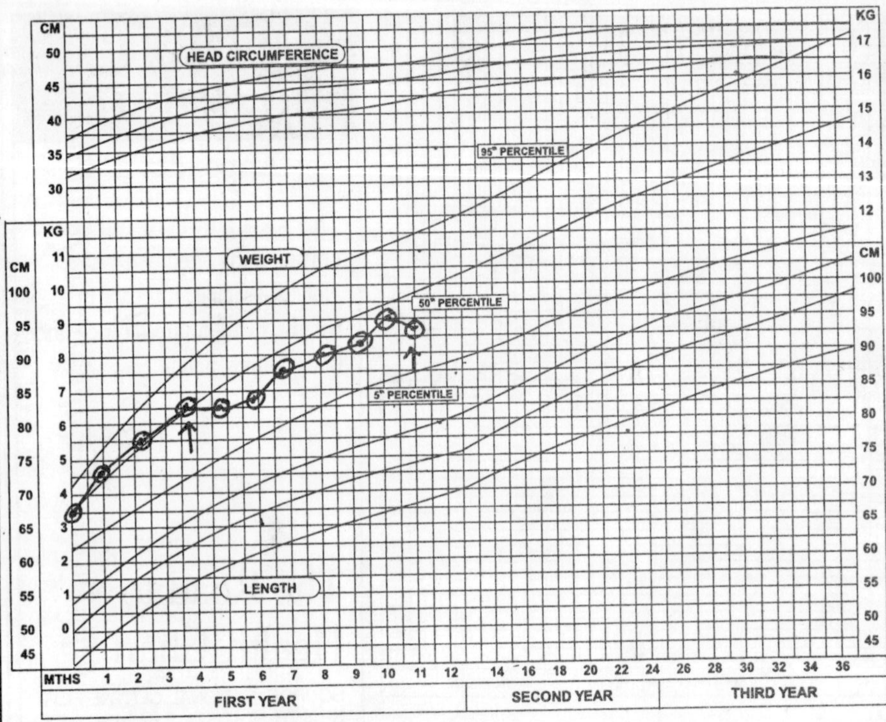

GROWTH RECORD

Appendix a (ii)

This is the growth record of a two year old who fell ill frequently with respiratory and GI infections. See how the growth parameters have faltered as compared to the chart in the previous example.

The Road to Health Chart

SOURCE: NATIONAL CENTRE FOR HEALTH STATISTICS (NCHS)

Appendix b.
Immunisation Schedule recommended by I.A.P

Age	Vaccine (s)	Comments
0 – 2 months	B.C.G. O.P.V. 0 H.B.V. 1	See note 2 below
1 ½ months	O.P.V. 1 D.P.T. 1 H.B.V. 2 Hib 1	Hib vaccine is an optional vaccine and may be offered to those who can afford it. See note 3 below. See also note 4.
2 ½ months	O.P.V. 2 D.P.T. 2 Hib 2	--
3 ½ months	O.P.V. 3 D.P.T. 3 Hib 3	--
4 ½ months	O.P.V. 4	May be combined with H.B.V. 3 at 6 months of age.
6 months	H.B.V. 3	--
9 months	Measles vaccine	This vaccine can be given anytime between 6 – 9 months in measles endemic countries/areas.

Immunisation Schedule recommended by I.A.P (contd.)

15 months	M.M.R. vaccine	May be given up to the age of 18 months
18 months (1 ½ years)	O.P.V. 5 D.P.T. 1st Booster Hib Booster	--
24 months (2 years)	Inj. Typhoid vaccine	Needs to be repeated *every* 3 years.
60 months (5 years)	O.P.V. 6 D.P.T. 2nd Booster	--
Any age after 1 year	Chicken pox vaccine	Additional vaccine for those who wish to give it to their children. Costly.
Any age after one year	Hepatitis A vaccine	Two doses 6-12 months apart. Addl. Vaccine costly.

Abbreviations:

B.C.G. Bacillus Calmette Guerin; D.P.T. Diphtheria-Pertussis-Tetanus (triple) antigen; H.B.V. Hepatitis B vaccine; Hib H. influenzae b; O.P.V. Oral Polio Vaccine; M.M.R. Measles-Mumps-Rubella Vaccine.

Notes:

1. This schedule is one of the many that are followed by Pediatricians in India. The reasons for the variability include non-updating of schedules in line with newer recommendations, additions of new vaccines to the roster, the socio-economic levels of the community served by the doctor, the needs of the community and many others.
2. One to two weeks after giving the B.C.G. vaccine, a red papule develops at the site; it grows gradually to the size of about 2-3 mm diameter, and its center turns soft and yellowish in colour. By 1 ½ months, the boils ruptures and discharges cheesy pus mixed with a few drops of blood. The papule collapses and heals over the next 1-2 weeks, leaving behind a papery scar.
3. The Hib vaccine schedule depends on the age of the child at the time of the 1st dose of this vaccine. If the first dose is delayed till after 6 months, only 2 and not 3 primary doses are needed. In the same way, if the first dose is delayed further, fewer doses are needed. Ask your doctor about it.
4. The D.P.T. vaccine causes local swelling, redness and pain, and may also cause the child to have fever and excessive crying. These side-effects are now reduced if one opts for a newer version of D.P.T. called the *acellular D.P.T. vaccine.*
5. Vaccinations must be given on time even when the child is suffering from cold, cough, loose stools, vomiting, weakness or any mild to moderate illness.

6. If vaccines are delayed for any reason, the doctor will suggest ways to re-schedule/combine/add or drop vaccines so that the child gets all the important vaccines.
7. The Hepatitis A and Chicken Pox vaccines are costly and therefore offered as "Additional vaccines" to those who can afford them.
8. Typhoid vaccine has been recommended to be included in the compulsory immunisation schedule but as of 2004, it is still an Optional vaccine.
9. The current recommendation for Hepatitis B vaccination is to begin at birth, give the second dose at 6 weeks and the third dose at 6 months; however, alternative schedules are also now available. One such schedule allows for the three doses to be given along with the three D.P.T. and Hib doses at 1 ½, 2 ½ and 3 ½ months, followed by a booster at 1 year of age. This facilitates a combination of all the vaccines to be given with the same syringe (conditions apply, please consult your Pediatrician).
10. One last point. Insist on knowing about the pros and cons of each vaccine before allowing the doctor to give the vaccine to your child.

Some useful links are given in Chapter 22.

Appendix c: Counting Calories

Table 1:

Calorie Consumption per hour

Activity	Calories used / hr
Driving	200
Teaching	200
Writing (sitting)	100
Badminton (singles)	310
Badminton (doubles)	270
Hill climbing	530
Running (11 km/hr)	625
Swimming (medium)	480
Walking (8 km/hr)	500
Yoga	200
Cooking	165
Eating	85
Sitting quietly	70
Sitting & talking	90
Sleeping	60
Waiting in a queue	90
Watching TV	80

Table 2 :

Calories in common cooked/ready to eat foods

Food item	Quantity (wt)	Quantity (serving)	Calories
Bread	100 g	2 slices	60
Chapati	40 g	1	100
Puri	15 g	1	100
Plain rice	50 g	1 cup full	150
Sambar	-	½ cup	105
Buttermilk	-	1 glass	25
Curd	100 g	½ cup	-
Chicken roast	50 g	2 small pieces	100
Egg boiled	35-40 g	1	55
Fish fried	70 g	2 small pieces	100
Samosa	100 g	1 piece	400
Idli	100g	3 big	130
Dosa (plain)	100 g	3 medium	360
Uthappam	100 g	2 big	330
Cheese pizza	100 g	5 " diameter	270

Appendix d: Recommended Dietary Allowances

The following table is adapted from Gopalan C, Rama Sastri BR's book called "Nutritive Values of Indian Foods", ICMR, 1980. All quantities are in grams/ml per day.

Table 1:
Recommended Quantities of Foodstuffs (uncooked) in children

Food Item	**1-3 years**	**4-6 years**	**7-9 years**	**10-12 years**	**13-18 years@**
Cereals	150	200	250	325	400-450
Pulses *	40	50	60	60	60
Green Leafy vegetables	50	75	75	100	100
Roots, tubers and other vegetables	30	50	50	75	150
Fruits	50	50	50	50	50
Milk@	200-300	200-250	200-250	200-250	200-250
Fats and oils	20	25	30	35	50
Meats, fish, eggs	30	30	30	30	60
Sugar, jaggery	30	40	50	50	50

Notes:

* Total vegetarians will need 10 grams more than the figures given herein.

@ The needs are greater in adolescent boys than girls of the same age.

The following table gives the RDA's of nutrients in children. It is based on the I.A.P. Text book of Pediatrics.

Table 2: Recommended Dietary Allowances of Nutrients in Children

Nutrient	Infants	Age 1–3	Age 4–6	Age 7–9	Age 10–12	Age 13–15	Age
Cal/day(B)	See	1287	1752	2075	2194	2447	2642
(G)	Table 3	1193	1630	1833	1965	2056	2064
Prot (g/d)	See	21	29	40 (B):	52	67	75
	Table 4			(G):	55	62	60
Ca (mg/d)	500	400	400	400	600	600	600
Fe (mg/d)	See $	11.5	18.5	26	30	40	50 *
Vit A(µg/d)	350	400		600			
Thiamine #	0.5						
Riboflavin #	0.6						
Niacinamide #	6.6						
Pyridoxine(mg/d)	0.3-0.4	0.9		1.6		2.0	
Folate (µg/d)	25	40	50	60	70	100	
Vit B 12 (µg/d)	0.2	0.2 – 1.0					
Vit C (mg/d)	25	40					
Iodine (mg/d)		100 – 150					
Zinc (mg/d)		4 - 6					

Notes:

: mg/1000 calories consumed; B : Boys; G: Girls; $: Fe (iron) requirement for infants is 1 mg/kg body weight/d after the 4th month of life;

* : Needs are for boys. Girls need about 10-15 mg less per day

Table 3:

Calories needed per day in Infants

Age	Calories/kg/day
0-3 months	115
4-6 months	99
7-9 months	95
10-12 months	101

Table 4:

Protein requirement in Infants

Age	Proteins g/kg/d
0-3 months	2.3
4-6 months	1.85
7-9 months	1.65
10-12 months	1.5

Table 5:
Nutritional Value of Foods (per 100g /ml)

Name of Food	Protein (g)	Calories (kcal)	Comments
Rice	7.0	350	Unpolished rice preferred. Do not discard cooking water
Wheat	11.0	350	Richer in protein. Do not use Maida.
Bajra	7.0 – 12	300 - 350	All these cereals should be given intermittently as they complement rice and wheat
Jowar			
Maize			
Nachni (Ragi)	7.3	328	Richest source of calcium and iron
Legumes/ Pulses	20-25	350	Good alternative to flesh foods. Sprouted legumes are more nutritious, with more iron, calcium, etc.
Ground nuts	25	567	Good protein, but fattening
Soyabeans	43	432	Excellent protein source
Green Leafy Veg	2.0-5.0	25-45	Rich in Folate, Calcium, Iron
Other Veg, Roots, Tubers	1.0-3.0	50-100	Prefer to have brightly coloured vegetables
Apples	0.2	65	Good in iron and B-vitamins
Bananas	1.2	120	Rich in potassium
Dates	2.5	317	-

Table 5:
Nutritional Value of Foods (per 100g /ml) *(contd)*

Flesh Foods	20	150-200	Fish meat is rich in Phosphorous, Iodine; White meats preferred to red meats.
Shrimp	68	349	
Egg	13	180-200	A complete meal! Rich in Vit A,D, and Calcium, Iron too
Milk (cow)	3.5	67	-
Milk (buffalo)	4.3	115	Richer, creamier milk.
Ghee and Oil	-	900	Fats
Sugar	-	400	Carbohydrate
Water	-	-	There is no evidence that "mineral water" is indeed better for health. Ensure

Appendix e:
Height / Weight Norms for Children

The following charts give the average weight and height of Indian children from birth to 18 years. Data is separately listed for boys and girls. Here are a few formulas for estimating expected measurements at any given age:

Weight at birth: 3.2 kg
3 – 12 months: [Age (months) + 9] ÷ 2 kg
1 – 6 years: [Age (yrs) x 2] + 8 kg
7 – 12 years: [Age (yrs) x 7] – 5 ÷ 2 kg

Height at birth: 50 cm
At 1 year: 75 cm
From 2 – 12 years: [Age (yrs) x 6] + 77 cm

i) HEIGHT NORMS FOR CHILDREN

Age	Indian Affluent Children (India)		National Centre For Health Statistics (U.S.A.)	
	Boys	Girls	Boys	Girls
Birth	50.4	50.3	50.5	49.9
3 months	59.4	59.1	61.1	59.5
6 months	65.9	65.5	67.8	65.9
9 months	70.6	70.0	72.3	70.4
1 year	74.3	73.5	76.1	74.3
1 ½ years	80.7	79.8	82.4	80.9
2 years	86.0	85.0	87.6	86.5
2 ½ years	90.5	89.9	92.3	91.3
3 years	94.4	93.3	96.5	95.6
4 years	100.8	99.8	102.9	101.6
5 years	106.2	106.0	109.9	108.4
6 years	113.6	113.1	116.1	114.6
7 years	119.7	117.4	121.7	120.6
8 years	123.6	123.2	127.0	126.4
9 years	128.2	129.2	132.2	132.2
10 years	133.6	135.2	137.5	138.3
11 years	139.6	140.9	143.3	144.8
12 years	145.8	146.0	149.7	151.5
13 years	152.0	150.4	156.5	157.1
14 years	157.6	153.8	163.1	160.4
15 years	162.5	156.0	169.0	161.8
16 years	166.3	156.8	173.5	162.4
17 years	168.7	157.0	176.2	163.1
18 years	169.8	-	176.8	-

On the following page is the table for norms of weight in children.

ii) WEIGHT NORMS FOR CHILDREN

Age	Indian Affluent Children (India)		National Centre For Health Statistics (U.S.A.)	
	Boys	Girls	Boys	Girls
Birth	3.1	3.2	3.3	3.2
3 months	5.7	5.4	6.0	5.4
6 months	7.4	7.0	7.8	7.2
9 months	8.5	8.1	9.2	8.6
1 year	9.3	9.0	10.2	9.5
1 ½ years	10.7	10.4	11.5	10.8
2 years	11.9	11.6	12.6	11.9
2 ½ years	12.9	12.6	13.7	12.9
3 years	13.8	13.5	14.7	13.9
4 years	15.4	15.1	16.7	16.0
5 years	17.1	16.8	18.7	17.7
6 years	19.2	18.9	20.7	19.5
7 years	21.0	19.0	22.9	21.8
8 years	22.6	20.8	25.3	24.8
9 years	25.6	25.1	29.7	30.5
10 years	27.0	26.9	31.4	32.5
11 years	30.6	30.9	35.3	37.0
12 years	34.8	35.0	39.8	41.5
13 years	39.4	39.1	45.0	46.1
14 years	44.1	42.7	50.8	50.3
15 years	48.6	45.7	56.7	53.7
16 years	52.4	47.7	62.1	55.9
17 years	55.5	48.4	66.3	56.7
18 years	58.6	-	68.9	-

Source: I.A.P. Textbook of Paediatrics

Appendix f: Teething Chart

Teeth buds are formed as early as 6th week of intrauterine life. The first set of teeth is called deciduous or milk teeth; it starts erupting by the age of 6 months and all the 20 teeth have erupted by 2 ½ to 3 years. This set of teeth lasts for about 5 – 6 years; the teeth are shed sequentially from the age of 6 years; shedding of primary teeth overlaps the eruption of permanent or secondary teeth. Shedding of primary teeth is completed by 10 years. The first permanent tooth erupts by the age of 6 – 6 ½ years; all but the last 4 teeth (the third molars or wisdom teeth) have erupted by the age of 12 – 13 years. The wisdom teeth erupt around the age of 17 – 22 years.

The following chart shows the naming, eruption sequence and shedding of teeth.

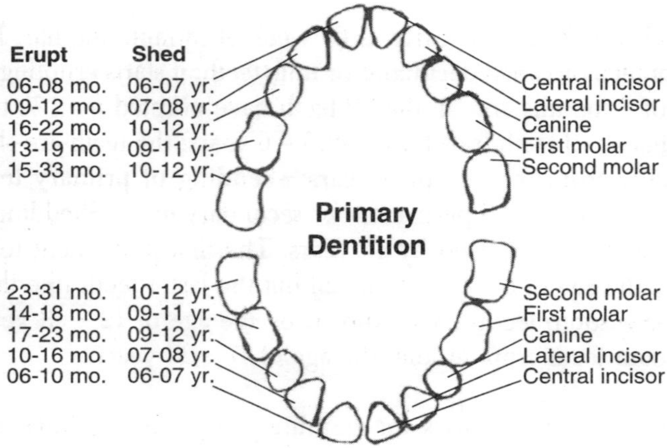
Erupt
Shed
06-08 mo. 06-07 yr.
09-12 mo. 07-08 yr.
16-22 mo. 10-12 yr.
13-19 mo. 09-11 yr.
15-33 mo. 10-12 yr.
Central incisor
Lateral incisor
Canine
First molar
Second molar
Primary Dentition
23-31 mo. 10-12 yr.
14-18 mo. 09-11 yr.
17-23 mo. 09-12 yr.
10-16 mo. 07-08 yr.
06-10 mo. 06-07 yr.
Second molar
First molar
Canine
Lateral incisor
Central incisor

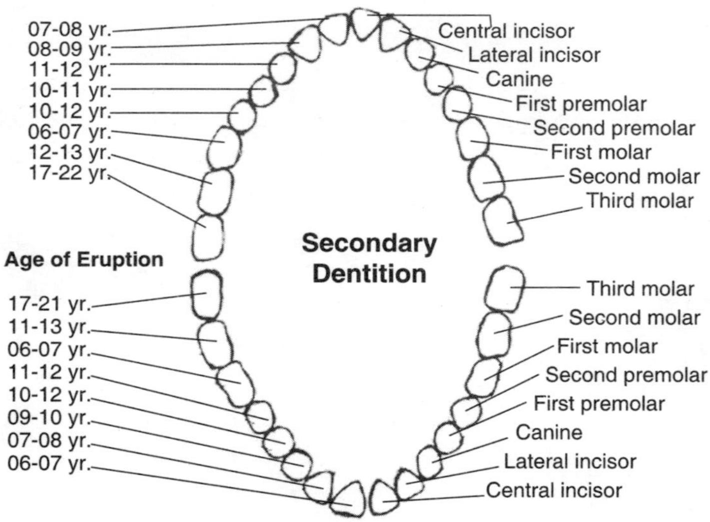
07-08 yr.
08-09 yr.
11-12 yr.
10-11 yr.
10-12 yr.
06-07 yr.
12-13 yr.
17-22 yr.
Central incisor
Lateral incisor
Canine
First premolar
Second premolar
First molar
Second molar
Third molar
Secondary Dentition
Age of Eruption
17-21 yr.
11-13 yr.
06-07 yr.
11-12 yr.
10-12 yr.
09-10 yr.
07-08 yr.
06-07 yr.
Third molar
Second molar
First molar
Second premolar
First premolar
Canine
Lateral incisor
Central incisor

Appendix g: Weaning foods

Some simple recipes of commonly used weaning foods are discussed here for parents who do not have proper information of the same.

A few tips first:

- Breastfeeding must continue for as long as possible. Weaning should be started from the seventh month of life.
- Commercially available weaning foods are too tasty and "addictive" for the infant. As a result, many infants stop feeding at their mothers' breast *even when she is getting a good quantity of milk. This is very undesirable.*
- See chapter 9 for more information about the how, why and what of weaning foods.
- The below-mentioned recipes are modifiable, taking into consideration the local mores and individual tastes.
- Until the end of the first year of the infant's life, breast milk continues to be a major source of nutrition for the infant.
- Try and give *bland* weaning foods right from the start; this will prevent the baby learning to covet only a particular taste to the exclusion of all others.

1. *Khimati:* This is a traditional Maharashtrian weaning food made from different cereals and food-grains. If the food-grains are first germinated, dried and then milled to prepare the flour for this recipe, the nutritional value of this food is increased manifold, as is its digestibility and acceptance (see the footnote below).

Ingredients	Amount
Ragi (*nachni*) flour	1 tsp
Jowar flour	1 tsp
Maize flour	1 tsp
Wheat ARF*	1 tsp
Ghee	½ tsp
Jaggery	to taste
Water	to 1 cup

Method: 1) Clean the raw form of ragi, jowar and maize and roast them on low flame for 5-10 minutes. 2) Mill them all with a hand pounder or an electric grinder. 3) Sieve the above flour and add it in one cup of water. Put all this in a cooking pan and boil for 2-3 minutes. Now add crushed jaggery and ghee along with the wheat ARF (amylase-rich flour, see the footnote *). 4) Cook for a few more minutes and remove from the stove. The above-mentioned amounts give one portion of a weaning food for a seven month old infant.

Goodness: Ragi and jaggery are excellent sources of iron. Ragi is also very rich in calcium. The ARF makes this food pre-digested and thus easy to assimilate.

**Note:* The term ARF refers to "Amylase Rich Flour". When wheat is soaked overnight in water, and left in a cool, dark place to sprout, it becomes nutritionally far superior to virgin grains of wheat. At the same time, as the endosperm has grown, it is a living plant, with much higher amounts of the enzyme amylase in it. This enzyme breaks down the complex carbohydrates within the wheat into smaller, more easily digestible sugars. This, in turn, makes the food less viscous, less bulky and nutritionally more concentrated. This is the advantage of using pre-germinated grains and pulses to prepare weaning foods.*

2. Vegetable Soup: Cooked, mashed vegetables provide a ready source of minerals and vitamins when cooked in the proper way.

Ingredients	Amounts
Spinach leaves	100 gm
Tomato	50 gm
Bottle gourd	50 gm
Sprouted, cooked, whole green gram	10 gm
Rice kanjee	1 cup
Salt	to taste

Method: 1) Clean and wash the vegetables. 2) Cook all the vegetables together along with the green grams in the pressure cooker with the desired quantity of water for 5-15 minutes. 3) Cool and grind the mixture in the large jar, using the rice kanjee as the base liquid. 4) Add salt. 5) Serve to the infant.

Note: You might want to add a few potatoes also to the soup. Another tip is to add a few black peppercorns and a dozen-odd mint leaves to increase the digestibility of this soup.

3. *Khichri:* The cereal (rice) and the legume (*moong* or green gram) in this recipe complement each other so that the food is near-perfect in nutritional value.

Ingredients	Amount
Rice	50 gm
Sprouted *moong*/ split green gram	20 gm
Salt	to taste
Oil for cooking	½ tsp
Jeera powder	One pinch
Turmeric	One pinch
Water	250 ml

Method: 1) Wash and soak moong for a half to one hour in one vessel. Do likewise with rice for about 15 minutes in another vessel. 2) In a large cooking vessel, add the rice, the *moong*, the oil, the salt and turmeric in 250 ml of water. Stir the contents and cover the vessel with an appropriate lid. 3) Cook over high flame till the water nearly dries up and the rice and the *moong* become tender. *Do not throw away the rice water. If it is in excess, store it in a glass bottle and ask for it to be saved in the fridge. It can be used as a base to prepare mixed vegetable or non-vegetarian soup.* 4) Take off the stove; add a few leaves of coriander or mint on the top as a garnish. 5) After it cools a bit, it can be served to the infant.

4. Egg Custard: Egg yolk is an excellent source of Vitamins A and D, as also iron, phosphorus and protein. Soft custard is a suitable way of introducing egg yolk.

Ingredients	Amount
Egg yolk	Half of an egg
Milk	75 ml
Sugar	1 tsp (5 gm)
Salt	to taste

Method: 1) In a bowl, beat the egg yolk with salt and sugar till all the ingredients are thoroughly mixed. 2) Bring milk to a boil in a cooking pot and take it off the stove once it is boiled completely. 3) Add the hot milk little by little over the egg in a new container and keep stirring all the time. 4) Allow the mix to cool. The custard will thus be ready.

5. ***Idli:*** Rice that is soaked for an hour or two is dried and milled to prepare the rice flour for idli. A small quantity of black gram (*udad*) flour is also added to the rice flour for that unique taste of idli.

Ingredients	Amount
Rice flour	30 gm
Split udad flour	10 gm
Fenugreek (*methi*) seeds	a pinch
Salt	to taste

Method: 1) Grind the pre-soaked rice coarsely in a grinder. 2) Grind the pre-soaked (one to two hours) udad dal *with* the fenugreek seeds with some quantity of water over a grindstone till the mix is light and frothy. 3) Mix the two flours with a small amount of water and leave overnight. 4) In the morning, check the batter. Add salt to it, mix thoroughly and pour it into *idli* moulds. 5) Put the moulds on the *Idli* stand and put the entire stand into a pressure cooker. 6) Add water at the bottom, cover with a lid and steam for five to ten minutes. Turn off the gas and let the lid open on its own. 7) The idlis will be ready to be removed when the cooker lid opens.

6) ***Poha:*** This is another traditional recipe made with rice flakes.

Ingredients	Amount
Rice flakes	30 gm
Onions (finely chopped)	One, medium
Potato (peeled and diced)	One, medium
Turmeric	a pinch
Oil	Two tsps
Cummin seeds (*jeera*)	½ tsp
Salt	to taste
Coriander leaves (chopped)	for garnish
Coconut (grated)	– do –

Method: 1) In a cooking pan (*kadhai*), keep the oil for heating. 2) Add the chopped onions and stir fry till they are golden-brown. 3) Add the cummin seeds to the hot oil and wait till they start spluttering. 4) Now add the potatoes and sauté till they are partly tender. 5) Add the salt and turmeric and cook further. 6) Take the rice flakes in a colander and moisten them lightly under a running tap of water for about ½ a minute, taking care to avoid completely wetting them. Let the water drain off. 7) Now add the flakes to the cooking pan and stir them into the previously cooking ingredients. Cover the pan with a lid and cook further for about 10 minutes. 8) Turn off the stove after confirming that the potatoes and the rice flakes are both well-cooked. 9) Pour the *poha* into a serving bowl. 10) Garnish with chopped coriander leaves and grated coconut and serve. (The last step may be omitted when preparing this item for an infant below the age of ten months.)

Understanding Medical Terms

Note: The list below is by no means an exhaustive one, and the more interested reader is advised to consult one of the standard medical dictionaries that are available in the market. However, an attempt is being made to simplify medical jargon in simple, easy to understand language. The entries are listed alphabetically. Within an entry, words that are written in **bold** may be found with independent entries elsewhere.)

Abscess: An abscess is a collection of pus in any part of the body, either internally or externally. Pus anywhere in the body MUST be removed surgically if the person is to become healthy.

Acne: The skin problem that surfaces in children of both sexes in and around **adolescence**. It is a hormonally induced problem; the spots are seen on the face, shoulders, back, etc. After the age of 18-20, most children's acne problem subsides. The major impact is healing of acne with scars. Teenaged children are very conscious about how they look.

AIDS (Acquired Immune Deficiency Syndrome): Caused by the HIV viruses, AIDS is a full blown disease that eventually has the potential to kill the affected person, either through the agents of infection by virulent, rare germs, or through the occurrence of fast-progressing cancer. Unsafe sex (without a condom), sharing of IV needles (as in drug addicts), transfusion with HIV-infected blood or blood products, and vertical transmission to a baby from a HIV positive mother can all lead to HIV positivity and AIDS. We are a long way from curing this deadly epidemic of the third millennium.

Adenoids: Situated just behind the back of the nose and the uppermost attic of the throat, the adenoids comprise lymphatic tissue similar to tonsils. The adenoids swell up in response to infection. This can block the passage of air from the nose into the airways and choke up the person's breathing, leading to mouth breathing, noisy breathing, nose infection and so on. Sometimes, this can cause the child to have a typical look called *"adenoid facies"*.

Adolescence: The age period from 10-16 years in girls and 11-17 years in boys is called adolescence. This is the age when the child matures into an adult physically, mentally, socially, intellectually and sexually.

Allergy: It is the state of altered responsiveness to otherwise inert or harmless substances. It is said that humans can be allergic to anything under the sun, and the sun itself. The most common substances include dust, inhaled pollen, cosmetic applications, drugs of all kinds, the sun's rays, different types of fabrics and insects, cats and dogs, and food substances like eggs, milk, etc. Anti-allergic treatment makes the effects of allergy more bearable, while avoiding the article that causes allergy will help prevent the symptoms. Symptoms can be local (rashes, skin darkening) or general (asthma, running nose, red eyes, loose motions, etc). **Immunotherapy** is aimed at "teaching" the body to "unlearn" an allergy and enable it to tolerate the allergic substances without any harm.

Alopecia: Absence of hair locally, in patches or all over the body.

Amblyopia: Normal looking eyes but with variable blindness, **squint** and flickering eyeballs (see **nystagmus**, below).

Amenorrhoea: Absence of monthly periods in a girl or woman. Usually indicates pregnancy if the person had normal periods previously and if the history is suggestive. Amenorrhoea, however, may also be seen if an individual has an imperforate (closed) hymen, a hormonal problem, or a congenital absence of the uterus.

Amniocentesis: The medical procedure by which, with the help from **ultrasonological** guidance, some fluid is collected from around the developing fetus for testing. This procedure has immense value, and the risk of an accident causing fetal loss is about 5 %. It is done in the 4th month of pregnancy.

Anemia: Anemia is the condition caused by a low **hemoglobin** percent in our blood or the loss of a large quantity of blood through a hemorrhage. In our country, the commonest cause is nutritional iron deficiency.

Anorexia: Loss of appetite. It is the commonest symptom for which a child is brought to a pediatrician. In *anorexia nervosa*, the adolescent girl refuses to eat to an extent that while she remains active, she loses weight rather rapidly. This needs intensive psychiatric care.

Antibiotic: Literally, "*anti-life*", an antibiotic is a substance obtained from cultured germs in a laboratory, and is used to kill disease-causing bacteria. Usually, antibiotics are anti-bacterial only, and have no effect on viruses, fungi or other types of microbes.

Appendicitis: Is a painful **inflammation** of the appendix, a small tubular structure with no definite function situated in the right lower part of the abdomen. Usually, the condition causes an acute emergency, sometimes needing surgery to remove the appendix (an *appendicectomy*).

Arthritis: Joint pain and inflammation is called arthritis. Can be a harbinger of serious disease if it persists; most commonly, arthritis is due to injury or viral infection, and has a good outcome.

Asthma: A chronic, persistent inflammation of the airways that is caused by a mix of hereditary vulnerability, exposure to allergens and occurrence of precipitating agents. The condition is characterised by difficulty in breathing, cough and wheezing. Inhaled drugs are currently recommended in treatment of asthma.

Attention Deficit Disorder with or without Hyperactivity (ADD-H): Impulsive behaviour, attention deficit and purposeless fidgetiness and hyperactivity characterise this difficult to treat disorder; happily, most children improve as they grow older, but all need counselling and special education during childhood. Some may need medication.

Autism: An increasingly commonly seen behavioural disorder characterised by reduced social interaction, intense liking for a stable, unvarying home environment and normal mentation. The child avoids eye contact and does not answer when spoken to. She finds happiness in her own world. She does not like to be cuddled, and most often, she will not exude warmth.

Bacteria: Living micro-organisms that exist all around us. Only some are harmful or cause disease, while the rest are either harmless or actually useful to us. The disease-causing ones are inhibited or killed with **antibiotics**.

Birth Asphyxia: A dreadful condition caused in the newborn baby by lack of oxygen to it before, during, or just after birth. The symptom is a delayed cry at birth, with rapid development of other complications as the time to cry is progressively prolonged. This illness can be fatal, despite it being managed by a specialist well-versed with neonatal care. If the child survives, she may well end up with **mental retardation**, spastic **cerebral palsy**, movement disorders, hearing or seeing deficit or a **convulsive disorder (fits)**.

Booster: This term is used in **immunisation.** It refers to a dose of a **vaccine** that is given some months to years *after* a **primary immunisation course**. Its purpose is to *boost* the antibody levels in the body, so that the duration of protection is prolonged. Boosting is a result of the body's previous memory of being exposed to the vaccine before.

Bow legs: In infancy, most babies have lower legs that seem bowed or curved, with the curvature outwards. This is physiological; it disappears as the child starts walking and running. Bowing beyond the age of two is abnormal and may be due to many causes, the chief one being **rickets**.

Bronchiolitis: It is inflammation of the small airways of the lungs that is caused by viruses. It affects infants and small children. Most children recover within 7-10 days, although some may require hospitalisation for oxygen therapy and other supportive care.

Candida: A type of fungus that can produce oral thrush (white, painful coating of the tongue), diaper-area rashes and occasionally, loose stools. It belongs to the yeast family.

CPR (Cardio-pulmonary Resuscitation): In the event of an impending death, CPR is the standardised method of trying to revive that person by ensuring that he/she continues to get oxygen by artificial breathing, and survives till medical help arrives. It can be learned by anyone, even a commerce graduate, even a housewife, for example. If you are trained to do a CPR, you should announce this when you see someone dying and start CPR without delay. You may well save a life.

Caries: Decay of the teeth. Initially, there is staining, followed by formation of plaque and finally, formation of cavities. Poor oral hygiene and indiscriminate eating habits foster dental decay. Bottle-feeding can cause caries of the upper front incisors (*bottle feeding caries*).

Cerebral Palsy: A disorder of the brain and the nervous system that is characterised by delay in achievement of major milestones and abnormal muscle tone, (most often, **spasticity** or increased tone). The disorder is static (does not worsen with age) and may be accompanied by mental retardation, hearing loss, fits or other neurological problems. **Prematurity** is a predisposing cause. The child needs physiotherapy and medication for life. When there is no mental handicap, the child may be educable to the fullest possible extent.

Chicken pox: A viral illness caused by the chicken pox virus. It is highly contagious and infectious. The rashes are marked by fluid within a blister. Most children have itching. The illness recovers in most of the children. One natural attack offers lifelong immunity.

Circumcision: A surgical procedure where the foreskin of the penis is removed, either for medical or religious purposes.

Club foot: An inborn abnormality of the feet where the feet point downwards and towards each other instead of being at right angles to the legs. This may need plastering or surgery if simple manipulation does not set the feet right.

Colostrum: The yellowish milk secreted by the mother in the first few days after delivery. It is rich in immunoglobulins and must be given to the baby.

Congenital: Present since birth. The occurrence may be due to hereditary or non-hereditary factors.

Convalescence: The period of recovery following an illness. During this period, rest and increased nutrition are essential for the patient.

Convulsion (Fit or Seizure): Sudden, involuntary twitching of some or all parts of the body, at times associated with loss of consciousness, frothing at the corners of the mouth, uprolling of both eyes and passage of urine or stool. Children who have repeated fits may be suffering from **epilepsy** or may have some disease inside their brains or elsewhere.

Cradle-cap: Formation of thick, yellowish crusts on the top of the scalp in infancy in some babies. It is a type of "dandruff" and is medically called "seborrhoeic dermatitis".

Cretin: A baby affected by low thyroid hormones (*hypothyroidism*). It may be caused by deficiency of iodine in drinking water and food.

It can be diagnosed at birth or soon thereafter by clinical examination and a single drop of blood. The disorder may lead to irreversible growth and mental retardation if left untreated. It may be associated with **goiter** (*thyroid gland enlargement*). Fortunately, it is easy to treat and the child will be completely normal if treated from a very early age.

Croup: A respiratory illness characterised by a harsh, barking cough and a "croupy" sound that is heard with each intake of breath. The sound is created by an inflamed voice box and air-pipe. The most common cause is viral infection, and the illness is most often seen in winter.

Cyanosis: It is the bluish discolouration of the skin and mucous membranes that is a sign of lack of oxygen delivery to the body tissues, either due to a respiratory, cardiac or general circulatory failure. In winter, babies' hands and feet may turn cold due to a sluggish peripheral circulation. This is called *acrocyanosis.*

Dandruff (*roosi*): This is flaking and scaling from the scalp that is sometimes seen in children. Like **cradle cap**, it can cause itching. It needs aggressive management, and is difficult to treat.

Dehydration: The state of the body where there is a loss of water and **electrolytes** from it is called dehydration. Many illnesses may produce this problem, but by far the most important one is acute **gastroenteritis** or **diarrhoea**. Treatment involves rapid replacement of lost fluid and salts by **oral rehydration.** Some children may need hospitalisation and **intravenous** therapy.

Dengue fever (break-bone fever): This is a viral illness that occurs due to infection by one of the three types of dengue viruses. It is transmitted to human beings through the bite of a mosquito (*Aedes aegypti*). It is characterised by high fever, severe body aches and pain in the eyes. The illness runs in two phases, with a fever-free interval in between the two phases. Although the child recovers in most cases, at times, the disease gets complicated by bleeding and circulatory shock, and may lead to fatality.

Diarrhoea (Loose motions): Diarrhoea is defined as the passage of one or more loose stools in a setting of **gastroenteritis.** A change in the established frequency of passing stools will herald the onset of watery diarrhoea. The illness may be life threatening if the water and salts that are passed out in the stool are not replaced quickly. **Dehydration** may then set in, which may need hospitalisation.

Dysentery *(pechis)*: Blood and mucus in stool, often with a griping pain in the stomach, is described as dysentery. This illness is caused by various kinds of microbes and protozoa.

Eczema: It is an allergic illness of the skin. The illness causes a weeping, itchy rash of the face and scalp in small babies. Often, an eczema-affected child goes on to develop other allergic illnesses like allergic conjunctivitis, **asthma** and so on.

Electrolytes: These are the various salts that exist in our body. They include Sodium, Potassium, Chloride and others. Deficiency of sodium is seen in gastroenteritis, diarrhoea and many other illnesses. Rapid replacement of decreased electrolytes is the cornerstone of therapy in such illnesses and can save lives.

Encopresis: This is a psychological disorder that stems from the reluctance of a child from passing her stools normally. She tends to "hold back her stools" and gets constipated. Then, there is an involuntary passage of stools in the child's panties from time to time. The child may develop abdominal distension. The condition is frequently a consequence of punitive toilet training.

Enuresis: Bed-wetting.

Epilepsy: Occurrence of repeated convulsions in an individual is called epilepsy. Usually, no cause can be found despite a diligent search thereof.

Epistaxis: Bleeding from the nose. This can be a normal symptom in some children, especially in summer. At other times, there may be a local cause, such as a dilated blood vessel. Picking the nose can rupture such a vessel and cause bleeding. The correct way to treat this condition is to take the child to a shaded place, make her sit down on a chair with the head bent forwards, and then pinch her nose with your thumb and forefinger. Ask her to open her mouth and breathe slowly through her mouth. If she is running a fever, apply ice over her head in an ice-bag. With these measures, the bleeding usually stops.

Failure to thrive: Failure of a child to grow in weight and height as per the normal trends for that age.

Febrile convulsion: A fit or convulsion that occurs during fever caused by an illness. This condition is most often seen in infants and young children between the ages of 6 months and 4 years. Usually, the child does not have any future after effects on his mental development. No fit - medicines are usually indicated.

Fever: Rise in internal body temperature beyond 99.6 degrees Fahrenheit is called fever. Fever is usually a symptom of infections, but there are many non-infective causes of fever too. Fever in infection is actually helpful in that it helps the body fight the disease-causing germs. A very high fever may lead to a **febrile convulsion**.

Fontanel: It is a window in the skull. A newborn baby has a large fontanel up in the front of her skull (the anterior fontanel). There are many such windows or soft spots in the baby's skull. They are actually gaps between the different small skull bones, and are areas that allow the brain inside to grow outwards, without being hampered by the skull box. The anterior fontanel closes by 12-24 months of age.

Gastritis: Inflammation of the internal lining of the stomach. This is a rare illness in isolation, but with inflammation of the bowel, it is called **gastroenteritis**, which is exceedingly common. Gastritis may occur due to drugs, viruses or bacteria.

Gastroenteritis: Inflammation of the stomach and the bowel; see **diarrhoea**.

Genetic disorders: This is another term for hereditary or inheritable diseases, for example, **hemophilia** and **thalassemia**.

Goiter: Swelling of the thyroid gland is called goiter. It is often, but not always accompanied by a low thyroid status (**hypothyroidism**).

Headache: This is an uncommon symptom in children, so that when it does occur, it has a more sinister implication than when it occurs in adults. Older children may suffer from psychological causes like anxiety (at the time of exams), tension etc. or even from migraine.

Heat exhaustion: The tiredness that comes in children from playing too much in the sun's heat. There is sweating, cold hands and feet and weakness accompanied by a mild **headache**. Replacement of water containing electrolytes is sufficient to herald recovery.

Heat stroke: This is more serious than a **heat exhaustion**. The sweating mechanism is rendered ineffective, so the skin temperature remains high, while the inner temperature may reach to 105 degrees F or even higher. The child may rapidly become drowsy and go on to become comatose or develop **convulsions**.

Hematemesis: Presence of blood in the vomit.

Hematoma (Bruise): A blood clot in the tissues, e.g. after an injury.

Hematuria: Presence of blood in the urine. If the blood loss is minimal, the patient may not be aware of it.

Hemophilia: A hereditary bleeding disorder seen in males. It is caused by deficiency of a specific clotting factor (known as Factor VIII) in the blood. Children with this disorder bleed heavily even after a minor injury. Every episode of bleeding needs close observation and/or hospitalisation for replacement therapy with Factor VIII.

Hemoptysis: Presence of blood in the sputum. A rare occurrence, it points to the presence of some abnormality in the airways or lungs.

Hemorrhage: Simply put, it means bleeding from anywhere in the body. For example, a gastric hemorrhage is bleeding in the stomach.

Hepatitis: Inflammation of the liver, most often caused by viruses, toxins or an internal disease of the body of the affected child. The chief symptoms are loss of appetite, vomiting, jaundice, fever and abdominal pain. Enlargement of the liver is an important finding on examination. Most children recover from a Viral Hepatitis.

Hernia: This is an outward protrusion of some internal structure (s) of an individual through a weak spot in the abdominal wall. An **umbilical hernia** protrudes through the navel; it is common in the first few months of life and in 9 out of 10 cases, it gets "self-cured" by the age of one year.

Hiccups: A sudden, spasmodic twitch of the *diaphragm*, the curtain like muscle situated between the chest cavity and the abdomen, is called a hiccup. Hiccups are common in early infancy, and are caused by distension of the stomach immediately after a feed.

Hydrocele: This is collection of fluid within the scrotal sac. The fluid is usually gravitated from the abdominal cavity, but it takes many months to gradually disappear. Sometimes, it may *not* go on its own, in which case, it may need a surgical removal.

Hydrocephalus: Collection of excessive fluid inside the brain of a child causes enlargement of the head. This is called hydrocephalus. Down-rolling of eyes and enlargement of veins over the head and face are seen. Usually, a hydrocephalus needs surgery.

Hyper- and Hypo-thyroidism: These are states of increased and decreased thyroid hormone activity in the body. While a hyperthyroid child may or may not have **goiter**, the hypothyroid child usually does not have it. The symptoms are diverse and beyond the scope of this glossary.

Immunisation: Is the process of providing protection against communicable (infectious) diseases by injecting the subject with antigens derived from the microbes themselves. The **primary immunisation course** is completed in the first year of life, barring some special **vaccines**; the **boosters** are generally given in later years of life.

Impetigo: This is a skin infection characterised by the occurrence of boils. It is exacerbated (worsened) by summer and by poor personal cleanliness.

Infection: Occurrence of a situation where a microbe enters the body and causes the latter to "react" to it by forming an immune response against it. An illness may or may not result, depending upon the body's immune response and memory of previous exposure to that microbe or similar microbes.

Inflammation: This is the classical problem with swelling, pain, redness and heat of a particular part or organ of the body. Infection is one of the causes, but other illnesses may also cause it.

Inhaler Therapy: This is the treatment where a special device called an *inhaler* is used to deliver medication directly into the lungs. The commonest illness for which inhalers are used in children is **asthma**.

IQ (Intelligence Quotient): This is a measure of the intelligence of an individual. To get the Quotient, we divide the child's *mental age* by her *chronological age* and express it as a percentage. The normal IQ of children varies between 90-110.

Jaundice: This is a clinical condition characterised by yellowish discoloration of the eyes and skin, passing of dark brown coloured urine and symptoms of vomiting, pain in the right side of the upper abdomen and fever. Most commonly, jaundice is caused by **hepatitis.**

Knock-knees: Most infants have a *physiological* knock knees condition: their knees come together at the middle while their ankles are < 5.0 cm away from each other. A distance >5.0 cm and/or age more than 2 years suggests that the knock-knees need medical supervision and work- up.

Leukemia: This is commonly termed as blood cancer. It is a disorder of the blood-forming tissues in the bone marrow. There is unregulated production of blood cells and their precursors; often, these cells are abnormal in appearance. It can occur in any age group, from newborn to old age.

Malaria: This is an acute, potentially life-threatening infestation caused by the injection of malarial parasites by the anopheles mosquito's bite. Malarial parasites are detectable in the blood during a fever episode; the victim suffers from chills and high fever, body aches, headache and at times, a complicated course with fatality.

Measles (*Khasra, govar, gobri*): This is an acute, communicable, contagious viral illness that affects infants and older children. The illness begins with a running nose, fever and red eyes, and is followed by a spotted rash that begins on the face and spreads to affect the whole body over the net three days. The rash then declines in the same direction and is followed by recovery of the child.

Meningitis: This is inflammation of the *membranes* (or inner coverings) that surround the brain and the spinal cord. It is an acute condition that can be caused by many microbes like bacteria, viruses, fungi and so on. The condition can be fatal, or it can cause lasting disability if it is not detected early or treated incorrectly.

Mental retardation: This means a subnormal intelligence. It may be associated with many inherited as well as acquired conditions. In many cases, no cause can be discovered despite a diligent search.

Microcephaly: This means a small head, and it is usually, but not always associated with either **spasticity** or **mental retardation.**

Mongolism (Down syndrome): This is a chromosomal anomaly in which there is extra genetic material of the 21st pair of chromosomes in an individual. The child is born with "mongoloid" facies, small head, slanted eyes and mental retardation. The **IQ** is subnormal. Children with this disorder are happy-go-lucky types, affable and trainable in most cases.

Mumps (*kaanpedey*): This is a viral, communicable disease that causes pain and swallowing difficulty with swelling of both the parotid glands, situated just below both the ears and by the sides of the cheek. Recovery is spontaneous and as a rule, complete.

Neonate: A neonate is a baby from birth to 28 days of age.

Newborn: A baby is called a newborn from birth to the age of seven days.

Osteomyelitis: Infection of the bone due to germs. It is a very indolent infective process and may take weeks to months to get eradicated.

Otitis Media: Infection of the middle ear either from an external focus (the air around us) or an internal focus (such as the throat, **adenoids** or the meninges). This usually presents as pain and pus discharge from the affected ear.

Phimosis: This is a condition where the foreskin of the penis cannot be drawn backwards due to some inflammation of the prepuce skin.

In infants up to the age of two years, the skin is normally not retractable.

Pica: This is a habit disorder of children where there is a tendency to eat mud, chalk or other substances on a routine basis. It may be due to iron deficiency.

Pneumonia: Infective process involving the lung(s) and causing fever with chills, cough with sputum (in older children), chest pain and difficulty in breathing.

Poliomyelitis: One of the vaccine preventable diseases, this illness is caused by the polio viruses. It used to be an important cause of paralysis of the upper or lower limbs in many children until the advent of the Oral Polio Vaccine, which has succeeded in reducing the incidence of this disease to a minor illness present in less than 20 countries worldwide.

Pre-term, Term and Post-term infant: According to the period of gestation, a newborn will be one of these at birth. A term baby is born after 40 weeks of gestation. A pre-term baby is born before 37 weeks, while a post-term baby is born later than 42 weeks.

Primary Immunisation Course: This is the prescribed course of primary vaccines that is compulsory in every child almost all over the sub-continent. It consists of a B.C.G. vaccine given soon after birth, three doses of oral polio vaccine and three shots of the D.P.T. vaccine between 1 ½ and 3 ½ months and one shot of the Measles vaccine at nine months of age. Recently, Hepatitis B vaccine, M.M.R. and Typhoid vaccine are sought to be added to the list of essential vaccines.

Puberty: Puberty is that stage of development during which a child attains the ability to sire children, that is when he/she becomes sexually mature and grows up into an adult. This is usually achieved by 12-14 years in a girl, and 15-16 years in a boy.

Rabies: A disease caused by the bite of a rabid dog. This disease is also called "*hydrophobia*" because the victim has fear of water. It is 100 % fatal. A vaccination course must be undertaken upon getting bitten if one wants to prevent rabies.

Rheumatic fever: This is a systemic disease caused by the after-effect of a sore throat caused by a certain type of germs. The main characteristics are joint pains, heart inflammation, development of nodules under the skin, and occasionally, development of involuntary body movements called a *chorea.* While some of the children recover without any sequelae, most develop chronic heart disease with damage to the valves of the heart.

Rickets: A bone disease caused by the deficiency of Vitamin D. Most of the times, this leads to weakening of the bones. If detected and treated with Vitamin D, there is no lasting problem.

Rubella (German measles): This is a viral rash illness similar to measles (but different from it in many ways). The affected child recovers in just 3-5 days. If the child has not had rubella in childhood and not received the rubella vaccine (which is a part of the MMR vaccine), she can transmit rubella to the unborn baby if she catches the infection in adulthood when she is pregnant. The fetus may be born deformed and retarded as a result.

Scabies: This is a skin infestation caused by the *itch mite.* The main symptom of this is incessant itching. The female mite resides in a burrow that she makes in the human skin and she lays her eggs within this burrow. The disease is transmitted by close personal contact between the victim and other persons.

Spina Bifida: In this developmental disorder, there is failure of the spinal canal to fuse around the developing nervous tissue during fetal life. As a result, the spine remains "open" and the damaged nervous tissue may flop out through the defect either covered by skin or totally open. The child will invariably have some functional loss of either the bladder or bowel, or of the use of her legs.

Squint: This is what we call "cross-eyed"-ness. A normal baby may show a varying squint of one or both of her eyes during the first 6-8 months of life, but this disappears soon after. A squint may either be a problem on its own, or may be accompanied by other eye problems like, for example, a refractive error.

Thalassemia: This is a blood disorder of a hereditary nature. It is caused by the formation of defective hemoglobin and is characterised by the development of **anemia** refractory to usual iron therapy. Repeated blood transfusions are the usual way of treatment, but later on in life, the child may need other, more expensive forms of treatment. Both parents usually carry one defective gene for this illness and it is possible to screen prospective couples for this disorder.

Thrush: This is an infection caused by a fungus called candida albicans (see **candida**).

Tonsillitis: Inflammation or infection of the tonsils is called tonsillitis. Frequent attacks of tonsillitis may require their removal (a *tonsillectomy*).

Typhoid fever: A common gastrointestinal infection caused by typhoid germs (salmonella). This illness is transmitted by the fecal-oral route and is seen during hot, humid summer and monsoon. The symptoms are a rising fever, abdominal distension and pain, enlargement of the liver and spleen and loose stools. Treatment is with specific antibiotics.

Urticaria (hives): Development of red, raised blotches that itch. This symptom is usually seen as a result of some allergy. Children with recurrent urticaria keep missing school because of the discomfort. Occasionally, recurrence may be a harbinger of something more serious, but usually, it is due to physical factors like cold, heat, etc.

Vaccines: These are preparations that children get to protect themselves against the vaccine preventable diseases. See **Immunisation.**

Viruses: These are small, ultramicroscopic germs that cause many illnesses of mankind such as **measles**, **chicken pox**, **rabies** and the common cold.

Vitamins: These are nutritional elements that are necessary in a balanced diet.

Warts: Warts are thick, rough papules caused by a type of virus. Untreated, they may either linger on for months, or disappear on their own.

Wheezing: This is the sound heard by bystanders who are close to a child suffering from asthma or a similar disorder. The doctors call it "bronchospasm" or "rhonchi".

Whooping cough (Pertussis): Fortunately, this disease entity has declined in recent times, thanks to Pertussis vaccine, which is a part of the D.P.T. vaccine. Whooping cough is a deadly illness characterised by onset like a common cold; the symptoms progress rapidly as the child starts getting intense bouts of spasmodic cough that causes discomfort to the point of producing oxygen deficiency of the whole body. The muscles of the trunk bulge outwards, the eyes become bloodshot and the face becomes progressively red, then blue. The prolonged bout ends with a forceful intake of breath which is called a "whoop". The child may get dehydrated and exhausted as a result of these repetitive bouts of cough and is at risk of dying from it.

Further Reading

Books:

1. Sutcliffe, Jenny **Baby Bonding** Virgin Publishing Ltd, 1994 ISBN 1 85227 429 8

2. **NCT's Complete Book of Baby Care** Harper-Collins 1999 ISBN 000 414053 2

3. Karst, Patricia **The Single Mother's Survival Guide** Crossing Press 2000 ISBN 1 58091 063 7

4. Balaskas, Janet **New Natural Pregnancy** Gaia Books 1998 ISBN 1 85675 074 4

5. Morse, P.S. and Brand, L.B. **Young Children at Home and in School: 212 Educational Activities for Their Parents, Teachers, and Caregivers**. Boston, MA: Allyn & Bacon, 1995.

6. Trainer, M. **Differences in Common: Straight Talk on Mental Retardation, Down Syndrome, and Life**. Rockville, MD: Woodbine House, 1991.

7. Healey, J.M. **Your Child's Growing Mind: A Parent's Guide to Learning from Birth to Adolescence**. Garden City, NY: Doubleday, 1987

8. Murphy, Tim **The Angry Child**
Three Rivers Press NY 2001 ISBN 0 609 80751 X

9. Markova D. **How to Make Your child Smart**
Magna Publishing Co Ltd 2001 ISBN 81 7809 094 5

10. Morris, Desmond. **Babywatching**
Jonathan Cape UK ISBN 0 224 06011 2

11. Stoppard Dr. Miriam **Complete Baby and Child Care**
DK Books London ISBN 0 7513 1233 9

12. Bharadwaj, Dr. Ashwini **A complete Guide to Baby and Child care** Goodwill Publishing House (India) ISBN 81 7245 306 X